Jews Out of the Question

SUNY SERIES, PHILOSOPHY AND RACE
Robert Bernasconi and T. Denean Sharpley-Whiting, editors

JEWS OUT OF THE QUESTION

A Critique of Anti-Anti-Semitism

Elad Lapidot

Published by State University of New York Press, Albany

©2020 State University of New York
All rights reserved

No part of this book may be used or reproduced in any manner whatsoever without written permission. No part of this book may be stored in a retrieval system or transmitted in any form or by any means including electronic, electrostatic, magnetic tape, mechanical, photocopying, recording, or otherwise without the prior permission in writing of the publisher.

For information, contact State University of New York Press, Albany, NY
www.sunypress.edu

LIBRARY OF CONGRESS CATALOGING-IN-PUBLICATION DATA
Names: Lapidot, Elad, author.
Title: Jews out of the question : a critique of anti-anti-Semitism / Elad Lapidot.
Description: Albany : State University of New York, 2020. | Series: Suny series, philosophy and race | Includes bibliographical references and index.
Identifiers: LCCN 2020001221 (print) | LCCN 2020001222 (ebook) | ISBN 9781438480459 (hardcover) | ISBN 9781438480466 (ebook) | ISBN 9781438480442 (pbk)
Subjects: LCSH: Antisemitism—Philosophy. | Philosophy—Political aspects. | Antisemitism—History. | Antisemitism—History—21st century.
Classification: LCC DS145 .L3225 2020 (print) | LCC DS145 (ebook) | DDC 305.892/4—dc23
LC record available at https://lccn.loc.gov/2020001221
LC ebook record available at https://lccn.loc.gov/2020001222

10 9 8 7 6 5 4 3 2 1

Contents

Acknowledgments   vii
Introduction   1

PART I   ANTI-ANTI-SEMITISM   23

1. Anti-Heidegger: Anatomy of Anti-Anti-Semitism   25
2. Anti-Semitic Creation of Jews: Adorno & Horkheimer to Sartre   53
3. Jewish Creation of Anti-Semitism: Arendt and Badiou   85
4. The Anti-Anti-Semitic Jew: Jean-Luc Nancy   149

PART II   ANTI-SEMITISM   185

5. Renan's Anti-Semitic Science   195
6. Aphenomenology of the Jewish Question: Bauer and Marx   223
7. Triumph of Judaism: From Marr to Hitler   255

Epilogue. The End of Anti-Anti-Semitism
as Introduction to Talmud   285

Bibliography   305
Index   325

Acknowledgments

KNOWING IS PLURAL; WRITING IS TOO. *"Seit ein Gespräch wir sind,"* since we are a conversation. I wish to express my deep gratitude to the colleagues who were the first to acknowledge this book, a fragile creature, by being its first readers, and with their comments, questions, suggestions, critiques, and encouragement helped me to give it its final form: Luca Di Blasi, Menachem Lorberbaum, Gil Anidjar, Elliot Wolfson, Michael Fagenblat, and Sarah Ross.

I further wish to acknowledge the friends who, in many conversations and exchanges, in different places, times, and settings, have discussed with me various aspects of this book, gave me their time, attention, support, and good advice, and have thus become those to whom I speak when I write: Jan Eike Dunkhase, Ron Naiweld, Oded Schechter, Hannah Tzuberi, Aviva Ronnefeld, Ivan Segré, Sergey Dolgopolski, Micha Brumlik, Hans Ruin, Itamar Ben-Ami, Karma Ben-Johanan, Frederic Brenner, Gabriel Levy, Yemima Hadad, Brian Crawford, Louis Blond, Roi Bar, and Amir Engel.

I am also grateful to Paul Mendes-Flohr, Phil Getz, and David Myers for their help in looking for a suitable venue for publishing this work, and to Robert Bernasconi and Tracy Denean Sharpley-Whiting, who accepted it into their Philosophy and Race series at SUNY Press, as well as to Rafael Chaiken and Ryan Morris, my editors at SUNY Press, for making this publication happen.

Last but not least, thank you, Eva, my beloved partner, and you, Alma, my beloved daughter, for your love and support, in all weathers, every day.

Introduction

THIS BOOK INTERVENES NOT ONLY IN A DEBATE, but in a war, a real one, fierce and ongoing. In such conditions, claiming neutrality is—even unwittingly—an act of aggression. I therefore begin by declaring my position: the present critique of anti-anti-Semitism does not intend to defend anti-Semitism. On the contrary, it suggests a fundamental affinity, and so a certain complicity between a dominant critique of anti-Semitism and the criticized object, anti-Semitism itself, a complicity between these two wars. This book critiques a certain discourse that frames, organizes, and generates both anti-Semitism and anti-anti-Semitism.

It offers a philosophical meditation on anti-Semitism, which counters what Alain David recently described as "the absence of anti-Semitism in philosophy and among philosophers—for whom anti-Semitism doesn't seem to be a theme for reflection or discussion, but rather a pathology, a sort of pendant to Jewish particularism."[1] Indeed, this relation—the actual, possible, and impossible relation—of philosophy, theory, or thought to anti-Semitism, and to the Jewish, is a fundamental question underlying the following reflections.

---

1   Alain David, "Die Abwesenheit von Antisemitismus genügt keineswegs," in *Heidegger, die Juden, noch einmal*, ed. Peter Trawny and Andrew J. Mitchell (Frankfurt am Main: Vittorio Klostermann, 2015), 224. For an important recent exception, which tries to consider Nazism and anti-Semitism philosophically, this too in the context of Heidegger, see Elliot Wolfson, *The Duplicity of Philosophy's Shadow: Heidegger, Nazsim, and the Jewish Other* (New York: Columbia University Press, 2018).

Indeed, even as the following pages not only acknowledge the topicality of the debate on anti-Semitism but explicitly take a position in the struggle against it, they nonetheless take a step back from the immediacy of current affairs and attempt a more systematic contemplation.

This book therefore does not directly (although indirectly it does nothing but this) deal with or try to answer questions such as whether or not specific statements, actions, or positions (the BDS movement, critiques of the State of Israel, anti-Zionism or pro-Zionism and more) are anti-Semitic, or whether there is or isn't a rise of new or old anti-Semitism in Europe or in the United States or elsewhere and whether or not the government does enough to fight it. Rather, it examines the basic categories and notions that underlie and pre-configure this discourse, namely the way in which anti-Semitism is talked about, thought about, and fought against. It examines how these categories are interconnected to the basic categories that shape contemporary culture—first and foremost its politics and its knowledge. It is a basic critical observation of this book, concurring with Alain David, that discussions of anti-Semitism tend to avoid or even preclude this kind of examination. Engaging in such a questioning is thus in itself engaging in polemics.

POLITICAL EPISTEMOLOGY

The present inquiry suggests a defined conceptual framework for the critique of anti-anti-Semitism, so to speak, for its "anti-anti-anti-Semitic" thought. The critical effort of this book, its underlying anti-, is indeed situated within a concern that is designated throughout this book as "political epistemology" or "epistemo-politics." As arises from its concept, political epistemology concerns the relations between the ways we understand and perform what was named in Greek *episteme* or *logos*, i.e., knowledge, science, philosophy, and so forth, and the ways we understand and perform—conceptually still Greek—*polis*, i.e., our political, communal existence.

The term "political epistemology" has been used over the preceding decades, with a noticeable increase in recent years, but without attaining any systematic or standard meaning. A common feature of current uses is that they presuppose the concept and thus the phenomenon or phenomenal complex, either of politics or of knowledge or of both, and engage in a more or less empirical observation of, say, the role of "political ideas and knowledge" in "political action."² The present critique of political epistemology aims, in contrast, at problematizing the conceptual matrix regulating the interrelations of politics and knowledge. It is closer to how Bruno Latour used the term "political epistemology" to characterize the basic question of Science Studies as not extending "politics to science, nor science to politics," but rather trying "to understand where the difference comes from and how the distribution of skills among the different domains has been adjudicated."³ Nonetheless, Latour seems to reduce both knowledge and politics to the categories of the social, which is perhaps the categorical difference between the sociology of science and the project envisioned here as "political epistemology."

Political epistemology may be deemed as the philosophical pendant of political theology; the question of epistemo-politics or logo-politics is troubled by the same hyphen as theo-politics, which is perhaps also the same hyphen of bio-politics. Performed, however, within the realm of knowledge, within the institution or *polis* of knowledge, inside the university and academic discourse, the epistemo-political reflection is self-reflection, which experiences this troubled hyphen more readily as an *internal* split. In the present context, of particular interest for the following inquiry is a critical meditation on the *modern and contemporary* epistemo-political condition. In other words, it tries to observe and describe a certain difficulty, deficiency, or dislocation in the relation between knowledge and

---

2   See the petition to create a section devoted to political epistemology that was submitted in 2013 to the American Political Science Association: "The purpose of the section will be to encourage the empirical and normative study of political knowledge and information. Since the definition of 'knowledge' is often contested, political epistemology means the study of (1) the empirical role in political behavior of perceptions, theories, and other ideational factors; (2) the sources of these factors; (3) the accuracy of political actors' perceptions and other ideas (the value of their knowledge and information); and (4) the normative implications of items 1–3" (https://www.politicalepistemology.org). The recently founded, more philosophically oriented "Political Epistemology Network" makes a more general call to "scholars working at the intersection of epistemology and political philosophy"; see https://www.politicalepistemologynetwork.com/about-us.

3   Bruno Latour, "The Netz-Works of Greek Deductions," *Social Studies of Science* 38, no. 3 (June 2008): 449; see Duncan Kennedy, "Knowledge and the Political: Bruno Laltour's Political Epistemology," *Cultural Critique* 74 (2010): 83–97.

politics in modernity, a fundamental disconnection, disassociation, and dis-relation between *episteme* and *polis*. Similar or perhaps the identical disconnection has been already noticed and analyzed by Hannah Arendt, who traced the split back to the very origin of philosophy: "The gulf between philosophy and politics opened historically with the trial and condemnation" of Socrates.[4]

The *locus* of the present critical reflection on modern political epistemology is the field of modern episteme that does explicitly concern the *polis*, namely political thought. Methodologically, its contemplation of contemporary political thought does not set out from the current doctrinal formulation of political science or political philosophy, nor does it attempt to offer such a formulation of political epistemology itself. Rather, the present investigation focuses on political thought itself as a happening, an *event* within the polis, a political, historical event of thought, knowledge, or discourse, an event of logos. The paradigmatic event of knowledge is not just "discovery" or "invention," although these are no doubt constitutive happenings, but, so this book suggests, rather the *polemos*, the *machloykes* (Yiddish for "disagreement")—the controversy. There is here an obvious epistemo-political affinity to the perception of the Political—by Carl Schmitt, for instance—as founded on war, *polemos*, against which however—and this is not a small war—I insist on *polemics*.[5] The contemporary polemics taken here as the evental site for contemplating contemporary political thought is a double or second-order polemics, a war on war: anti-anti-Semitism.

Of course, it is easy to see how, since World War II, this polemics has functioned as a foundation of Western political thought. In the apocalypse of Auschwitz, anti-Semitism has become the paradigm of dystopia; the anti-

---

4   Hannah Arendt, "Philosophy and Politics," *Social Research* 71, no. 3 (2004): 427. See also Arendt, *The Human Condition* (Chicago: University of Chicago Press, 1970); Alireza Shomali, *Politics and the Criteria of Truth* (London: Palgrave Macmillan, 2010), which focuses on the normative search for a "new epistemology," providing a "criterion of truth that is attentive to the sociopolitical conditions that determine meaning" (6).

5   For a more articulated polemics with Schmitt, see Elad Lapidot, "Carl Schmitt's Warring Wars: On the Political Epistemology of Political Theology," *Philosophical Journal for Conflict and Violence* (2020): 36–53.

Semitic state, Nazi Germany, has become the paradigm of the bad state, the *kako-polis*, the exact opposite of the ideal *kalo-polis*. Anti-Semitism has thus become, for post–World War II political philosophy, a sort of negative *Politeia*; and war on anti-Semitism, accordingly, a fundamental operation of politics and political thought. In this context, reflecting on anti-anti-Semitism is a basic critical operation of contemporary political thought.

This is the horizon in which can also be located related critiques (see discussion below) on the War on Anti-Semitism (Gil Anidjar) or the Philosemitic Reaction (Ivan Segré) as figures of the West. The epistemological emphasis of the present inquiry, however, is particularly interested in the *conceptual* quality of what it therefore declaratorily calls "anti-anti-Semitism," namely not primarily as a *figure* of the West but, on the contrary, as a conceptual constellation, an epistemology, or contemporary political epistemology, of which "the West" would be a figure.

ANTIHYPHEN

Examining anti-anti-Semitism as epistemology means examining it as knowledge of knowledge. That anti-anti-Semitism *is* knowledge seems to be obvious, surely for anti-anti-Semites, who *oppose* anti-Semitism, which assumes they *know* it. In fact, the "anti-," a relation of opposition, resistance, and negation, would seem to constitute a central *epistemic* figure, a figure of knowledge, cognition, or consciousness, namely to use Husserl's definition of *Bewußtsein*, an intentional relation *to* something, *Bewußtsein von*, knowledge *of*. Intentionality is graphically marked by the hyphen, a staple of phenomenological texts, i.e., the anti"-." *Anti*-anti-Semitism is therefore knowledge, and what it knows is itself, once again, knowledge—*anti*-Semitism. Anti-anti-Semitism is accordingly knowledge of knowledge, epistemology. It is *political* epistemology insofar as the epistemic figure that it knows, anti-Semitism, is a political figure, a movement, ideology, or politics. Indeed, the "anti-" seems to constitute a foundational epistemo-political figure, a phenomenon of knowledge-based political existence, a community of *polemos*.

One simple formulation of this book's basic thesis, however, is that anti-anti-Semitism constitutes *negative* political epistemology, which opposes political knowledge per se, namely rejects any positive relation between knowledge and politics and actively *effects* their disconnection. This means that anti-anti-Semitism is a paradoxical, self-negating political epistemology, and this book does perhaps nothing more than articulate this paradox. Its basic observation is that anti-anti-Semitism's fundamental "anti-" against anti-Semitism, its basic adversarial knowledge of anti-Semitism, namely what it asserts to know *of* and *against* anti-Semitism, is that anti-Semitism itself is *no* knowledge, and that the fundamental problem with anti-Semitism is that it claims to know. For anti-anti-Semitism, the fundamental problem with anti-Semitism is not its "anti," but its hyphen.

In anticipation of the detailed textual analyses to follow, as a preliminary demonstration, the basic operation of anti-anti-Semitic political epistemology may in fact be called de-epistemization by de-hyphenation: denying the anti-Semitic hyphen. In explaining this de-hyphenation, namely their explicit decision to avoid the admittedly "more popular term 'anti-Semitism'" for "antisemitism," Julia Schulze Wessel and Lars Rensmann, in their essay "Arendt and Adorno on Antisemitism," thus argued: "Arendt used 'antisemitism,' not 'anti-Semitism' throughout her work, for the good reason that, as she observes in *Origins of Totalitarianism*, antisemites do not oppose any 'Semitism,' as the more popular term 'anti-Semitism' suggests. As Arendt points out ... 'antisemitism' is an ideology that constructs a Jewish enemy but has nothing to do with any opposition to 'Semitic' ethnic origins or language communities. In the original German usage, *Antisemitismus* is never hyphenated."[6]

---

6   Julia Schulze Wessel and Lars Rensmann, "The Paralysis of Judgment: Arendt and Adorno on Antisemitism and the Modern Condition," in *Arendt & Adorno: Political and Philosophical Investigations*, ed. Lars Rensmann and Samir Gandesha (Stanford, CA: Stanford University Press, 2012), 329n.5. See also the editors' note in Roger Berkowitz, Jeffrey Katz, and Thomas Keenan, eds., *Thinking in Dark Times: Hannah Arendt on Ethics and Politics* (New York: Fordham University Press, 2010): "Hannah Arendt intentionally wrote *antisemitism, antisemitic,* and *antisemite* instead of *anti-Semitism, anti-Semitic,* and *anti-Semite* throughout her work. She did so for the simple reason that, as she wrote in *The Origins of Totalitarianism*, there is a difference between 'Jew-hatred' on the one hand and 'antisemitism' on the other. There is no such thing as a pro-Semitic 'Semitism' that an 'anti-Semitism' opposes, but only an ideological 'antisemitism.' Following Arendt's reasoning and her practice, the essays in this volume will speak of antisemitism, antisemitic persons and ideas, and antisemites."

Dehyphenation of anti-Semitism denies its epistemic quality, denies it knowledge. The analyses below show why, in contrast to Wessel and Rensmann, I think that Adorno may be more easily invoked in support of this position than Arendt. In this context, one also wonders about the exact kind of support for the de-hyphenation of anti-Semitism sought by the invocation of "the original German usage." (Is it meant to suggest that the original and explicit intention of the original German anti-Semites, by calling themselves *Antisemiten* rather than *Anti-Semiten*, was to declare that their movement has nothing to do with any opposition to Semites? Is not, however, "German usage" *not* to use the hyphen? What German *Anti-* are hyphenated? What German word compositions in general are hyphenated? Would lack of hyphen in German always indicate lack of conceptual relation? Would *Antisemitismusforschung*, for instance, have nothing to do with the research of anti-Semitism?)

What is important to highlight at this point, however, is the extent of anti-anti-Semitic de-epistemization of anti-Semitism. De-hyphenated, antisemitism would know nothing of Semitism, namely would have nothing to do with the entire political epistemology that has been historically generated around the figure of the Semite (which Anidjar, as I discuss below, identified as "the West"). It is in this sense that anti-anti-Semitism obliterates Semitism. Further, however, and this is a basic claim of the present book, anti-anti-Semitic de-epistemization of anti-Semitism also concerns its relation to *Jews*. For anti-antisemitism, anti-Semitism would not only be a declaration of war against Semitism that has nothing to do with Semitism, but also, as Wessel and Rensmann write, an "ideology that *constructs* a Jewish enemy" (my emphasis), which means, in the Arendtian sense of "ideology," that it has nothing to do with reality—knows nothing of real Jews. Indeed, as the analyses in this book will show, a fundamental motif in anti-anti-Semitism has been the assertion that anti-Semitism has in fact *no* actual knowledge of real Jews. This is the epistemological foundation for an entire *Antisemitismusforschung* that will consequently know nothing of Semites and nothing of Jews, nor therefore of anti-Semitism, but only of "antisemitism" in the exclusive sense of anti-Semitic acts and people, a science of anti-Semites. And the fundamental anti-anti-Semitic accusation and critique against anti-Semitism does not accordingly concern its "anti," namely its *animosity* toward Jews, but rather its hyphen, its anti"-"Semitism," its asserted knowledge *of* Jews.

ANTI-"JEWISH"

Pending textual analyses, it may be helpful in this introduction to provide a preliminary articulation of anti-anti-Semitic epistemology, which decries anti-Semitic views on Jews as mere construction, projection, imagination, and figuration. Indeed, even if there is a historical basis for claiming that anti-Semitism, as a political movement, in fact has never explicitly campaigned against "the Semites," all anti-anti-Semitism describes anti-Semitism, be it antisemitism, as a certain intentionality directed toward "Jews." Wessel and Rensmann speak of *construction* "of a Jewish enemy." The currently most common institutional anti-anti-Semitic definition of "Antisemitism" states: "Antisemitism is a certain perception of Jews, which may be expressed as hatred toward Jews."[7] In other words, the attitude of "hate," the negative axiology of anti-Semitism, its "anti," expresses a more fundamental, foundational—to use here Husserlian epistemology—*doxic* relation to Jews: "perception." Before being a negative attitude toward Jews, anti-Semitism is a certain way of perceiving Jews. Husserl would agree. Nonetheless, this definition hardly intends to contradict the basic anti-anti-Semitic position, as it will be demonstrated in this book, whereby anti-Semitism is actually antisemitism, namely *no* real relation to real Jews, by insisting that it *does* consist in the cognitive act of "perceiving" Jews. "Perception of Jews" is meant in anti-anti-Semitic discourse as a purely subjective view, fantasy, imagination, or construction, which would stand in contradistinction to the objectively real Jews, to what may be called in terms of Kantian epistemology Jews *an sich*.

Of course, thinking this through with Kant and Husserl, one could say that perception, *Wahrnehmung*, is nevertheless the closest we can ever get to anything (Kant) or even the very mode in which the thing itself is "given"

---

7   Formulated in 2005 by the European Monitoring Centre on Racism and Xenophobia, it has been adopted by European Parliament Working Group on Antisemitism (https://ep-wgas.eu/ihra-definition), the International Holocaust Remembrance Alliance (https://www.holocaustremembrance.com/stories/working-definition-antisemitism), and by its members states, including the US (https://www.state.gov/defining-anti-semitism), the UK (https://commonslibrary.parliament.uk/home-affairs/communities/uk-governments-adoption-of-the-ihra-definition-of-antisemitism/), and Germany (https://www.auswaertiges-amt.de/de/aussenpolitik/themen/kulturdialog/06-interkulturellerdialog/-/216610).

to us as such, i.e., in itself becomes our object, exists for and known by us (Husserl). A "certain perception of Jews" would accordingly mean a certain basic way of cognitively relating to Jews, of having Jews as an object of consciousness. Speaking Husserl's hermeneutical language, anti-Semitism, as "a certain perception of Jews," would consist in a way of understanding, namely constructing the very sense of what "Jewish" is, of the idea or essence "Jewish," as the basis for any perception of Jews, namely for any perception of something that may be called "Jewish." Put differently, anti-Semitism may be said to be *necessarily* based on certain—problematic and partial as it may be, but nonetheless—*knowledge* of Jews. It is precisely this knowledge, with its specific mode of knowing, that would be expressed by the designation "Semites." Anti-Semitism would perceive—and hate—Jews *qua* Semites.

It is, however, a basic observation of this book that anti-anti-Semitism fundamentally rejects anti-Semitic knowledge of the Jewish, categorically rejects in fact *any* knowledge of the Jewish: as *mere* perception, construction, projection, imagination, fantasy, and myth. As already noted, this book will indicate how anti-anti-Semitism most fundamentally tends to criticize anti-Semitism not for thinking *against* Jews, but for thinking *of* Jews at all, namely for engaging Jews as an object of thought, as an epistemic entity. In other words, so the claim, anti-anti-Semitism has criticized anti-Semitism for introducing "the Jews" or "the Jewish" as entity of thought: as a category, idea, concept, or more commonly as a *figure* of thought, a figural Jew, a "Jew," with scare quotes. To formulate it provocatively, the analyses below will show anti-anti-Semitism to be anti-"Jewish."

With respect to this anti-anti-Semitic rejection of "the Jewish," i.e., rejection of the Jewish from the realm of thought, the following chapters make two basic claims: first, that at work in this rejection, and therefore in anti-anti-Semitism, is a specific radical type of *negative* political epistemology; second, that this rejection, and the negative political epistemology that underlies it, is what anti-anti-Semitism shares with anti-Semitism. It is this epistemo-political complicity that the present anti-anti-anti-Semitic critique wishes to bring to light.

As for the first claim, on anti-anti-Semitism's negative political epistemology, what it argues is that anti-anti-Semitic critique against the introduction of Jews into the realm of thought, the rejection of the "figural" Jew, as the supposed essence of anti-Semitism, is itself based on a certain figuration or "construction," a certain perception of Jews. Quickly stated, the analyses to follow will show how this figuration consists in a fundamental *dis-figuration*, namely in a perception of the Jews as a historical human collective, whose existence, as a collective, lies outside the epistemic realm, outside the realm of knowledge, philosophy, and thought, and so, strictly speaking, outside of any perception or imagination, a non-figure or dis-figure. It would be for this reason illegitimate or rather invalid *in principle*, epistemically fallacious, to criticize, antagonize, or oppose this human collective, to be *anti*-Jewish, not because Jews are essentially "good," i.e., not because the "anti" is wrong, but because "the Jewish" stands for, manifests, or "figures" no specific content, no specific idea. Strictly speaking, there is no "Jew." In other words, the anti-anti-Semitic "Jews" are a radically de-epistemized collective, and in this sense a radically negative epistemo-political figure. Furthermore, this book argues that in and through anti-anti-Semitic discourse the epistemo-politically negative category of "the Jew" emerges as a *paradigm* of contemporary political epistemology, a contemporary paradigm for the figure of "the people."

As for the second claim, on the epistemo-political complicity of anti-anti-Semitism and anti-Semitism, what it argues is that the dis-figured, de-epistemized Jew, the anti-anti-Semitic real Jew *an sich*, a paradigm of contemporary negative political epistemology, is a realization, consummation, and perfection of the category of "the Semites." It is in this sense that I subscribe to Gil Anidjar's observation (see below) that anti-anti-Semitism as well as anti-Semitism are forms of Semitism, and therefore, in this perspective, "the Semitic perspective," they tend to converge. Whereas Anidjar focuses on the Semite as concealing the Muslim, this book focuses on the Semite as dis-figuring the Jew, and the ways in which this dis-figuration becomes a gateway between anti-anti-Semitism and anti-Jewish anti-Semitism. As it will be shown, the (anti-anti-Semitic) critique against (anti-Semitic) attempts to inscribe the Jews as an epistemic entity within theoretical or philosophical discourse must lead to the realization that the attribution of epistemic value and meaning to Jewish being has been an exercise carried out, more often than by anti-Semites, by self-identifying Jews themselves, precisely *as* the performance of what they perceive to be their Jewishness. Accordingly, the critique of anti-Semitism for the very conceptualization, imagination, or construction of the Jewish—and my claim is that this is *the center of contemporary anti-anti-Semitism*—quickly veers into a critique of Jewishness itself, into anti-anti-Semitic anti-Judaism.

KNOWN ANTI-ANTI-ANTI-SEMITES

The main analytic category of this book, "anti-anti-Semitism," which designates its principal object, is already in use. It was explicitly introduced to the academic discourse, with the same meaning in which it is used here, more than a decade ago, by Jonathan Judaken, in *Jean-Paul Sartre and the Jewish Question: Anti-antisemitism and the Politics of the French Intellectual*.[8] Judaken introduced this concept (or, more precisely, the concept of "anti-antisemitism"; and the grammatological significance of this difference was already indicated) as the organizing category of his inquiry, aiming "to evaluate the conceptual and perceptual 'biases' that animate the *opposition* to antisemitism" (20). Judaken's purported evaluation of anti-anti-Semitism was accordingly, from the outset, *critical*, so to speak anti-anti-anti-Semitic, not, however, in defense of anti-Semitism, but, on the contrary, just like the present contemplation, in defense of the opposition to anti-Semitism: "The risk of anti-antisemitism is that it merely reverses the dictums of antisemitism without problematizing the axiology and doxology that underpin antisemitism and can thereby end up duplicating aspects of the problem that anti-antisemites seek to resist" (20).

In other words, Judaken suggested an epistemological communality or solidarity between anti-Semitism and anti-anti-Semitism, and it is precisely this communality that the term "anti-anti-Semitism" implies in the present inquiry. "Any anti-," to quote Heidegger, must "originate from the same essential ground as that against which it is anti-."[9] This quote is especially pertinent here as it is taken from one of the most controversial *anti-Semitic* passages of the *Black Notebooks*, the specific "anti-" in question there being the "anti-Christ," who, like the Christ, would "originate from the Jewry," which, Heidegger writes, "was, in the period of the Christian West, namely of metaphysics, the principle of destruction" (20). Would the essential sameness or communality of the anti- and that against which it is anti- also apply to anti-Semitism? Would this mean anti-Semitism has some intima-

---

8   Jonathan Judaken, *Jean-Paul Sartre and the Jewish Question: Anti-antisemitism and the Politics of the French Intellectual* (Lincoln: University of Nebraska Press, 2006).
9   Martin Heidegger, *Anmerkungen I–V (Schwarze Hefte 1942–1948)*, ed. Peter Trawny (Frankfurt am Main: Klostermann Verlag, 2015) (= GA, Bd. 97), 20.

Introduction   11

cy of essence with Semitism, or, if anti-Semitism is a form of anti-Judaism, with Judaism? These are hard but, so it seems, necessary questions for any anti-anti-Semitism to ask itself, lest, as Judaken warned, it "end up duplicating aspects of the problem that [it] seek to resist."

The theoretical critique of anti-anti-Semitism was further developed by Gil Anidjar, who, following Judaken, pointed at the broad significance of "the anti-anti-Semitic movement," a phenomenon Anidjar described as "the war on anti-Semitism" ("WAS"), similar to "the war on drugs, the war on poverty and the war on terror."[10] It is the *political* question that Anidjar placed at the center of his inquiry: "It has become imperative today at least to attempt to explain the political significance of the anti-anti-Semitism movement." Writing on the unity of "Anti-Semitism and its Critiques," Anidjar, like Judaken, asked about the "continuities ... between the history of anti-Semitism and the current struggle against it" (8). It is noteworthy that Anidjar, like Heidegger, argued for a conceptual, *necessary* communality between the anti- and its adversary, which he accordingly deployed as a methodological principle: "WAS [War on Anti-Semitism] must be treated as a social and political movement, one that is related and in fact comparable (for obvious reasons having to do with the mimetic dynamism at work in adversarial relations) to that which it has historically opposed" (5). This conceptual insight highlights all the more Anidjar's further observation, which is particularly pertinent for the reflections in the present book, namely beyond or next to the political problem of anti-anti-Semitism, also of its epistemological problem, i.e., "the near complete absence ... of reflective and indeed concerted gestures on the part of those of us who struggle against anti-Semitism" (5), or as he formulated it more recently: "The war against antisemitism as a movement that does not know itself."[11] If "know thyself" is a founding principle of philosophy, anti-anti-Semitism would accordingly be something like an anti-philosophical politics.

In what would this negative epistemology of anti-anti-Semitism consist? What exactly would it fail to know and how is this continuation of anti-

---

10   Gil Anidjar, "When Killers Become Victims: Anti-Semitism and Its Critics," *Cosmopolis: A Review of Cosmopolitics* 3 (2007), http://agora.qc.ca/cosmopolis.
11   Gil Anidjar, "Antisemitism and Its Critics," in *Antisemitism and Islamophobia in Europe: A Shared Story?*, ed. James Renton and Ben Gidley (London: Palgrave Macmillan, 2017), 204.

Semitism? Anidjar, author of *A History of the Enemy*,¹² analyzed the problem as properly politico-epistemological one, i.e., as the failure to properly *know* the enemy of anti-Semitism—the object of its anti-. The deficiency for Anidjar lies in the gap between the enemy of anti-Semitism according to its concept, namely "the Semites," and the enemy of anti-Semitism according to its historical performance, i.e., "the Jews." "Anti-Semitism" would be a political performance that disregards, forgets, or obliterates its own concept. It is this fundamental operation through which "the Semites" are obliterated by the politics pertaining to "the Jews," which would constitute the continuity between hate of Jews in the name of anti-Semitism and defense of Jews in the name of anti-anti-Semitism. The basic epistemological deficiency that Anidjar observes in the joint discourse of anti-Semitism and anti-anti-Semitism is therefore, paradoxically, the oblivion of Semitism, namely "the lack of attention directed at the history of the category of 'Semites', its sources and its enduring effects."¹³

It has in fact been a feat of Anidjar's work, against this oblivion, to open up and articulate the "Semitic perspective" (17), namely the basic dynamics of the historical and still contemporary discourse or knowledge that has emerged from and been organized—also and often negatively—around the notion of "Semites." What makes Anidjar's analysis so powerful, and essential for the present book, is that it interrogated and displayed the discourse of the "Semites," i.e., Semitism, as foundational for basic categories of modern and contemporary knowledge. *Semites: Race, Religion, Literature*, he wrote.¹⁴ Semitism is the logos of race, religion, and literature, and this means of contemporary episteme itself. Anidjar has designated this episteme analytically as "Christian,"¹⁵ meaning "Western Christendom," and identified it in various forms, such as "Roman Catholicism, Reformation, Secularism, WAS,"¹⁶ i.e., the war on anti-Semitism (to which one may no doubt also add anti-Semitism), but perhaps most comprehensively "the

---

12   Gil Anidjar, *The Jew, The Arab: A History of the Enemy* (Stanford, CA: Stanford University Press, 2003).
13   Anidjar, "When Killers," 18.
14   Gil Anidjar, *Semites: Race, Religion, Literature* (Stanford, CA: Stanford University Press, 2008).
15   Cf. Gil Anidjar, *Blood: A Critique of Christianity* (New York: Columbia University Press, 2014).
16   Anidjar, "When Killers," 17.

West," meaning *Us*, e.g., the "understanding of politics in which we have all come to share" (10).

The aspect of Semitism that has been the most central to Anidjar's analysis, and also crucial to his critique of anti-anti-Semitism, is the nature of the figure that Semitism constitutes as its object, namely "the Semites." Anidjar's basic observation was that the unity of the category "Semites" has been generated and performed through differentiation between two Semitic paradigms: Semitism is the (Western Christian) double invention of "Judaism and Islam—the Jew, the Arab."[17] Semitism would be the generation of the Semites in the double figure of the Jew and the Arab or Muslim. The Semites, however, have been and still are generated essentially as *enemies*, namely as objects of hate, of anti-. Semitism *is* anti-Semitism. It follows that the two figures of Semitism, the Jew and the Arab, would be constituted by two interrelated discourses of hate: anti-Jewish and anti-Arab or anti-Muslim, Anidjar to follow Edward Said in pointing at the intimacy between (anti-Jewish) anti-Semitism and Orientalism, or Islamophobia.[18]

The fundamental epistemological or politico-epistemological problem underlying both (anti-Jewish) anti-Semitism and Islamophobia, both forms of anti-Semitic hate, would therefore be precisely the concealment or oblivion of their epistemological identity, i.e., Semitism, through their conceptual, analytical, and political division, the division between anti-Semitism and Islamophobia, between Arab and Jew. This division, Anidjar claims, has been generated by historical anti-Semitism, which targeted specifically "Jews," and is further maintained and reproduced by contemporary anti-anti-Semitism, which targets specifically hate against Jews: "to uphold the division between Jew and Arab, between Jew and Muslim is to reproduce the origins of racism and of anti-Semitism at once" (19). Anidjar's analysis was developed by Gil Hochberg, who, in "Re-Membering Semitism," suggested a correlation between two contemporary forms of Western anti-anti-Semitism, namely the campaign against the "new," Muslim anti-Semitism, and the critique against Zionist, Jewish anti-Arabism: "Europe's way to cleanse itself from its two modern historical

---

17   Anidjar, *Semites*, 49.
18   Anidjar, "Antisemitism and its Critics," 205. Cf. Edward Said, *Orientalism* (London: Penguin Books, 2003 [1978]), 27–28.

crimes—anti-Semitism, on the one hand, and colonialism on the other—by transferring their weight onto its primary historical victims."[19]

A similar, politically somewhat counter-intuitive, conceptual correlation between anti-anti-Semitism and anti-colonial anti-Zionism has also been made visible by the work of Ivan Segré, working in the contemporary French discourse.[20] Segré characterized the twenty-first-century campaign of French authors against the "new" anti-Semitism, anti-anti-Semitism that he called "philosemitism," as *reactionary*. In *The Philosemitic Reaction*,[21] Segré, similarly to Anidjar, identified in this war a contemporary figure of the "defense of the West" (11), a West that, in converting from pre-Auschwitz anti-Semitism to post-Auschwitz anti-anti-Semitism, would nonetheless preserve "an imperialist vision of the world, a xenophobic ideal of society, a police-like conception of knowledge" (12). Noteworthy for the present inquiry is how and where Segré located the epistemological problem of anti-anti-Semitism. Segré focused less on what anti-anti-Semitic discourse disregards and forgets, namely "the Semites," and the categorical unity of Jews and Muslims, and more on what anti-anti-Semitism, at least in its French, "philosemitic" version, does seem to remember, defend, and assert, does, in other words, claim to know: "the Jews."

Segré's critique of anti-anti-Semitism thus targeted more directly not just its political workings but its epistemic structure. The epistemic problem of anti-anti-Semitism, according to Segré, is not just ignoring the Muslim; it is also a "betrayal of Jewish particularism" (11). In other words, the continuity between anti-anti-Semitism and anti-Semitism would be not only Semitism, but also anti-Judaism. The significance of this point is epistemologically crucial. What it means is that anti-anti-Semitism, and anti-Semitism, and Semitism, "the West," may be criticized not only as a closed discourse, based on its own internal play of *différance* (Jewish/Muslim), but also as a relation to or *knowledge of* Others, here the Jew, which would be consequently more than a mere Western Semitic, anti-

---

19   Gil Hochberg, "Remembering Semitism" or "On the Prospect of Re-Membering the Semites," *ReOrient* 1 (2016): 194.
20   For his recent critique of anti-colonial anti-Zionism, see Ivan Segré, *Les pingouins de l'universel: antijudaïsme, antisémitisme, antisionisme* (Paris: Lignes, 2017).
21   Ivan Segré, *La Réaction Philosémite, ou La Trahison des Clercs* (Paris: Lignes, 2009), trans. David Fernbach as "The Philosemitic Reaction," in Alain Badiou, Eric Hazan, and Ivan Segré, *Reflections on anti-Semitism* (London: Verso, 2013).

Semitic, and anti-anti-Semitic invention. The Semitic fiction would be a betrayal of the Jew, who is accordingly suggested by Segré's critique, in contrast, as a figure of non-Semitic, and so non-Western political epistemology, namely that is not based on the sole discourse of "the Semites."[22]

It is precisely in the effacement of the Jew *as* a figure of alternative epistemology that Segré sees the fundamental "betrayal" of anti-anti-Semitism. This effacement is not effected by way of disregard, like the effacement of the Muslim, but, on the contrary, by way of disguise, i.e., by presenting the Jew as a positive figure—that exists outside of thought. In *What Is Called Thinking Auschwitz?*,[23] Segré thus showed how theoretical attempts, such as Heidegger's and Arendt's, to *think*, to philosophically "critique" what is seemingly the apocalyptic figure of anti-Jewish anti-Semitism, "Auschwitz," has depended on extracting the essential event of Auschwitz from its supposedly contingent, non-essential anti-Jewish context ("anti-Semitism therefore is contingent: it doesn't inform the philosopher about what Auschwitz is in its essence" [67]), and inscribing it in a non-Jewish conceptual discourse, e.g., "modern technology." Thinking Auschwitz, an operation of philosophical anti-anti-Semitism, is thus positing the Jewish outside of thought, de-epistemizing the Jew. As a paradigm of the *critique* of anti-anti-Semitism, Segré accordingly posited the French philosopher Philippe Lacoue-Labarthe (to whom I will return later), in "his insistence on thinking the singularity of Nazism such that, essentially, the Extermination was of *Jews*" (77). The critique of anti-anti-Semitism thus emerges in the form that will guide the present book, namely as the concern "to inscribe the name *Jew* in the philosophical text" (79, 85).

ANTI-ANTI-ANTI-SEMITIC ACTS

By the rules of formal logic, the present critique of anti-anti-Semitism, "anti-anti-anti-Semitism," might be said, decried, to affirm anti-Semitism. This is correct only to the extent that "anti-Semitism" is equally understood not as hate of Jews or Semites, but as the fundamental resistance to "Semitism" as the discourse that perceives the Jewish—and Muslim, and

---

22 Cf. Alain David, *Racisme et Antisémitisme: Essai de philosophie sur l'envers des concepts* (Paris: Ellipses, 2001).

23 Ivan Segré, *Qu'appelle-t-on penser Auschwitz?* (Paris: Lignes, 2009).

any—collective existence through the category of "the Semites." Nor is the present anti-anti-anti-Semitism therefore a critique of philosemitism or any other allosemitism.[24] Anti-allosemitism has most often tended to share and reaffirm, so it seems to me, the basic "Semitism" of anti-anti-Semitism, namely the basic dis-figuration of the Jew. "Dis-figuration" means here, once again, first and foremost the elimination of the figure, namely the abolishment of any idea and thus of any epistemic value, any concept and content of the signifier "Jew," which thus becomes necessarily a matter of *indifference*, something inessential, beyond love and hate, beyond anti- and philo-. The anti-anti- is in this sense, beyond binary logics, where negation of negation means affirmation, a double negation that means *stronger* negation, anti-anti- that is more negative—not to say more *exterminatory*—than anti-.

In not just revealing and critiquing but also resisting anti-anti-Semitic disfiguration of the Jewish, anti-anti-anti-Semitism does not therefore proceed to *affirmation* of "Semitism." I subscribe to the need identified by Anidjar to remember and by Hochberg to "re-member" the Semites, the Jew, the Muslim. My analysis further supports the project of subverting the Semitic construction in an attempt to reconfigure the Jewish and the Muslim. My claim is, however, that Semitism is not just a specific set of figures, but a specific regime of figuration, i.e., it does not only attribute and distribute sets of predicates, for instance to the Jewish, but determines its mode of appearance—or rather disappearance, what I call here "dis-figuration." Consequently, subverting Semitism requires more or something different than revaluating its tropes, by deeming nomads, for instance, against anti-Semitic slur, as virtuous. What needs to be subverted or overcome, and first made visible, is the epistemology that underlies the discourse of Semitism. The challenge is not only to remember the Jew and the Muslim, but to access Jewish and Muslim memories, where Jewish and Muslim do not only exist as Christian others, as "Semites."

The critical operation of anti-anti-anti-Semitism is finally distinguished also from the act of categorically rejecting the use of the Semitism discourse altogether, by, for instance, replacing the term "anti-Semitism"

---

24   Cf. Zygmunt Bauman, "Allosemitism: Premodern, Modern, Postmodern," in *Modernity, Culture, and 'the Jew'*, ed. Bryan Cheyette and Laura Marcus (Stanford, CA: Stanford University Press, 1998), 143–156.

by the term "(racial, modern, etc.) anti-Judaism." This kind of intervention would in fact, at best, be none, and at worst be a reconfirmation of Semitism. Resistance to Semitism must *also* intervene directly on the given Semitism discourse. Taking the position of anti-anti-anti-Semitism, instead of simply not using the concepts Semitism and anti-Semitism, is to acknowledge the essential temporality, processuality, or historicity of thought, its inherent givenness and thus fundamentally hermeneutical operation. Thinking is thought reading.

I recall that the basic concern of the present act of thought is the political epistemology of which the disfigured Jew is a figure, namely a contemporary *negative* political epistemology, as disconnection between *episteme* and *polis*, between knowledge and thought, on the one hand, and, on the other hand, the collective human project. Designating the critique of the disfigured Jew "anti-anti-anti-Semitism," an expression that sounds like a parody on Hegel (until you read Hegel), performatively attempts to reinscribe the de-epistemized Jew, disrobed of all concept, back into the epistemic realm, not only remembered but reintroduced into thinking, into the conceptual event of opposition, of contradiction and negation, and negation of negation, of *machloykes*, which is the element of knowledge insofar as it is temporal, insofar as it is *thought*. Anti-anti-anti-Semitism is accordingly an introduction to Jewish thought, to thinking as it has historically been deployed in and as Jewish being, to thinking as *machloykes*.[25] Anti-anti-anti-Semitism is introduction to Talmud.

STRUCTURE OF THE BOOK

The basic anti-anti-anti-Semitic operation is taking a distance from and in this way revealing, rendering visible, and describing anti-anti-Semitism. Anti-anti-anti-Semitism is a phenomenology. Phenomenology is the challenge of looking at the seemingly invisible, namely at thought. Like all phenomenology, the present investigation too is faced with the basic question of how and where precisely thought *appears*. Anti-anti-Semitism appears in a variety of phenomena: a variety of contemporary approaches

---

25 See Elad Lapidot, "People of Knowers: On Heideggerian and Jewish Political Epistemologies," in *Heidegger and Jewish Thought: Difficult Others*, ed. Elad Lapidot and Micha Brumlik (New York: Rowman and Littlefield, 2018), 269–289.

to and performances of anti-anti-Semitism—and of Jewishness. Indeed, contemporary Jewishness is to a significant extent a performance of anti-anti-Semitism. Nonetheless, the present phenomenology focuses on the most conceptual form of anti-anti-Semitic thought, namely on explicitly formulated and articulated critical theories of anti-Semitism, as offered textually by prominent political philosophers after World War II. What this book offers is thus a series of intertwined readings, a hermeneutical exercise.

Part I of this book reads anti-anti-Semitic thought. Chapter 1 begins with a first overview of the dynamics of anti-anti-Semitic discourse as it has unfolded in an especially intensive and transparent manner in the recent controversy on Heidegger's anti-Semitism. It traces the basic outline and central moments of the way in which the category of "anti-Semitism" has generated within the debate, even as it engaged in denunciation and critique of anti-Semitism, a specific relation to or perception of Jews, which, at least in its epistemo-political aspects, manifested a conceptual complicity with the denunciated anti-Semitic discourse itself.

For better and further articulating the inner logic of this discursive dynamic of anti-anti-Semitism, the investigation then examines in more detail its manifestation within broader systematic attempts undertaken in post–World War II theoretical discourse at critically thinking anti-Semitism. The order, logic, and method of the readings arise from their phenomenological purpose, namely of displaying the discursive dynamics that is at work in and through them. The order of reading thus follows the order of the conceptual articulation of anti-anti-Semitism. The different readings feature different positions within anti-anti-Semitic discourse. The interrelations between these positions, however, are not only typological, but dialectical, i.e., they feature not just various types of anti-anti-Semitism, but different and interdependent moments of one anti-anti-Semitic logos.

Dialectics is temporal, such that the logical order of the texts featured by the following readings is also chronological, i.e., historical. The focus, however, will not be on direct personal influences, on how later authors explicitly reacted to earlier authors, but on the discursive effects of conceptual chronology, by virtue of which, for instance, anti-anti-Semitism succeeds anti-Semitism. Although affirmatively operating in and on the dimension of history, the claim of the present inquiry is not *disciplinarily* historical. The texts read will not be contextualized beyond their own self-contextualization, with respect both to nontextual history (world events, biographies, etc.) and to textual history (texts of other authors, other texts of the same author).

Chapter 2 is dedicated to the first, basic anti-anti-Semitic position, which denies anti-Semitism any epistemic value by reducing "the Jewish," namely the Jewish idea or principle, to which the anti-Semite is anti, to the anti-Semite's own subjective fantasy. There is no Jew *an sich*, only for the anti-Semite. The Jew would be a creation of the anti-Semite. The first, weaker version of this conception will be articulated through a reading of Adorno and Horkheimer's *The Dialectic of Enlightenment*, and described as the *imaginary* anti-Semitic creation of the Jew, by an act of *projection*. Jewishness would be the epistemic content projected by the anti-Semite on the knowledge-free, concrete living Jew. The second, stronger version of this conception is the *actual* anti-Semitic creation of the Jew, which will be presented through Sartre's *Réflexions sur la question juive*, which describes how through intersubjective interaction the anti-Semitic projection of Jewishness in fact generates actual Jewish self-consciousness.

The greatest conceptual difficulty of the first anti-anti-Semitic position lies in the exact relation between the projected, imaginary Jew and the real, concrete, flesh-and-blood Jew. There must still be something in the living Jew that makes possible the projection, which provides the screen or surface of the projection, the *Projektionsfläche*. Why the Jews?

This question moves the anti-anti-Semitic discourse to its next position, which is discussed in Chapter 3. The second anti-anti-Semitic position, in an attempt to identify the condition of possibility of the anti-Semitic projection *in the Jew*, performs a second, inverse reduction, and retraces anti-Semitism to a Jewish origin: the Jewish creation of anti-Semitism. A first version of this argument will be indicated in Hannah Arendt's *The Origins of Totalitarianism*, where the genealogy of anti-Semitism leads back to a Jewish consciousness of a separate ethnic identity. A more recent instance of the same argument will be outlined in Alain Badiou's writings on *Uses of the Word 'Jew'* (*Portées du mot 'juif'*), as well as in his readings of Saint Paul, where Jewishness is portrayed as the universal principle of particularity, as conceptual source both for anti-Semitism, by way of reproduction, and for Christianity, by way of negation.

Chapter 4 discusses a third anti-anti-Semitic position, which, like the second position, traces back the anti-Semitic idea of Jewishness to a Jewish episteme. The third position, however, does not posit Jewish episteme as identical to anti-Semitism, but as *opposite* to it. Notwithstanding the opposition between anti-Semitic and Jewish knowledge, the third position remains within anti-anti-Semitic discourse, since the Jewish knowledge that it posits is nothing but anti-anti-Semitism itself, i.e., the negation of any Jewish knowledge, a negation that would thus paradoxically constitute Jewishness. This position, which posits Jewishness as anti-anti-Semitism, is, so the claim goes, one of the most powerful current conceptions of Jewish being. Its contour and dynamics are presented through a reading in Jean-Luc Nancy's recent analyses on anti-Semitism in the wake of the Heidegger debate, where against the anti-Semitic, Christian, and Western principle of "self," he posited a Jewish principle of "alterity," of a "self" that is constituted by "dispersion of the self," in epistemo-political terms: "a people of no people."

Having criticized anti-anti-Semitism in Part I, Part II of the book offers a direction and first outline for a non-anti-anti-Semitic critique of anti-Semitism. The basic attempt is to reinscribe the historical discourse of political anti-Semitism into modern and contemporary epistemology. It is an exercise in re-membering the Semites. The basic claim is that anti-Semitism arises from a modern negative political epistemology, a central operation of which has been the obliteration, effacement, or disfiguration of the Jewish, such that anti-Semitism may in fact be said to contain the roots of anti-anti-Semitism, as analyzed in Part I.

Chapter 5 contemplates the emergence of the category "anti-Semitic" and the discourse arranged around it from within nineteenth-century science. Focusing on the works of Ernst Renan, as the first self-proclaimed "anti-Semite," my readings retrace the conceptual movements that generated the appearance and meaning of "the Semites" as a central figure of human sciences. A basic motif revealed by these readings, which draw a connection between Renan's early Semitic philology and his later advocacy of the Nation, is the powerful political epistemology underlying the rise of scientific Semitism *eo ipso* as political anti-Semitism. "The Semites" emerge as the negative epistemo-political paradigm of modernist Christology, as the spirit of race to be superseded by the race of spirit; "the Jews" emerge as the site of modern supersession in the form of emancipation; emancipation emerges, in this discourse, as disfiguration by way of assimilation.

Chapter 6 looks more closely at the idea of Jewish emancipation as advent site of modern political epistemology. It does so through readings in generative texts of the polemics on Jewish emancipation and assimilation, and the resistance, opposition, and *anti* to which it gave rise, namely generative texts of "The Jewish Question." Next to Renanian science, the mid-nineteenth-century emergent discussion on the Jewish Question is analyzed as a second discursive root of political anti-Semitism. The readings focus on the famous debate between Bruno Bauer and Karl Marx. The articulation of the conceptual tension between Bauer and Marx on the Jewish Question will allow distinguishing between their respective political epistemologies and the roles that they give to the Jews. My analysis will suggest a close intimacy between Bauer and Renan in deploying the discourse of modern state, race, and religion, which is generative of anti-Semitism. It will further indicate a significant difference between Bauer and Renan to Marx, whose anti-Jewish text nonetheless, so is the claim, resists race-state discourse and points at the direction of an alternative, possibly positive, perhaps even Jewish-y political epistemology.

The last chapter, Chapter 7, is dedicated to readings in the seminal texts of political anti-Semitism, anti-Semitism proper, from Wilhelm Marr to Adolf Hitler. If Chapter 6 attempts to render visible the politics of Semitic science, this chapter tries to work out the epistemological framework, presuppositions, and stakes of anti-Semitic politics. It thus indicates central categories and moments in which anti-Semitic politics in fact constitutes consummation and materialization of modern political epistemology, as analyzed in Chapters 6 and 7. The various readings reveal at the basis of anti-Semitism a political epistemology of *the invisible*, which arises from and gives ultimate effect to modern race theology, as presented in Renan and Bauer. Anti-Semitic political epistemology in fact identifies the essence of race in its invisibility and consequently deems the disappearance and disfiguration of the Jews through assimilation not as the passing away but as the highpoint and omnipresence of Jewish being, as "The Triumph of the Jews." This epistemology, so it will be claimed, provided the conceptual framework for the disfiguration of the Jews by way of the Final Solution.

The epilogue to the book goes back to where it started, both existentially and structurally, to the debate on Heidegger's anti-Semitism. Having identified, articulated, analyzed, and critiqued anti-anti-Semitic discourse, this concluding section indicates at least a direction for overcoming it, by drawing the outlines for a non-anti-anti-Semitic approach to this debate. It will demonstrate, in other words, how instead of countering Heidegger's anti-Semitism by banning the Jewish from thought, it is possible to respond by engaging on and in Jewish thought.

Part I

ANTI-ANTI-SEMITISM

1 Anti-Heidegger

Anatomy of Anti-Anti-Semitism

FROM FEBRUARY 2014 TO MARCH 2015 the German *Klostermann Verlag* has published the first four volumes of what will come to be generally known as Martin Heidegger's *Black Notebooks*.[1] The *Black Notebooks* are a collection of notes written by Heidegger between the years 1931 to 1975, which he himself before his death prepared for posthumous publication, as the last volumes, 94–102, of the integral edition of his collected works, the *Gesamtausgabe*. The four published volumes contain the notes from 1931 to 1948. These notes could be generally characterized as philosophical fragments; however, their characterization has been controversial. Indeed, immediately upon publication, in fact even before they were published,

---

1   Martin Heidegger, *Überlegungen II–VI (Schwarze Hefte 1931–1938)*, ed. Peter Trawny (Frankfurt am Main: Klostermann, 2014) (GA 94), trans. Richard Rojcewicz as *Ponderings II–VI Black Notebooks 1931–1938* (Bloomington: Indiana University Press, 2016); Heidegger, *Überlegungen VII–XI (Schwarze Hefte 1938–1939)*, ed. Peter Trawny (Frankfurt am Main: Klostermann, 2014) (GA 95), trans. Richard Rojcewicz as *Ponderings VII–XI: Black Notebooks 1938–1939* (Bloomington: Indiana University Press, 2017); Heidegger, *Überlegungen XII–XV (Schwarze Hefte 1939–1941)*, ed. Peter Trawny (Frankfurt am Main: Klostermann, 2014) (GA 96), trans. Richard Rojcewicz as *Ponderings XII–XV: Black Notebooks 1939–1941* (Bloomington: Indiana University Press, 2017); Heidegger, *Anmerkungen II–V (Schwarze Hefte 1941–1944)*, ed. Peter Trawny (Frankfurt am Main: Klostermann, 2015) (GA 97).

the *Black Notebooks* sparked off a heated controversy. The debate started in the *feuilleton* sections of European press, followed by international media, then transported to academic venues, conferences, journals, and books, to take the shape of a scholarly and philosophical conversation, an extraordinary intellectual event.[2] The entire controversy concerned a handful of notes, mostly from the years 1939–1941, covering together about three pages of text, out of about 1,800 pages of all so far published *Black Notebooks*. What is common to all the controversial notes is that they refer to Jews or "Jewish" things. All these references constitute negative statements and have been thus almost unanimously recognized as *anti-Semitic*.

In what follows, I will show how the controversy concerning Heidegger's *Black Notebooks*, built up around and in opposition to anti-Semitism, unfolding, that is, as *anti-anti-Semitic* discourse, has been forming a contemporary site of non-encounter between the philosophical and the Jewish. I will in particular identify the underlying epistemo-political pre-

---

2   Among the important monographs published so far: Peter Trawny, *Heidegger und der Mythos der jüdischen Weltverschwörung* (Frankfurt am Main: Klostermann, 2014); Donatella Di Cesare, *Heidegger, die Juden, die Shoah* (Frankfurt am Main: Klostermann, 2015); F.-W. von Herrmann and F. Alfieri, *Martin Heidegger. Die Wahrheit über die Schwarzen Hefte*, übers. Pascal David (Berlin: Duncker & Humbolt, 2017); Elliot Wolfson, *The Duplicity of Philosophy's Shadow: Heidegger, Nazism, and the Jewish Other* (New York: Columbia University Press, 2018). To name some of the collected volumes that have appeared so far: Joseph Cohen and Raphael Zagury-Orly, ed., *Heidegger et "les juifs," La Règle du Jeu*, no. 58–59 (Paris: Grasset, 2015); Peter Trawny and Andrew J. Mitchell, ed., *Heidegger, die Juden, noch einmal* (Frankfurt am Main: Vittorio Klostermann, 2015); Marion Heinz and Sidonie Kellerer, ed., *Martin Heideggers "Schwarze Hefte." Eine philosophische-politische Debatte* (Berlin: Suhrkamp, 2016); Ingo Farin and Jeff Malpas, ed., *Reading Heidegger's Black Notebooks 1931–1941* (Cambridge, MA: MIT Press, 2016); Walter Homolka and Arnulf Heidegger, ed., *Heidegger und der Anti-Semitismus. Positionen im Widerstreit* (Freiburg/Basel/Wien: Herder, 2016); Hans-Helmuth Gander and Magnus Striet, ed., *Heideggers Weg in die Moderne. Eine Verortung der »Schwarzen Hefte«* (Frankfurt am Main: Vittorio Klostermann, 2017); Mårten Björk and Jayne Svenungsson, ed., *Heidegger's Black Notebooks and the Future of Theology* (New York: Palgrave Macmillan, 2017). For a good review of some of these volumes, see Jan Eike Dunkhase, "Beiträge zur neuen Heidegger-Debatte" (book review), *H-Soz-Kult*, March 13, 2017, http://www.hsozkult.de/publication review/id/rezbuecher-27447.

conceptions of this anti-anti-Semitic operation, and indicate moments where it echoes or threatens to converge with tropes of a discourse that may be designated, by this very same anti-anti-Semitic discourse itself, as *anti-Semitism*. This will be just an initial indication, performed in the corpus of a still ongoing conversation. Key concepts, positions, and dynamics of this anti-anti-Semitic discourse will be examined more closely in the following chapters. The main topic here is the critique of anti-Semitism, i.e., anti-anti-Semitism. The focus for now is therefore the *debate* concerning Heidegger's anti-Semitic fragments and not these fragments themselves, nor their anti-Semitism. I will come back to the question of anti-Semitism in the second part of this book, and to Heidegger's anti-Semitism in the epilogue. Presently, as a passage to the controversy, I will simply quote the four most central notes that have been discussed in the current debate:

1 "But the temporary increase in the power of Judaism [*Judentum*] is grounded in the fact that Western metaphysics, especially in its modern development, offered the point of attachment for the expansion of an otherwise empty rationality and calculative capacity, and these thereby created for themselves an abode in the 'spirit' without ever being able, on their own, to grasp the concealed domains of decision. The more originary and inceptual the future decisions and questions become, all the more inaccessible will they remain to this 'race.' (Thus Husserl's step to the phenomenological attitude, taken in explicit opposition to psychological explanation and to the historical calculation of opinions, is of lasting importance—and yet this attitude never reaches into the domains of the essential decisions; instead, it entirely presupposes the historical tradition of philosophy. The necessary result shows itself at once in the turning toward a neo-Kantian transcendental philosophy, and this turn ultimately made inevitable a progression to Hegelianism in the formal sense. My 'attack' on Husserl is not directed to him alone and is not at all directed inessentially—the attack is directed against the neglect of the question of being, i.e., against the essence of metaphysics as such, the metaphysics on whose ground the machination of beings is able to determine history. The attack establishes a historical moment of the supreme decision between the primacy of beings and the grounding of the truth of beyng.)" (GA 96: 46; Rojcewicz, 37)

2 "The Jews, *with their accentuated talent for calculation*, have for the longest time already been 'living' according to the principle of race, which is why they are also offering the most vehement resistance to its unrestricted application. The instituting of racial breeding stems not from 'life' itself, but from the overpowering of life by machination. What machination pursues with such planning is a complete deracializing of peoples through their being clamped into an equally built and equally tailored instituting of all beings. One with the deracializing is a self-alienation of the peoples—the loss of history, i.e., the loss of the domains of decision regarding beyng." (GA 96: 56; Rojcewicz, 44)

3 "The question of the role of *world-Judaism* [*Weltjudentum*] is not a racial question, but a metaphysical one, a question that concerns the kind of singular human existence [*Menschentümlichkeit*] which, being utterly unattached [*schlechthin ungebunden*; Rojcewicz translates "in an utterly unrestrained way"], can undertake as a world-historical 'task' the uprooting of all beings from being." (GA 96:243; Rojcewicz, 191)

4 "The anti-Christ must, like any 'anti-', originate from the same essential ground as that against which it is 'anti-'—namely like 'the Christ'. He originates from the Jewish collective [*Judenschaft*]. The latter has been, in the era of the Christian Occident, i.e., of Metaphysics, the principle of destruction. The destructive element in the turning of the consummation of Metaphysics—i.e., of Hegel's metaphysics through Marx. Spirit and culture become the superstructure of 'life'—i.e., of economy, i.e., of organization—i.e., of the biological—i.e., of the 'people'. When the essential 'Jewish' in the metaphysical sense begins to fight against the Jewish, the summit of self-annihilation was reached in history; provided that the 'Jewish' has everywhere completely seized control, such that also fighting 'the Jewish'—and primarily it—comes under its dominion." (GA 97; 20)

ANTI-SEMITISM, THE END OF PHILOSOPHY

The primary anti-anti-Semitic operation effected by the ongoing debate concerning the above passages has been hermeneutic, namely pertaining to the basic relation to the text as such or, more radically, an operation revealing the basic relation to thinking *as* a relation to text, as a relation of reading. Designating the controversial passages as "anti-Semitic" has led to questioning the essence of this text, of text in general, and more precisely the nature of the *philosophical* text, or, on the side of reception, of *philosophical reading*. Through a hermeneutic procedure, similar to earlier ones already performed in previous Heidegger controversies with respect to the question of National Socialism, the question of anti-Semitism triggered an operation of differentiation and separation, within the Heideggerian text, within the seeming consistency of its texture, between the philosophical and the non-philosophical. In this operation, it is by means of the category "anti-Semitism" that the Jews have come to signify the limit or end of philosophy.

What is meant by this is not the diverging appreciations of how central to Heidegger's thought, in general or as expressed in the *Black Notebooks*, are his discussions of Jews, starting with the explicit passages and variously expanding the scope of this corpus through more or less far-reaching semantic extrapolations (whereby Jews are also intended or should be understood as signified by terms such as "calculation," "machinations," "uprootedness," "groundlessness," "enemy," "beings" etc.). One easily joins, for instance, Karsten Harries's rejection of Richard Wolin's exaggerated assertion of Heidegger's "obsession with World Jewry."[3]

---

[3] See Karsten Harries, "Nostalgia, Spite, and the Truth of Being," in *Reading Heidegger's Black Notebooks*, 207–222, quoting and critiquing Wolin on 208; cf. Richard Wolin, "Vernunftkritik nach den Schwarzen Heften," in *Martin Heideggers "Schwarze Hefte,"* 397–415, reading in the *Black Notebooks*, in an equally excessive manner, that "for Heidegger, the Jews are the pillars [*tragende Säule*] of modernity" (409). Elliot Wolfson too rejects "the claim that the *Black Notebooks* reveal anti-Semitism at the core of Heidegger's philosophy as sensationalistic and inaccurate"; see Wolfson, *The Duplicity*, 31.

What I mean is rather the various conceptual devices deployed in order to trace within the Heideggerian text and Western corpus or thought in general a clear separation between anti-Semitism or anti-Judaism and philosophy—both in Heidegger's defense or against him. Thus, on the apologetic side, Friedrich Wilhelm von Hermann considers all Heidegger's texts pertaining to Jews to be "philosophically without import."[4] Rosa Maria Marafioti understands "the non-philosophical passages

---

4   Friedrich-Wilhelm von Herrmann, "The Role of Martin Heidegger's Notebooks within the Context of His Oeuvre," in *Reading Heidegger's Black Notebooks*, 93. See also Friedrich-Wilhelm von Herrmann und Francesco Alfieri, *Die Wahrheit über die Schwarzen Hefte*, 39–40. In their book, von Herrmann and Alfieri make the worthy attempt of enhancing the philosophical discussion of the *Black Notebooks* by enlarging its scope beyond what they justly consider as the marginality of the "Jewish-related" [*Juden-bezogen*] passages to the more central questions, and by intensifying the philological rigor, principally by reading the *Black Notebooks* in the context of Heidegger's more systematic works on the *Seinsgeschichte*. This worthy cause notwithstanding, von Herrmann and Alfieri's attempt remains to a large extent unconvincing, and even counterproductive. Their text is highly polemic (repeatedly denouncing the "instrumentalization" of the *Black Notebooks*, the exact nature of which—an instrument for *what?*— is never really explained) and often of a rather baroque style (the first chapter, for instance, is titled "Necessary Elucidations to the *Black Notebooks*, beyond the Naïve Instrumentalization that was Staged Based on Conjectures of Convenient Positions"). The authors' central and recurrent argument is that Heidegger's anti-Jewish statements arise from a more general critique of modernity, which doesn't only target Jews but also Christianity, natural sciences, technology etc., and for this reason cannot be considered as anti-Semitism. My obvious answer to this argument is that even if it is indeed incorrect to consider Heidegger's philosophy or critique of modernity as anti-Semitic, his anti-Jewish statements can still arise from anti-Semitic notions, as I think they do.

In the present context, it should be noted that von Hermann and Alfieri's anti-anti-Semitic hermeneutics is extreme. Thus, in a "Preliminary Remark," von Hermann divides the text fragments contained in the *Black Notebooks* into two groups: 1. Philosophical or "pure" thoughts; and 2. Personal or private views ("everything that belongs to 2 is for me completely *redundant!*" [26]). With respect to the current debate, von Hermann formulates the hermeneutical principle guiding this division as follows: "As long as Heidegger's comments to his 'diagnoses of modernity', i.e., to 'calculative thought', appear in the notebooks *without reference* to

critical of Jews" as the "opinions of a private person."⁵ Jeff Malpas uses the distinction between "philosophical" and "personal/political," and Daniela Vallega-Neu finds the controversial passages not to represent "originary thinking."⁶ In contrast and in breach of this original level of philosophy, the anti-Semitic text represents an external and alien element, which can only enter the philosophical text by the effect of "infection" or "contam-

---

the 'Jews', they belong to Heidegger's 'pure' thought. They only become political-private *when* and *inasmuch as* he refers them to the 'Jews'" (27).

Similarly, Alfieri's close reading of the "Jewish-related" passages of the *Black Notebooks* is often perplexing, eliciting from the texts the exact opposite of what they seem quite plainly to say. Thus, for instance, concerning the text "The question of the role of *world-Judaism* [*Weltjudentum*] is not a racial question, but a metaphysical one, a question that concerns the kind of singular human existence [*Menschentümlichkeit*] which, being utterly unattached, can undertake as a world-historical 'task' the uprooting of all beings from being" (GA 96:243), Alfieri comments: "*Nowhere* in the notebooks *is the slightest trace to be found, that Heidegger ascribes a metaphysical essence to the Jews*" (172). With respect to the words "the Jewish collective [*Judenschaft*] … has been, in the era of the Christian Occident, i.e., of Metaphysics, the principle of destruction" (GA 97; 20), Alfieri writes: "As Judaism cannot be separated from the Christian Occident, so Judaism cannot be integrated in metaphysics: to claim otherwise means to intentionally falsify the texts—here as elsewhere" (205). His conclusion, whereby "it is proven that no trace of anti-Semitism is to be found in Heidegger" (228), is thus unconvincing.

5   Rosa Maria Marafioti, "Heideggers vielsagendes, 'Schweigen'", in *Heidegger und der Anti-Semitismus*, 285 and 278, respectively.

6   Jeff Malpas, "On the Philosophical Reading of Heidegger: Situating the *Black Notebooks*," in *Reading Heidegger's Black Notebooks*, 12; Daniela Vallega-Neu, "The Black Notebooks and Heidegger's Writing on the Event (1936–1942)," in *Reading Heidegger's Black Notebooks*, 136.

ination."⁷ "A small, but highly poisonous dose," Dieter Thomä called it.⁸ Stamped "anti-Semitic," these texts are completely banished from the realm of thought, meaning, and intelligibility. Reading them, the hermeneutical expert Jean Grondin can do nothing more than "shake the head" and identify them as "Nazi war propaganda," of which Heidegger was the "victim."⁹ While the apologists use the separation of anti-Semitism and philosophy for surgically removing the malignant passages and thus salvaging the otherwise healthy corpus, the more prosecutorial voices use the exactly same separation for disqualifying the entire oeuvre. Thus, invoking Emmanuel Faye's 2005 excommunication of Heidegger's work from philosophy on the charge of National Socialism ("Such a work may not remain in philosophy libraries: it rather belongs to the historical archives of Nazism and Hitlerism"),¹⁰ Marion Heinz upholds the sentence by ruling that "there can be no 'anti-Semitic *philosophy*.'"¹¹

BAN OF THE COLLECTIVE

For such an operation as this, which determines the limits of philosophy, which thus in a way decides on the definition and essence of philosophy, either a very elaborate reasoning is required—or the certainty of

---

7   Vallega-Neu, "The Black Notebooks and Heidegger's Writing on the Event (1936–1942)," 128, 137; Peter Trawny, *Heidegger and the Myth of Jewish World Conspiracy*, 12: "The contamination attacks the boundaries of thoughts and dissolves, blurs them." In the Epilogue to the 2nd edition of his book, Trawny distances himself from the term "*Kontamination*," which he considers to be too close to "the logic of purification" that he criticizes in Heidegger. It remains unclear, however, in what way Trawny's suggested alternative, "*Mitberührt-, Miterfasstwerden*," provides anything more than a literal German translation of the term "contamination," thus perhaps avoiding the cultural-historical connotations of this term, but not its underlying logic of relation between *alien* elements.
8   Dieter Thomä, "Wie antisemitisch ist Heidegger? Über die Schwarzen Hefte und die gegenwärtige Lage der Heidegger-Kritik," in *Martin Heideggers "Schwarze Hefte,"* 211.
9   Jean Grondin, "Warum ich Heidegger in schwieriger Zeit treu bleibe," in *Heidegger und der Anti-Semitismus*, 233, 239.
10   Emmanuel Faye, *Heidegger, l'introduction du nazisme dans la philosophie* (Paris: Albin Michel, 2005), 513.
11   Marion Heinz, "Einleitung," in *Martin Heideggers "Schwarze Hefte,"* 27.

self-evidence. The current debate most often seems to hold the mutual exclusion of philosophy and anti-Semitism as self-evident. In any case, no elaborate reasoning has been so far provided for this virtually universal gesture. The desire to distance oneself and one's discourse from anti-Semitism, in particular in the historical context of Heidegger's *Black Notebooks* entries, is no doubt self-evident. As I explained above, however, the way of anti-anti-Semitism is ambiguous, and may also lead to the opposite of the desired direction. For this reason I find it essential to insist on asking the explicit question: why is anti-Semitism excluded from philosophy? Or better: what in anti-Semitism excludes it from philosophy? Or yet better: what in anti-Semitism, as understood by the current discourse, excludes it from philosophy?

My basic argument, which I will quickly state at the outset, before demonstrating it in the texts, is that this crucial component is not the "anti-," namely is not the negative attitude of anti-Semitism toward Jews, not *what* statements anti-Semitism makes about Jews, but rather *that* it makes any statements about Jews at all, whether negative or positive. In other words, I argue that the problematic component of anti-Semitism, which in the eyes of the current discourse excludes anti-Semitism from philosophy, is the Jews. This means that the current anti-anti-Semitism as it expresses itself in the current Heidegger controversy is grounded on "a certain perception of the Jews" as something, a collective being, with respect to which no philosophically relevant statements may be made, namely as something that lies outside of thought.

For demonstrating my claim, I start by referring to one of the most important and omnipresent voices in the current debate, to whom I will continue to refer often in this chapter. Indeed, the basic terms of this debate were set in advance, a few months before the actual publication of the *Black Notebooks*, through a chain of interactions triggered by their editor, Peter Trawny. Trawny's essay on the *Black Notebooks* was published simultaneously with the *Notebooks* themselves, but pre-circulated as a draft a few months earlier, and is—as are his editor's notes in the *Gesamtausgabe* volumes themselves—the most often explicitly and inexplicitly quoted authority and source on the matter.[12] It was Trawny who opened and framed

---

12   Peter Trawny, *Heidegger und der Mythos der jüdischen Weltverschwörung* (Frankfurt am Main: Klostermann, 2014).

the discussion by initially introducing the accusation of "anti-Semitism" that had allegedly "contaminated" Heidegger's thought. As far as I know, Trawny has been so far the only participant in the discussion who also offered an explicit definition of what he meant by "anti-Semitism," which has not been contested or further discussed, and so seems to express a general consensus.[13] I should emphasize that if my critique of the current discourse often refers to Trawny's work, it is not because I find it to be more problematic that others, but, on the contrary, the best articulated and so the most interesting to engage with, the best *Gegner*, as Heidegger would have it.[14]

The first part of this definition focuses on the "anti-," the negative component of "hate": "Anti-Semitic—was and is anything affective or administrative directed against Jews based on rumors, prejudices and pseudo-scientific (race-theoretical or racist) sources, and which leads to (a) defamation, (b) a general hostile stereotype [*Feindbild*], (c) isolation—occupational ban, ghetto, camp, (d) expulsion—emigration, (e) extermination—pogroms, mass executions, extermination camps." This first part already raises different questions, for example concerning the requirement that the anti-Jewish measures be "based on rumors, prejudices and pseudo-scientific (race-theoretical or racist) sources": would there be more legitimate sources? Or is it implicitly assumed that *any* negative attitude ("affective or administrative") toward Jew is *eo ipso* based on problematic sources, pseudo-sources, is in fact necessarily groundless, by definition unfounded? And would this mean that banning anti-Semitism commands an unconditional *positive* attitude toward Jews, or rather, at least on the affective and administrative levels—no attitude at all? It is precisely in this direction that the second, supplementary part of Trawny's definition points at, going beyond any specific negative or positive attitude, beyond "anti-" and "pro-," touching the more fundamental level of perception: "*Nowadays* should be also designated as anti-Semitic whatever is meant to characterize the Jews as 'the Jews.'"[15]

---

13   Trawny, 11. Trawny refers in this context to Wolfgang Benz, *Was ist Anti-Semitismus?* (Munich: C.H. Beck, 2004). In the introduction to the collective volume on the controversy that was edited by Trawny and Andrew J. Mitchell, the editors laconically refer to "universal standards of anti-Semitism research," with no further specifications; see *Heidegger, die Juden, noch einmal*, 7.
14   Cf. GA 94: 179.
15   Trawny, *Heidegger und der Mythos*, 11.

It is this last part that has been most central for the current Heidegger controversy. Its terse formulation contains the entire problem *in nuce*. Anti-Semitism is understood here as characterizing, namely referring to or perceiving the Jews as "the Jews." This definition does not concern any specific value or content attributed to the Jews. It rather concerns the basic mode of relation to Jews, the fundamental way of understanding the kind of being, thing or object designated by the collective name "the Jews." The difference between the non-anti-Semitic and anti-Semitic conception is made and signified by the scare quotes around the expression "the Jews." This profoundly semantic difference of "" appears very often in the discourse concerning anti-Semitism, including the current Heidegger debate. I would even venture to say that this semantic difference is foundational for this discourse, for its specific mode of discursivity, of signifying. The scare quotes around "the Jews" in fact signify here the mode of signification itself: the same sign (the Jews) functions, signifies in one mode in Trawny's sentence ("whatever is meant to characterize the Jews etc."), and in another mode ("as 'the Jews'") in the allegedly anti-Semitic discourse. Anti-Semitism would consist in mixing or confusing these two semantic functions: characterizing the Jews as "the Jews"; Anti-anti-Semitism would consist in keeping them apart.

To get a more precise idea of the nature of this basic separation or difference, I refer to one of the most famous and already canonic uses of scare quotes to differentiate between modes of signification concerning the Jews, as it was made by Jean-François Lyotard in the context of the last great Heidegger controversy in the late 1980s. Lyotard titled his intervention "Heidegger and 'the jews'" [*Heidegger et 'les juifs'*] and opened it by explaining his semantic operation: "I write 'the jews' this way neither out of prudence nor lack of something better. I use lower case to indicate that I am not thinking of a nation. I make it plural to signify that it is neither a figure nor a political (Zionism), religious (Judaism), or philosophical (Jewish philosophy) subject that I put forward under this name. I use quotation marks to avoid confusing these 'jews' with real Jews."[16]

I disregard for now the greater complexity of Lyotard's operation—the lowercase, the plural—and focus on the specific function of the scare

---

16   Jean-François Lyotard, *Heidegger and "the jews,"* trans. Andreas Michel and Mark Roberts (Minneapolis: University of Minnesota Press, 1990), 3.

quotes: they are intended to distinguish between, on the one hand, the Jews as signifying a theme of the philosophical, theoretical, conceptual discourse, an entity or being that pertains to the kind of discourse Lyotard is engaged in, "the Jews" (or "the jews"), and, on the other hand, the Jews as something that exists outside of this order of discourse, an entity the pertains to a different region of being altogether, the region of being as reality, namely the Jews of reality—the "real Jews" (the need to use here the scare quotes, in quoting Lyotard writing "real," does not generate but rather represents the fundamental difficulty of this semantic preclusion of reality from the order of discourse).[17] It is precisely this difference between Jews as reality and Jews as ideality, a concept, an entity of discourse or of *knowl-*

---

17   Lyotard's operation on 'the jews' has generated its own debate—see references and discussion in Sarah Hammerschlag, *The Figural Jew: Politics and Identity in Postwar French Thought* (Chicago: University of Chicago Press, 2010), 8–10. While some criticism tended to accuse Lyotard of "latent anti-Semitism" (Hammerschlag, 9), I agree with Hammerschlag's analysis (11n.34) that the discourse Lyotard deployed arises from postwar French philosophy's self-conscious *opposition* to anti-Semitism, what I call "anti-anti-Semitism," in which I nonetheless observe conceptual similarities to anti-Semitism. I will deal more closely with the discourse of and on what Hammerschlag called "The Figural Jew" in Chapter 4, focusing on the most current voice of this discourse, Jean-Luc Nancy.

At this point, I want to note that my critique of Lyotard's split between the Jews and "the jews" is similar—not identical—to Hammerschlag's. Hers is formulated in response to such critics as Daniel and Jonathan Boyarin, who criticized Lyotard's—and postmodern philosophy's—operation as Paulinian "allegorization," appropriation, and ultimately supersession of the Jews in the flesh (Daniel and Jonathan Boyarin, "Diaspora: Generation and the Ground of Jewish Identity," *Critical Inquiry* 19, no. 4 [1993]: 697–700; see also Daniel Boyarin, *A Radical Jew: Paul and the Politics of Identity* (Berkley: University of California Press, 1994), 149–152. For two similar critical positions as the Boyarins', see Geoffrey Bennington, "Lyotard and 'the Jews,'" in *Modernity, Culture, and 'the Jew'*, ed. Bryan Cheyette and Laura Marcus (Stanford, CA: Stanford University Press, 1998), 188–196; and in the same volume, Max Silverman, "Re-Figuring 'the Jew' in France," 197–207).

Hammerschlag's book argues, in contrast, in favor of the "trope of the Jew"—"The Figural Jew"—as developed in postmodern French philosophy. What she criticizes in Lyotard's "the jews" is not being trope *enough*, since the scare quotes *eo ipso* mark and limit the trope ("the jews") in view of the non-figurative, real Jews (the Jews). Hammerschlag accordingly suggests overcoming this separation between figurative and real when she calls to "engage with being Jewish as a liter-

edge, that Trawny too makes and seeks to fixatate through the operation of scare quotes. Both Lyotard and Trawny, while producing or re-producing this difference, namely this double Jewish being, at the same time observe the imperative of strictly separating between the real Jews and the conceptual "Jews," or rather avoiding and resisting their confusion, a confusion that Trawny defines as anti-Semitism.

In the context of the current debate, this discursive operation has been carried out most explicitly and fully by a second important voice, Donatella Di Cesare's. Di Cesare limited her analysis to the specific case of Heidegger's anti-Semitism, which she characterized as "metaphysical anti-Semitism," thereby attributing its mechanism to the specific tradition of Western metaphysics.[18] Di Cesare draws the difference between "the Jews" and the Jews as a difference between "the specter, the projection, the *figure* of the Jew, the *figural Jew*" and the "concrete Jews," "real Jews," or "flesh-and-blood Jews."[19] This last expression, "flesh-and-blood," is a further specification of the category "real," suggesting that the specific reality of the real, non-conceptual Jews consists in their organic existence, in life. There might be here a question of translation, of the German term "*leibhaftig*," which "flesh-and-blood" perhaps seeks to render in Di Cesare's English essay. This Husserlian term expresses the mode in which the object of our consciousness is given or present to us, to our perception, not just in a mediate way, through a photo or a sign, for instance, but directly in itself—"in flesh," *leibhaftig*. Famously, the conceptuality of life shapes

---

ary figure, ... treat it as a trope" (266). Jewish *being* itself, i.e., the Jews, would be a figure—no need for extra scare quotes.

As I will show in Chapter 4, I believe both positions—the Boyarians' radical defiguration and Hammerschlag's radical figuration of the Jewish—to be in fact more complex and ultimately arrive at surprisingly similar notions of Jewishness.
18   Donatella Di Cesare, *Heidegger, die Juden, die Shoah* (Frankfurt am Main: Klostermann, 2016); Di Cesare, "Heideggers metaphysischer Anti-Semitismus," in *Heidegger und der Anti-Semitismus*, 212–219; Di Cesare, "Das Sein und der Jude. Heideggers metaphysischer Anti-Semitismus," in *Heidegger, die Juden, noch einmal*, 55–74; Di Cesare, "Heidegger's Metaphysical Anti-Semitism," in *Reading Heidegger's Black Notebooks*, 181–194.
19   Di Cesare, *Heidegger, die Juden, die Shoah*, 254–263; Di Cesare, "Heidegger's Metaphysical Anti-Semitism," 189. Di Cesare may be said to express here the position of the Boyarins against Hammerschlag's "Figural Jew"—see note 17 above. See a more detailed discussion in Chapter 4.

in Husserl's thought the paradigm of immediate presence. Live, lived and *leibhaftig*, i.e., immediately present, is for Husserl however not primarily the "real," in the sense of sensual, spatio-temporal bodies, but rather entities such as ideas (*Ideen*) or essences (*Wesen*).[20] For Di Cesare, who I think in this point expresses the common anti-anti-Semitic discourse, it is rather the opposite: the *leibhaftig*, immediately present and concrete, is precisely *not* the idea or concept of the Jew, but the "real," literally "flesh-and-blood," living Jew. She thus describes the confusion between the two, namely anti-Semitism or according to her "metaphysical" anti-Semitism, as follows: "One seeks to define the Jews, in order to reduce [to this definition] the corporeal [*leibhaftigen*], concrete Jews. . . . The *metaphysics of the Jews* leads to the *metaphysical Jew*, to an abstract figure, to whom qualities are attributed, which are inherent to the 'idea', to the model of the Jew."[21]

Of course, this motif of fighting anti-Semitism by rejecting stereotypes, generalizations, and essentializations etc. is well known and omnipresent and in no way confined to the philosophical discourse in the Heidegger controversy. Nonetheless, the conceptual accuracy and logical commitments of the philosophical discourse provide a more precise articulation of this anti-anti-Semitic strategy and enable to better assess its internal difficulties. In fact, considered with philosophical rigor, there seems to be a deep paradox in not just differentiating, but strictly separating between and denouncing the confusion of real Jews and the concept, idea, or definition of the Jews, i.e., in forbidding the characterization of the Jews as "the Jews." How can this very prohibition, this reference to the Jews, the so-

---

20   Husserl, *Logische Untersuchungen. Zweiter Band. Untersuchungen zur Phänomenologie und Theorie der Erkenntnis* (Den Haag: Martinus Nijhoff, 1984), 144; Husserl, *Ideen zu einer reinen Phänomenologie und phänomenologischen Philosophie. Erstes Buch. Allgemeine Einführung in die reine Phänomenologie* (Den Haag: Martinus Nijhoff, 1976), 10.

21   Di Cesare, *Heidegger, die Juden, die Shoah*, 258. See also Christian Geulen's distinction between Jews as "abstraction" and "real Jewish life reality" [*Lebenswirklichkeit*], "Gewollt willenlos. Heideggers Schwarze Hefte als historisches Dokument" in *Martin Heideggers "Schwarze Hefte,"* 285. As we shall see, the category of "life" plays a central role in this debate. Also note that Di Cesare's description echoes Lyotard's portrayal of European anti-Judaism: "'The jews' are the object of a dismissal with which Jews, in particular, are afflicted in reality" (*Heidegger and "the jews,"* 3).

called real Jews, be at all understood, how can something like "real Jews" be perceived in the world, without any concept, idea, definition, model, or figure of "Jews"? With all philosophical rigor, the notion of perception, cognition, or any other form of epistemic condition, of knowledge, without any idea or concept, challenges the basic epistemology of the entire philosophical tradition, pushes philosophy to its limit. This challenge is all the more striking, considering that the liminal object of this supposedly pure, pre- or non-conceptual intuition is not something like Being, Time, I, the Other, or God, but "the Jews," namely a collective, a set of individuals joined by some form of common generality.

This paradox or difficulty is not just a theoretical deficiency that would undermine the ability of anti-anti-Semitic discourse to conceptualize or to *account* for a preliminary, pre-conceptually given fact, figure, or perception of "the Jews." On the contrary, my point is precisely that the discursive-conceptual paradox is coherent with or even generative for a specific *perception* or image of the Jews or the Jewish. I claim that the aforesaid paradox is the conceptual device by which anti-anti-Semitic discourse *posits* the Jews as an epistemo-political paradigm, a negative paradigm of political epistemology: i.e., as a collective devoid of concept, a political existence with no *episteme*. This negative Jewish paradigm thus serves as the general paradigm for understanding a series of concepts, all designating the collective subjectivity of the political existence, the collective political subject: the people, the *ethnos*, the nation, the "we." The rejection of anti-Semitism through the division between the reality and the ideality of the Jewish collective, between the Jews and "the Jews," thus shows itself to be but the figure of the more general, universal separation or even—since this epistemo-political operation is as *political* as it is epistemological—banishment of the collective subjectivity from the realm of knowledge and discourse of philosophy. In the current controversy, this can be clearly observed in the way in which the accusation of "anti-Semitism" against Heidegger universally and virtually without exception is translated into—and thus submerged in—the general denouncement of Heidegger's reference to collective subjectivities in his philosophical discourse, the philosophical nature of which being allegedly compromised and "contaminated" precisely by this reference.

And so, next to "the Jews," Peter Trawny extended the scare quotes in his discussion of Heidegger's *Black Notebooks* to "the Greeks," "the Germans," "the Romans," "the Christians," "the Jesuits," "the Protestants," "the Catholics," "the Russians," "the English people" [*die Engländer*], "the French people" [*die Franzosen*], "the Americans," "the Europeans," and "the Asians." "For us today," Trawny proclaims-observes, "the use of such collective concepts has become problematic."[22] This formulation of itself forces the question concerning the precise identity or mode of signification of "us today," for which such collective concepts have become problematic. May this "we" be designated by any of the collective concepts it finds problematic, or by similar "such" concepts? Would there be any other kind of collective concepts more appropriate for "us today"? Or are "we today" to be defined as the collective that rejects all collectivity, at least *conceptually*?

Insofar as Trawny's "we" designates the community of knowledge, of philosophers and scholars, which has expressed itself in the current Heidegger controversy, its reaction to anti-Semitism has in fact been an almost unanimous, virtually constitutive banishment of the afore-mentioned collective subjects from the epistemic realm of philosophy, condemning the contamination of Heidegger's discourse by such concepts. Thomas Rohkrämer, for instance, denounced Heidegger's "sweeping associations between nations and metaphysical positions," while Andrew Bowie condemned the "pernicious nonsense" of bringing together "ontological difference" and "politico-historical issues"; for Markus Gabriel, "Germans" and "Jews" are nothing but "figments of imagination" [*Hirngespinst*], and Thomas Vašek decried the use of "dark, mystifying [*raunende*] concepts such as 'soul', 'blood' or 'people.'"[23]

In fact, the basic question that has been shaping the main contours of the current anti-Semitism controversy refers neither to the Jews nor to the collective in general, be it "people," "nation, "race," or other, themes with respect to which there seems to prevail a quasi-consensus that they do not

---

22   Trawny, *Heidegger und der Mythos*, 27.
23   Respectively: Thomas Rohkrämer, "Heidegger and National Socialism: Great Hopes, Despair, and Resilience," in *Reading Heidegger's Black Notebooks*, 248; Rohkrämer, "Heidegger, Kulturktirik und völkische Ideologie," 274; Andrew Bowie, "Philosophy, Science and Politics in the Black Notebooks," in *Reading Heidegger's Black Notebooks*, 258; Markus Gabriel, "Heideggers antisemitische Stereotypen," in *Heidegger und der Anti-Semitismus*, 225; Thomas Vašek, "Schluss mit Heidegger?," 393.

belong to philosophy.²⁴ Rather, the basic question has concerned the extent to which these concepts contaminate Heidegger's philosophy. On the one extreme, there are those who, like Wilhelm Friedrich von Hermann and Rosa Maria Marafioti, protect the purity of the philosophy by simply classifying all the problematic passages as non-philosophical (private, personal opinions etc.). More nuanced, both Peter Trawny and Donatella Di Cesare, for instance, do identify a contamination, but diagnose it as inconsistency or self-betrayal within Heidegger's philosophy, Trawny a betrayal of the ontological difference, and Di Cesare as Heidegger's "falling back" into the metaphysical tradition that his philosophy precisely purports to surmount.²⁵ On the other extreme, a group of scholars has taken up the task already defined by Emmanuel Faye of showing how the collective subject has been not at all contaminating but rather underlying Heidegger's thought from its inception, for the sake of reaffirming Faye's aforementioned sweeping conviction of Heidegger's entire project and ensuing call to ban it from the philosophical discourse and community.

At this point I would like to indicate the intimacy between the anti-anti-Semitic exclusion of the collective from the philosophical episteme and the intertwined exclusion of history. In fact, the textual epicenter of the controversy on Heidegger's anti-Semitism, the period and section of his writings in which "the Jews" and all the other collectives emerge, the conceptual environment that so to speak facilitated the "contamination" of the philosophical by the non-philosophical, is what Heidegger called the *Seinsgeschichte*. Translating this term opens up to the difficulty it stands for. It may be translated the "history of being." This translation is not false, insofar as it correctly indicates the historical dimension that during this period Heidegger lends to his philosophy of being, which for him is thought per se. Collectivity thus appears in the dimension of historicity. And yet, translating Heidegger's *Geschichte* by "history" is insofar problematic as this term derives much of its semantic thrust precisely from its differentiation from *Historie*. I cannot discuss here the exact nature of this difference and

---

24   See, for instance, the critique of Tracy Strong, "On Relevant Events, Then and Now," in *Reading Heidegger's Black Notebooks*, 223–238.
25   Trawny, *Heidegger und der Mythos*, 75–76; Trawny, "Heidegger and the Myth," 171; Di Cesare, "Heidegger's Metaphysical Anti-Semitism," 188; Di Cesare, "Das Sein und der Jude," 68.

Anti-Heidegger   41

the alternative translations it may generate to the term *Seinsgeschichte*. The main point now is that Heidegger distinguishes between two concepts and modes of historicity, the one, *Geschichte*, more intimate to philosophy, and the other, *Historie*, more distant and estranged.

The interpretations of this historical dimension of philosophy in the current debate, and the forms of resistance to it, have depended on the question of the collective, inasmuch as the different positions with respect to the nature of Heidegger's *Seinsgeschichte* differed in their attitude toward the one common ground, namely the exclusion from philosophy of the historical dimension in which exist such collective subjects as "the Jews" (and such phenomena as anti-Semitism). The apology extended the surgical separation between "philosophy" and "personal opinions" to the separation between pure *Seinsgeschichte* and a non-philosophical history, what Vallega-Neu called "representable historical events or 'incidents.'"[26] It is in the terms of this surgical operation for salvaging the *Seinsgeschichte* that Ingo Farin, for instance, could write that "not one iota in [Heidegger's] history of being would have to be changed if one removed all references to Jewish matters."[27]

The critical tone increases the more inseparable from *Seinsgeschichte* one finds the historical collectives to be. Peter Trawny thus reads the *Seinsgeschichte* as a basic "narrative" that "conveniently presents itself to the philosopher" [*kommt dem Philosophen entgegen*].[28] The narrative "presents itself" to the philosopher, namely as something from the outside, something foreign to philosophy itself, an alien discourse, a *myth*.[29] The *Seinsgeschichte* itself would be the original contamination. It is precisely of this myth that the collective subjects referred to in the *Black Notebooks* would be, according to Trawny, the "actors" or "protagonists"; it is the appearance therein of "the Jews" that Trawny famously diagnoses as what he considers to be the specific kind of Heideggerian anti-Semitism, "*seinsgeschichtliche* anti-Semitism," i.e., anti-Semitism predicated on the

---

26   Vallega-Neu, "The Black Notebooks," 136.
27   Ingo Farin, "The Black Notebooks," 311; see also von Herrmann, "The Role," 90.
28   Trawny, *Heidegger and the Myth*, 17.
29   It was Heidegger himself who, quoting Plato, pronounced that philosophy is "not to tell stories"; see Martin Heidegger, *Sein und Zeit*, 6.

Seinsgeschichte.³⁰ An equally categorical rejection of the entire historical dimension that Heidegger was attempting to lend to or unveil in philosophy was expressed also, for instance, in Andrew Bowie's sharp distinction between "ontology" and "ontic history" or "empirical history," and in Marion Heinz's more dismissive one between "the so called [*die sogennante*] *Seinsgeschichte*" and the "empirical state of things."³¹

"THE JEWS"

In the last step of my demonstration, in the context of the Heidegger controversy, of the ambiguous nature of the anti-anti-Semitic discourse in its underlying perception of the Jews, I wish to point at several consequences that arise from its objection to anti-Semitism by way of excluding the historical collective subject from the realm of philosophy. All these consequences pertain to the factual existence of this discourse itself, more precisely to the discourse's necessity of accounting for its own specific existence as a historical discourse. What I mean is the way in which anti-anti-Semitic discourse, while denying the *legitimacy* of anti-Semitic tropes within the epistemologically normative boundaries of philosophical discourse, beyond its moral or hygienic denunciations, nonetheless needs to explain or account for the factual existence of "anti-Semitism" in (here Heidegger's) philosophy, and thus for its own existence as a reaction thereto. How does philosophy understand the nature and sources of its anti-Semitic "infection," "contamination," or "poisoning"?

The first ambiguous consequence concerns the way in which the anti-anti-Semitic discourse understands the basic epistemic nature of anti-Semitic discourse. As I demonstrated above, in the current Heidegger controversy, anti-Semitism has been epistemologically defined and objected to as the illegitimate attribution of an epistemic value to the political collective subject (the people, the nation), which is paradigmatically ex-

---

30   See critique by Harries, "Nostalgia, Spite, and the Truth of Being," 214–215; see critique from the opposite direction, Michèle Cohen-Halimi and Francis Cohen, *Le cas Trawny. À propos des 'Cahiers Noirs' de Heidegger* (Paris: Sens & Tonka, 2015).
31   Andrew Bowie, "Philosophy, Science and Politics," 257; Heinz, "Einleitung," 10–13.

pressed in the categorical confusion between the Jews and "the Jews," i.e., the real Jews and the Jews as a concept or idea. This definition itself, as I claimed, is based on the ontological separation between the form of being of concepts and ideas and the form of being of the Jews, or any other historical collective. The latter are conceived of as existing in the form of "reality," and more precisely in the mode of organic reality, of "life." This means that the paradigm of Jewish reality is the organically living, "flesh-and-blood," i.e., *individual* Jewish person. For the anti-anti-Semitic discourse, which denies any *concept* of Jewish being, i.e., any Jewish knowledge or *episteme*, to speak of such collective knowledge, i.e., to attribute any common concepts or ideas to "real" Jews, necessarily implies the notion of specific, explicit, and abnormal coordination of all Jewish individuals, for which one of the most common figures is the *conspiracy*.

Nota bene: obviously, I'm not saying that anti-anti-Semitism asserts that there *is* a Jewish conspiracy. What I'm saying is that for anti-anti-Semitism, as I analyzed it in the current Heidegger controversy, to speak about "Jewish" ideas that are common to Jews as Jews must imply some kind of explicit or implicit assertion of conspiracy between Jews. This is precisely the figure that Trawny has in mind when he titles his essay, in which he diagnoses Heidegger's speech as anti-Semitism, "Heidegger and the Myth of Jewish World Conspiracy."[32] The consequence of this conception is its awkward solidarity with anti-Semitism itself, in considering that the paradigmatic text (falsely) portraying something like (in reality nonexistent) "Jewish" thought—a text to which Trawny links also Heidegger's statements[33]—is "The Protocols of the Elders of Zion." In Chapter 7 of this book, I will analyze the internal logic and function of the notion of conspiracy as a key element within the political epistemology of anti-Semitic discourse.

A second ambiguous consequence of the "contamination" logic of anti-anti-Semitism pertains to the attempt, not to characterize the epistemic

---

32   Peter Trawny, *Heidegger und der Mythos*; see also Micha Brumlik, "Die Alltäglichkeit des Judenhasses—Heideggers Verfallenheit an den Anti-Semitismus," in *Heidegger und der Anti-Semitismus*, 205; Di Cesare, "Heideggers metaphysischer Anti-Semitismus," 215; Hermann Schmitz, "Heidegger und der Nationalsozialismus," 341.
33   Trawny, *Heidegger und der Mythos*, 45–48.

nature of anti-Semitic contamination of philosophy, but to explain its causes or sources. In fact, it is the constitutive dialectics of any discourse of contamination, infection, poisoning, interruption etc., that it posits an irreducible divide inside/outside, internal/external, natural/unnatural etc., in order to describe nonetheless an event of contact, mixture, and the undoing of separation. In other words, the discourse of contamination, of breached separation, is actually a negative form of conceptualizing unity. Any such discourse thus necessarily proceeds to account for the possibility or potentiality of contact within separation, i.e., the interior's internal exteriority and vice versa. It is to this form of account that belongs the explanation by sources and causes, why's and how's. In the context of anti-anti-Semitism, this procedure is carried out as the *explanation* of anti-Semitism, which necessarily means the internalization of the supposedly external anti-Semitic discourse through the mechanisms of explanation.

This procedure of internalization is set in motion by the implicit and explicit question, which ultimately commands the entire anti-anti-Semitic discourse, and to which accordingly the question of "why anti-Semitism?" inevitably refer back: "Why the Jews?" What this question asks about is the condition of the possibility that, notwithstanding the ontological divide between the bare reality of historical collectives and the ideal realm of concepts and knowledge, real Jews could nonetheless be confused with or characterized as "the Jews," to produce anti-Semitism. It is through this inevitable question that the real Jews are incorporated into the conceptual, philosophical discourse, which, through the logic of explanation, is required to posit a certain general characterization, a model or figure of the Jews, namely similarly to anti-Semitic discourse itself, generate or maintain a general idea of "the Jews."

It is here in fact that the proximity of anti-anti-Semitism and anti-Semitism becomes more palpable. The inevitable anti-anti-Semitic conceptualization of the Jews is effected on the basis of the paradigm of the historical collective's reality in the sole mode of life. The real Jews are consequently conceptualized exclusively in the form of "the real Jews," namely through categories of reality and subsistence of collective organic life. This is the conceptual environment of the *socioeconomic* explanations of anti-Semitism, which is intertwined with the socioeconomic characterization of the Jews, or differently formulated the conceptualization and *perception* of the Jews as a primarily and essentially socioeconomic phenomenon. It is here that the anti-anti-Semitic perception converges with the anti-Semitic perception of Jews, for which a certain pathological, asocial economic behavior is a central characteristic of the Jews. In Chapter 6, I will outline this anti-Semitic notion and highlight its fundamental difference from Marxist analysis, including Marx's infamous socioeconomic portrait of the Jews in "On the Jewish Question."

This perceptual convergence is in any way clearly visible in the current Heidegger controversy. Central to the debate has been one of the main characteristics that the controversial *Black Notebooks* passages attribute to the Jews, namely the tendency toward "calculation." Much hermeneutic effort has been invested in interpreting it. The image that has been often invoked for decoding this concept has been that of Marx's *Schacherjude*, the haggling Jew, the money Jew, "the Rothschilds," even though this figure is not mentioned in Heidegger's text, which remains rather abstract. The invocation is not unlikely.[34] However, in the current discourse it has not only been suggested that the anti-Semitic figure of the money Jew is the underlying perception of the Jews for Heidegger's conception of Jewish "calculative" talent, but this suggestion was without exception accompanied by the confirmation of this perception. In other words, it was not suggested that Heidegger had been influenced by anti-Semitic perception of Jews, but rather that Heidegger's anti-Semitism, like anti-Semitism in general, is based on the true perception of real Jews, who in fact, at least in Heidegger's times, have been characterized by their affinity to money.[35] This is where anti-anti-Semitic and anti-Semitic perceptions of Jews

---

34   That the figure of the money Jew was not foreign to Heidegger is demonstrated in a letter of 1920 from Heidegger to his wife, where he writes: "They [*Man*] speak here often about how much livestock from the villages is now bought away [*fortgekauft*] by the Jews.... The farmers here too become gradually shameless and everything is flooded by Jews and pushers" (*Briefe Martin Heidegger an seine Frau Elfriede 1915–1970*, ed. Gertrud Heidegger [Munich: Deutsche Verlags-Anstalt, 2005], 112). It is interesting how in his relation to Jews Heidegger completely adopts the discourse of the *Man* ("they," "one"), which seven years later he will completely condemn in *Being and Time* as improper (see *Being and Time*, §27).

35   See, for instance, Trawny, *Heidegger und der Mythos*, 35–36; Silvio Vietta, "Heideggers seinesgeschichtliche Kovergenztheorie," in *Heidegger und der Anti-Semitismus*, 422; Andrew Bowie, "Philosophy, Science and Politics in the Black

meet. The difference is in the interpretation of this perception. Anti-anti-Semitism denounces anti-Semitism for postulating Jewish mind behind Jewish money, namely for linking the specific nexus of real Jews with money to any specifically Jewish concept, thought, intention, or epistemic agency. Rather, the paradigmatic anti-anti-Semitic conception consists in *explaining* the real Jewish affinity to money by referring it to other real socioeconomic conditions, namely by providing a *causal* explanation. The epistemic agent of the socioeconomic causality, the mind behind it, is not Jewish, but external to the Jews, belongs not to sheer reality, but to the realm of knowledge, and is most often identified as medieval Christianity. The epistemic reproach addressed by anti-anti-Semitism to anti-Semitism in this context, including to Heidegger, is ignoring, overseeing, or mistaking the real situation and erroneously attributing agency to the Jews, who in fact have none.[36]

Anti-anti-Semitic discourse arrives at its ultimate and most ambiguous epistemo-political consequence, however, when it unfolds its constitutive dialectics to its extreme. I will analyze the conceptual dynamics of this discursive movement in the next three chapters. At this point I provide only an initial indication of its factual occurrence in the current Heidegger controversy. The first step of anti-anti-Semitism is to reject any conceptualization of the Jews by separating between concrete, real, living Jews and the abstract concept or idea of "the Jews." The second step was to account for the confusion of the two ("why the Jews?") by pointing at anti-Semitism's erroneous attribution of epistemic agency to the merely real (socioeconomic) and passive Jewish existence. By the very dialectics of "confusion" and "error," which is akin to the logic of "contamination," the third step leads the confusion back to the Jews themselves, which thus become the source of contamination. This step involves a modification of the

---

Notebooks," 258; Françoise Dastur, "Y a-t-il une 'essence' de l'antisémitisme?," in *Heidegger, die Juden, noch einmal,* 88.

36   A similar structure of elimination of agency is detectable in the explanations based on the perception of Jewish dispersion and homelessness, which is typically identified with passivity; in the context of the current Heidegger controversy, see Klaus Held, "Heidegger und das 'Politische,'" in *Heidegger und der Anti-Semitism,* 264–267; Schmitz, "Heidegger und der Nationalsozialismus," 340. For an anti-anti-Semitic perception of Jewish dispersion as expressing Jewish *agency*, a Jewish political epistemology, see Chapter 4 below.

epistemo-political ontology of the Jews: the paradigm of Jewish existence is still flesh-and-blood reality, but this organic or socioeconomic reality itself now gains its own conceptual dimension, a dimension of knowledge. The ontological modification entails a perceptual one: it is at this point that a certain form of Jewish epistemic agency, Jewish knowledge, conceptions, and texts, Jewish *voices*, enter the discussion. What these voices produce as heard by the anti-anti-Semitic discourse is nothing but the original confusion between historical collective reality and ideal conceptuality, between politics and knowledge. In other words, notwithstanding Sartre's famous statement, whereby "it is the anti-Semite who creates the Jew," which will be discussed in the next chapter, it is Jewish voices who appear to produce anti-Semitism or at least to be co-original to it. Indeed, at least one important historical corpus that in various ways characterizes the Jews as "the Jews" is of course—once the Jewish is perceived as *episteme*—Jewish texts and discourses themselves.

Thus, in the discourse of the current Heidegger controversy, various authors in fact, having identified Heidegger's litigious passages as anti-Semitic, proceeded to further identify, in different forms and without necessarily claiming any direct influence, Jewish sources for the same kind of anti-Semitism. Peter Trawny, again as an instance of a common and as I claim structurally inherent motif of the discourse, in almost every occasion in his book where he speaks of Heidegger's anti-Semitic passages, immediately makes—often in a footnote—reference to Jewish authors who made similar statements: Heidegger's use of the collective concepts "Jews" and "Germans" is matched with Hermann Cohen's (28); Heidegger's talk about Jewish "calculation" is glossed by a reference to Buber and Herzl complaining about the pathologies of Jewish economy (35–36n.7);[37] traces for Heidegger's racism are coupled with the reflection on the potential racist dimension of Jewish conscience of chosenness (40–41n.15);[38] Heidegger's note on "Jewish" psychoanalysis is supported

---

37 Tracy B. Strong, in "On Relevant Events, Then and Now," 243, to make sense of Heidegger's talk about Jewish "uprootedness," proposes an analogous reference to Joachim Prinz' call for Jewish "purity of nation and race," which would express Jews' own sense of not belonging to their host nations.

38 See also Babette Babich, "Heidegger's Black Night: The Nachlass and Its Wirkungsgeschichte," in *Reading Heidegger's Black Notebooks*, 77–78, which extends these reflections to the politics of the State of Israel.

by Freud (44n.21); the Protocols of the Elders of Zion, possible influence on Heidegger, are traced back to Zionist World Organization (45);³⁹ Heidegger's use of the anti-Semitic term *Verjudung* ("Jewification") is balanced through Rathenau's earlier use of the same term, and Heidegger's admission of being "anti-Semitic in questions concerning the university" in a letter to Arendt is soothed by Arendt's own implied understanding thereto (86–87n.6). The frequent use of the footnote is very conspicuous and significant here: a certain thesis or thought, which is rather systematic and *fundamentally crucial* for the entire topic and claim of the essay, is nonetheless repressed and pushed to the margins, present-absent on the page, semi-allowed only as the passing shadow of by-the-way.

An amplified, more explicit and more developed version of the same conceptual shift goes beyond mere parallelism between Heidegger's anti-Jewish discourse and Jewish discourse itself, to suggest the latter as the proper source for the conceptions underlying the former. Thus, Françoise Dastur, for instance, starts by seeking inspiration in Heidegger's own alleged resistance to "essentialist thinking," in order to reject the essentialist conception of what Hannah Arendt, to whom Dastur refers, called "eternal anti-Semitism," a conception which Arendt, as I will discuss in Chapter 4, criticized in Jewish discourse.⁴⁰ Having thus answered to the negative the question she posed in her essay's title—"Is There 'Essence' of Anti-Semitism?"—Dastur then, again in Arendt's footsteps, proceeds to trace essentialist thinking about the Jews (what Trawny called characterizing the Jews and "the Jews," and which for the current discourse defines anti-Semitism) back to Jewish episteme itself. In the "Old Testament," she thus finds, inherent to "Jewish self-conscience," notions of "blood" and "soil," rooted in "the principle of separation, founded on the biblical doctrine of election," which, she adds *by the way*, in a footnote, "a universal religion doesn't acknowledge."⁴¹

A similar insight has led John Caputo, engaged like Trawny in "demythologizing" Heidegger, to hold, years before the publication of the *Black Notebooks*, that Heidegger's "narrative of being" was borrowed from "the

---

39   See also Babich, "Heidegger's Black Night," 65.
40   Dastur, «Y a-t-il une 'essence' de l'antisémitisme?,» 78.
41   Dastur, 79, 87, and 88n.30. To demonstrate the relevance of these notions for twentieth-century Jews, she refers—in a footnote—to Franz Rosenzweig's understanding of the Jewish people as a "blood community" (87n.29).

narratives of the Jews and their God in the Tanach" about the divine call "that defines and identifies a sacred people: one God, one people, one place."[42] Oblivious to its "Jewish *Urquel*," in Heidegger's version "the call was addressed to a rival chosen people, not the Jews but the Greeks and their spiritual heirs, the Germans, in a rival new Jerusalem, not Israel but the Third Reich, with a rival prophet, not Hosea but—if truth be told and with all due modesty!—Heidegger."[43] Caputo's own final call illustrates how close denouncing Heidegger's *Seinsgeschichte* may come to a harsh critique of Judaism: "We need to break with ... the myth of the originary language, the originary people, the original land, by means of which Heidegger reproduces the myth of God's chosen people, of God's promised land, ... the murderous twin myths of the people of God and of the people of being, myths which license murder in the name of God or in the name of the question of being."[44]

The same ambiguity, in a milder, more meditative form, is also voiced by Trawny. Establishing that Heidegger's occasional use of "race" doesn't have a biological but an ethnic meaning, Trawny still finds this is "coming close to the ideology of National Socialism," since "what meaning has the belonging to a people, beyond the linguistic community?"[45] This leads him to raise—in a footnote—the question of a possible "Jewish kind of 'racism'": "It is a social-psychological question whether and how the 'passive claim to exclusivity'—to be the 'chosen people'—can be a trigger to react in a racist manner to the constant distinction between belonging and non-belonging."[46] Another footnote at the end of the book explicitly suggests "another way to approach Heidegger's *seinsgeschichtlichem* anti-Semitism," namely of a "peculiar affinity": "The thought (which at times is no doubt to be designated as messianic) of the 'last god' as a non-universalistic god of a people reminds Judaism's conception of god (an utterly provisional claim of course). Didn't Heidegger consider the Germans as a 'chosen peo-

---

42 John Caputo, "People of God, People of Being: The Theological Presuppositions of Heidegger's Path of Thought," in *Appropriating Heidegger*, ed. James E. Falconer and Mark A. Wrathall (Cambridge: Cambridge University Press, 2000), 88, 96.
43 Caputo, 90.
44 Caputo, 99.
45 Trawny, *Heidegger und der Mythos*, 39–40.
46 Trawny, 41n.15.

ple'? What is the relation of the 'last god' to this 'chosenness'? Is there in Heidegger an unacknowledged closeness to Judaism?"[47]

This chapter examined the conceptual complex of anti-anti-Semitism as it was articulated in the current controversy around Heidegger's *Black Notebooks*. It pointed at several central motifs in this discourse, which were presented as various moments of one and the same conceptual movement, with its own inner logic and discursive necessity. This inner logic, so the claim, is governed by a basic perception or conception of the Jews as constituting an epistemo-political paradigm, i.e., a paradigm of the relation between knowledge and the collective subject. I tried to show in what way this Jewish epistemo-political paradigm is a *negative* one, and in what way it consequently instills a basic necessary ambiguity in anti-anti-Semitic discourse, which at central moments brings it close, in respect of its own proclaimed anti-anti-Semitic intentions, to a critical attitude toward Jews, making visible a certain complicity or entente with anti-Semitism itself.

Different elements of this claim still require further demonstration, not the least through the examination of anti-Semitic discourse itself, which will be undertaken in Part II of this book. But prior to that, with greater urgency, the various conceptual moments of the claim, and most importantly the inner logic and necessity of their unified discursive movement, require further elucidation. This chapter only indicated their existence and regulative significance within the current Heidegger controversy. It has not yet or not sufficiently analyzed them in themselves, per se. This mode of existence of the concepts, "per se," does not mean existence outside or independently of discourse, of a *given* discourse. Rather, it designates the quality of the relation between the concepts and the discourse that they generate and regulate. It indicates a higher level of explicitness or self-reflexivity in this relation, namely a discourse—here, an anti-anti-Semitic discourse—that explicitly concerns and deals with the basic concepts that animate it.

The discourse analyzed in this chapter was not explicitly about anti-Semitism, much less anti-anti-Semitism. It was about Heidegger. Being from its inceptive stages (and with obvious justification) determined through the category of "anti-Semitism," it has committed itself to the

---

47   Trawny, 94n.21.

logic of anti-anti-Semitic discourse, which, however, has operated to a large extent implicitly, in the discursive subconscious only. As I tried to show, this non-reflexivity is not just an accidental feature of the analyzed discourse, not just a *lack* or default; rather, it constitutes a positive discursive operation of repression of anti-Semitism—and the Jews—outside of the discourse of philosophy, a repression inherent to the principle of anti-anti-Semitism.

The next three chapters examine a different field of philosophical discourse, of which anti-Semitism and resistance thereto do constitute the explicit theme. They look at texts written by central authors of post–World War II philosophy, theory, and thought, who in these texts dedicated their thought to reflect on anti-Semitism. These thinkers developed some of the most systematic and influential political epistemologies of our time. It is within these epistemologies that their discussion of anti-Semitism is embedded. This of course means that no complete and entirely fair account of their discussion of anti-Semitism can do without contextualizing it within the broader horizon of their thought—and perhaps of their time. This cannot be done here. My purpose is also not to use their different epistemo-political conceptions, *in general*, in order to understand what they say on the *particular* case of anti-Semitism. It is rather the contrary: I'm suggesting there's inner logic to the discourse organized around the basic category of "anti-Semitism," which regulates also anti-anti-Semitic discourse, operating also within these texts by producing "the Jews" as a general epistemo-political paradigm, which can thus function as a hermeneutical key for an epistemo-political reading, or questioning, of these authors—and perhaps of their time.

2 Anti-Semitic Creation of Jews

Adorno & Horkheimer to Sartre

TWO OF THE EARLIEST ATTEMPTS to think of anti-Semitism in view of Auschwitz were "Elements of Anti-Semitism: Limits of Enlightenment," by Theodor Adorno and Max Horkheimer (part of their *Dialectics of Enlightenment*) and *Reflections on the Jewish Question* (translated as *Anti-Semite and Jew*) by Jean Paul-Sartre.[1] Both texts are in fact explicit attempts to have philosophy and more generally the philosophical and scientific episteme, the *episteme* in its original, Aristotelian meaning, engage on the phenomenon and discourse of anti-Semitism. In other words, they are not just talking about anti-Semitism, but self-reflectively asking about the sort of access philosophy might at all have to anti-Semitism or, more precisely, on the sort of phenomenon that anti-Semitism might be understood to be for the philosophical gaze. Both texts consequently admit anti-Semitism as an issue for philosophy, which the current Heidegger controversy, as I showed in the previous chapter, for the most part denied.

In the philosophical text I will examine now, anti-Semitism is admitted into philosophy through the front door: namely as an epistemic phenom-

---

1   Max Horkheimer and Theodor Adorno, *Dialektik der Aufklärung. Philosophische Fragmente* (Frankfurt am Main: Fischer, 1988; New York: Social Studies Association, 1944); translated into English by Edmund Jephcott as *Dialectic of Enlightenment* (Stanford, CA: Stanford University Press, 2002); Jean-Paul Sartre, *Réflexions sur la question juive* (Paris: Gallimard, 1954; Paris: Paul Morihien, 1946); translated to English by George Becker, *Anti-Semite and Jew* (New York: Schocken Books, 1976 [1948]).

enon, a phenomenon of knowledge. In fact, as I already noted above, one way of characterizing philosophical discourse would be through its reflectivity: as a self-reflective knowledge, knowledge of knowledge or self-knowledge, which would be one way of translating the very expression epistemo-logy, i.e., the discourse/knowledge about knowledge. Anti-Semitism is thus analyzed as a certain constellation, condition, or situation of knowledge, with a paradigmatic, universal import. This epistemological universalization of anti-Semitism must be contemplated within the historical epoch opened by the emerging awareness and shock in view of the destruction of the Jews during World War II. In this epoch of radical self-reflection of an entire civilization, it became manifest that the universal catastrophe and rupture, the event signifying the end and limit of its collective project of knowledge, reason, and consciousness, the end of "enlightenment," was intimately connected with anti-Semitism. In fact, the examined texts integrate and universalize anti-Semitism in the philosophical discourse not just as one epistemological constellation among others, but as the epistemic negativity par excellence, as the pathological condition of knowledge, marking the inner limit of reason. In other words, anti-Semitism is admitted into philosophy as marking the end of philosophy. This admittance is necessarily ambiguous, with the same ambiguity through which I characterized the current anti-anti-Semitic discourse on Heidegger.

The ambiguity of the philosophical discourse on anti-Semitism arises from the anti-anti-Semitic interpretation of anti-Semitism not just as a negative, distorted, or pathological episteme, but more radically as something like a non-episteme, a form, structure, or appearance of knowledge, which is no knowledge at all, but rather a psychological effect, hallucination, or fantasy. What characterizes this form of (non)knowledge is that its seeming object, i.e., that which it claims to know, has no real being—does not exist. And so, the radical epistemic negation of anti-Semitism implies radically negating the existence of the object to which the anti-Semitic episteme refers, namely the Jews. The Jews, *of whom anti-Semitism speaks, of whom it asserts knowledge*, become for anti-anti-Semitism "the Jews." "The Jews" having been thus denied any epistemic existence, any real being for knowledge, the only epistemic subject, the only agent of knowledge involved in and implied by anti-Semitism, for the anti-anti-Semitic eye, is the anti-Semites themselves. This means that "the Jews," as an epistemic entity, as a concept or knowledge, have nothing to do with any *real* Jews, but only with the anti-Semites. "The Jews" become a figment of the anti-Semitic mind, which accordingly emerges as the creator of the Jews. This conception is consummated by the perfection of the anti-Semitic creator's power to create not just figments but realities, namely to produce actually existing Jewish episteme, actual Jewish consciousness, and so to create Jewishness, which would thus appear as a deeply dubious creation. The readings that follow will try to retrace this story of creation in two of its most powerful narratives.

ADORNO AND HORKHEIMER ON THE IMAGINARY CREATION OF THE JEWS

Adorno and Horkheimer's *Dialectic of Enlightenment*, written during World War II, is profoundly epistemo-political insofar as it is dedicated to investigating the relation between, on the one hand, the paradigm of knowledge as it has constituted and guided modernity, or rather as it has constituted and guided the West in the eyes of modernity, i.e., "enlightenment," and, on the other hand, the fundamental project of a collective human world, "civilization." The basic observation of this investigation, which has been one of the basic challenges to any epistemology situated enough to be aware of its own time, is the *inverse proportion* between the actual, historical developments of the two projects, the epistemic and the civilizatory. "The goal that we had set for ourselves was nothing less than the knowledge of why humanity," ever more *enlightened*, "instead of entering a truly human state, is sinking into a new kind of barbarism."[2] The correlation between enlightenment and barbarism, however, does not lead Adorno and Horkheimer to renounce the project of enlightenment. On the exact contrary, not only they affirm the basic civilizatory power of enlightenment, of the human knowledge project, but they also attribute to it the opposite, negative, barbaric, and anti-civilizatory power. Barbarism is not opposed to enlightenment, but is rather one of the two contradicting forces within enlightenment. There would be a *Dialectic of Enlightenment*.[3]

---

2   Adorno and Horkheimer, *Dialektik*, 1.
3   Helmut König, in *Elemente des Antisemitismus. Kommentare und Interpretationen zu einem Kapitel der* Dialektik der Aufklärung von Max Horkheimer und Theodor W. Adorno (Weilerswist: Velbrück Wissenschaft, 2016), notes the probable inspiration from Walter Benjamin's *Thesen über den Begriff der*

The object of Adorno and Horkheimer's investigation of twentieth-century barbarism, of the collapse of the human collective project, is thus given the name "the self-destruction of enlightenment." The method of investigation is Hegelian, consisting in observation of various modern realities as manifestations, as *phenomena*, of the fundamental concept, "the self-destruction of enlightenment." Adorno and Horkheimer call it "contemplation of the destructive." Whereas, therefore, Hegel's is a phenomenology of negative phenomena of the positive, absolute knowledge, what manifests itself in Adorno and Horkheimer's negative phenomenology is itself negative—the self-destruction of enlightenment. Considering both phenomenologies are also eschatological narratives, if the *Phenomenology of Spirit* is the gospel of the coming of absolute knowledge, the *Dialectic of Enlightenment* is its apocalypse—a vision of the coming as end, or rather a vision of destruction without promise of resurrection, destruction that is perhaps not even the end. This "sad science," as Adorno described it in *Minima Moralia*,[4] his "reflections on a damaged life" (yet another concept for negative phenomenology), which he had begun to write in the same year as the *Dialectic of Enlightenment*, 1944, testifies to the glory of enlightenment by contemplating all cultural elements contemporary to Auschwitz as revelations of enlightenment's self-destruction: "There is no longer beauty or consolation except in the gaze that is looking for horror, withstanding it, and in unalleviated consciousness of negativity holding fast to the possibility of what is better" (26).

Minima Moralia's strongest thrust lies perhaps in the realization that this destruction reveals itself most powerfully not in the most barbaric elements of culture but quite on the contrary in the elements that this essentially barbaric culture considers to be the most civilized and *schön*: *Die Gesundheit zum Tode*, "Healthy unto Death" (65). In *The Dialectic of Enlightenment*, however, the exemplary phenomenon of enlightenment's self-destruction is anti-Semitism, which Adorno and Horkheimer describe as "the return of the enlightened civilization to barbarism *in reality [in der*

Geschichte, a copy of which was given in June 1941 by Hannah Arendt to Adorno, who sent it to Horkheimer, noting that "none of Benjamin's works shows him to be closer to our own intentions" (quoted in König, *Elemente*, 243).

4   Theodor W. Adorno, *Minima Moralia. Reflexionen aus dem beschädigten Leben*, Gesammelte Schriften, Bd. 4 (Frankfurt am Main: Suhrkamp Taschenbuch Wissenschaft, 2003 [1951]), 13.

Wirklichkeit]"⁵ (my emphasis). This phenomenological election is not explained or justified, rather appears as intuitive, perhaps self-evident. Its evidence for Adorno and Horkheimer pertains no doubt to the fact that anti-Semitism has been the unique feature of the exemplary barbarism that has damaged their own lives, National Socialism, a feature that affected them personally, ended their existence as German scientists, so to speak executed their epistemological selves. Such self-evidence notwithstanding, the central role given to anti-Semitism in this epistemo-political apocalypse is significant.

What Adorno and Horkheimer purport to deliver in their "Elements of Anti-Semitism," which appeared as the fifth chapter of the *Dialectics of Enlightenment*, is "a philosophical pre-history [*Urgeschichte*] of anti-Semitism" (7), namely to expose the philosophical, conceptual, epistemological genesis and infrastructure of the *reality* that is anti-Semitism.⁶ There is room here for asking about the precise nature of this distinction between philosophy and reality, *Wirklichkeit*, and the assignment of anti-Semitism to the latter, which echoes the separation between philosophy and anti-Semitism in the current Heidegger controversy. The subtitle that Adorno and Horkheimer give to their seven theses on anti-Semitism, "Limits of Enlightenment" [*Grenzen der Aufklärung*], also seems to point at this direction, namely of placing anti-Semitism beyond or outside of enlightenment and its dialectics.⁷ Nevertheless, the concept of *Grenze*, limit, or border, as also analyzed by Hegel in his *Logic*,⁸ designates the otherness that constitutes the self. As marking the "limit of enlightenment," anti-Semitism would be a certain definition and consummation of enlightenment, namely the consummation of its self-destructive movement. In

---

5   Adorno and Horkheimer, *Dialektik*, 6–7.
6   For a recent comprehensive commentary and study of the *Elements of Anti-Semitism*, their place and genealogy in the broader context of the work of Adorno and Horkmeimer, as well as the Frankfurt School, before and after World War II, and their reception in Germany, see Helmut König, *Elemente des Antisemitismus*. See also Lars Rensmann, *The Politics of Unreason. The Frankfurt School and the Origins of Modern Antisemitism* (Albany: State University of New York Press, 2017).
7   See König, *Elemente*, 215–219.
8   Georg Wilhelm Friedrich Hegel, *Wissenschaft der Logik. Erster Band. Die objektive Logik* (1812/13), Werke 5 (Frankfurt/M.: Suhrkamp Taschenbuch Wissenschaft, 1969), 131–139.

fact, the aim of Adorno and Horkheimer's "philosophical pre-history of anti-Semitism" is to show how anti-Semitism, the most concrete manifestation of barbarism in 1944, arises "from the essence of dominant reason itself."[9] The conceptual self-destruction of enlightenment reaches its most accomplished realization in the concrete social, political, historical, technical acts of anti-Semitism, which Adorno and Horkheimer thus understand as the "self-annihilation" [*Selbstvernichtung*] of civilization.[10]

In the proximity of the current Heidegger controversy, this inevitably invokes Heidegger's much quoted *Black Notebook* entry of the same immediate postwar period, whereby "when the essentially 'Jewish' in metaphysical sense fights against the Jewish, the highpoint of self-annihilation in history is reached."[11] It is a question to what extent understanding Auschwitz as "*self*-annihilation" renders irrelevant the distinction between anti-Semites (or anti-Jews) and Jews, and thus the semantic difference between Heidegger's and Adorno and Horkheimer's formulation.[12] Similar

---

9   Adorno and Horkheimer, *Dialektik*, 7.
10 The idea of anti-Semitism as epitomizing the state of civilization was expressed by Adorno and Horkheimer in the years preceding the *Dialektik*. On October 3, 1941, for instance, Horkheimer wrote to the British political philosopher Harold Laski: "As true as it is that one can understand Antisemitism only from our society, as true it appears to me to become that by now society itself can be properly understood only through Antisemitism." Quoted in König, *Elemente*, 210. See also Anson Rabinbach, "Why Were the Jews Sacrificed? The Place of Anti-Semitism in Dialectic of Enlightenment," *New German Critique* 81 (2000): 53–54.
11 Heidegger, GA 97, 20.
12 Helmut König indicates a similar logic in Horkheimer's earlier text, *The Jews and Europe* (*Die Juden und Europa*), in *Gesammelte Schriften*, Bd. 4 (Frankfurt am Main: Fischer Verlag, 1988), 308–331), where Horkheimer writes, in 1939, in reference to the Jews: "Whoever … held to a limited human order, should not be surprised when he himself occasionally falls under the limitation" (quoted in König, *Elemente*, 227). König's interpretation: "The Jews themselves were those who over a long period phase of history appeared as the protagonist of the same logic that now buries them" (227). Jonathan Judaken observed this logic also in the *Elements of Anti-Semitism*, where "anti-Semitism as the ultimate result of the logic of the dialectic of enlightenment, and reflective of the limits of enlightenment, simultaneously has its origins and its end in a Jewish impulse," i.e., of liberation from myth; see Judaken, "Blindness and Insight: The Conceptual Jew

ambiguity inheres Adorno and Horkheimer's eschatological anti-anti-Semitic vision, according to which "a step away from the anti-Semitic society…[and] toward the human one" would be to realize that "the Jew is a human being," which could equally mean a step away from the Jewish society. This immediately invokes all the difficulties that constitute the discourse of the "Jewish Question," a paradigmatic epistemo-political site of Enlightenment, as I will show in Chapter 6. Adorno and Horkheimer are aware of this ambiguity when they immediately add: "Such a step would also fulfill the fascist lie, as its very contradiction: the Jewish question would indeed prove the turning-point of history."[13] The refutation of anti-Semitism does not lie in giving an opposite, positive answer to the Jewish question, but in abolishing the question, which means abolishing the reference to the Jews, both as perception and signification, i.e., making Jews disappear.

I would like to point at the operation of this epistemic abolishment of the Jews more precisely in Adorno and Horkheimer's "philosophical prehistory of anti-Semitism." As aforesaid, this philosophical historiography is a phenomenology, which presents the concrete reality of anti-Semitism as the manifestation of the conceptual destruction of enlightenment by enlightenment itself. In the first, conceptual part of the *Dialectic of Enlightenment*, "The Concept of Enlightenment," Adorno and Horkheimer famously posit as a counter-concept to enlightenment the concept of the "myth." The analysis of the current Heidegger controversy already revealed, in the anti-anti-Semitic discourse, the solidarity between philosophy's op-

---

in Adorno and Arendt's Post-Holocaust Reflections on the Antisemitic Question," in Lars Rensmann and Samir Gandesha, eds., *Arendt and Adorno: Political and Philosophical Investigations* (Stanford, CA: Stanford University Press, 2012), 194. Accordingly, in contrast to the anti-Semitic creation of the Jew that I analyze in the *Elements of anti-Semitism*, Judaken identifies in this text, notwithstanding its "foundational thesis … that antisemitism is a paranoid projection of fascism's own worldview" (192), Adorno and Horkheimer's own "conceptual Jew," which "rather than critically undermine Western civilization's image of 'the Jew' and Judaism, [reinforces] it by repeating the negative construction of Jews that facilitated their destruction" (195). I find it easier to second Judaken in observing this motif in Arendt's analysis; see Chapter 3.

13   Adorno and Horkheimer, *Dialektik*, 209.

position to anti-Semitism, its opposition to the myth and, ultimately, its consequent opposition to the Jews. Adorno and Horkheimer's enlightenment, however, is dialectic, namely it already contains its own negation, its own counter-concept. They thus describe enlightenment's self-destruction as "enlightenment's fall *back* into mythology" (3; my emphasis). In fact, the first of the authors' theses is that myth is the beginning of enlightenment, or as they put it, "myth is already enlightenment" (6).

The already enlightening function of the original myths—both Greek and Jewish, the authors emphasize—is to give to humanity control and domination over the feared unknown through the tool of *explanation*: "the myth wanted to report, name, tell the origin: therewith present, establish, explain" (10).[14] The authors' basic argument is that later enlightenment, through its very attempt to break with mythology, creates a new, 'enlightened' myth, one of the most achieved forms of which is *positivism*. The central figures of this mythology are the very anti-mythological categories of enlightened epistemology: the "facts" and the "clarity" of scientific explanation. The mythological effect of these categories, according to Adorno and Horkheimer, lies in the sanctification of the immediately accessible, present, and "factual" reality. Enlightenment, a myth of science, thus tends to produce absolutization and idolization of what is already existing [*das Bestehende*] and given [*das Vorfindliche*]:[15] "In the terseness of the mythical image, as in the clarity of the scientific formula, the eternity of the factual is confirmed and mere existence is declared to be the meaning it obstructs."[16] This epistemic absolutization of the existing order of the world operates as what Marx and Engels called "ideology," namely the

---

14   "In this, the Jewish story of creation and the Olympic religion correspond" (14).
15   The conspicuous closeness to Heidegger's description of improper, inauthentic existence (*Uneigentlichkeit*) in *Being and Time* resonates also in Edmund Jephcott's translation of Adorno and Horkheimer's *Vorfindliche* as "what is immediately at hand" (20), which calls to mind Macquarrie and Robinson's translation of Heidegger's *Vorhanden* as "present-at-hand"; Martin Heidegger, *Being and Time*, trans. Johan Macquarrie and Edward Robinson (Oxford: Blackwell, 1962), 520; Joan Stambaugh's translation, *Being and Time* (Albany: State University of New York Press, 1996), rendered "what is objectively present" (14).
16   Adorno and Horkheimer, *Dialektik*, 33.

perpetuation of prevailing structures of domination and political power by perceiving them as natural and necessary.[17]

It is of this epistemo-political self-destruction of enlightenment that anti-Semitism would be the manifestation *in reality*. Of the seven "theses" that Adorno and Horkheimer formulate in their "Elements of Anti-Semitism," mainly the last two, the longest, can be read as substantiating this claim. The crucial element of Adorno and Horkheimer's "philosophical pre-history" is the diagnosis of anti-Semitism as an *epistemic* condition, namely as a certain condition, more specifically a negative, perverse condition of knowledge. Anti-Semitism, they write, is a "pathology of cognition" [*Pathologie der Erkenntnis*] (203). Although the authors do not make this correlation explicit, this epistemic "pathology" corresponds to the inner counter-concept of enlightenment, the "myth." In fact, like the myth, anti-Semitism too, as a pathological condition of knowledge, is characterized by a fundamental discrepancy between knowledge and reality.

However, and this is central for my own argument, this analogy—and with it the assertion of anti-Semitism as the real manifestation of enlightenment's self-destruction—breaks in one crucial point. As said above, the *enlightened* form of the myth, "positivism," consists in the absolutization of factual reality, which prevents from perceiving and understanding this reality as the product of human conceptions and political decisions. In contrast, when Adorno and Horkheimer, in their sixth thesis, characterize the epistemic pathology of anti-Semitism as a "projection without reflection" or "false immediacy," they do not mean to say that the anti-Semite correctly perceives the factual reality of Jews, but fails to understand it as the product of historical socioeconomic and political processes. Rather, what they mean is that anti-Semitism consists in projecting one's own ideas on reality so as to *prevent* one from seeing reality as it positively is, i.e., the actual facts. We can even say that for Adorno and Horkheimer anti-Semitism constitutes the radical epistemic perversity in which knowledge develops not to better access reality but to conceal reality. What the anti-Semite perceives and condemns as "the Jews" is thus nothing but the projection

---

17 Cf. Karl Marx und Friedrich Engels, *Die deutsche Ideologie. Kritik der neuesten deutschen Philosophie in ihren Repräsentanten Feuerbach, B. Bauer und Stirner, und des deutschen Sozialismus in seinen verschiedenen Propheten*, in Marx-Engels Werke, Band 3 (Berlin: Dietz, 1961), 26–27.

of his own condemnable self. This would be the paradigm of "sickness of mind" or counter-mind, of *para-noia*, which is the explicitly clinical term that Adorno and Horkheimer use for diagnosing anti-Semitism. Like God, they write, the paranoid anti-Semite "creates everything in his own image."[18]

Using God as a metaphor is never trivial, much less as a metaphor for the anti-Semite, a link, however, that, as we will see, is a recurrent motif in theories of anti-Semitism. For Adorno and Horkheimer, unlike God's, the anti-Semite's creation is not absolute reality but absolute unreality.[19] Consequently, anti-Semitism for them is not a phenomenon of enlightenment's science, of positivism, but of "half-erudition" [*Halbbildung*] and the other syndromes of "mass culture," such as "stereotyped thinking," as explained in their seventh thesis of 1947 (210). Mass culture is the epistemological apocalypse of late capitalism, in which knowledge becomes completely perverted: "Illusion has become so concentrated that to see through it objectively assumes the character of hallucination" (214). Adorno and Horkheimer characterize this condition of non-knowledge as "blind intuition and empty concepts," which is the radical negation of the two fundamental conditions for any possible experience, knowledge, and science in Kant's epistemology (211). Consequently, anti-Semitism would not be a *negative* perception of Jews but more fundamentally *non*-perception of Jews, namely stereotypes and ready-made clichés of "the Jews," for which "the individuals' experience of Jews plays no role" (210).

The passage from the conceptual analysis of enlightenment's self-destruction to anti-Semitism as the alleged manifestation of this self-destruction in reality does not, however, entail only a shift from the epistemic pathology of "positivism" (idolizing facts) to the pathology of "paranoia" (idolizing illusions). I suggest that in their analysis of anti-Semitism as paranoia, Adorno and Horkheimer themselves engage in

---

18   Adorno and Horkheimer, *Dialektik*, 200. Note the conceptual intimacy of understanding anti-Semitism as paranoia with its diagnosis by others as "conspiracy theory"; see discussions in Chapter 1 and Chapter 7.

19   Cf. König, *Elemente*, 315–316, who also observes the similarity to Sartre's *Reflections on the Jewish Question*, which I discuss below. König insightfully notes that Adorno and Horkheimer's more limited, only psychological, and unreal anti-Semitic creation of the Jews required them to provide at least some account of real historical Jewish existence, from which Sartre's theory on the *real* creation of the Jew by the anti-Semite was exempted.

positivism.[20] According to their own definition, positivism is the absolutization of immediate, factual reality, which fails to see facts as mediated by concepts. It is precisely this conceptual mediation that Adorno and Horkheimer, however, *refuse* to recognize in anti-Semitism. By denying anti-Semitism any epistemic value, i.e., as nonperception, nonknowledge, nonexperience of Jews, anti-Semitism is denied any mediation, namely any reference to anything outside of itself, and thus in fact is no longer perceived as an epistemic condition, as a state of knowledge, but rather as an immediate, positive fact: as the psychological condition of the anti-Semitic person.[21] This explains why *Elements of Anti-Semitism* refers to no anti-Semitic text, speech, or statement.[22] It is precisely this positivism that will guide a few years later the scientific project of *The Authoritarian Personality*, carried out in the late 1940s under the supervision of Horkheimer, as the director of the American Jewish Committee's Department of Scientific Research, and with the participation of Adorno. This post–World War II sociopsychological study of prejudice, anti-democratic tendencies, fascism, ethnocentrism, and authoritarianism, which focused its investigations on the phenomenon of anti-Semitism, opened by declaring: "The authors, in common with most social scientists, hold the view that anti-Semitism is

---

20   The more common critique of *The Dialectic of Enlightenment* has been, in contrast, that its authors were too entranced by their own conception to see reality as it is, i.e., their text is *paranoid*. For example: "Wie können die beiden Aufklärer, die sie immer noch sind, den vernünftigen Gehalt der kulturellen Moderne so unterschätzen, daß sie in allem nur eine Legierung von Vernunft und Herrschaft, Macht und Geltung wahrnehmen?" Jürgen Habermas, *Der philosophische Diskurs der Moderne. Zwölf Vorlesungen* (Frankfurt am Main: Suhrkamp, 1985), 146.

21   As Helmut König writes: "The central statement of the *Elements* is that ultimately anti-Semitism can only be driven by a psychological energy. Anyway it may not be explained strictly rationally, politically or economically. It follows that anti-Semitism may only be decoded in looking at its function for the anti-Semite. This function consists primarily in positing one's own despised interiority outside and fighting it there. Thus, behind anti-Semitism stands a mix of defense and projection" (11).

22   As was observed by Jeffrey Herf, "*Dialectic of Enlightenment* Reconsidered," *New German Critique* 117 (2012): 86, where Herf also points at the failure to mention "the obvious," "namely, that the Nazis drew on centuries of Jew-hatred rooted in Christian belief." See my own discussion of anti-Semitism in Part II.

based more largely upon factors in the subject and in his total situation than upon actual characteristics of Jews, and that one place to look for determinants of anti-Semitic opinions and attitudes is within the persons who express them."[23]

Adorno and Horkheimer's positivism becomes even more radical, however, with respect to the Jews. The de-epistemization of anti-Semitism, i.e., the denial of any epistemic value to the anti-Semitic concept of "the Jews," insisting that it has nothing to do with factual reality, necessarily raises the question concerning the notion of "real Jews." The reality of the Jews in the seven theses on anti-Semitism is, however, neither conceptual nor epistemic, i.e., they stand for no Jewish knowledge, nor even is it psychological or cognitive, like the reality of the anti-Semite. Rather, against the anti-Semitic concept of the Jews, Adorno and Horkheimer posit the purely nonconceptual, nonepistemic Jews, Jews as pure facts, which could be best characterized, so it seems to me, through the already analyzed category of the "living Jews."[24] This becomes visible in their answer to the crucial question, which reveals the dependency of any analysis of anti-Semitism on a pre-conception of the Jews, namely, "Why the Jews?" The main answer of the theses is given in the form of the paradigmatic positivist (we may say, together with *The Dialectic of Enlightenment*, mythological) explanation, which, as the sole singular characteristic of the Jews, identifies their socioeconomic situation.

The second thesis of the *Elements of Anti-Semitism* thus points at liberalism, which granted rights and property to the powerless Jews, who henceforth—in particular as bankers and intellectuals—enjoyed "happiness without power" (*Glück ohne Macht*) and so provoked the envy of the underprivileged masses.[25] The third thesis links anti-Semitism to re-

---

23   T. W. Adorno, Else Frenkel-Brunswik, Daniel J. Levinson, and R. Nevitt Sanford, *The Authoritarian Personality* (New York: Harper and Row, 1950), 2. Adorno too, throughout his own sections, repeats the basic premise that "anti-Semitism is not so much dependent upon the nature of the object as upon the subject's own psychological wants and needs" (609). The project was already conceived and outlined in 1939; see König, *Elemente*, 210; Jay, *The Jews and the Frankfurt School*, 141–143; Rensmann, *Politics of Unreason*, 65–143.
24   See Chapter 1.
25   Horkheimer and Adorno, *Dialektik*, 141.

sentment toward the economic role of the Jews as "bearers of capitalist modes of existence" (143). The role of the Jews as "agents of circulation" was also at the center of Horkheimer's *Die Juden und Europa* of 1939. Anson Rainbach indicates how in the *Dialektik*, "the emphasis . . . is no longer on the *presence* of the Jews in the sphere of circulation, but on the Jews in the mental 'imagery' of Nazism, which metaphorically substitutes the Jews as the 'hated mirror image of capitalism.'"[26] Helmut König noted a significant shift from the Marxist, socioeconomic ("functionalist") explanation framework, toward what he calls a "genealogical" framework, of Nietzschean and Freudian inspiration, in the *Dialektik*. This "prehistory" (*Urgeschichte*) traces anti-Semitism back to archaic mechanisms in human psyche and culture, deems it as a "ritual of civilization."[27] Of obvious application to the anti-Semite's psychology, the "genealogical" explanation of "why the Jews" is less trivial. As König notes, its main deployment takes place in the fifth thesis, via the notion of *mimesis*: anti-Semitism arises from civilization's aversion toward traces of man's natural origins manifest in "mimetic expressions," i.e., remains of human imitation of nature. Why Jews? According to the fifth thesis, Jews tend to manifest such mimetic features, which they "inherited through an unconscious process of imitation in early childhood from generation to generation, from the Jewish rags-and-bones man to the banker" (149). König is no doubt right that mimetic genealogy provides a nonracial theory of heritage.[28] Positing unconscious mimesis as the *paradigm* of Jewish tradition, however, whose content would thus be imitation of pre-civilizational instincts, does raise the question of the ultimate difference between mimetic and race theory in accounting for Jewishness.[29]

I already discussed in Chapter 1 the figure of the "real," "living" Jews in the anti-anti-Semitism of the current Heidegger controversy, and prob-

---

26   See Rabinbach, 52. For a broader view and reflection on Marxist and other accounts of anti-Semitism in the Frankfurt School, see Martin Jay, "The Jews and the Frankfurt School: Critical Theory's Analysis of Anti-Semitism," *New German Critique* 19 (1980): 137–149.
27   Horkheimer and Adorno, *Dialektik*, 171.
28   König, *Elemente*, 268.
29   Cf. Rabinbach, *Anti-Semitism*, 61. I discuss the question of race in Chapters 5 and 7.

lematized its epistemo-political significance. I now wish to briefly mention another recent discursive instance of this same figure, which raises the same difficulties, and which makes explicit reference to Adorno and Horkheimer's analysis, namely David Nirenberg's monumental history of "anti-Judaism."[30] This work deserves a much more careful discussion, to which the very rudimentary remark I must here limit myself to certainly can do no justice. I only wish to call attention to Nirenberg's basic premise, whereby "anti-Judaism" (and the distinction from anti-Semitism is of course not without significance) can and should be analyzed as a "Western Tradition," namely as a figure of Western thought, which has nothing to do with real Jews. This premise is based on the distinction and absolute separation between the "Judaism of Thought," which has been generated by anti-Judaism, and the "living Jews," which are accordingly stripped of any epistemic existence in Nirenberg's history of Western thought.[31] In addition to all the epistemo-political difficulties that arise from using "life" as the determinant category for collective existence, as discussed throughout the present book, of particular interest in Nirenberg's analysis is the extent to which his own historiography tends to reproduce the very fundamental anti-Jewish principle that it identifies in the Western tradition, namely the preclusion of the Jews—as representing materiality and worldliness, as *carnal life*—from the realm of "spirit."[32]

In support of his methodology of studying anti-Judaism as completely independent of Jews, Nirenberg rejects Hannah Arendt's attempt to explain

---

30   David Nirenberg, *Anti-Judaism: The Western Tradition* (New York: W. W. Norton, 2013).

31   "My history of thinking about Judaism speaks scarcely at all about the thoughts and actions of people who would have identified themselves as Jews. My focus here is how people—only a tiny minority of whom were Jews—thought with and about Judaism, and how that thinking affected (and was affected by) the possibilities of existence for Judaism in the world. Sometimes that thinking took place in interaction with *living Jews*, but often it did not." Nirenberg, *Anti-Judaism*, 10 (my emphasis).

32   "The Middle Ages created for the Jews a political and legal status analogous to their hermeneutic one. The Jews already represented for Christian exegesis a form of relation to text, an extreme literalism that turned them into *living flesh* unconnected to spirit." Nirenberg, *Anti-Judaism*, 115 (my emphasis).

anti-Semitism by reference to "something that Jews *really* were, something that they *really* did,"[33] and subscribes to Adorno and Horkheimer's more radical epistemology of anti-Semitism as a "projection" lacking any relation to reality. Adopting their epistemological definition of anti-Semitism as "projection without reflection," Nirenberg understands it as the "resistance to reflection about the gap between our ideas about Jews, Judaism, or Jewishness, and the complexity of the world."[34] It is noteworthy that for Nirenberg "Jews" thus become a paradigm for "the complexity of the world," and anti-Judaism in consequence becomes a paradigm for human perception *in general*, namely as essentially based on inadequate conceptual projections, which inevitably oversimplify a world too complex for us to understand: "our prodigious cognitive and computational abilities are inadequate to a full comprehension of our complex world," so we "reduce complexity to intelligibility by projecting our mental concepts onto the world" (34). This epistemology of "complex" reality beyond intelligibility tends toward a certain form of empirical positivism, which is indeed consistent with Adorno and Horkheimer's analysis of anti-Semitism. However, as I showed above, it can hardly represent the general epistemology underlying the *Dialectic of Enlightenment*, but on the contrary constitutes the very object of its critique, which discredits as "myth" any positing of factual, given (social) reality as existing immediately, detached from all human conceptions.

Against the positivist myth, "the claim of knowledge," according to Adorno and Horkheimer, "consists not in mere perception, classification and calculation, but precisely in the determined negation of the relevant immediacy."[35] This means that their remedy to modern myth, including the anti-Semitic one, is not the rejection of concepts in favor of facts, by means of whatever historical, sociological, or anthropological empiricism, but on the exact contrary the rejection of any pretention that facts are irreducibly and immediately given reality, and the insistence on thinking factual realities "as mediated conceptual moments, which are only fulfilled in the development of their social, historic, human meaning" (33). Indeed, the

---

33   Nirenberg, *Anti-Judaism*, 267–268.
34   Nirenberg, *Anti-Judaism*, 268.
35   Adorno and Horkheimer, *Dialektik*, 33.

critical school founded by the *Dialectic of Enlightenment*, at least nominally, will not aspire to criticize the "false absolute" of the myth with better facts, but with critical "theory." In the case of anti-Semitism, this would mean, instead of condemning the very conceptualization of Jews as such as paranoid projection and positing against it the "real" Jews, as Adorno and Horkheimer seem to do in the "Elements of Anti-Semitism," criticizing the bad conceptualization of Jews by anti-Semitism and offering a better or alternative conception.

To conclude my discussion of Adorno and Horkheimer, I wish to very briefly suggest that their text actually provides at least a blueprint, direction, or beginning of such critical theory of Jewishness not just as the fact of living Jews, but as belonging to the order of concepts and knowledge, i.e., as a specific episteme. This beginning is found outside their analysis of anti-Semitism, beyond the confines of their anti-anti-Semitic discourse. It appears at a certain moment in the "Concept of Enlightenment," the only moment in fact that features or hints at something like a break with the self-destructive history of enlightenment. If the myth of Odysseus is presented as an "allegory for the dialectic of enlightenment" (41), the break with this dialectic, or at least with its self-destructive dynamic, is featured, very briefly, in the figure of the "Jewish religion" (29–31).

In the "Jewish religion," Adorno and Horkheimer recognize an epistemic principle, a nucleus of Jewish episteme, which counters enlightenment's self-destructive tendency to sacralize the factually given, positive reality. This principle is the prohibition on idolatry or, as the authors describe it, "the prohibition to invoke falsity as God, the finite as the infinite, lie as truth" (31). This prohibition, a fundamentally *negative* commandment, is, so they claim, the only epistemic practice to which the Jewish religion "attaches hope." The through and through Hegelian founders of the Frankfurt School interpret the Jewish prohibition on idolatry as expressing the basic methodological maxim of the Hegelian project of knowledge, the principle of dialectic movement, namely the "specific negation" [*bestimmte Negation*]. This means knowledge only advances through the constant negative operation of rejecting any achieved, positive state of knowledge, which is never a total rejection, but always specific, aspiring not backward but always forward, toward a less positivist, more self-conscious state of knowledge. It is this principle, under the name of "negation of reification," that Adorno and Horkheimer declare in the preface to the *Dialectic of Enlightenment* to be the "true concern" of the *Geist*, namely of the human epistemic project.

Thus, not only do they recognize a Jewish episteme, Jewish epistemology looms as the historical paradigm of critical theory itself.[36]

There are of course many questions that should be raised in this regard, such as the basic characterization of the Jewish episteme as "religion," with the ensuing consequences and difficulties for its relations to Adorno and Horkheimer's own project; and more patently the understanding of the prohibition on idolatry as the fundamental principle of the Jewish religion, provoking difficulties concerning the relations of this religion to its historical others, in particular Christianity and Islam, in which the same prohibition plays an equally central, and in some variants arguably even greater, role.[37] But most importantly in the epistemo-political context, I wish to point at the difficulty of identifying the Jewish episteme—and with it, since it is granted here a paradigmatic status, the basic human project of knowledge—with a purely negative principle, a difficulty that I will discuss in detail in Chapter 4. The difficulty refers more specifically to the possibility of this radically negative epistemic project, which Adorno and Horkheimer explicitly attribute to a specific historical collective, the "Jewish," to manifest itself in some *positive* historical phenomenon, in some actual collective reality, as real Jews. It is, however, precisely this positive epistemo-political figure that is excluded from their phenomenology through the analysis of anti-Semitism as paranoid projection with no connection to living Jews.

---

36   Even more than Hegel, who "however, by finally postulating the known result of the whole process of negation, totality in the system and in history, as the absolute ... violated the prohibition and himself succumbed to mythology." See Adorno and Horkheimer, *Dialektik*, 30. König (*Elemente*, 327–345) provides indications to ways in which ideas related to this notion of the essential negativity of "Jewish religion" continue to significantly operate and fashion the post-World War II work and thought of Horkheimer—e.g., religion as the "yearning for complete justice"; cf. Max Horkheimer, "Die Sehnsucht nach dem ganz Anderen. Gespräch mit Rudolf Ringguth und Georg Wolff," in *Gesammelte Schriften*, Bd. 7 (Frankfurt am Main: Fischer Verlag, 1985), 393, quoted in König, *Elemente*, 331; and Adorno (e.g., the notion of "redemption," *Erlösung*—see *Minima Moralia*, 333). See also Jay, *The Jews and the Frankfurt School*, 148–149.

37   Adorno and Horkheimer follow here the footsteps of Freud, *Der Mann Moses und die monotheistische Religion* (Frankfurt am Main: Fischer, 1999 [1939]); translated by James Strachey as *Moses and Monotheism* (London: Hogarth, 1939). See Rabinbach, *Anti-Semitism*, 57.

The idea of anti-Semitic creation of the Jew, which governed Adorno and Horkheimer's analysis in the sense of pure fantasy, is perfected by Jean-Paul Sartre's idea of anti-Semitic real creation of real Jews. In fact, the object of Sartre's meditations of 1944 was not perceived and identified initially as anti-Semitic but as pertaining to the Jews. His thoughts were titled *Reflections on the Jewish Question*.[38] Nonetheless, the ambiguity of the concept "the Jewish Question" is that "Jewish" seems to describe the question itself but almost always refers rather to the *object* in question. This ambiguity is reproduced in the title of the English translation, *The Anti-Semite and the Jew*, which suggests a story with two seemingly equal protagonists. As has been most often the case, however, Sartre too does not understand the Jewish question as asked by the Jews, as pertaining to Jewish discourse, consciences, and knowledge, but to a different subjectivity, agency, and episteme, the anti-Semitic, which—and this is significant for the epistemo-political investigation—is represented by the individual figure of the anti-Semite. The anti-Semite is the first and primary theme of Sartre's *Reflections*: "The primary phenomenon, therefore, is anti-Semitism."[39]

Similar to Adorno and Horkheimer, Sartre too approaches anti-Semitism as an epistemic phenomenon, as a form or structure of knowledge. More specifically, Sartre too does not characterize the anti-Semitic episteme primarily through its specific object, "Semites" or "Jews," but through its

---

38   For a comprehensive study of the Jewish in Sartre's work, including a chapter on the *Réflexions*, see Jonathan Judaken, *Jean-Paul Sartre and the Jewish Question: Anti-antisemitism and the Politics of the French Intellectual* (Lincoln: University of Nebraska Press, 2006). As the book's title suggests, and as I already mentioned in the Introduction, Judaken's perspective is similar to mine, in identifying and examining Sartre's "anti-anti-Semitism" as a central site of his political thought: "Every time [Sartre] fundamentally rethought the underlying principles that defined his politics and his role as a public intellectual, Sartre did so by reflecting on 'the Jewish Question'" (3). Another excellent and relevant discussion of "Sartre's Jew" is Chapter 2 in Sarah Hammerschlag's *The Figural Jew* (2010), 68–116.

39   Sartre, *Réflexions*, 103.

unique epistemology, as an epistemological paradigm. Anti-Semitism, he writes, is not just an "opinion" but a "method of thought and a conception of the world" (23). Further in unison with Adorno and Horkheimer, for Sartre too anti-Semitism designates basically the *negative*, perverse epistemic principle. The anti-Semite chooses "passion" over "reason," thus "reasons falsely," and therefore is "impervious to reason and experience" (12), as well as to "historical facts" (10). This means that the anti-Semitic episteme is a form of knowledge that in fact negates knowledge, is but a seeming, pseudo-knowledge. The anti-Semite has no real knowledge of Jews. Consequently, like Adorno and Horkheimer, Sartre too basically diagnoses and describes anti-Semitism less as a form of knowledge than as a mental state, a sick mind, *para-noia*. What the anti-Semite thinks he knows of the Jews has nothing to do with any real experience with real Jews, but solely reflects "the *idea* of the Jew that one forms for himself" (11). It is this subjective idea that the anti-Semite projects on reality, generating a false, paranoid perception of the real: "Far from experience producing his idea of the Jew, it is the latter which explains his experience" (8).

In my analysis of Adorno and Horkheimer's anti-anti-Semitism, I already indicated the conceptual correlation between the de-epistemization of anti-Semitism, diagnosed as a psychological syndrome, and the de-epistemization of the Jews, who are only perceived as real, living Jews. Sartre is much more explicit in articulating this correlation. In fact, it is as a general epistemo-political paradigm that he characterizes the basic "principle" of anti-Semitism, namely the basic *falsity* of anti-Semitic pseudo-knowledge. According to Sartre, anti-Semitism fundamentally consists in perceiving human collectives not just as a collection of individuals, but as a "whole" that "is more and other than the sum of its parts; a whole that determines the meaning and underlying character of the parts that make it up" (24). Sartre does not provide here a further conceptual development of this paradigm. I suggest that what Sartre *rejects* here as anti-Semitism is the basic condition of the possibility of acknowledging *any* form of positive epistemo-politics, i.e., which acknowledges the collective reality of knowledge and the epistemic reality of the collective.

This can be observed, first of all, in the one concession that Sartre makes to the thought of collectives, when he accepts to think of the collective as a "synthetic reality." This notion of course conceptually reduces the collective reality to the reality of the individuals. Furthermore, Sartre makes this concession in the name of Marxist thought, to the crucial significance of which I will later return, such that the sole reality he recognizes for the synthesis of the individuals is the reality of "economic functions," the paradigmatic collectives thus being the "bourgeoisie" and the "working class" (25).

Sartre's rejection of the epistemic collective is articulated even more clearly, however, in his analysis of how the general anti-Semitic principle applies to the anti-Semitic perception of the collective that is the specific object of anti-Semitism, namely the Jews, who thus serve as the paradigm for Sartre's critique of epistemo-politics. "For the anti-Semite," he writes, "what makes the Jew is the presence in him of 'Jewishness' [*Juiverie*], a Jewish principle analogous to phlogiston or the soporific virtue of opium" (26). Sartre continues to characterize the "Jewish principle" posited by anti-Semitism as a negative principle, a principle of "evil." Anti-Semitism is a "purely negative" attitude to the Jewishness it invents. However, as I already showed in Chapter 1, with respect to the current Heidegger debate, for Sartre too the fundamental problem of the anti-Semitic principle is the invention of a Jewish principle, namely the very perception of any epistemic reality that would be Jewish. For Sartre, as I claimed was the case also for Adorno and Horkheimer, the basic problem with anti-Semitism is that it creates Judaism. And whereas the conceptual consequences of this thesis for the positive perception of the Jews remained in Adorno and Horkheimer's text implicit and even ambiguous, Sartre explicitly denies any "Jewish principle," namely any intellectual or moral dimension of Jewish existence *qua* Jewish, and declares that "the sole ethnic characteristics of the Jews are physical" (85). The real Jews would be, once again, the living, "flesh and blood," biological Jews, whose collective Sartre categorizes as "race" (43).

Nevertheless, Sartre makes a crucial step beyond Adorno and Horkheimer, when he identifies in France 1944, in the reality beyond the anti-Semitic mind, some kind of Jewish existence that exceeds pure biology, "the French Jew," and when he sets out to describe and account for this *epistemic* Jewish existence.[40] His negative account, i.e., the descriptions

---

40 It has been already noted that the actual anti-Semitism—and consequential Jewishness—that Sartre seems to have before his eyes in his descriptions is

that he eliminates, is, albeit very brief, as instructive as his positive. In fact, in his brief discussion of what the Jews in France are *not*, Sartre offers two further collective categories, beyond "class" and "race," which could have hypothetically also applied to the Jews. The two new categories are "nation" and "religion," which constitute what Sartre calls "concrete historical communities": "concrete historical community is basically *national* and *religious*" (47). The exact meaning of these epistemo-politically crucial concepts, in particular their status for the Marxist discourse of "synthetic realities" and "economic functions," remains here undeveloped. The only indications for Sartre's understanding of these concepts can be drawn from his explanation of why they do not apply to the French Jews. Interestingly, the explanation is not that the Jews, as Sartre explicitly declared earlier in the text, are only a "race," joined by nothing but common physical traits, namely pure biology with no conscience and no history. Rather, Sartre does recognize a historical Jewish community, both a nation and religion, which he however perceives as pure past: "Certainly at a remote time in the past there was a religious and national community that was called Israel. But the history of that community is one of dissolution over a period of twenty-five centuries" (46). There would be much to say, too much for this stage of my discussion, about this epistemo-political *topos*, which, while acknowledging fundamental phenomena of epistemic collectivity, "religion," "nation," "history," nonetheless subordinates them all absolutely to the political condition of state sovereignty. Indeed, in Sartre's narrative, the loss of Jewish political sovereignty with the Roman destruction of the Kingdom of Judea has necessarily entailed the loss of all collective episteme, the dissolution of the Jewish collective subject itself. What was lost in this Jewish history of loss is nothing shorter than Jewish history itself: "Its twenty centuries of dispersion and political impotence forbid its having a historic past. If it is true, as Hegel says, that a community is historical to the degree that it remembers its history, then the Jewish community is the least historical of all, for it keeps a memory of nothing but a long martyrdom, that is, of a long passivity" (47). This paradoxical de-historicized Jewish historical

---

not situated in the context of Nazism but rather in the context of the Dreyfus affair; see Hammerschlag, *The Figural Jew*, 92; Maurice Samuels, *The Right to Difference: French Universalism and the Jews* (Chicago: University of Chicago Press, 2016), 145.

community Sartre calls "abstract historical community." This state of fundamental negativity should have been highly suggestive for a philosopher who a year earlier, in his magnum opus, *Being and Nothingness* (1943), attached a constitutive significance to negativity in the very being of human consciousness, and even, as Sarah Hammerschlag notes, went "so far as to call the structure of consciousness 'diasporic.'"[41] Instead, in the negation of Jewish polity, religion, and history that characterizes the condition of the assimilated French Jews, Sartre is able to perceive nothing but race.

Whence his positive account for what he nevertheless identifies, beyond physiology, as a factually existent French Jewish consciousness, namely a collective Jewish episteme. Since the historical Jewish episteme has been lost without a trace, current Jewish consciousness for Sartre necessarily derives from a non-Jewish consciousness, "the Jew is one whom other men consider a Jew," which is the foundation for his famous thesis, whereby "it is the anti-Semite who *makes* [*fait*] the Jew" (49). In fact, beyond Adorno and Horkheimer's anti-Semitic creation of the Jew as an imaginary, fantasmatic figure, anti-Semitism for Sartre is the creator of real Jews as epistemic subjects, of real Jewish conscience, of Jewishness. In this process of creation of the Jew by the non-Jew, the anti-Jew, the anti-Semitic projection is interiorized and appropriated by its object, who consequently identifies himself as 'Jew,' acquires something like 'Jewish' self-consciousness.

This process, which Sartre describes in 1944, essentially reproduces what one year earlier, in *Being and Nothingness*, he described as the basic constitutive dynamics of self-conscience in general, and for which the Jew was already a central paradigm. In a nutshell, the basic ontological character of consciousness in *Being and Nothingness* is "being for itself," namely always being in reflection on, "conscious to," and thus in distance from its factual being ("being in itself"). This means that, as I mentioned above, human consciousness is ontologically characterized by negativity—it "is what it is not and is not what it is,"[42] which translates itself existentially to a fundamental human condition of *freedom*. Sartre argued that the essentially negative human consciousness acquires a positive and factual being

---

41 Hammerschlag, *The Figural Jew*, 79, in reference to Jean-Paul Sartre, *L'être et le néant* (Paris: Gallimard, 1943), 131–132, 182; translated by Hazel E. Barnes as *Being and Nothingness* (New York: Washington Square, 1992), 138, 195.

42 Sartre, *L'être et le néant*, 70, 106.

through its "being for others," i.e., the process of being perceived and treated in certain ways by other people, through "the look of the other": "In order for me to be what I am, it suffices merely that the Other look at me" (262, 301). Thus, human consciousness' fundamental freedom is always limited by the social position in which it is situated, by its "situation," in which the others ascribe to me some specific factual being, a certain identity, which does not emerge from my absolute freedom, which I am not absolutely free to choose. One of the central examples that Sartre provides for the situated identity, which is imposed on me by the others, is indeed the Jew; and next to the Jew, and this is quite significant for a philosophical treatise published during the Nazi occupation, "the Aryan": "Here I am—Jew, or Aryan, handsome or ugly, one-armed, etc." (523, 568). I note in passing, that the disturbing depoliticization (or on a second, more disturbing thought, the *specific* politicization) of these two categories, already by the very act of positing them side by side, reaches its climax in an absurd moment, almost ironic and so exonerating, where Sartre names examples for the way in which the situated identity is imposed on the individual through "the encounter with a prohibition": "('No Jews allowed here' or 'Jewish restaurant. No Aryans allowed', etc.)" (524, 569).

The intimacy between Sartre's general theory about the constitution of the self by the other and his thesis on the creation of the Jew by the anti-Semite generates a double effect of the former on the latter and vice versa.

On the one hand, the general theory of the self provides fundamental legitimacy to the alleged act of anti-Semitic creation. If for Adorno and Horkheimer anti-Semitism ultimately remained a sickness of mind, for Sartre the creation of the Jew through the anti-Semite transpires as a paradigm for the normal way in which collective identities are created. Consequently, and here lies one of the most powerful ambiguities of the *Reflections on the Jewish Question*, the understanding that the Jew is created by the anti-Semite does not lead Sartre to renounce this creation but on the contrary to acknowledge it, to give it recognition.

Thus, he categorically rejects what he designates as the position of the "Democrat." The latter, declining in principle all "collectivities" and recognizing only individuals, consistently resists to and repudiates the anti-Semitic creation, solving the "Jewish Question" by simply saying: "There are no Jews" (40). It seems to me that this position (or certain variations thereon) is ultimately the one dominating the current Heidegger controversy, as I attempted to show in Chapter 1, and Sartre too is well aware of the ambiguity by the force of which this kind of anti-anti-Semitism may easily veer in anti-Judaism, becoming "hostile to the Jew to the extent that the latter thinks of himself as a Jew" (41).[43]

In contrast to the position of the "Democrat," Sartre's own position with respect to the Jewish creation of the anti-Semite is rather one of acknowledgment and recognition, such that his analysis can be read as an existentialist interpretation on the theological themes of creation and election. As I will show later in my analysis of Hannah Arendt's and Alain Badiou's theories of anti-Semitism, the metamorphosis and structural reproduction of the theological *topos* of the divine election of the Jews in the narrative of the anti-Semitic election of the Jews is in fact an inherent motif of anti-anti-Semitic logic. The Jew, Sartre writes, "cannot choose not to be a Jew.... To be a Jew is to be thrown into—to be *abandoned* to— the situation of a Jew; and at the same time it is to be responsible in and through one's own person for the destiny and the very nature of the Jewish people" (64). In the context of this book, it would be no doubt suggestive to reread the biblical myth of "the Chosen People" with such concepts as "being-thrown," which Sartre explicitly draws from the Heideggerian analysis of human existence.[44]

The cardinal analytic gain of Sartre's own existential interpretation of Jewish (anti-Semitic) election is the description of Jewish self-consciousness itself, of Jewishness, as a reaction and response to this unchosen chosenness. The horizon of Jewishness is thus analyzed as the horizon of the Jew's possible responses to his election by the anti-Semite. Sartre sketches the general contours of this horizon through a fundamental distinction between two archetypes or arche-modes of response, using Heidegger's distinction between the two basic modes of the human being's attitude toward its own existence, constituting two basic modes of existence, the "inauthentic" and the "authentic."[45] In the Sartrean variation

---

43   Maurice Samuels compellingly shows how Sartre's "democrat" quite precisely corresponds to the position, not so much of "Revolutionaries like Clermont-Tonnerre and Robespierre," but of the famous Dreyfusiard Émile Zola; see Samuels, *The Right to Difference*, 154.
44   Heidegger, *Being and Time*, §29.
45   One should be aware of the difficulty of translating Heidegger's *Eigentlichkeit* and *Uneigentlichkeit* with "authenticity" and "inauthenticity." This

on Heidegger's *Existenzanalytik*, the "inauthentic Jew" is inauthentic inasmuch as he denies his election and attempts to escape his situation by developing epistemic attitudes and personal characteristics such as "reflection," "irony," "detachment," "bad faith," tending in general to the "abstract, rationalist, intellectual" and "universal" (66–91). The "authentic Jew," in contrast, seizes his thrownness and chooses to assume his unchosen anti-Semitic election, by "choosing oneself *as Jew*—that is, in realizing one's Jewish condition": "The authentic Jew *makes himself a Jew*, in the face of all and against all" (98–99). The anti-Semite's Jew thus practically becomes an existential paradigm of human being in general. This explains the constitutive significance that Sartre's *Reflections* could have had on at least one generation of French Jews, as attested by Jean Daniel: "We are many, from François Jacob to Simone Veil, from Edgar Morin to Claude Lanzmann and Robert Misrahi, to have recognized ourselves in the Sartrean text."[46]

---

difficulty arises not the least from Sartre's own reservations from the terms "authentique" and "inauthentique," which he finds to be "questionable and not very sincere due to their implicit moral content" (*L'être et le néant*, 575), even as he, without raising the question of translation, attributes these French expressions directly to Heidegger himself, who in *Being and Time* (§9) nonetheless insisted on the "rigorous literal meaning" of these expressions.

46   In his introduction to *Le Nouvel Observateur*'s special dossier on Sartre of January 2000, quoted by Judaken, *Sartre*, 240. It is here that also Sarah Hammerschlag justly identified the political potential of Sartre's "authentic Jew" "as a response to the potential dialectic between universalism and particularism": "Sartre's prescription for authenticity in *Réflexions* seems to advocate a nonnaturalized pluralism, a respect for difference founded on historical and cultural context that does not at the same time reinscribe the language of nature and essence, a position that Sartre referred to as *concrete liberalism*" (*The Figural Jew*, 93). The same observation was expressed in 1947 by Emmanuel Levinas, who indicates that Sartre's existentialism, in the notion of the situation, "recognizes for spirit engagements that are not elements of knowledge [*des savoirs*]," and thus, vis-à-vis the "anticartesian and antispinozist" racist anti-Semitism, existentialist humanism is able to provide a response that is not limited to the abstract rationalism of Descartes and Spinoza (represented by "the Democrat" in Sartre's text); see Levinas, "Existentialisme et Antisémitisme," in *Les imprévus de l'histoire* (n.p.: Fata Morgana, 1994), 103–106. Maurice Samuels formulates a similar insight in terms of "universalism": "Sartre broke new ground by rejecting universalism outright and by theorizing the implications of this stance" (*The Right to Difference*, 140).

Furthermore, to fully appreciate the force and effect of Sartre's "creationist" thesis in this book, it would be imperative to consider the influence that it had on postcolonial thought, which has provided some of the central epistemo-political paradigms of our time. I only point here at the constitutive role that the *Reflections on the Jewish Question* has played in the development of Frantz Fanon's thought. His *Black Skin, White Masks* is in constant conversation with Sartre's text, and the idea that it is the anti-Semite who creates the Jew is the explicit inspiration for Fanon's assertion that "it is the racist who creates his inferior,"[47] namely that the "Negro" is a construct of the "white," which led Fanon to take a distance from the search for a specific black episteme, of "négritude." It is instructive that Fanon nonetheless perceived a profound difference between Jews and Blacks in this regard, insisting that the case of the latter is dominated by the physical and biological in a way that Jews, *pace* Sartre, don't: "I am the slave not of the 'idea' that others have of me but of my own appearance" (87). Sartre's negative creationism also echoes in *The Wretched of the Earth*, which was originally published with a preface by Sartre, and in the first pages of which Fanon states: "It is the colonist who *fabricated* and *continues to fabricate* the colonized subject."[48] In this context it would no doubt be important to reflect on the conceptual nexus between this thesis and the question of violence as indispensable means of decolonization and liberation.[49]

This is how Sartre's thesis about the anti-Semitic creation of the Jew, which is consistent with his general philosophy of self-consciousness, is normalized into a universal epistemo-political paradigm. However, on the other hand, the constellation in which the paradigmatic "other" that acts as the original agent for the constitution of the self is the fundamentally problematic figure of the anti-Semite must obviously generate some difficulties

---

47 Frantz Fanon, *Peau Noire, Masques Blancs* (Paris: Seuil, 1952), translated by Charles Lam Markmann as *Black Skin, White Masks* (New York: Grove Press, 1967), 69.

48 Frantz Fanon, *Les damnés de la terre* (Paris: Fançois Maspero, 1961), translated by Richard Philcox as *The Wretched of the Earth*, with commentary by Jean-Paul Sartre and Homi Bhabha (New York: Grove Press, 2004), 2.

49 See Bennetta Jules-Rosette, "Jean-Paul Sartre and the Philosophy of Négritude: Race, Self, and Society," *Theory and Society* 36, no. 3 (2007): 265–285; Linda A. Bell, "Different Oppressions: A Feminist Exploration of Sartre's 'Anti-Semite and Jew,'" *Sartre Studies International* 3, no. 2 (1997): 1–20.

for the nature and value of the thus constituted self. In epistemo-political terms, if the basic problem with anti-Semitism is precisely that it *wrongly* asserts the existence of a Jewish principle or episteme, beyond mere biology, how can the collective Jewish consciousness created by this anti-Semitic projection not be fundamentally tainted by the exact same problem?

In Sartre's analysis, this difficulty is most clearly visible with respect to the "Authentic Jew," who supposedly responds to his election by the anti-Semite by making a choice to actively assume his imposed identity and to "make himself" as a Jew. The basic question that this idea raises is whether the Jewish self-choice is not and cannot be but the reenactment of the anti-Semitic choice, such that "authentic" Judaism would constitute the consummation of anti-Semitism. That this conclusion is hard to avoid can be seen in Sartre's—admittedly limited—attempt to positively contemplate this kind of authentic, self-conscious Jewish collective. The most concrete conception that he offers for this collective is a "Jewish national community," namely some kind of Zionism (100–101). However, other than the dangerous—but obvious—complicity that Sartre's notes might develop between Zionism and anti-Semitism in contesting the Jews' belonging to a non-Jewish nation, for example, the French, it is unclear what positive episteme can grow on the basis of pure race, as Sartre's anti-anti-Semitism understands the Jews ultimately to be. Indeed, at an earlier passage in the text, Sartre already indicates that a community based on race can hope to be nothing but racist: "If the Jews want to draw a legitimate pride from this community, they must indeed end up by exalting racial qualities, since they cannot take pride in any collective work that is specifically Jewish, or in a civilization properly Jewish, or in a common mysticism" (61).[50]

In fact, the inner consistency of Sartre's theory does not allow any place for the Jewish collective in his epistemo-political program.[51] According to

---

50 On Sartre's later attitude toward and relations to the actual accomplishment of Zionism, the State of Israel, as characterized by "ambivalent commitments," see Judaken, *Sartre*, 184–207. In his homage to Sartre after the latter's death in 1980, Levinas pointed at Sartre's scrupulous fidelity toward the "existence of the State of Israel" as "probably already revealing a different position than the one he expressed in *The Jewish Question*." See Levinas, "Un langage pour nous familier," in *Les imprévus*, 131.

51 I therefore do not share Maurice Samuels's sense of "surprise" at what he describes as a "last-minute reversal," in which "Sartre seems to advocate the

his eschatological vision, as he lays it down in the *Reflections on the Jewish Question*, the final solution of the Jewish Question lies in the dissolution of both anti-Semites and Jews in the "classless society" (108). The mere eschatology of abolition of all social differences and particularities at the end of history does not of course in itself preclude, but on the contrary in principle enables, recognizing and sustaining the "historical communities," which by definition belong to history, before it ends.[52] I have already pointed at the conceptual nexus between the recognition of epistemology's collective dimension and the recognition of epistemology's historical dimension.[53] The profound tension that manifests itself in Sartre's text is rather between the epistemo-political paradigm of something like a historical Jewish collective, on the one hand, and arguably the most powerful

---

very procedure he denounces: he ends the text by calling for assimilation after all" (Samuels, *The Right to Difference*, 155). Consequently, I also cannot accept Samuels explanation of this "surprise" by "Sartre's allegiance to Marxism [that] thus motivates him to accept a political category he has just renounced (universalism)" (156).

52 It is at this conceptual point that I locate the tension between Judaken's and Hammerschlag's analysis of Sartre's argument. Judaken clearly identifies and criticizes the basic *negativity* of Jewish being in Sartre's conception: "The problems of *Réflexions sur la question juive* result from the strict dialectical logic that structures Sartre's anti-antisemitism. 'The Jew' is a negation, the antisemite is the negation of the negation, and the synthesis is Sartre's utopian revolution" (Judaken, *Sartre*, 145). Hammerschlag sees this negativity but at the same time, in a truly Hegelian move, identifies it as the essential condition for the emergence of the concept, idea, or *figure* of the Jew in postwar French philosophy, which will ultimately, also in Sartre's own later "Hope Now," "revalorize" Jewish negativity to a political ideal. She thus deems Sartre's *Réflexions* as "a turning point in the history of the Jewish question in France": "Sartre made it possible to disentangle the idea of the Jew from the real Jew, allowing for the idea to function as a metaphor for the outsider and, thus, for Sartre as an ideal. Ironically, by describing the Jew as society's other, Sartre in fact facilitated a description of the Jew that made this figure worthy of emulation" (Hammerschlag, *The Figural Jew*, 72). Whereas Judaken in his later work on theories of anti-Semitism, such as in Adorno and Arendt, criticizes, similarly to the Boyarins, the very procedure of conceptualizing Jewish being, what he calls the "conceptual Jew," my epistemology acknowledges the potential of Hammerschlag's "figural Jew," with respect to which I will in Chapter 4 nonetheless present my critical analysis.

53 See Chapter 1.

historical epistemo-politics in modern times, Marxism. Marxist theory, as Sartre applies it, in fact offers its own paradigm of historical collective, the "class." Class struggles, which according to Marx are the motor of history, have been carried out by Marxism to a large extent not exactly as struggles between classes, but as epistemic struggles between the very notion of the "class" or "class consciousness" and other collective paradigms.

It would be an important and difficult task to examine the various conceptual and historical, actual and potential relations of the "class" and other Marxist epistemo-political paradigms, such as the "party," which Sartre does not discuss in this text, to different understandings of the Jewish collective. Chapter 6 will propose some reflections on this question. In the specific context of Sartre, I have already pointed at the conceptual complicity between his understanding of the class collective as an "economic function" and his general concept of the collective as "synthesis," namely of individuals. In other words, the "class" seems to serve Sartre as a concrete paradigm for a collective that is completely reducible to its individuals, i.e., devoid of proper collective or general episteme, such as the "Jewish principle" attributed by the anti-Semite to the Jews. This observation may lead to a general (and somewhat paradoxical) question as to the basic ability of Marxist theory, the historical agent of "communism," to provide the necessary epistemic basis for a collective subject. Indications that this may well be the case at least for Sartre's Marxism can be found in the larger Sartrean oeuvre, such as the limited analysis in *Being and Nothingness* of the "we" as "a plurality of subjectivities," or when in *Critique de la raison dialectique* Sartre "repeats with Marxism" that "there is nothing but humans and real relations between humans; from this point of view, the group is in a certain sense nothing but a multiplicity of relations and of relations between these relations."[54]

To conclude my discussion of Sartre's anti-anti-Semitism, I should, first, state that no appreciation of the *Reflections on the Jewish Question* could be complete without also taking into account its long history of reception, through several generations of French thinkers and philosophers, Jews and none, who sometimes offered critiques not unsimilar to mine.[55] Second, I

---

54 Sartre, *L'être et l'étant*, 453; Sartre, *Critiqe de la raison dialectique*, Tome I (Paris : Gallimard, 1960), 55.
55 For an excellent overview, see Judaken, *Sartre*, Chapter 8. See also in Hammerschlag, *The Figural Jew*, 68–73.

should equally point at Sartre's own critical reflections on his *Reflections* in his later years, most famously in his controversial last conversations with Benny Lévy, first published in *Le nouvel observateur* in 1980, a very short time before Sartre's death, and later independently as *L'Espoir Maintenant*, "Hope Now."[56] In these interviews, Sartre was directly confronted by Lévy for holding in his *Reflections* "that the Jew—let's put this provocatively—was an invention of anti-Semites. In any event, according to you there was no such thing as Jewish thought, no such thing as Jewish history" (100). Sartre confirmed in response that the book had been intended as "a declaration of war against anti-Semites, nothing more" (101), i.e., was interested primarily in anti-Semites, not in Jews, much less Jewish knowledge, such that *Reflections on the Jewish Question* was written by Sartre "without reading one book about Jews" (102).

Thirty-six years later, in the interviews with Lévy, Sartre modified his view. His account of the change still mentions no books ("Most of the significant things about Jews are written in foreign languages, especially in Hebrew, sometimes in Yiddish"), but is rather focused on his postwar encounters with individual living Jews ("It came from meeting more Jews after the Liberation"), like Claude Lanzmann, his adoptive daughter, Arlette ("who is Jewish, and I've spent a lot of time with her and know how she thinks"), and Benny Lévy himself (101). Nonetheless, Sartre does recognize in the interviews a "Jewish reality beyond the destruction inflicted by anti-Semitism on the Jews," a reality which he characterizes as "metaphysical"—like the "Christian reality"—and which consists in the "relation of the Jew to the infinite," namely God (104). Most importantly for the epistemo-political question, in this Jewish principle or "religion" he perceives a "Jewish finality," which through categories such as the "resurrection of the dead" and "messianism" aspires to "a new world" that will "ultimately reunite humanity" (105–106). In this Jewish eschatology Sartre identifies "the goal of non-Jews, those I agree with," namely "revolution": "Doing away with the present society and replacing it by a juster society" (107). Significantly, from the interviews it arises (and here lies

---

56   Jean-Paul Sartre and Benny Lévy, *L'Espoir maintenant. Les entretiens de 1980* (Paris: Verdier, 1991); translated by Adrian Van den Hoven as *Hope Now: The 1980 Interviews* (Chicago: University of Chicago Press, 1996). For the controversy around and reception of this text see Judaken, *Sartre*, 226–239; Hammerschlag, *The Figural Jew*, 109–116.

no doubt at least some of their controversial nature) that in his late days Sartre finds this Jewish episteme to be not just comparable but superior to the Marxist doctrine, in that it offers "ethics" that goes beyond the "economic problems" of Marxism (107). Even more profoundly, at least from the epistemo-political perspective, recognizing a positively Jewish epistemic reality entails for Sartre the necessity of re-thinking historicity. More precisely, Sartre deems it necessary to think beyond the "history of a sovereign political being" ("the history that Hegel introduced into our intellectual landscape," Benny Lévy suggests), in order to *perceive* a positive historical Jewish epistemo-political existence, namely "a real unity of the Jews in historical time, and this real unity is due not to their being gathered together in a historical land, but to actions, writings, relations that don't derive from the idea of a homeland, or have only been so for the last few years" (104).[57]

This chapter has looked at the first position or configuration of the anti-anti-Semitic discourse, i.e., the anti-Semitic creation of Jewish being—either as imagination, a fantasy of the anti-Semitic mind (Adorno and Horkheimer), or as reality, a real Jewish consciousness and collective consciousness (Sartre). The fundamental conceptual, namely internal difficulty of this anti-anti-Semitic position pertains to the relation between internal projection and external reality. "Reality" emerges in the anti-Semitic mind in two main forms: first, the very name "Jew" as the name for the anti-Semitic projection; second, the real people, individuals and collectives, on which this projection is projected—the "real," concrete, flesh-and-blood Jews. Even after total de-epistemization, there must still be something in the

---

57 Thus, for Levinas, vis-à-vis Sartre's *Réflexions*, where "it is under the gaze of the anti-Semite and through this gaze that the Jew would receive his obstinate essence" and "perpetuity" ("Langage pour nous familier," 130), *Hope Now* is "a complete turn," where against Hegel's exclusive "history of states," Sartre discovered "another history" (132), namely the "Holy History" born by the Jewish people. Quoting Sartre himself in the interviews with Lévy: "If Jewish history exists, Hegel is wrong. And Jewish history exists" (see Levinas, "Quand Sartre Découvre l'Histoire Sainte,» in *Les imprévus de l'histoire*, 134–137). For a detailed discussion of Sartre's rereading of Hegel in this context, see Hammerschlag, *The Figural Jew*, 94–109.

living Jew that provides the minimal support for the name "Jew," which continues to inscribe *bios* in *episteme*, body in knowledge, and which thus provides the screen or surface for the projection, the *Projektionsfläche*, a *specific* screen for this *specific* projection. This conceptual difficulty emerges in anti-anti-Semitic theory in the image of the factual question: "Why the Jews?" It is this question that connects Adorno and Horkheimer's last three theses on anti-Semitism to the first four, their Freudianism to their Marxism; it led Sartre from *Reflections* to *Hope*. It is this question that thus drives anti-anti-Semitic discourse to its next configuration.

3 Jewish Creation of Anti-Semitism

Arendt and Badiou

THE SECOND ANTI-ANTI-SEMITIC POSITION arises from the consistent attempt to explain the possibility of anti-Semitic projection from the epistemic Jew onto the living Jew. This position identifies the condition for this possibility in the living Jew herself: it traces anti-Semitism back to a Jewish origin. I call this position the Jewish creation of anti-Semitism. It is epistemo-politically more complex than the first position, the anti-Semitic creation of the Jew, since it does recognize Jewish knowledge, a Jewish episteme. Furthermore, as I will show in this chapter, it recognizes a Jewish political epistemology. This position thus opens up a horizon for understanding Jewishness in epistemo-political terms, as a configuration of the political vocation of knowledge. Nonetheless, for the second anti-anti-Semitic position, Jewish political episteme remains negative—it is conceived primarily as the origin of anti-Semitism, "the Jewish creation of anti-Semitism," which means that it *is* essentially anti-Semitic, analogous to anti-Semitism or manifests itself ultimately in anti-Semitism. In this position the complicity of anti-anti-Semitism and of anti-Semitism is manifest. For this reason, this second anti-anti-Semitic position is never explicated as such by its authors. It comes to light in polemics, which these authors in fact provoked, and through deconstructive hermeneutics. It is with such hermeneutics that I will now approach two authors: Hannah Arendt and Alain Badiou.

HANNAH ARENDT AND THE JEWISH ORIGINS OF ANTI-SEMITISM

With respect to Arendt, more than other thinkers discussed in this book, it is especially important to methodically clarify the hermeneutical operation performed here. The goal is to expose the inner dynamics of anti-anti-Semitic discourse, by pointing at and interlinking different elements of this discourse as they emerge in texts of prominent post–World War II political thinkers. This means that only distinct moments in the broad oeuvre of these thinkers are illuminated. I do think and to some extent argue that these anti-anti-Semitic moments are central, perhaps crucial for their thought. At the same time, however, I am also aware of the complexity, synchronic nuances and of course diachronic development in their work. My analysis focuses mostly on the synchronic tensions, while the diachronic transformations are only hinted at. In no way does this presentation claims to provide any exhaustive, sufficient, or comprehensive analysis of these thinkers, nor do I suggest that anti-anti-Semitism primarily characterizes their project. All I say is that—a certain version of—anti-anti-Semitic discourse emerges at and may account for a central moment in it.

This clarification, I said, is especially important with respect to the work of Hannah Arendt. This is so, because of all the thinkers discussed here, it seems that Arendt's work has been in the most profound, sustained, and differentiated manner concerned with "the Jewish Question," as Richard Bernstein titled it.[1] The last part of this book will indicate how "the Jewish Question" is a paradigmatic category for Jewish being in *modernity*. In fact, Bernstein's book convincingly demonstrates how contemplation of various aspects of the phenomenal and historical complex of modern Jewish existence has been present in and often preconfigured Arendt's thought. Moreover, Arendt's positions with respect to key events in modern Jewish

---

1   Richard Bernstein, *Hannah Arendt and the Jewish Question* (Cambridge, MA: MIT Press, 1996), arguing that "approaching Arendt from the point of view of her understanding and response to the Jewish question and the political forms of anti-Semitism that arise in the nineteenth and twentieth centuries is, to use her own language, an essential *perspective* for gaining an understanding of the most characteristic themes in her thinking" (9). See also Jennifer Ring, *The Political Consequences of Thinking Gender and Judaism in the Work of Hannah Arendt* (Albany: State University of New York Press, 1998).

being, such as the Holocaust and Zionism, in particular around her book on the Eichmann trial, have been controversial and influential for the reception of her work.[2] This controversy is one of the events in which the problematic complicity of anti-anti-Semitic with anti-Semitic discourse has in fact been noticed, brought to light—and at times reproduced by Arendt's critics.[3] One may therefore say that the epistemo-political ques-

---

2   On Arendt and Zionism, see Amnon Raz-Krakotzkin, "Jewish Peoplehood, 'Jewish Politics' and Political Responsibility: Arendt on Zionism and Partitions," *College Literature* 38, no. 1 (2011): 57–74, observing Arendt's critique of Zionism "from a national Jewish point of view" (66). See also Shiraz Dossa, "Lethal Fantasy: Hannah Arendt on Political Zionism," *Arab Studies Quarterly* 8, no. 3 (1986): 219–230. For a vehement polemic against Arendt's relation to Zionism and to the Eichmann trial as a "moral failure," see Elhanan Yakira, "Hannah Arendt, the Holocaust, and Zionism: A Story of Failure," *Israel Studies* 11, no. 3 (2006): 31–61; for a counterposition and response, see Idith Zertal, "A State of Trial: Hannah Arendt vs. the State of Israel," *Social Research* 74, no. 4 (2007): 1127–1158.

The literature on Arendt and Eichmann is vast. For a review of the original debate, see Richard I. Cohen, "Breaking the Code: Hannah Arendt's 'Eichmann in Jerusalem' and the Public Polemic: Myth Memory and Historical Imagination," *Michael: On the History of the Jews in the Diaspora* 1993, 29–85; Anson Rabinbach, "Eichmann in New York: The New York Intellectuals and the Hannah Arendt Controversy," *October* 198 (2004): 97–111; Amos Elon, "The Excommunication of Hannah Arendt," *World Policy Journal* 23, no. 4 (2006/7): 93–102. Important works from the last two decades include Seyla Benhabib, "Identity, Perspective and Narrative in Hannah Arendt's 'Eichmann in Jerusalem,'" *History and Memory* 8, no. 2 (1996): 35–59; Dan Diner, "Hannah Arendt Reconsidered: On the Banal and the Evil in Her Holocaust Narrative," *New German Critique* 71 (1997): 177–190; Bernard Bergen, *The Banality of Evil: Hannah Arendt and "The Final Solution"* (Lanham, MD: Rowman and Littlefield, 1998); Michael Mack, "The Holocaust and Hannah Arendt's Philosophical Critique of Philosophy: 'Eichmann in Jerusalem,'" *New German Critique* 106 (2009): 35–60.

3   See recently Emmanuel Faye, *Arendt et Heidegger. Extermination nazie et destruction de la pensée* (Paris: Albin Michel, 2106). Even though some of my readings are close to Faye's, in particular his analysis of the role ascribed to Jewish political and intellectual agency in Arendt's history of anti-Semitism (49–88), I do not draw the same critical conclusions. I have already indicated in Chapter 1 the anti-anti-Semitic nature, to my eyes, of Faye's own position on the question of Heidegger's anti-Semitism. I identify the same logic in Faye's polemics against

tion embodied by the figure of the Jew has been central both to Hannah Arendt's political thought and to her political performance.

Political Epistemology of Totalitarianism

At the center of the present discussion stands Arendt's analysis of anti-Semitism in *The Origins of Totalitarianism* of 1951,[4] which belongs with Adorno and Horkheimer's *Dialectics of Enlightenment* and Sartre's *Reflections on the Jewish Question* in the same intellectual hour of post–World War II crisis. This is one of Arendt's central works, and it is so crucial for the development of her political philosophy that Margaret Canovan could claim that in this book "the entire agenda of Arendt's political thought was set by her reflections on the political catastrophes of the mid-century."[5] In fact, like Adorno, Horkheimer, and Sartre, Arendt belongs to this same epistemo-political event, in which political thought has directly arisen from and was itself an integral part of the historical happening of the *polis*. Arendt's project too was explicitly defined as an attempt of engaging, performing, and exercising *episteme*—knowledge, thought, and intelligibility, what she calls "comprehension"—on the negative political event, the twentieth century's event of the *polis*'s negation, which Arendt, like Adorno and Horkheimer, in fact understands as the collapse of the very political project of humanity, the collapse of "civilization." This anti-political event

---

Arendt, which, as the book's title and introduction make explicit, significantly draws from his polemics against Heidegger.

4 Hannah Arendt, *The Origins of Totalitarianism* (New York: Harcourt Brace and Co., 1979 [1951]). This book has had several different editions in the course of sixteen years, in which it has undergone significant modifications. For a genetic analysis of the book's structure, see Roy Tsao, "The Three Phases of Arendt's Theory of Totalitarianism," in *Hannah Arendt: Critical Assessments of Leading Political Philosophers*, vol. 1, Arendt and Political Events, ed. Garrath Williams (New York: Routledge, 2006), 195–223. On Arendt's book in the context of theories of totalitarianism of its time, see in the same volume Alfons Söllner, "Hannah Arendt's *The Origins of Totalitarianism* in Its Original Context," 265–285.

5 Margaret Canovan, *Hannah Arendt: A Reinterpretation of Her Political Thought* (Cambridge: Cambridge University Press, 1992), 7. Seyla Benhabib described the book as "the crowning achievement of Arendt's political, as opposed to more strictly philosophical, reflections"; see *The Reluctant Modernism of Hannah Arendt* (Lanham, MD: Rowman and Littlefield, 2000), xlii.

determines the temporality of Arendt's text itself, namely renders its own operation temporal, historical, by defining its temporal location, its 'now,' as situated in the immediate presence of this negative event: "The essential structure of all civilizations is at the breaking point" (vii). The book's original title, in the initial British edition, was *The Burden of Our Times*.[6] It is significant to note that, considering the book was published in 1951, the apocalypse Arendt perceived and described as *present* was not limited to World War II and the Shoah, but survived both and extended well into the Cold War period.

It is indeed one of Arendt's most important operations in this book to have *named* and so identified the essence of the twentieth century's negative political event. For the purpose of my investigation, it is highly significant that in the first pages of Arendt's preface to the book's first edition, she explicitly diagnoses the essence of this event in epistemological terms. The collapse of the political, of civilization, is a collapse of meaning, a negation of understanding, of "*comprehension.*" In this sense, the book's attempt to "comprehend" in fact emerges as a direct act of epistemic intervention in the political realm, a political act of epistemological resistance, whose aim is "to discover the hidden mechanics by which all traditional elements of our political and spiritual world were dissolved into a conglomeration where everything seems to have lost specific value, and has become unrecognizable for human comprehension, unusable for human purpose" (vii–viii).

It should be nonetheless noted from the outset that Arendt's epistemological intervention, "comprehension," does not simply seek to reassert knowledge against absence of knowledge, human mind against the eruption of inhuman, elemental forces of nature or the bare real. On the contrary, Arendt's "comprehension" is an intervention within the epistemic realm itself, an act of resistance that is primarily directed against a certain form of knowledge. Moreover, Arendt's epistemic resistance is to a certain extent formulated as resistance to the force of knowledge itself, namely as resisting or at least postponing intelligibility for the sake of facing raw, hard politico-historical reality: "examining and bearing consciously the burden which our century has placed on us—neither denying

---

6   Hannah Arendt, *The Burdon of Our Times* (London: Secker and Warburg, 1951).

its existence nor submitting meekly to its weight" (viii). Unlike Adorno and Horkheimer, for Arendt, resisting the twentieth century's collapse of the political by "comprehending" it therefore does not mean a Hegelian *Aufhebung* of the immediate, nonconceptual reality by raising it to the level of mediated concepts, but precisely the opposite: an anti-Hegelian resistance to the concept—and, at least for Hegel, to knowledge—itself, in other words "comprehension," that is virtually defined as the attempt of rendering visible the incomprehensible: "Comprehension, in short, means the unpremeditated, attentive facing up to, and resisting of, reality—whatever it may be" (viii). Arendt's anti-Hegelianism in *The Origin of Totalitarianism* remains nonetheless Hegelian in that it posits the incomprehensible, i.e., the negative epistemo-political event of the twentieth century, as *absolute*. Of course, antithetical to Hegel's triumphant absolute, absolute knowledge, Arendt's, much as Adorno's, is the absolute *negative*—"absolute evil" (viii).[7]

The famous name Arendt gives to this absolute evil at the end of all human civilization is, however, not at all a sign of incomprehensibility, of surplus reality beyond any concept, of the singular and proper beyond all generality, i.e., it is not a *proper* name, not "Auschwitz." Nor is this name even the concept of singularity or particularity, of any specific, historical evil, such as "anti-Semitism" or "National Socialism." On the contrary, the name Arendt gives to twentieth-century absolute evil is a concept of generality and universality, of complete and total comprehensibility:

---

7   For a discussion of the concept of "evil" in Arendt's thought, in particular its development from "absolute evil" or "radical evil" in *Origins* to "the banality of evil" in *Eichmann*, see Bernstein, *Arendt and the Jewish Question*, 137–153. Revisiting Arendt's own statement, in her letter to Scholem of 1964, whereby this conceptual change reflected a change of her mind concerning the nature of evil—"that evil is never 'radical', that it is only extreme, and that it possesses neither depth nor any demonic dimensions" (138)—Bernstein rather asserts the *continuity* between the two concepts. He indicates how both concepts "differ from the main traditional Western understandings of evil because [they have] nothing to do with humanly understandable 'evil motives'—indeed, [they have] nothing to do with *human* motives at all" (145). I agree with Bernstein insofar as *human* means *individual*, i.e., insofar as both "radical" and "banal" evil in Arendt in fact designate extreme *political* evil, in which evil becomes the norm, such that the individuals operating within the evil system may not be and most commonly are not motivated by any "evil motives," and far from "demonic," may even, as Eichmann, actually claim to act profoundly ethically.

Totalitarianism. Indeed, calling absolute evil "Totalitarianism," the doctrine of the total, is, at least on the level of the concept, which is here the heart of the matter, entering into fundamental polemics with an entire epistemology epitomized in Hegel's dictum: *Das Wahre ist das Ganze*, "The true is the total."[8]

At first sight, the "Totalitarianism" that Arendt identifies in twentieth-century politics as the end of civilization does not seem to be characterized epistemologically. On the contrary, Arendt describes Totalitarianism not in terms of knowledge, but in terms of force, conquest, domination, and rule. Totalitarianism is the "attempt at global conquest and total domination,"[9] at "total domination and global rule" (389). The evil totality Arendt sees in Totalitarianism is not total knowledge, but total power. Consequently, when, in the preface to the book, she briefly states her own vision of the new, better world order that is designed to counter the total destruction

---

8   Hegel, *Phänomenologie des Geistes*, 24. Arendt was of course not the first to use the concept of "Totalitarianism" as a central category of political theory, and more specifically in analyzing Nazism and Stalinism. On Arendt's book in the context of theories of totalitarianism of its time, see Alfons Söllner, "Hannah Arendt's *The Origins of Totalitarianism* in Its Original Context," in *Arendt: Critical Assessments*, 265–285. What interests me here is how Arendt deploys "Totalitarianism" not only as a political but also as an *epistemological* category, which, notwithstanding the novelty and unprecedentedness of totalitarian regimes, reveals their link to and to some extent coherence with the history of Western thought. I would therefore like to qualify Steven Aschheim's claim, whereby Arendt "dismissed any notion of the complicity not only of German— but also European—culture and tradition in what had transpired" ("Nazism, Culture and the Origins of Totalitarianism: Hannah Arendt and the Discourse of Evil," *New German Critique* 70 [1997]: 127), even though backed by Arendt's own statements of 1946 and 1951. I find more accurate Canovan's observation that "by understanding Nazism in terms not of its specifically German context but of modern developments that could be linked to Stalinism as well, Arendt was putting herself in the ranks of the many intellectuals of German culture who sought to connect Nazism with Western modernity" (*Reinterpretation*, 20). Canovan indicates how Arendt's project for a sequel book on "Totalitarian Elements in Marxism," which was never realized, was supposed to provide, in Arendt's own words, "the missing link between the unprecedentedness of our present situation and certain commonly accepted traditional categories of political thought" (quoted in Canovan, 64).

9   Arendt, *Origins*, viii.

meted out by Totalitarianism, this vision, this "new political principle," as a counter political knowledge to global Totalitarianism, is formulated in the most total, global, comprehensive terms: "a new political principle, a new law on earth, whose validity this time must comprehend the whole of humanity" (ix). In other words, with respect to its content and validity, to its *epistemic* value, Totalitarianism seems not have been total and universal enough. Accordingly, it is not on the conceptual, epistemic level that Arendt wishes to counter the global totality of politics. Rather, the limitation should only apply to power. The new, anti-totalitarian political principle, the "new law on earth," should be global, universal, and total, "while its power must remain strictly limited, rooted in and controlled by newly defined territorial entities" (ix).

This distinction between the content or epistemic value and validity of the political principle, on the one hand, and its power, on the other hand, a distinction that seems to significantly underlie Arendt's political thought, here and elsewhere, is profound and far from evident. It raises at least all the difficulties that, seven years later, in *The Human Condition* of 1958, Arendt herself will indicate and criticize in the Western tradition of distrusting power: "Perhaps nothing in our history has been so short-lived as trust in power, nothing more lasting than the Platonic and Christian distrust of the splendor attending its space of appearance, nothing—finally in the modern age—more common than the conviction that 'power corrupts.'"[10] In fact, it is a question to what extent the universal polis, which is based on a universal human principle, should *not* be global and total, and what precisely is the nature and meaning of limiting the total application and force of political universality through "territorial entities."

Nevertheless, one of the main theses of *The Origins of Totalitarianism* is that the essence and therefore the absolute evil of Totalitarianism lie precisely in its aspiration to surpass and ultimately abolish the power limitation of political universalism through "territorial entities," namely in Totalitarianism's opposition to *the nation-state*. Indeed, Arendt's famous—and controversial—claim was that, in contrast to common perception, the evil of twentieth-century politics, the absolute, "unforgivable" evil, as it transpired for instance in Nazi Germany, was not particularistic nation-

---

10   Hannah Arendt, *The Human Condition* (Chicago: University of Chicago Press, 1958), 204–205.

alism, was not the total state of fascism. The evil in National Socialism, according to Arendt, was not its national character, which distinguished it from the international character of communist socialism. Rather, the absolute evilness of Nazism, as totalitarian, lies in its super- or transnationalism, the global character that, on Arendt's account, it *shares* with Communism.

In terms of political epistemology, Arendt's analysis of totalitarian absolute evil can be initially read as suggesting that totalitarian dissolution of the state means dissolution of the epistemic order, destruction of the realm of knowledge. In Arendt's description, the modern (nation-) state stands for the stability and determinability of the objective, rational, intelligible order, for regularity and certainty, for positive laws. Against static statism, super-statist Totalitarianism is described by Arendt as "movement." Totalitarianism's total movement—such as Arendt identifies both in Nazism and in Communism—dissolves all positive laws, all established order. It is the movement at work in "the hidden mechanics by which all traditional elements of our political and spiritual world were dissolved into a conglomeration where everything seems to have lost specific value, and has become unrecognizable for human comprehension, unusable for human purpose" (vii–viii). It undoes all bonds of humanity, consequently turns human beings into atomized, uprooted, lonely individuals, existing in a global condition of statelessness, worldlessness, and lawlessness, "the condition of savages," subject to the sole rule of terror, denuded of all will and action.

On closer reading, however, the dissolution of the state by the totalitarian movement in Arendt's analysis, especially in the third part of *The Origins of Totalitarianism*, is not dissolution or destruction of the *episteme*. Totalitarianism entails epistemic destruction only to the extent that, on the contrary, it more fundamentally arises from total *empowerment* of the epistemic order. The totalitarian state of mind or *credo*, as Arendt succinctly formulates it, that "everything is possible" (427), does not mean an anarchic state of total chaos and absolute uncertainty. On the contrary, curiously in synch with a central theological motif, for Arendt, "everything is possible," i.e., *omnipotence* rather signifies total, cosmic, super-human order.[11] Thus, the abolition of the state's positive laws by the totalitarian

---

11   Nonetheless, in Arendt's essay on "The Concept of History: Ancient and Modern," in *Between Past and Future: Six Exercises in Political Thought* (New York:

movement is done in the name of higher laws, the "laws of movement," which are not divine but laws of history. In other words, if we follow Arendt's analysis, the dissolution of the nation-state's territorial limits by Totalitarianism is done in the name of *higher* knowledge, which consists in perceiving a higher, more comprehensive, and complete objective order. The condition of uprootedness and worldlessness generated by Totalitarianism is in fact not completely devoid of all action but rather is characterized by the paradigmatic activity of "logical deduction" (469) or "logical reasoning" (477).[12]

Viking Press, 1961), 41–90, the precept of "everything is possible" is interpreted epistemologically to imply, as founding principle of modern epistemology, the "production" of facts and truth: "The axiom from which the deduction is started does not need to be, as traditional metaphysics and logic supposed, a self-evident truth; it does not have to tally at all with the facts as given in the objective world at the moment the action starts; the process of action, if it is consistent, will proceed to create a world in which the assumption becomes axiomatic and self-evident" (88). It is here that one can observe the link between the old theological (Augustinian and nominalistic) notion of omnipotence as arbitrary free will, i.e., the "frightening arbitrariness" that would be "the exact counterpart of consistent logical processes," and the technological essence of natural science. The epistemological precept of the latter would be "I know only what I have myself made" (88).

12 Cf. the much more nuanced political epistemology presented by Arendt in *The Human Condition*, where "logical reasoning," due to its worldlessness, is placed at the bottom of the epistemic hierarchy, under philosophical thought and scientific cognition. Interestingly, it is nonetheless precisely due to human thinking's capacity of detaching itself from the world, i.e., due to its potential worldlessness, that Arendt considers it as the highest of all activities, namely as being most essentially action, pure and sheer action, which is not only an instrument for something else, for non-action, for a thing in the world: "Acting and speaking are still outward manifestations of human life, which knows only one activity that, though related to the exterior world in many ways, is not necessarily manifest in it and needs neither to be seen nor heard nor used nor consumed in order to be real: the activity of thought" (95). This ambivalence arises from the more basic ambiguity of *The Human Condition* concerning the position of thinking in the *polis*. The epistemo-political tension between *The Human Condition* and *The Origins of Totalitarianism* could be worked out conceptually around the tension between *action* and *movement*.

Indeed, Arendt's analysis offers key elements for what can be called a political epistemology of Totalitarianism, in which the absolute political evil of twentieth century's Totalitarianism and its savagery transpire as a fundamentally *epistemic* condition, much like Adorno and Horkheimer portray the twentieth century's barbarism as arising from enlightenment. Nonetheless, *The Dialectics of Enlightenment* and *The Origins of Totalitarianism* seem to suggest two, in a certain sense exactly opposite, epistemo-political accounts of evil. Adorno and Horkheimer identify the epistemo-political evil in the myth of positivism. Arendt on the other hand identifies the epistemic condition of Totalitarianism as "ideology," whose pathology she diagnoses as claiming knowledge beyond "verifiable experience," i.e., as noncompliance with a rather *positivist* criterion of truth. If Adorno and Horkheimer criticize the mythology of facts, it is in contrast precisely in the name of "reality and factuality" (458), of experience and sense perception, that Arendt condemns in Totalitarianism the aspiration to "total explanation" (470), the search for "supersense" (458) that would "make the world consistent" (458). As noted above, there is in Arendt's epistemology a deep suspicion and rejection of comprehensibility, a concept of science that *resists* understanding, a sort of anti-gnostic episteme, that counters an entire Western epistemo-political tradition that Arendt at one point designates as "prophetic," when she decries Totalitarianism's "prophetic scientificality" (458).[13]

---

13 Drawing on a short passage in Arendt's *Denktagebuch* of March 1953 (Hannah Arendt, *Denktagebuch. 1950 bis 1973*. Band 1, hg. v. Ursula Ludz und Ingeborg Nordmann [München/Zürich: Piper, 2002], 331–332), Michael Mack ("The Holocaust and Hannah Arendt's Philosophical Critique of Philosophy," see above) points out how Arendt's very concept of *Verstehen*, "comprehending" or "understanding," in fact stands in contrast to "meaning." Accordingly, Arendt's "comprehending" would mean "knowing," insofar as "the real demands of us the act of knowing, but knowledge of the real does not bestow meaning on the world: on the contrary, it brings to the fore its inconsistency and its meaninglessness, and this knowledge of inconsistency enables the work of critique and judgment" (42–43). Mack convincingly shows how this epistemic concept of understanding and knowledge is intimately connected to an ethical resistance to the Christian notion of "forgiving," opening instead the way to "reconciliation" (43).

Knowing Anti-Semitism

This hint of epistemological affinity between Totalitarianism and the "prophetic" tradition reinvokes the cardinal question of my present discussion, namely the role of anti-anti-Semitism in Arendt's account. The choice to identify twentieth-century political evil not only in National Socialism but more broadly in Totalitarianism so as to also include Stalinism, seems to diminish the role of anti-Semitism in the basic plot. Thus, when Arendt suggests that the "true central institution of totalitarian organizational power" (438) is the concentration and extermination camps, her observation must also include Soviet camps. However, including Stalinism in Totalitarianism does not necessarily mean limiting the role of anti-Semitism—it may just as well mean expanding it.

In fact, anti-Semitism is the first of two basic elements of Totalitarianism that Arendt analyzes in *The Origins of Totalitarianism*, the second being imperialism, in which, as I will show, anti-Semitism also plays for Arendt an important role. From the outset, Arendt's point of departure is—for the present discussion of anti-anti-Semitism—radically different than that of the authors analyzed in the previous section, about the anti-Semitic creation of the Jew, namely Adorno and Horkheimer as well as Sartre.[14] Arendt's observation of "the political significance of anti-Semitic

---

14 My analysis of Arendt thus emphasizes the opposite motif to the one highlighted by Julia Schulze Wessel and Lars Rensmann, "The Paralysis of Judgment: Arendt and Adorno on Antisemitism and the Modern Condition," in Rensmann and Gandesha, *Arendt and Adorno*, 197–225, i.e., Arendt's observation that in the final, totalitarian formation of anti-Semitism, "'The Jew' became exclusively an expression of the modern anti-Semite's fantasy world" (218), which converges with Adorno and Horkheimer's analysis. For a detailed interpretation of Arendt's understanding of anti-Semitism along these lines, see Julia Schulze Wessel, *Ideologie der Sachlichkeit. Hannah Arendts Politische Theorie des Antisemitismus* (Frankfurt am Main: Suhrkamp, 2006), which is also the most comprehensive work written thus far on Arendt's theory of anti-Semitism. Schulze Wessel reads in Arendt a history of "the successive disappearance of hostility towards Jews [*Judenfeindschaft*] in anti-Semitism" (14), which would thus be "detached from experience" (67), i.e., of Jews, such that Arendt completely agrees with Adorno and Horkheimer (140–141, 223).

Besides my diverging reading of Arendt, it seems to me that Schulze Wessel's reading itself is guided by an anti-anti-Semitic discourse. Thus, what she means

movement" (8) in the twentieth century's political evil does not lead her to recognize and highlight the special political agency of the anti-Semites. Rather, the political force of anti-Semitism is connected to the presence of another political actor, a collective subject, the object of anti-Semitic animus, "the Jewish people." The Jewish people is for Arendt, on the most basic level, a real historic entity, subject and actor, and not an anti-Semitic creation. The exact mode of being of this political entity, and its exact mode of action—or non-action—in the event of anti-Semitism, and so of Totalitarianism, nonetheless remain ambiguous in Arendt's account. For instance, in the "Preface to Part One: Anti-Semitism" of 1967 she notes: "Twentieth-century political developments have driven the Jewish people into the storm center of events" (xiv). The ambiguous nature of this "drive"—movement or action?—pertains to a central question that is con-

---

by "hostility towards Jews," which would be based on a real and concrete experience of Jews, she designates as "subjective ressentiment against Jews" (14) or, in the case of Eichmann, "feeling of hate" against Jews (15). In contrast, abstract ideological "anti-Semitism" would mean loss of "concrete content orientation" and increase in "elements, visions and desirable fantasies about population politics about a new model of social order, a society, in which man may intervene as he wishes" (14). In other words, real experience of Jews means a *personal* and emotional experience of Jewish individuals, "flesh and blood." Political, ideological, and *sachlich* discourse must necessarily abstract from any Jewish content, and anti-Semitism would lie precisely in *failing* to perform such abstraction.

It seems to me that the exact same anti-anti-Semitism also guides the exact opposite reading of Arendt's treatment of anti-Semitism by Peter Staudenmaier, "Hannah Arednt's Analysis of Antisemitism in *The Origins of Totalitarianism*: A Critical Appraisal," *Patterns of Prejudice* 46, no. 2 (2012): 154–179. Staudenmaier, in contrast to Schulze Wessel and similarly to my own reading, underlines Arendt's acknowledgment of Jewish agency in the history of anti-Semitism. Nonetheless, similarly to Emmanuel Faye, Staudenmaier appraisal of Arendt is highly critical, reproaching her of neglecting the "basic postulate," which he proclaims in anti-anti-Semitic terms of the Adorno and Horkheimer's school: "The purely contingent relationship between antisemitic perceptions and actual Jewish behavior, between antisemitic convictions and the real world of Jewish-Gentile interactions, is a fundamental characteristics of antisemitism *per se*.... Antisemitism is an ideology about Jews that is autonomous from and only tangentially related to the true conditions of Jewish existence" (173).

stitutive also of Arendt's later work and certainly underlies its analysis of anti-Semitism.

It is easy to show how Arendt, too, like the authors discussed above, understands anti-Semitism most fundamentally as an epistemic condition, as a configuration of knowledge. In fact, this epistemic conception is clearly visible in Arendt's analysis, in that in all of her discussions of anti-Semitism she approaches the phenomenon principally as a phenomenon of knowledge, namely the appearing, given knowledge *about* anti-Semitism, wherein anti-Semitism appears essentially as an object or element of knowledge. The primary object of Arendt's analysis of anti-Semitism is this given knowledge or theories of anti-Semitism, namely the ways in which anti-Semitism has become a known entity, has been perceived, conceived of, understood, and accounted for, or, as Arendt herself designates it, the offered *"explanations"* of anti-Semitism, which is the exact same object of my own analysis here.

It is crucial to note that the basic epistemic category by which Arendt thinks this knowledge about anti-Semitism, a category that perhaps commands Arendt's epistemology in general, is *"history."* The primary object of Arendt's thinking of anti-Semitism is accordingly the historiography of anti-Semitism. Arendt's *assertion* of anti-Semitism as an element of historical—and not, for instance, socio-psychological[15]—knowledge is significant. She is fully aware of the epistemological problem that anti-Semitism, precisely *as episteme, as a configuration of knowledge,* poses to historiography, namely the problem of acknowledging the historical existence and value of the object of anti-Semitism: the Jews. In fact, Arendt recognizes that the basic problem posed by anti-Semitism to knowledge and to thinkers or historians is not the antagonism against Jews, but more basically the very perception of Jews as a historical entity. The "Outrage to Common Sense" that twentieth century's anti-Semitism presents, as the title to Chapter 1 on anti-Semitism of 1951 states, lies in "the fact that of all the great unsolved political questions of our century, it should have been this seemingly small and unimportant Jewish problem that had the dubious honor of setting the whole infernal machine in motion. Such discrepan-

---

15   For an assessment of Arendt's critical attitude towards the social sciences, see Peter Baehr, "Identifying the Unprecedented: Hannah Arendt, Totalitarianism and the Critique of Sociology," in *Arendt: Critical Assessments*, 224–264.

cies between cause and effect outrage our common sense, to say nothing of the historian's sense of balance and harmony" (3). In other words, the acknowledgment of anti-Semitism as a central moment and force, a central *agent* of history, calls for acknowledging a significant historical role of the Jews (the "Jewish problem"), a proposition which is, however, as Arendt observes, "outrageous" for common sense, for a certain common perception of Jews and understanding of history.

The initial object of Arendt's critique of the common knowledge of anti-Semitism is accordingly common "explanations" of anti-Semitism, which, like the theories discussed above, attempt to completely eliminate the epistemic value of anti-Semitism itself, by denying any existence to its object, namely the Jews. Such explanations are the "attempts to escape the seriousness of anti-Semitism and the significance of the fact that the Jews were driven into the storm center of events" (7). Under this title Arendt first rejects theories that reduce anti-Semitism to the more general phenomenon of nationalist xenophobia, which would have nothing specific to do with Jews. Against this theory, Arendt famously claims—and demonstrates in detail in her book—that anti-Semitism has been rather linked not to the rise, but rather to the decline of nationalism, and to the emergence of supernational imperialism (see below). The second kind of theories that Arendt rejects as escape from reality are the "scapegoat" explanation of anti-Semitism, according to which the Jews were the *arbitrarily* chosen victim of anti-Semitism. Her rejection of arbitrariness manifests a noteworthy acknowledgment of the epistemic value of "ideology," i.e., totalitarian episteme, which is connected to its political performance: "an ideology which has to persuade and mobilize people cannot choose its victims arbitrarily" (7). Persuasion requires evidence. And so, inversely, the fact of anti-Semitism's persuasiveness indicates that it is based on some evidence, and thus on some reality, on some truth.[16]

---

16 Interestingly, the specific evidence and truth, the specific knowledge reflected in anti-Semitism, is revealed to Arendt precisely in contrast to the specific non-truth, the evident lie of anti-Semitism: "If a patent forgery like the 'Protocols of the Elders of Zion' is believed by so many people that it can become the text of a whole political movement, the task of the historian is no longer to discover a forgery. Certainly it is not to invent explanations which dismiss the chief political and historical fact of the matter: that the forgery is being believed" (7). In other words, it is precisely the obvious fictitiousness of the canonic anti-Semitic

By far the most important "explanation" of anti-Semitism that stands at the center of Arendt's critique, however, is of another, almost opposite kind. In 1951 Arendt calls this explanation "eternal anti-Semitism." With this concept, Arendt does not refer to claims whereby anti-Semitism is an independent, mental disposition, which has nothing to do with Jews. On the contrary, by "eternal anti-Semitism" she means the conception that "Jew-hatred is a normal and natural reaction to which history gives only more or less opportunity" (7). In other words, the supposed "eternity" of anti-Semitism, according to this kind of explanations, would lie in its being a *natural reaction* to Jews, who are thus posited as a primary, equally natural, nonhistorical, or rather meta-historical entity. The problem with the notion of "eternal anti-Semitism" is that it entails the notion of the eternal Jew. In fact, both in Arendt's earlier essay on "Anti-Semitism" of 1938/39,[17] and in her 1967 preface to *The Origins of Totalitarianism*, she criticizes jointly the notion of "timelessness of anti-Semitism" and the inseparable notion of "timelessness of the Jewish mission in the world" (48) or of a "secret Jewish society that has ruled, or aspired to rule, the world since antiquity" (1967, xi).

What is the meaning of this notion of "timeless" Jewishness for Arendt, and what is the problem that she identifies in it? "Timelessness" and "eternity" refer to a non- or meta-temporal and so non- or meta-historical dimension, something like a Platonic realm of ideas, of intellectual being, which would be separated from the realm of sensual being, of temporality and change. "Timelessness" would be the realm of philosophy. Arendt does not dismiss here timelessness as such, only timeless *Jewish* being. More precisely, what she rejects is the conception that "Jewish," which is a historical phenomenon, a historical collective being, stands for any specific idea or epistemic value. Surely, for Judeo-Christian theology, that Jews are linked to divine transcendence is banal. Such a conception indeed implies something like a specific meta-historical Jewish agency, a "mission in the

---

text, its patently fictional nature, namely its evident non-correspondence with the historical facts, evident non-truth, that forces the realization of its validity in another, superior, "chief" realm of factuality and truth, an epistemic realm of political and historical effectiveness. Cf. my discussion of the epistemology of the *Protocols* in Chapter 7.

17 Hannah Arendt, "Anti-Semitism," *The Jewish Writings*, ed. Jerome Kohn and Ron Feldman (New York: Schocken Books, 2007), 46–124.

world." For Arendt (and perhaps for all Platonism), this notion immediately evokes the image of *conspiracy* ("secret Jewish society" aspiring to rule the world), in complete synch with anti-Semitic imagination, as will be shown in Part II. As for Plato, for Arendt too, at first sight at least, asserting ideas in the realm of temporal existence amounts to "myth," of which the "eternal Jew" would be a paradigm, most exemplary articulated in the "Protocols of the Elders of Zion." I already indicated this motif in the current Heidegger debate (Chapter 1) and in Adorno and Horkheimer's discourse (Chapter 2), and will examine it later in anti-Semitic discourse itself (Chapter 7).

It is instructive to note how Arendt's critique of the "timeless Jewish mission" in fact leads her to explicitly formulate her historical project in Platonic terms. Whereas Plato defended philosophical knowledge, the knowledge of timeless ideas, against the ancient sophists, Arendt saw herself as defending the knowledge of temporal facts, historical knowledge, against modern sophists:

> The most striking difference between ancient and modern sophists is that the ancients were satisfied with a passing victory of the argument at the expense of truth, whereas the moderns want a more lasting victory at the expense of reality. In other words, one destroyed the dignity of human thought whereas the other destroy the dignity of human action. The old manipulators of logic were the concern of the philosopher, whereas the modern manipulators of facts stand in the way of the historian. For history itself is destroyed, and its comprehensibility —based upon the fact that it is enacted by men and therefore can be understood by men—is in danger, whenever facts are no longer held to be part and parcel of the past and present world, and are misused to prove this or that opinion.[18]

There are many questions that can be raised here about this conception, which attempts to reconcile philosophy and history, by appointing both the philosopher and the historian to be the defenders of their dividing border, each from his own side, the eternal and the temporal. First and foremost, we should ask whether this conception itself is philosophical or historical, eternal or temporal, and acknowledge the obvious historicity of Arendt's distinction between ancient and modern sophism, a historical-

---

18   Arendt, *Origins*, 9.

philosophical, *geistesgeschichtliche* observation or knowledge, i.e., precisely *history*, that seems already to transcend the Platonic distinction between non-temporal and temporal, to already be receptive to something like the "eternal Jew."[19]

Timeless Jew

Nevertheless, Arendt's historico-philosophical epistemology, and thus her understanding of the figure of the "timeless Jew," had its own history in the development of her work on anti-Semitism. In the 1938/39 essay, the basic problem that she sees in this notion is in fact the very attribution of any epistemic agency to the historical Jewish collective, which would thus account for anti-Semitism as the negative reaction to Judaism. Very similarly to the anti-anti-Semitic conception analyzed above, whereby Judaism is the creation of anti-Semitism, young Arendt too identifies the notion of original Jewish episteme, which would be the "source" of anti-Semitic reaction, as the very core of anti-Semitism: "That the Jews are the source of anti-Semitism is the malicious and stupid insight of anti-Semites."[20] Accordingly, anti-Semitism would consist precisely in producing the "abstraction" of "the Jew" as "evil principle of history," namely in inscribing Jewish being in the realm of ideas, definitions and principles, in the realm of philosophical knowledge (64–65). This abstraction would have "no connection whatever with any germinal knowledge about Jews" (69), whose actual being is limited to the realm of factual, temporal, sensual, non-eternal reality, the realm of "life," who are namely in fact "living human beings" (64), who exist in the paradigm of the "living individual" (65).[21]

---

19 Cf. Arendt's discussion in "The Concept of History," where she indicates a "gap of time between past and future" as a "non-time-space in the very heart of time," which "is not a modern phenomenon, it is perhaps not even a historical datum but is coeval with the existence of man on earth" (13).
20 Arendt, "Anti-Semitism," 47–48.
21 Cf. Arendt's description of her own self-understanding as Jewish, in response to Scholem's critique of *Eichmann in Jerusalem* of 1963: "Being Jewish [*Judensein*] for me belongs to the undeniable givens of my life and I never wished to change anything in such facticities. Such a mentality of basic gratefulness for what is, as it is, given and not produced, *physei* and not *nomoi*, is pre-political, but does have, in extraordinary circumstances, like those of Jewish politics, also so to

The "reality of Jews," which could thus be the only legitimate object of "concrete knowledge of Jews," i.e., of Jewish history, on the one hand, and on the other hand the only legitimate object, basis, or "source" of anti-Judaism, of "hatred of Jews," is economic, namely "the role Jews played in commerce and banking" (68–69).

It is noteworthy that anti-Semitism, this epistemic *locus* of abstraction, i.e., of creating the epistemic entity of Jewishness from the concrete living individual, anti-Semitic knowledge itself *is* located by young Arendt historically. The historical address of anti-Semitic episteme is for Arendt *Germany*, which would be "the classic land of anti-Semitism," "a model to the whole world" (64–65). The German thus arises in history as point of detachment from history, a suitable location for the "absolute evil" of twentieth-century totalitarianism, conceptually akin to the Jewish as "evil principle of history."[22]

Further noteworthy is that this conceptual kinship doesn't remain purely potential or implied, but as a matter of fact makes up the very center of Arendt's earlier text. Indeed, the main target of Arendt's critique in her early essay "Anti-Semitism" is not anti-Semitism but, as already indicated, the explanation of anti-Semitism as "eternal" reaction to the "timeless" Jew, a notion she indeed denounces as anti-Semitic, but identifies historically—in 1938/39—rather in *Jewish* knowledge or "historiography." Thus, like

---

speak negative political consequences: it renders certain behaviors impossible, and it seems to precisely those that you read into my analyses." Hannah Arendt/ Gershom Scholem *Der Briefwechsel*, hg. v. Marie Luise Knott (Frankfurt am Main: Juedischer Verlag, 2010). See also her response to Scholem's complaint about her lack of *Ahabat Israel*, i.e., love to the Jewish people: "I have never in my life 'loved' any people or collective, neither the German nor the French nor the America, nor something like the working class or anything similar. Indeed, I only love my friends and am incapable of any other love" (439). See further Arendt's response to Golda Meir's statement, "I believe in the Jewish people": "The greatness of this people once was to believe in God.... And now this people no longer believes but in itself? What will become of that?—So, in this sense I do not 'love' Jews and do not 'believe' in them, but only belong by nature and factually to this people" (440).

22 Emmanuel Faye noted how from this early German locus of anti-Semitism, in *The Origins* Arendt relocates her analysis of historical anti-Semitism to France, omitting authors such as Marr and von Treitschke in favor of Gobineau and the Dreyfus affair—see Faye, *Arendt et Heidegger*, 72–73.

an equivalent of the conspiracy myth from the *Protocols*, Arendt indicates the attempts of nationalist Jewish historiography "to dress a persecuted, pogromized people and turn it into a fairy tale of princes and princesses" (48). The myth, the "fairy tale" of the Jewish principle in history is not necessarily anti-Jewish, but also—not yet primarily—Jewish.

For Arendt, and this is a crucial point, what epitomizes the *self-knowledge* of the eternal Jew is the Jewish *national* movement, Zionism, which as a matter of fact has laid exclusive claim to represent historical "Jewish agency." She thus criticizes Zionist thinkers, like Herzl and Buber, for perceiving Jewish being as "Jewish substance" (54), an "inalterable," "unified, eternal substance" (56), a conception that would be (in accordance with Arendt's Platonism as suggested above) simultaneously "pseudophilosophical" (54) as well as "unhistorical" (55). Her critique of Zionist notion of "autonomous Jewish politics" and "auto-emancipation" as illusory thus seems to arise not only from her historical observation of Zionist role in serving British imperialism (57–58), but from her rejection in principle of a specific Jewish epistemic agency. The same applies to Arendt's critique of the racist tendencies of the Zionist conception of the Jew, which manifests a dangerous resemblance to anti-Semitic conception of the Jew, a resemblance that will lead Arendt to note in her preface from 1967 that the direct consequence of anti-Semitism is not Nazism, but a "counterideology," Zionism.[23]

If Arendt's prewar critique against the notion of "timeless" Jewishness in fact tends to contest historical Jewish agency and epistemic being and to reduce it to an anti-Semitic operation of abstraction, to anti-Semitic creation, her postwar argumentation takes the—almost—opposite direction. In her 1967 preface to the *Origins of Totalitarianism* she explicitly dismisses the suggestion "that Jewish self-consciousness was ever a mere creation of anti-Semitism," "a myth that has become somewhat fashionable in intellectual circles after Sartre's 'existential' interpretation of *the Jew* as someone who is regarded and defined as a Jew by others" (xv). Already in 1951, the basic problem that *The Origins of Totalitarianism* identifies in the notion of "eternal anti-Semitism," which, as demonstrated above, is intertwined with the notion of timeless—and epistemic—Jewishness, is not the mythical exaggeration of Jewish agency, but on the contrary its elimination.

---

23 Arendt, *Origins*, xv.

Or more precisely, acknowledging "timelessness" in Jewish being is now understood as problematic because it eliminates "responsibility" both on the side of the anti-Semites—and on the side of Jews. This is so, because, as Arendt understands it, again Platonically, attributing "timelessness" to Jewish being, like *any* being, necessarily means removing it from the realm of history and thus—this is the crux of the matter for Arendt—of human action and politics.

The liquidation of human activity and thus the destruction of the political, by means of intellectual abstractions from factual reality ("ideology"), is precisely how in 1951 Arendt understands Totalitarianism, as explained above. Accordingly, one of the first figures of Totalitarianism to appear in her book is the abstraction, the principle, or the—"timeless"—concept of "the Jew." Here again, as already in the earlier essay, the historiographical agency for this specific figure of Totalitarianism (and it is simultaneously the precise point and the great paradox of *The Origins of Totalitarianism* that Totalitarianism itself *has* a specific historical agency, i.e., appears in history as or through one or more specific historical collectives) is remarkably a joint agency of anti-Semites and Jews. Furthermore, the later text, in particular the 1967 preface, underlines in a more accentuated manner those Jewish historiographies of the type Saul Baron designated as the "lachrymose," which "embellish and manipulate facts and historical records" (xii–xiii), i.e., engage in modern sophism, to reproduce yet another "myth," namely the perverted history, the pseudo-history, the simulacra of historical knowledge of the Jews, which is perhaps the paradigmatic myth *tout court*, namely the "myth of chosenness."

Anti-Totalitarian History of Totalitarianism

It is against this pseudo-historiography, at once anti-Semitic and Jewish, this *totalitarian* mythology, of timeless anti-Semitism and timeless Jewishness, that Arendt deploys her anti-totalitarian historiography. Her primary task is a historical account of anti-Semitism, as an element of Totalitarianism, namely a non-totalitarian history of Totalitarianism, which essentially entails an "impartial, truthful treatment of Jewish history" (xiv).

Upon a closer look, the task of history of Totalitarianism, as Arendt understands it, presents a paradox. The basic epistemological problem with Totalitarianism, I recall, is the disassociation of totalitarian knowledge, of ideology, from "factual reality," namely from history. Totalitarian episteme is not just ahistorical, it is the (false) perception and presentation of the historical, the temporal, as non-historical, timeless. At its extreme, Totalitarianism operates even on its own already dehistoricized knowledge and ideology, and abstracts it from the remaining link, source, or "basis" it has in history, an operation that can be understood as the dehistorization of dehistorization, a forgetfulness of forgetfulness:

> Totalitarian politics—far from being simply anti-Semitic or racist or imperialist or communist—use and abuse their own ideological and political elements until the basis of factual reality, from which the ideologies originally derived their strength and their propaganda value—the reality of class struggle, for instance, or the interest conflicts between Jews and their neighbors—have all but disappeared. (xv)

The very notion of such a complete and absolute detachment from factual reality, from history, in itself presents conceptual questions, which remind of the paradoxes of freedom in history or in nature, and in this sense ironically seems to position Totalitarianism itself as the very paradigm of human action, which is not conditioned by history, namely free. Be that as it may, there is certainly some paradox in wishing to account historically for the historically detached, that is without acknowledging the *limitation* of history. This is no doubt the basic problem of Arendt's book, namely the attempt to counter Totalitarianism through historiography.

This difficulty is so fundamental for Arendt's entire project and for the question of political epistemology that it merits a closer examination. What is exactly the problem of writing the history of Totalitarianism? Arendt herself explicitly identified and formulated this problem in her famous reply to Eric Voegelin's critical review of *The Origins of Totalitarianism* in 1953.[24] Arendt's reply in fact suggests two formulations of the problem. The first one, which has become the better known, to the virtual obliteration of the second, was that "all historiography is necessarily salvation and frequently justification; it is due to man's fear that he may forget and to his striving for something which is even more than remembrance.... Thus my first problem was how to write historically about something—totalitarianism—which I did not want to conserve but on the contrary felt engaged to destroy" (77). Historiography conserves the past from oblivion,

---

24 Hannah Arendt, "A Reply," *Review of Politics* 15, no. 1 (1953): 68–85.

saves and redeems it, which makes it contradictory to write the history of something, of anything you want to destroy, for example Totalitarianism. There would be a general problem in historiography *of evil*.

This, however, raises a more fundamental question concerning historiography *tout court*. How can historiography, the writing of history, of factual reality, be affected by the evilness or goodness of its object? Does writing history depend on a preliminary *moral* decision as to the value of its object and as to the *purpose* historiography should serve? If there is a problem with history for the sake of destruction, is there not a similar, even a greater problem with history for the sake of edification? Where is "factual reality"? In fact, upon closer look, Arendt's above formulation reveals a difficulty with historiography itself: it strives to history "beyond remembrance," namely beyond simple record or documentation of the past, beyond factual reality—beyond history. Historiography itself engages in the operation of rendering the historical trans- or meta-historical: timeless. Whether destructive or edifying, historiography itself is problematic. It is noteworthy that the example Arendt gives in her reply to Voegelin is the problematic intimacy between the historiography of anti-Semitism, with destructive intentions, and the edifying, "apologetic" historiography of the Jews (77).

This problem is more explicitly stated in a second, more profound formulation of the difficulty of writing the history of Totalitarianism in Arendt's reply to Voegelin. In fact, this *is* her direct reply to Voegelin. Voegelin's critique merits here attention, as it addresses the basic question that animates my present reading of Arendt, namely, as Voegelin termed the basic issue in dispute between himself and Arendt, the question of "essence in history."[25] Voegelin's basic critique of Arendt's historiography of Totalitarianism was indeed its historicity, i.e., its proclaimed focus on the "factual level of history" (85). For him, "the stream of history" is unable to provide to knowledge, to science "theoretically justifiable units" (85), i.e., "essence." This is not just a theoretical, epistemological problem, but a *political* one. In Arendt's "factual history" Voegelin identifies a broader modern rejection of transcendence ('timelessness'), what he calls pure "immanentism," which is both fatalistic and "nihilist." Next to Arendt's "liberal"

---

25   Eric Voegelin, "Concluding Remark," *Review of Politics* 15, no. 1 (1953): 84–85.

historicism, the second significant figure of immanentism that Voegelin identifies in modernity is none other than Totalitarianism itself. As antidote to both, Voegelin points at science that would account for historical phenomena not exclusively from within history, but from the ahistorical perspective of "philosophical anthropology" that would provide knowledge of a trans-historical "human nature."[26]

It is in Arendt's direct reply to Voegelin's assertion of intimacy between historicity and Totalitarianism that she expresses her own recognition of this very same intimacy, from which would arise the fundamental epistemo-political paradox of any anti-totalitarian historiography of Totalitarianism. If Voegelin deems Arendt a representative of liberal historiography, Arendt in return sees in his critique the reflection of "the present state of the historical and political sciences."[27] In contrast to Voegelin, the problem Arendt identifies in contemporary historiography is not the loss of essence and philosophy in the "stream of history," but on the exact contrary, the loss of "phenomenal difference" resulting from historiography that is guided by the "essential sameness of a doctrinal nature" (80). It is through *historiography* that facts lose their "particular historical background. The result is a generalization in which the words themselves lose all meaning . . . a kind of confusion—where everything distinct disappears and everything that is new and shocking is (not explained but) explained away either through drawing some analogies or reducing it to a previously known chain of causes and influences" (83).

In other words, in contrast to Voegelin, who criticizes historiography as totalitarian for not being philosophical enough, Arendt considers contemporary historiography to be too philosophical—and precisely in this to *accommodate* Totalitarianism. Michael Mack has indicated the conceptual intimacy between Arendt's critique of the totalitarian nature of philosophy (in her *Denktagebuch* of 1953 she writes: "Totalitarianism signifies the victory of 'philosophy' over politics—and not the other way round")[28] and of what Mack designates as "constructing consistent narratives,"[29] namely

---

26   Eric Voegelin, "The Origins of Totalitarianism," *Review of Politics* 15, no. 1 (1953): 68–76.
27   Arendt, "A Reply," 82.
28   Arendt, *Denktagebuch*, 43.
29   Mack, "The Holocaust and Hannah Arendt's Philosophical Critique of Philosophy," 43.

writing the past "beyond remembrance," what Arendt identifies in *historiography*. Writing history would construct meaning and consistency that transcend history as temporal and factual, as real, and in this sense historiography is deeply related to the mythology of totalitarian ideology. It is here that emerges in Arendt's text the profound problematization of the very notion of "history," which distances her from any positivist view of "factual reality" and brings her closer to Adorno and Horkheimer's suspicion toward positivism as enlightened myth.

This, however, requires rethinking Arendt's aforesaid conception of the epistemological problem of Totalitarianism as breaking with history and "factual reality." It now seems that it is precisely *anti-totalitarian* historiography that demands to break with history, i.e., as the alleged consistent and evident "factual reality." Seyla Benhabib quoted in this respect Arendt's late formulation of her project, in the posthumously published *The Life of the Mind* of 1978, as seeking "to dismantle metaphysics, and philosophy with all its categories, as we have known them from their beginning in Greece until today."[30] There is indeed a strange resemblance between this project and Arendt's description of Totalitarianism's impact on our times in *The Origins* as the operation "by which all traditional elements of our political and spiritual world were dissolved into a conglomeration where everything seems to have lost specific value, and has become unrecognizable for human comprehension, unusable for human purpose."[31] This totalitarian "dissolution" of tradition seems to be precisely what Arendt in *The Life of the Mind* named as the *historical pre-condition* for her own project of "dismantling": "Such dismantling is possible only on the assumption that the thread of tradition is broken and that we shall not be able to renew it.... What has been lost is the continuity of the past as it seemed to be handed down from generation to generation, developing in the process of its own consistency."[32]

Arendt's anti-totalitarian history of Totalitarianism is in this sense *anti-historical writing*: it seeks to break with the consistent narrative of the past. This break with history strangely builds on the break with history carried out by Totalitarianism itself, which left us with what Arendt in

---

30   Hannah Arendt, *The Life of the Mind*, vol. 1, *Thinking* (New York: Harcourt Brace Jovanovich, 1978), 212. Quoted in Benhabib, *Reluctant Modernism*, 93.
31   Arendt, *Origins*, vii–viii.
32   Arendt, *The Life of the Mind*, 212.

The Life of the Mind calls "a fragmented past." It is as referring to this fragmented past that Arendt's anti-totalitarian historiography was described by Benhabib as "fragmented historiography."[33] The exact nature and purpose of this historiography remained obscure. Arendt herself, in her reply to Voegelin, explained that her historical account in *The Origins* focused on "facts and events instead of intellectual affinities and influences," and was looking for the essence of Totalitarianism not so much in its ideology, but rather in its "event."[34] In anticipation of the following discussion of Alain Badiou, one may perhaps identify in Arendt a shift from the paradigm of "history" to the paradigm of the "event." It is hard for me to agree with Michael Mack in that the ultimate goal of the epistemology Arendt had in mind is "knowledge of the contradictory plurality that is humanity,"[35] which, if developed no further, calls to mind the nihilistic tendencies of which both Voegelin and Arendt warned in contemporary science. I tend to agree more with Benhabib, who in Arendt's "fragmented historiography" as "storytelling" discerns not absolute break with all narrative, but a promise for "alternative archaeology of modernity."[36] It is such a promise, a promise of an end, of hope, without call to action, or rather with a call only to the extreme action that is patience, that I hear in the passage quoted by Mack: "The best that can be achieved is to know precisely what it was, and to endure this knowledge, and then to wait and see what comes to knowing and enduring."[37]

Jewish Origins of Anti-Semitic Elements

Be that as it may, to return to *The Origins*, the response that Arendt provides to the challenge of anti-historical history of Totalitarianism, a response that less solves its inherent difficulty than—to use what Richard Bernstein called one of Arendt's "favorite metaphors"[38]—"crystallizes" it, is the concept of *"origin."* The "origins" of Totalitarianism are those bases that

---

33 Benhabib, *Reluctant Modernism*, 94.
34 Arendt, "A Reply," 80.
35 Mack, "The Holocaust and Hannah Arendt's Philosophical Critique of Philosophy," 45.
36 Benhabib, *Reluctant Modernism*, 94.
37 Hannh Arendt, *Men in Dark Times* (New York: Harcourt, Brace, 1968), 20.
38 Bernstein, *Arendt and the Jewish Question*, 9.

Totalitarianism has in factual historical reality, from which however it detached itself, in order to become what it is, such that these historical facts are no longer present in it *as historical*, i.e., as sources and origins, but as building blocks, as *elements*. Totalitarianism does not *follow* from its origins, but is the "crystallization" of these origins as elements. "Origin" would thus be the concept of an origin that is not really one, what Arendt will call in hindsight, in her response to Voegelin, an "unfortunate" concept:

> I did not write a history of totalitarianism but an analysis in terms of history; I did not write a history of anti-Semitism or of imperialism, but analyzed the element of Jew-hatred and the element of expansion insofar as these elements were still clearly visible and played a decisive role in the totalitarian phenomenon itself. The book, therefore, does not really deal with the "origins" of totalitarianism—as its title unfortunately claims—but gives a historical account of the elements which crystallized into totalitarianism, this account is followed by an analysis of the elemental structure of totalitarian movements and domination itself. The elementary structure of totalitarianism is the hidden structure of the book while its more apparent unity is provided by certain fundamental concepts which run like red threads through the whole.[39]

This "unfortunate" nature of the category "origin" is nonetheless not at all contingent, it cannot simply be replaced by "element," since the force of Totalitarianism lies precisely in the conversion of origins to elements, of historical to timeless. The misfortune of "origin" is necessary, as demonstrated by the choice to keep it also in the title of the book's German version of 1955, "translated and revised by the author," this time next to its counter-concept: *Elemente und Ursprünge totaler Herrschaft*, "Elements and Origins of Total Domination."[40]

Accordingly, "anti-Semitism" in Arendt's account is an origin of Totalitarianism by being simultaneously a historical basis for Totalitarianism, a source and origin, and by being a non-historical, timeless component, an element of Totalitarianism. There would be two phenomena or realities of anti-Semitism, temporal and abstract: pre-totalitarian and

---

39   Hannah Arendt, "A Reply," *Review of Politics* 15, no. 6 (January 1953): 78.
40   Hannah Arendt, *Elemente und Ursprünge totaler Herrschaft. Antisemitismus, Imperialismus, totale Herrschaft* (München/ Zürich: Piper, 2008 [1986]).

totalitarian anti-Semitism, i.e., Jewish-hatred or historical anti-Semitism and anti-Semitism proper, modern or abstract anti-Semitism.[41] The history of anti-Semitism would be only the "prehistory of Totalitarianism." There would be a gap of timelessness separating between historical anti-Semitism, the hatred of Jews, and the abstract anti-Semitism of Nazism; and, correspondingly, between the real, factual, historical Jew, and the abstract, timeless Jew.

The great bulk of Arendt's writing on anti-Semitism is dedicated to portraying historical anti-Semitism, or more precisely the way in which the historical, pre-totalitarian hatred of Jews was in fact still historical, namely grounded in factual reality of history, in which domain Arendt situates human existence and action. In other words, Arendt's counter-totalitarian historiography focuses on how Jew-hatred was not just abstract or paranoid but connected to what Jews in fact were and did, or, as Arendt formulates it, is "still grounded in factual realities characteristic of Jewish-Gentile relations" (xvi). The real factual relations between Jews and Gentiles, i.e., non-Jews, are, at least for Arendt's historical approach that rejects the notion of "timeless" Jewishness, precisely what defines the Jewish, as a concrete human agency in history. Arendt's history of anti-Semitism thus amounts to a Jewish history, which, like all Jewish histories, amounts to a specific form of defining the Jewish.

Arendt's detailed analyses deserve a much closer reading than what can be offered here. All I will do is point at what seems to me as a fundamental difficulty in Arendt's attempt, which is common to an entire genre of Jewish historiographies. There is a certain conceptual necessity, by which the historization of the Jew, with the declared aim of de-mythologizing religious or other myths of eternal or timeless or essentialist Judaism, so radically precludes any ideal or epistemic content to the category "Jewish," that the only way of meaningfully holding to this designation as naming

---

41   Arendt, *Origins*, xv. Cf. Franz Neumann, *Behemoth: The Structure and Practice of National Socialism 1933–1944* (Chicago: Ivan R. Dee, 2009 [1942]), 121–122: "Anti-Semitism can be totalitarian or non-totalitarian. For the totalitarian Anti-Semite, the Jew has long ceased to be a human being. He has become the incarnation of evil in Germany, nay, in the entire world. In other words, totalitarian Anti-Semitism is magic and beyond discussion. Non-totalitarian Anti-Semitism preserves remnants of rationality and can, therefore, by analyzed. It exists in four forms: religious, economic, political and social."

a distinct reality is to *posit* the Jew as an all-the-more nonhistorical, nontemporal entity, which simply finds itself in history. It is thus that Arendt's historiography from the outset presupposes the factual differential existence of Jews and non-Jews, a factually given, real difference, which thus generates factual "differences of interests."[42] The effective, actual historical space in which her Jewish history takes place is thus the common space of Jews and non-Jews, in which the distinction Jewish/non-Jewish has neither reason nor justification, is nothing but *given*, and so basically generates an antithetical reaction, hatred, or, what is the other side of the same coin, calls for abolishment. This is the historical space of "emancipation" and "assimilation."[43]

Arendt's historiographical account of anti-Semitism thus sees the factual-historical basis of anti-Semitism, namely factual Jewish being and historical agency, in "the part Jews played in the development of the nation-state on one side and in their role in non-Jewish society on the other."[44] It is significant for my political epistemology that Arendt indeed conceives of Jewish being primarily in political terms. More specifically, her entire theory is based on the key-role of Jews for the formation of the central political form of modernity, the nation-state. It is precisely by the hostility of the imperialist totalitarian movements toward the nation-state that she explains totalitarianism's elemental anti-Semitism. The crucial point, however, is that in Arendt's narrative Jews play the essentially negative political role of outsiders, who are entirely defined by their *unjustified*—i.e., nonpolitical—exclusion from the sociopolitical order. It is this epistemo-political negativity that stands at the basis of Arendt's famous analysis of the Jews as "pariahs," whose isolation qualified them to function as abstract social elements—bankers and intellectuals—that were required for the emergence of the nation-state.[45]

---

42 Arendt, "Anti-Semitism," 51.
43 Cf. my own analysis of anti-Semitism in Part II of this book, which shares this observation with Arendt.
44 Arendt, *Origins*, xvi.
45 I thus identify a strong link between the political and the social analysis of anti-Semitism provided by Arendt, which Claude Lefort considered as too separated from one another—see "Hannah Arendt—Anti-Semitism in the Nazi System," trans. Anne O'Byrne, in *Arendt. Critical Assessments*, 174–194, 192. I do nonetheless find striking Lefort's observation that Arendt's account of the emer-

And so, already inherent to the conceptual infrastructure of Arendt's historiography, albeit dormant or implicit, is the abstract notion of the Jew, the notion of the Jewish as not completely contingent on history, but as a category that somehow belongs to the epistemic realm of ideas, a notion whose creation she nonetheless initially attributes to anti-Semitism, namely in its abstract, ideological, and later totalitarian form. According to a persistent motif in her narrative, it would be "the emergence of the first anti-Semitic parties in the 1870's and 1880's [that] marks the moment when the limited, factual basis of interest conflict and demonstrable experience was transcended and that road opened which ended in the 'final solution'" (xvi). Only proto-totalitarian anti-Semitism, that is, would transcend the factual basis of earlier Jew-hatred to create a trans-historical concept of Jewish being, as a necessary prerequisite for the break of absolute evil. However, I already pointed at the conceptual difficulties of maintaining this kind of anti-Semitic power of abstraction that has no basis whatsoever in its object, namely the Jews, and it is precisely this kind of anti-Semitic power of creation that Arendt herself declines to acknowledge. I already indicated above the complicity she underlines between anti-Semitic and Jewish historiographies in this regard. Now, it has become visible that Arendt's own narrative too shares this complicity, insofar as it tacitly presupposes the Jews as a historical constant, affected by history only with respect to its interests, not to its existence.

But this notion of the Jews so to speak as the origin and element of their own historical abstraction, and thus, potentially, of historical abstraction *tout court*, if anti-Semitism is indeed an origin and element of Totalitarianism, does not remain completely tacit in Arendt's text, even if it explicitly manifests itself relatively late. It is only in the 1967 Preface that this piece of the puzzle is added to Arendt's *Origins of Totalitarianism*. The summary historiography offered there prefatorily, as a sort of prehistory to the book's history of modern anti-Semitism, retains the demand to base all notions of Jew-hatred and Jews on the factual historical reality

---

gence of anti-Semitism and Totalitarianism from elements of modern politics omits the role of *democracy*. It is precisely in democracy that Lefort, in contrast, identifies an "origin" for the difficult interrelations between assimilation and anti-Semitism: "What haunts democratic society … is the image of a power that is *really* exterior, a foreign power, one thoroughly enmeshed in the intrigue of domination" (192).

of Jews' relations to non-Jews, places however this entire history under a certain condition, a Jewish condition, such that it appears as the history of "Jewish-Gentile relations under the conditions of Jewish dispersion" (xii).

Drawing mainly on the work of the Israeli historian Jacob Katz, in *Exclusiveness and Tolerance: Jewish-Gentile Relations in Medieval and Modern Times* (1961),[46] "who belongs among the younger generation of Jewish historians" with whom "the 'lachrymose' presentation of Jewish history...has indeed come to an end,"[47] Arendt now traces modern anti-Semitism back, as a "condition *sine qua non*," as *origin*, to pre-modern Judaism itself. It is in the late Middle Ages that would originally emerge, as "Jewish self-interpretation," the conception of "the alien character of the Jewish people" as—quoting Katz—"not one of creed and faith, but one of inner nature," "more likely to be racial in origin rather than a matter of doctrinal dissension" (xii). In other words, modern anti-Semitism would originate in premodern Jewish episteme, the central notion of which would be the non-epistemic, rather biological or racial essence of the collective Jewish being, of the Jewish people.

I underline this explicit figure, *negative* figure of Jewish political epistemology, which I think is central, albeit tacitly, to Arendt's discourse. The epistemic evil of totalitarian anti-Semitism, namely the abstraction of the Jew, would have its origin in Jewish self-abstraction, i.e., "the Jewish dissociation from the Gentile world, and more specifically from the Christian environment," which "has been of greater relevance for Jewish history than the reverse, for the obvious reason that the very survival of the people as an identifiable entity depended upon such voluntary separation and not...upon the hostility of Christians and non-Jews" (xiv). Jews would thus be the actual agent of Jewish political history. Jewish agency or Judaism would consist in the specific political episteme whose purpose and ultimate content is to sustain collective identity, the identity of a people, by "voluntary separation," namely by disassociation and abstraction of itself from the factual realities of "Jewish-Gentile relations," and so from history itself. "Jewish history" would accordingly be a history of anti-history, of detachment from history, a history "whose central con-

---

46   Jacob Katz, *Exclusiveness and Tolerance: Jewish-Gentile Relations in Medieval and Modern Times* (London: Oxford University Press, 1961).
47   Arendt, *Origins*, xii.

cern since the Babylonian exile has always been the survival of the people against the overwhelming odds of dispersion" (xv). The political category for the Jewish trans-historical abstraction is "exile," which Arendt, and this is crucial, because it manifests her profound agreement with Zionist historiography, interprets as sheer negativity, as historical agency whose essential action was to have "avoided political action for two thousand years" (8).

It is thus that in Arendt's historiography of anti-Semitism the primary epistemic vice of totalitarian anti-Semitism, namely the non-historical abstraction of the Jew, turning the Jew from a living individual into a concept, an epistemic entity, finds its origin—in the careful and complex sense given by Arendt to this term—in the proper Jewish episteme, whose agency would consist essentially in anti-historical self-abstraction. It should be emphasized that this is not the main point for Arendt in her account, and it is not even how Arendt herself formulates it, but rather a point that, with a specific deconstructive hermeneutics, can be shown—as I tried to demonstrate—to play a necessary and foundational role in the anti-anti-Semitic discourse that frames and sustains Arendt's argumentation.

The same hermeneutics would detect the same anti-anti-Semitic motif also in the other main parts of *The Origins of Totalitarianism*. Thus, much of Arendt's analysis of the second important origin and element of totalitarianism, *imperialism*, concerns *race*. On her account, racial thinking has played a central role in imperialist politics, because by replacing the "nation" with "race" it moved from a historically specific and limited collective to a biological collective bound by nothing but nature and thus potentially global. I will later argue against this stark opposition and indicate, at least within anti-Semitic discourse, a deeper affinity between "race" and "nation" (see Chapter 5). Be that as it may, Arendt's argument reveals a profound ambivalence, whereby racism, precisely by grounding imperialism, also entails a form of universalism. Arendt, however, focuses of course rather on the first, problematic aspect, of a small group that uses racial arguments to justify violently forcing its domination over others. She thus mentions the Boers, in the "African experience" of imperialism (Chapter 7), and in later "continental imperialism"—the great "pan-movements," Pan-Germanism and Pan-Slavism (Chapter 8). In both cases, she provides indications of how racist imperialist movements can be seen to relate, as their real historical paradigm, to the Jewish notion—or as she calls it, "myth"—of the chosen people.⁴⁸ At one point she points at this affinity to the idea of the "supernational" people as "what Himmler had in mind when he stated that 'we owe the art of government to the Jews'" (360).⁴⁹

It is important to notice that Arendt is mindful to differentiate between the Jewish paradigm and the imperialist application. She is thus pushed to identify an essential difference that would reveal a *positive* aspect in or perspective for Jewish epistemo-politics of the "people," which is radically opposed to what qualifies it to serve as model for the radical evil of the twentieth century. The redeeming element that Arendt identifies is the "Jewish-Christian faith in the divine origin of man" (233). This faith would thus not simply differentiate between Christian trans-ethnic universalism and Jewish ethnic particularism, but introduce universalism into ethnic politics itself, and thus mark "the difference between a Jewish mission in history to achieve the establishment of mankind and [the imperialist] 'mis-

---

48   With respect to the Boers, see *Origins*, p. 195: "The Boers simply denied the Christian doctrine of the common origin of men and changed those passages of the Old Testament which did not yet transcend the limits of the old Israelite national religion into a superstition which could not even be called a heresy. Like the Jews, they firmly believed in themselves as the chosen people,' with the essential difference that they were chosen not for the sake of divine salvation of mankind, but for the lazy domination over another species that was condemned to an equally lazy drudgery." With respect to the pan-movements, for instance, p. 239: "There existed an inherent affinity between the pan-movements' theories about peoples and the rootless existence of the Jewish people. It seemed the Jews were the one perfect example of a people in the tribal sense, their organization the model the pan-movements were striving to emulate, their survival and their supposed power the best proof of the correctness of racial theories."

49   Margaret Canovan refers to an "outline" that Arendt wrote in 1946 for her projected book, in which she explained "that the main theme of the first part would be the question of why antisemitism could be used by the Nazis as an 'amalgamator' for imperialism, and the answer was, she said, that the Jews who kept their identity without territory and without state, appeared as the only people that seemingly was already organized as a racial body politic. Modern antisemitism wanted not only to exterminate world Jewry but to imitate what it thought to be their organizational strength." See Canovan, *Hannah Arendt: A Reinterpretation of Her Political Thought* (Cambridge: Cambridge University Press, 1992), 43.

sion' to dominate all other peoples on earth" (240). This does not refute the paradigmatic quality of Jewish political epistemology; it rather means that the exact relation between the Jewish paradigm and the imperialist, say Nazi, application is not that of reproduction but, on the contrary, of "a complete reversion and perversion ... so that chosenness was no longer the myth for an ultimate realization of the ideal of a common humanity—but for its final destruction" (243).

The totalitarian, Nazi, or anti-Semitic perversion of the Jewish paradigm, once again, however, is conceptually dependent on and secondary to its *Jewish* perversion. It is this self-perversion, the reversion of Jewish episteme, of Judaism, in Jewish self-understanding that Arendt identifies in modern Jewish assimilation and secularization. Already in her 1938/39 essay she indicates how "Judaism, and belonging to the Jewish people," which "originally ... meant a specific religion, a specific nationality, the sharing of specific memories and specific hopes," through assimilation "degenerated into a simple fact of birth" (73). "Degeneration" means that Jewish epistemo-politics was not just replaced by bio-politics, but that Jewish episteme itself, Jewish self-knowledge, has become biopolitical, or in Arendt's terminology has turned from the collective knowledge of "Judaism" to "Jewishness," which is no more than a "psychological quality" (66) of individuals. This epistemic shift or perversion was enabled by and mediated through the idea of "chosenness," which secularization transformed from a messianic to a racial category, "tore down the strong bond of pious hope which had tied Israel to the rest of mankind" (74), and generated "Jewish chauvinism" and "perverted nationalism" (74).

Accordingly, in Arendt's 1951 analysis, if already preassimilated Jewish political existence served for the emerging totalitarian movements as "a perfect model of a nation without a state and without visible institutions," then continental "tribal nationalities," believing "that some mysterious inherent psychological or physical quality made them the incarnation not of Germany but Germanism, not of Russia, but the Russian soul," recognized that "the Jewishness of assimilated Jews was exactly the same kind of personal individual embodiment of Judaism and that the peculiar pride of secularized Jews, who had not given up the claim to chosenness, really meant that they believed they were different and better simply because they happened to be born as Jews, regardless of Jewish achievements and tradition" (240–241). This perceived symmetry or epistemo-political complicity can thus lead Arendt at one point to make a significant concession to (what she understands as fundamentally totalitarian) narratives of an overarching Jewish principle in history, and suggest that totalitarian anti-Semitism is "one of the most logical and most bitter revenges history has ever taken" (242). It is precisely at this point that Arendt's anti-anti-Semitism explicitly converges with "some truth" that she acknowledges in seminal writings of modern anti-Semitism: "For of course there is some truth in 'enlightened' assertions from Voltaire to Renan and Taine that the Jews' concept of chosenness, their identification of religion and nationality, their claim to an absolute position in history and a singled-out relationship with God, brought into Western civilization an otherwise unknown element of fanaticism (inherited by Christianity with its claim to exclusive possession of Truth) on one side, and on the other an element of pride that was dangerously close to its racial perversion" (242).[50]

To conclude by returning to the Arendt controversy, it should be noted that the above analysis of Arendt's argument in *The Origins of Totalitarianism* can be repeated, in its main articulations and with some modifications, also with respect to her account of the Eichmann trial.[51] I recall that according to Arendt it was precisely the (diasporic as much as Israeli) Jewish historiography of timeless anti-Semitism that was "at the root of all the failures and shortcomings of the Jerusalem trial" (267), in which justice of the individual doer ceded before collective history, such that "the case was built on what the Jews had suffered, not on what Eichmann had done" (6). It is this same understanding of anti-Semitism that supported, in Arendt's own

---

50   Cf. Canovan, *A Reinterpretation*: "The book as a whole traces the appalling consequences of understanding oneself and other in deterministic ways, and the moral of this chapter in particular is that by interpreting their Jewishness as a set of natural characteristics rather than as a religious or political commitment Jews contributed to the deadly antisemitism that destroyed them" (49–50). This specific and perhaps even originary Jewish agency is absent in Benhabib's account of Arendt's book. She thus describes the shift from "traditional anti-Judaism of Christian doctrine and practice" to "modern anti-Semitism" as a change in the *anti-Jewish* mind: "Enlightened opinion distances itself from traditional conceptions of the murder of the Son of God; however, Jewishness now becomes an undefinable 'essence,' a condition that is at once other and undeniable; Jewishness becomes a 'vice'" (*Reluctant Modernism*, 66). As quoted above, Arendt attributes this shift to the self-consciousness of *Jewish* assimilation itself.
51   Arendt, *Eichmann in Jerusalem: A Report on the Banality of Evil* (London: Penguin Books, 2006 [1963]).

account of the fact, the relations and actual cooperation between Nazis and Jews, such as Eichmann's "conversion" to Zionism (40–41) as well as the collaboration of Jewish communities with the Nazi authorities (10–11, 125), which led her to the suggestion of the blurred distinction between perpetrators and victims, later to be designated by Scholem as "perversion."[52]

It would be important, however, in any such analysis of Arendt's *Eichmann*, to notice and carefully trace the conceptual thread connecting the prevalence of historical over individual justice in the Israeli court with Eichmann's own absent individuality, i.e., his "sheer thoughtlessness,"[53] "word-and-thought-defying *banality*" (252), which in its turn would constitute precisely the dehumanizing effect of Totalitarianism—"and perhaps the nature of every bureaucracy" as "the rule of Nobody" (289). The failure of the Israeli court would accordingly only manifest "the inadequacy of the prevailing legal system" to deal with "acts of state" (294), whose perpetrators have no individual *mens rea*, are, in the legal sense, no longer perpetrators, *Täter*. In response to this, Arendt, in her own fictional 'judgment' of Eichmann, comes close to the notion of timelessness and objective order in history (and thus to the totalitarian notion of "objective enemy" she develops in *The Origins*),[54] beyond all positive law, ruling that "guilt and innocence before the law are of an objective nature, and even if eighty million Germans had done as you did, this would not have been an excuse for you" (278).

ALAIN BADIOU AND THE JEWISH FOUNDATION OF PARTICULARISM

A more recent instance of the same anti-anti-Semitic position as Arendt's, i.e., pointing at something like a Jewish creation of anti-Semitism, can be shown in the work of Alain Badiou.[55] Designating Badiou as "anti-anti-Semite" is not simple. In fact, the primary concern of Badiou's writings

---

52   Arendt/Scholem, *Der Briefwechsel*, 434.
53   Arendt, *Eichmann*, 287.
54   Arendt, *Origins*, 424.
55   Parts of this section appeared in Elad Lapidot, "The Word 'Jew,'" in *The Badiou Dictionary*, ed. Steve Corcoran (Edinburgh: Edinburgh University Press, 2015), 230–240.

on the issue of anti-Semitism has for the most part not been immediate opposition to anti-Semitism, but rather critique of (a certain discourse of) opposition to anti-Semitism. In other words, and from this perspective, Badiou's discourse could very reasonably be described less as anti-anti-Semitism, and more as anti-anti-anti-Semitism. Historically, unlike Adorno and Horkheimer, Sartre and Arendt, Badiou does not belong to the immediate reaction against the event of anti-Semitic politics, but, like this present text, to the reflection on this reaction. This historical positioning is also Badiou's own self-positioning, insofar as it was explicitly asserted, for instance, in the title of the volume in which appeared the English translation of Badiou's most recent intervention on this question, co-authored with Eric Hazan, "'Anti-Semitism Everywhere' in France Today," a volume titled *Reflections on anti-Semitism*,[56] an obvious reflection on Sartre's "reflections on the Jewish question." Nonetheless, my claim is that, precisely by the force of this reflection, Badiou's seeming anti-anti-anti-Semitism in fact remains within the anti-anti-Semitic discourse, with the basic operation of, in fact, reflecting and inversing, *mirroring* Sartre, namely, similarly to Arendt, switching the positions of the anti-Semite and the Jew.

Anti-Semitism Everywhere

Similarly to Sartre's reflections on the Jewish question, Badiou and Hazan's reflections too, on anti-Semitism, from the outset perceive their object as being itself a matter of thought or knowledge that is *no reflection*, a thought that reflects no reality, but rather consists of fantasy or imagination of something unreal, an empty or false thought, which is for this reason a concern for the philosopher. While "the Jewish" on whom Sartre reflects is a figment of the anti-Semite's imagination, Badiou and Hazan's reflections mirror Sartre's by looking in their turn not at "real" anti-Semitism, but at anti-Semitism that is only fantasized, only "imaginary." It is in fact a "hunt

---

56 Alain Badiou and Eric Hazan, Ivan Segré, *Reflections on Anti-Semitism*, trans. David Fernbach (London: Verso, 2013). The volume contains a translation of Alain Badiou and Eric Hazan, *L'antisémitisme partout—Aujourd'hui en France* (Paris : La fabrique, 2011), as well as a translation of Ivan Segré, *La Réaction philosémite ou la trahison des clercs* (Paris: Nouvelles Editions Lignes, 2009). The references below are to the French editions.

for an imaginary anti-Semitism" (39) that Badiou and Hazan critique. They do not say all anti-Semitism is only imaginary, rather distinguish the imagined from a real, as aforesaid, real anti-Semitism that I will later show to constitute a central element in Badiou's anti-anti-Semitism. Nonetheless, "'Anti-Semitism Everywhere' in France Today" focuses on 'Anti-Semitism Everywhere' in scare quotes, on a figment or specter of anti-Semitism, and more precisely on the medium in which this specter appears, a troubled, haunted, and disturbed medium, a disturbed mind or discourse. At the center of the essay stands "the discourse of the professional assailers of what they call anti-Semitism" (17), "those who have made a profession out of 'struggling against anti-Semitism'" (35). Badiou and Hazan do not characterize as "Jewish" the collective of "those" who carry the spectral discourse that they criticize. The inverse symmetry to Sartre, who deemed the Jew as anti-Semitic fantasy, does apply, however, inasmuch as on Badiou and Hazan's account, under the section "What Interests, What Aims?," the imagination of anti-Semitism would be intimately connected to, would be an element of, the same discourse as the assertion of the name "Jew."

The conceptual connection between anti-Semitism, the "imagined" one, and Jewishness is nonetheless not obvious in Badiou and Hazan's analysis. Their claim in fact consists to an important extent precisely in *denying* any connection between what is called in France today "anti-Semitism" and Jews. To them, it is precisely due to this lack of connection that the so-called "anti-Semitism," in contrast to real anti-Semitism, would be purely "imagined," or as an element of discourse, as a category or term, would be "a wrong term," a terminological error that nonetheless would not be arbitrary, a mere blunder or oversight, an epistemic nullity, but on the contrary pre-meditated, calculated, and deliberate—"a wrong term is deliberately chosen" (14)—and is thus not entirely wrong. It is in fact the (flawed) rationality, logic, or ideology behind the use of the (wrong) category "anti-Semitism" in France today, so to speak its (pathological) epistemology, that is the specific object of Badiou and Hazan's essay. Theirs is an inquiry on the "real and reactionary function. . .of this violent and shameless word 'anti-Semitism'" (42).

According to Badiou and Hazan, the wrong use of the word "anti-Semitism" functions in the service of a "new reactionary ideology," which would use also other names, such as, in the wake of the Cold War, "anti-totalitarianism" and "democracy." Arendt echoes strongly. It is indeed my own claim in this book that after World War II "anti-Semitism" has become a name and paradigm for political evil, and "the struggle against anti-Semitism" accordingly a requisite of any political agenda, reactionary or progressive. Badiou and Hazan's observation is, however, more specific. They rightly point out that the accusation of "anti-Semitism," "today in France" (and I think this applies also to Germany and elsewhere), is specifically directed against Arab and Muslim minorities, who are the socioeconomic-political weak, such that the campaign against anti-Semitism can be seen as "sowing distrust and hostility towards young people from the lower classes" (15). It is interesting to note how, to condemn anti-anti-Semitism for the (wrong) use of anti-Semitism, Badiou and Hazan themselves use anti-anti-Semitic discourse, when they speak of "populations viewed today with the same suspicious contempt that was displayed towards the Jews who arrived from central Europe before the Second World War.... It is these people who are responsible for all evils, starting with anti-Semitism" (41). The struggle against anti-Semitism would become so to speak the main weapon of anti-Semitism, a mirror effect that could further imply that the victims of anti-Semitism became its perpetrators.

This inversion corresponds to one of Arendt's central points whereby the explanation of anti-Semitism by Zionist historiographies ("eternal anti-Semitism") itself reproduces features of a totalitarian and anti-Semitic ideology. In Badiou and Hazan's account, too, it is Zionism that functions as link and location for the confluence of anti-Semitism and anti-anti-Semitism, of victims and perpetrators, of Jews and anti-Semites. Indeed, as indicated above, the (mis)use of the "wrong term" of anti-Semitism has its logic, which means that it is nonetheless not entirely arbitrary, has in other words *some* justification or reason. "Imaginary" and "real" anti-Semitism must have something in common, must share some fundamental common *image*. There must be something that connects anti-Semitism *in reality* to Muslim and Arab. This something is the Zionist project, the State of Israel, the Jewish state. Indeed, central to Badiou and Hazan's analysis is the observation that the war on anti-Semitism serves as a "diversion" from critique against the politics of the State of Israel (5). Of course, Israeli politics, or the political project of the Jewish State, namely, in Schmittian terms, its constitutive differentiation between friend and foe, has most immediately had adverse effects on Arabs and Muslims, who have thus been its most immediate opponents. It is due to this opposition to the Jewish State that Arabs and Muslims in France are accused, be that wrongly and wrongfully, of anti-Semitism. The specter of anti-Semitism is inseparably attached to the specter of the Jew, and the reflections on anti-Semitism necessarily lead back to reflections on the Jewish question.

Under the talk of "imaginary anti-Semitism," what Badiou and Hazan basically claim is that the opposition to the Jewish State is not necessarily anti-Semitic, because not necessarily anti-Jewish. To substantiate this claim, one needs to show that the critique against the Jewish State does not specifically criticize its Jewishness. To some extent, Badiou and Hazan do this by pointing out that in the anti-anti-Semitic discourse that they criticize, the State of Israel does not mean specifically the Jewish state, but rather functions as a paradigm and symbol for the entire political project of "the West," and thus "as an advance outpost of the West" in the Middle East in the war against the enemies of the West: "For the people we are talking about, whatever they say, what matters to them is not the name 'Jew' but rather 'the fate of the West'. This is the reason they identify 'Jew' with the State of Israel, and so eagerly support this state's war against the Palestinians and other Arabs" (30). In contrast, Badiou and Hazan question this association between the state of Israel, the West and the Jews, and more specifically raise the conceptual possibility of differentiation or even opposition between Jewish politics, i.e., Judaism as a political project, a political project carried out under and in the name of the "Jew," on the one hand, and on the other hand, the currently existing "Jewish State": "Was it necessary for this name, 'Jew'. . .to be dogmatically welded together with the state of Israel? Couldn't the same operation have been staged while leaving open the possibility of criticizing Israel, even doing so in the name of the name 'Jew'?" (29).

The Name "Jew"

This in fact is the fundamental question underlying Badiou and Hazan's polemic reflections on contemporary French anti-anti-Semitism. It concerns Jewish epistemo-politics, insofar as it asks about the semantics or epistemology of the word "Jew" and the nature of the political project that may be conceived of and carried out under that name. In this sense, Badiou and Hazan's 2011 reflections on anti-Semitism conceptually build on Badiou's earlier *Uses of the Word 'Jew'* (*Portées du mot 'juif'*).⁵⁷ This collection of essays, originally published in 2005, was, similar to "Anti-Semitism Everywhere," of a polemic nature. Badiou's polemic, mostly refraining from naming its concrete adversaries, encountered a vigorous counter-polemic in the journal *Les Temps Modernes*, under chief editor Claude Lanzmann.⁵⁸ Over the subsequent decade, this debate has been further developed in France by various authors in various media and forms, extending to an ever-broader perimeter of topics. Providing a point of reference and conceptual framework for the formation of thematic associations and intellectual alliances, the ongoing controversy around the word 'Jew' has come to define one line of confrontation currently shaping the intellectual public sphere in France. It is in this context that Badiou and Hazan's polemics of 2011 is situated.

---

57   Alain Badiou, *Circonstances, 3. Portées du mot « juif »* (Paris: Lignes & Manifeste, 2005); Badiou, *Polemics*, ed. and trans. Steven Corcoran (New York: Verso, 2011). The quotes refer to the English edition.

58   Éric Marty, "Alain Badiou: l'avenir d'une négation," *Les temps modernes* 635/636 (novembre-décembre 2005/janvier 2006): 22–58, accusing Badiou of a "hunt of the predicate 'Jewish'" (25). Also see Jean-Claude Milner, "Le juif de negation," 12–22, denouncing a perceived attitude of "no to the name Jew" (13). As my analysis shows, Badiou's position is more complex. The debate continued in the next issue of *Les temps moderns*, 637/638/639, no. 3 (mars-juin 2006), with Badiou's response to Marty, "*Le mot 'Juif' et le sychophante*" (733–747), as well as Marty's reply, "*Réponse à Alain Badiou et Cécile Winter*" (753–768).

See also Éric Marty and Yves Charles Zarka, "Les manipulations du nom de Juif," *Cités* 31 (2007): 151–170, where Zarka speaks of a "de-realization: the transformation of an existential question into another question concerning the 'word' or the 'name' 'Jew'" (151), i.e., "the exclusion of the reality of the Jews" (156). It nonetheless seems to me that the question of the name "Jew" is precisely the question of the "reality" of the Jews, i.e., what reality should be designated as "Jewish." As Zarka himself states later on in this text, emancipation and assimilation has destabilized Jewish self-understanding itself: "One doesn't know any more why one is Jewish. One doesn't know any more what it means 'to be Jewish'" (162). The reality more concretely in question in the debate with Badiou is the reality of the nation-state of Israel. Marty's texts were collected and published a little later as a book, *Une querelle avec Alain Badiou, philosophe* (Paris: Gallimard, 2007), trans. Alan Astro as *Radical French Thought and the Return of the "Jewish Question"* (Bloomington: Indiana University Press, 2015).

Before turning to *Uses of the Word 'Jew'*, and as a preliminary clue to its basic argumentation, the 2011 essay already signals that the problematic use of the name "Jew," which Badiou and Hazan identify at the basis of French anti-anti-Semitism, for them, once again, is not just an arbitrary mistake, but arises from the nature of this name itself. I already pointed at the question they raise at one point as to the possibility of criticizing Israeli politics in the name of the Jew, i.e., as to a potential political significance of the predicate "Jewish," which would be different than the identitarian naming underlying the nation-state. Nevertheless, more often in Badiou and Hazan's text the problem for them seems to be not that the name "Jew" is associated with *bad* politics (i.e., of the state of Israel); rather, the problem is the very use of "Jew" as naming politics, i.e., as being not just a proper name for a historical fact, but a category or concept of political thinking. Thus, in response to Jean-Claude Milner's ("the most original thinker among them") thesis on how instead of the "worker" the "Jew" has become the new "master-signifier" of political thought, by connecting universality and identity,[59] Badiou and Hazan argue for the "diametrically opposing aim" of these two names: whereas the "worker" signifies active opposition to power, the name "Jew" would stand for "collusion" with power and "allows a flock of people in a hurry to frequent the corridors of power" (27). Would "Jew" be the name of bad politics? A non-conceptual, non-philosophical and non-universal politics of names?

The question of naming can guide a reading of Badiou's *Uses of the Word 'Jew.'* The basic name that he uses as element, substance, or substrate for his reflections on the Jewish question in this collection, and in general, is not concepts of Jewish being, Jewishness, or Judaism, words that Badiou rarely uses, but "Jews," namely invoking no Jewish thought, but Jewish people. Badiou's questioning, however, does not refer directly to Jews. On the contrary, he explicitly declines what he considers to be a long intellectual tradition whose basic approach to Jews consists in putting them into question, and which would therefore require a certain solution. Instead Badiou approaches Jews fundamentally as a bare fact: 'there are Jews' (167). Jewish people are just another particular group of people, like any other. As such, for Badiou, Jews give rise to no special philosophical inquiry. It is precisely Badiou's observation that a certain contemporary discourse—which to

---

59   Jean-Claude Milner, *Le Juif de savoir* (Paris : Grasset, 2007).

a large extent overlaps with the discourse of "those who have made a profession out of 'struggling against anti-Semitism'"—does refer to Jews as a special theme of thought, which sets his own inquiry in motion, henceforth polemic in nature. The direct object of Badiou's reflection is thus not Jews as such but Jews in discourse: the word or the name "Jew." The fundamental question does not concern the *meaning* of this word. Strictly speaking, this word has no meaning, since it designates, for Badiou, no conceptual or epistemic content, but a fact, a thing, namely it is a word that doesn't mean but only designates, it is a pure, proper, particular name. Badiou's question thus concerns exclusively the *function* of this word: *Uses of the Word 'Jew.'*

For Badiou, since Jews are just a particular group of people, the name "Jew" ultimately designates nothing more than a person's adherence to this group. Badiou is aware of Jewish intellectual tradition. Nonetheless, this tradition or episteme he conceives generically as "religion," which according to him is "incompatible" with "the tradition of Enlightenment" and "contemporary universalism" and amounts to no more than "an identitary norm."[60] I suggest that this is Badiou's notion of negative knowledge, which is not entirely external to the epistemic realm, however it constitutes a deficient, perverse, or pathological phenomenon of knowledge or thought. In Badiou's terminology, this means that the word "Jewish" is just another "identity predicate." What Badiou observes in contemporary discourse is a certain use of this name as being more than that. He indicates that the name "Jew" seems to function in specific contexts as an "exceptional" or even "sacred signifier," which lies "above all usual handling of identity predicates" (159). It is noteworthy that a discourse that excludes "religion" from philosophy should nonetheless deploy paradigmatically theological categories such as the "sacred." This perceived "nominal sanctification" of the name "Jew" constitutes for Badiou, initially, however, not a theological but a *political* problem. To sanctify the name means to sanctify "the community claiming to stand for it," namely those who call themselves Jews. This particular group of people is thus "placed in a paradigmatic position with respect to the field of values, cultural hierarchies, and in evaluating the politics of states" (159). In other words, to sanctify the name "Jew" is to ascribe to those who identify themselves thus, the Jewish people, as such,

---

60   Alain Badiou et Alain Finkielkraut, *L'explication. Conversation avec Aude Lancelin* (Paris: Lignes, 2010), 92–94.

a special status in comparison to all other particular groups. For Badiou, this idea of "communal transcendence" contradicts what he conceives to be one of the basic categories of true politics in general, i.e., universality.

However, this use made of the name of the Jews is for Badiou not just another particular example of a problematic politics of names, but, as aforesaid, a certain exception in current discourse that deserves a special philosophical attention. Thus, according to Badiou, the alleged communal transcendence of "the Jews" does not merely challenge the general idea of universality, but in particular "contemporary" universalism (159). His position is articulated more concretely in his evaluation of the politics carried out in practice in the name of the "Jew," namely the *Jewish State*. It is here, in the debate concerning the State of Israel, that Badiou later localizes the fundamental problem that his intervention in this matter seeks to address (70). The particularistic politics of the State of Israel is not problematic just in itself, but, so Badiou, also in comparison to the "modern conception," which "is an open conception: a country is made up of all the people who live and work there" (214). "Truly contemporary states or countries" being "always cosmopolitan" (163), the Jewish State appears to Badiou as "a kind of archaism" (159).[61]

Badiou thus acknowledges the uniqueness of the very discourse that places the name Jew in a situation of exception, to which at one point he refers as a "French exception."[62] For him, this move is unjustified: Jews are no exception. He therefore identifies the factual unjustified exception that has *made* of the name "Jew." Consequently, the fundamental concept of Badiou's discussion of Jewish specificity is the *unjust* exclusion that has been historically made of and against Jews, namely *anti-Semitism*. The main *topos* selected by Badiou for his analysis is the concrete, factual, and historical reality of anti-Semitism, the real anti-Semitism, a real anti- against real Jews, namely the "extermination of the Jews by the Nazis." It is here that Badiou finds the common ground with the discourse that he criticizes. In fact, Badiou does not criticize the reference to the Nazis, which he identifies as the ultimate basis of the exceptional use made of the name "Jew." On the contrary, refusing to see in anti-Semitism a justification for

---

61   Badiou later clarified that his position is "for the disappearance of States" in general, and that "I said in my life infinitely more bad things about the French State than about the Israeli State"; see Badiou and Finkielkraut, *L'explication*, 76.
62   Badiou and Hazan, *L'antisémitisme partout*, 45.

this use, he sees anti-Semitism as the very origin of this use: "It was above all the Nazis who, before anyone else...drew all the consequences from making the signifier 'Jew' into a radical exception."[63]

It is in this sense that Badiou's reflection on the Jews, which is the basis for his reflection on "imaginary" anti-Semitism, in its turn draws on his reflection on real anti-Semitism, namely on the Nazis, in a very similar way to Sartre. Unlike the Jews, who are just another particular group, the basic object for Badiou's reflection on the Nazi question is not the multitude of "Nazi people" but the epistemo-politics of Nazism.[64] Badiou's criticism of the sanctification of the name "Jew" is formally similar to his criticism of a contemporary discourse that lends Nazism transcendence as—another echo of Arendt—"absolute Evil." However, the sanctification of Jews is criticized as an unjustified political exception made of a politically neutral (because not universal) reality, i.e., of mere particularity, which is external to the domain of what Badiou calls "truth." The absolutization of Nazism is criticized by Badiou, on the contrary, as not allowing us to think its real political singularity: "Even in the case of this Evil, which I would call extreme rather than radical, the intelligibility of its 'subjective' being...needs to be referred back to the intrinsic dimensions of the process of political truth" (175). For Badiou, to *think* Nazism as Evil is to acknowledge it not as nonpolitical but rather as a negative form of politics: as "criminal politics." In Badiou's categories, if the epicenter of politics is a true political event, then Nazism is its exact antipode: a non-event, a "simulated event."

---

63   Badiou, *Polemics*, 163–164.
64   Nonetheless, Éric Marty points out that the proper reaction advocated by Sartre to this anti-Semitic creation of the Jew is not rejecting or undoing this creation, which is the approach of what he calls the "Democrat" and the "inauthentic Jew," but rather its authentic appropriation, such that the Jew would fight anti-Semitism *as a Jew*. Badiou's position is thus closer to Sartre's "Democrat"; see Marty, "L'avenir d'une négation," 53–54; Marty/Zarka, "Les manipulations," 159. My above analysis of Sartre shows, however, the problematic and fragile status of this appropriation, such that ultimately the dissolution of the anti-Semite would also imply the dissolution of the Jew. Maurice Samuels identifies this more complex Sartrean position in Badiou's opposition to the French republican prohibition on wearing the veil in public spaces: "like Sartre, [Badiou] is willing to accept religious and cultural manifestations (especially when they come from oppressed groups, like Muslims) as a necessary stage on the path to a higher universal, the overcoming of capitalism." See Samuels, *The Right to Difference*, 180.

We touch here and must pause on a central element of Badiou's entire intellectual project, in a way an epistemo-political core of his thought, which shows it to be one of the important contemporary projects of political epistemology. In this framework I can only very briefly indicate a fundamental tension around which, so it seems to me, unfold both Badiou's anti-anti-Semitic discourse and the Badiouian possibility of going beyond this discourse, as I will show below.

On the one hand, Badiou may in fact be read as the proper contemporary thinker of critical political epistemology, i.e., as developing a critique of the cotemporary relations between knowledge and politics. Peter Hallward thus introduces Badiou as "rejecting the conjunction of politics and truth as inherently 'totalitarian,'" and so engaged in thinking and performing a "return to the politics of truth."[65] The basic operational notion in this "return" is that of truth as pertaining to the domain of temporal existence, of becoming or coming-into-being, of truth's being as an *event*: "a truth is something that *takes place* (from time to time)" (xxv). Truth "takes place" in human being or more precisely in the process of humans, of individuals *becoming* "subjects," *Subjects to Truth*, as Hallward's introduction is titled: "Truth, subject, and event are all aspects of a single process: a truth comes into being though the subjects who proclaim it and, in doing so, constitute themselves as subjects in their fidelity to the event" (xxvi). It is in the figure of *shared* fidelity that the event of truth is the foundation of politics: "This shared fidelity is the basis for a subjective community or being-together with no other criteria of inclusion than fidelity" (xxvi).

Reuniting politics and truth thus requires perceiving truth as coming-into-being in the figure of a *specific* community, enduring over time, over history by the force of "fidelity." The tension arises from the basic nature of truth as *universal* or "generic" (xxix). Thus, the universal nature or being of truth stands in tension to the *necessarily particular* communal existence of truth's becoming. If truth exists as coming to being in time, in history, its universality points against historical specificity, "against the current of history" (xxix). As Hallward formulates it, truth "takes place in a situation but is not 'of' that situation" (xxv). Against the necessary historical specificity and situatedness of truth as *event*, the event as *truth* generates

---

65   Peter Hallward, *Badiou: A Subject to Truth* (Minneapolis: University of Minnesota Press), xi.

in Badiou's thought a strong *opposition* to the specific historical collective as "particularity" opposed to the universality of truth. In a given situation, truth, to be universal, i.e., applicable to anyone, must, so it seems, refer to no one in particular. In a given situation, political truth may arise from no particular position in this situation.

There are therefore in Badiou's thought at least two figures of collective historical specificity: the generic community of fidelity to universalism and the community of collective particularism, of identity. The fundamental question would ultimately concern not the distinction between universalism and particularism, but the distinction between these two forms of particularity, which to some extent and in some essential respects *must look alike*, i.e., as specific historical collectives. There would be a necessary question of *seeming* and *simulation*: of distinguishing between actual, real procedures of truth, real events of universalism, and historical movements that only arises from *simulated* events. As Badiou explains with respect to the National Socialist movement, the simulated political event only *seems* to be universal, while in fact it consists in giving "substance" to a certain particular group and preserving it as such. This can only be done by imposing the void on everything else, universally: "What is addressed 'to everyone'...is death."[66] The simulated event is inherently an event of extermination.

The simulated event of Nazism, according to Badiou, referred to the particularity of the "Germans" or "Aryans." In order to lend substance to the Aryans, Nazism consisted in the universal extermination of all non-Aryans. However, he observes, "in the case of Nazism, the void made its return under one privileged name in particular, the name 'Jew'. There were certainly others as well: the Gypsies, the mentally ill, homosexuals, communists.... But the name 'Jew' was the name of names" (178). When Badiou rejects the view that "Nazi atrocities work in some way to validate...the election of the 'people'" (161), it is therefore not because there has never been any election, but because the election that did take place was originally Nazi: "inasmuch as it served to organize the extermination, the name 'Jew' was a political creation of the Nazis, without any pre-existing referent" (179). The Nazi election has led to the sanctification of the name "Jew" in the

---

66   Badiou, *Polemics*, 178.

twentieth century: "Once the Nazis were defeated, the name 'Jew' became, like every name of the victim of a frightful sacrifice, a sacred name" (168).[67]

This acknowledgment of the elected destiny of the Jewish people, be it through a Nazi election, of itself raises the fundamental question of any election: Why? Why the Jews? What is the reason for the Nazi election of the Jews? As Badiou affirms, "It was no accident" (168).

Of course, Badiou categorically rejects the Nazi discourse. The reason the Nazis elected the Jews is not because they are in reality non-Aryan: "But the Aryan doesn't exist. It is only a tautology of Nazi discourse that says: Aryans are Aryans" (213). For Badiou, the Jews are not conceived in Nazi categories, but in the categories of his own political analysis of Nazism. The Jews are not non-Aryan but non-Nazi. Since Nazism is the political non-event, namely the simulated event of particularity, then "the choice of [the name of the Jews by the Nazis] relates, without any doubt, to its obvious link with universalism" (178–179). In this way, by conceiving the Jews as that to which negative politics is opposed, Badiou arrives, in *Uses of the Word 'Jew,'* at a use of the word Jew, wherein it does not just designate yet another particular identity predicate, but names a specific aspect or moment within the process of universal truths: "a meaning for the word 'Jew' that would have universal import" (165).

Jewish Universal Particularism

This use comes closest to a Badiouian *concept* of the Jew, to his conception of what has been designated since early Christianity as *Judaism*, and which I call a Jewish knowledge or episteme. Badiou himself never explicitly formulates this concept as such, consistently refusing to recognize in proper Jewish intellectual tradition anything other than "religion," which supposedly lies beyond the realm of pertinent philosophical intervention. It is, however, precisely his reading of the foundational Christian text, *Saint Paul: The Foundation of Universalism*, that constitutes the second major Badiouian *topos*, other than Nazism, where the word "Jew" comes to name

---

67   Cf. Alain Badiou, *L'éthique, essai sur la conscience du mal* (Paris: Hatier, 1993), trans. Peter Hallward as *Ethics: An Essay on the Understanding of Evil* (New York: Verso, 2012), 75–77.

an essential aspect in the event of universality.⁶⁸ "Jew" once again is that in relation to which the process analyzed by philosophy takes place: in the formal event of the "Christian subject," the "Jewish community" constitutes its "site" (23). Badiou emphasizes that the Christian content of Paul's gospel—"Christ died and resurrected"—insofar as it constitutes a "fable" of "religion," precludes the Pauline movement from constituting a genuine event of "true universality." What Badiou reads in Paul is rather a formal "theory" of the event (77). In this framework, "Jew" names the "eventual site," if not of the real "Foundation of Universalism" properly speaking, as the admittedly "excessive title" of the book on Paul suggests, nonetheless of a "powerful watershed (*césure*)" in its historical emergence (115).

As the site of the Christian event, which as a Universal "traverses and transcends" (99) all particularities, Jewish particularity has "a kind of priority" (102) over other particularities, such as the Greek. "Jew" is the particularity from which Christian universality may emerge. The Jewish particularity is not just a matter of indifference to universality, like all other differences of "opinions and customs," including, we may assume, religion. As particular, it is an inherent moment of universality. More precisely, it is the particular that is the yet empty place, the "site," of the universal to come. How should we understand this? One may suggest that "Jew" names the particular that is the absent universal, the non-universal. As absence, within which its event is to take place, the universal appears as the "Jew," who is not yet the universal singularity of the Christian subject, but a uni-

---

68   Alain Badiou, *Saint Paul. La fondation de l'universalisme* (Paris: PUF, 1997); the following quotes are from *Saint Paul: The Foundation of Universalism*, trans. Ray Brassier (Stanford, CA: Stanford University Press, 2003). On theology in Badiou's thought see Hollis Phelps, *Alain Badiou: Between Theology and Anti-Theology* (Durham: Acumen, 2013), who asserts "a theological core and eschatological form that animate Badiou's philosophy, despite claims to the contrary" (2). For an illuminating contextualization of Badiou's turn to Paul, which began two decades before his Paul book with the theater play *L'incident d'Antioche* (Alain Badiou, *The Incident at Antioch / L'Incident d'Antioche. A Tragedy in Three Acts / Tragédie en trois actes*, trans. Susan Spitzer [New York: Columbia University Press, 2013]), as "the consequence of an acute disappointment of imminent expectation [*Naherwartungsenttäuschung*] … as a consequence of a double failure of a political messianism that was aroused in 1968"; see Luca Di Blasi, *Dezentrierungen. Beiträge zur Religion der Philosophie im 20. Jahrhundert* (Wien/Berlin: Turia + Kant, 2018), 26–33, 28.

versal particularity. On this reading, "Jew" is the particular with "universal import," particularity not just as a particular fact, but as a figure of the subject, i.e., the very thought of particularity.[69]

A precise articulation of this line of thought can be found in Badiou's novel *Calme bloc ici-bas*.[70] It is put in the words of one of the protagonists and should therefore be taken with caution, bearing in mind, however, that Badiou did choose to include the passage as an independent fragment in *Uses of the Word 'Jew.'* In this passage, Badiou has one of his fictional characters explicitly ask the fundamental Jewish Question: "What is Jewish/a Jew [juif]?"[71] The answer outlines a summary Jewish theology: "Imagine that there is a Law, which says that you are you, and that, in God's eyes, you alone are who you are. 'You' is something that comes from the mother."

The "law" is already a central theme of *Saint Paul*. There, subscribing to Paul's operation of "disjoining the true from the Law,"[72] Badiou explains that "the law is always predicative, particular and partial" (76). Being essentially "statist," the law is the constitutive principle of particular collectives, of "the particularizing multiplicity" (78). As a form of thought, a specific figure of the subject, "the law is what constitutes the subject as powerlessness of thought" (83), as stated by the third theorem of Badiou's "materialism of grace" (81). Constituting the subject as powerless thought, a dead thought, law is the principle of subjective life as *de facto* death. The law, like the letter, "mortifies," it "gives life to death" (82). Non-life under the law is precisely the site for the Pauline event of graceful "resurrection."

This site is specifically Jewish, because the "Jew" is not just another particularity operating under its own particular law. Rather, vis-à-vis the universal Christian event, "the Jews raise the question of the law" (28).

---

69 Sarah Hammerschlag notes how Badiou deploys his Pauline operation against "the cult of difference that he associates with Levinasian ethics" (*The Figural Jew*, 21; also 261–262). According to Hammerschlag, what Badiou "fails to see…is that Levinas himself offers us the resources for overcoming identity politics." See also Hammerschlag, "Bad Jews, Authentic Jews, Figural Jews," in Randi Rashkover and Martin Kavka, *Judaism, Liberalism, and Political Theology* (Bloomington: Indiana University Press, 2014), 221–240; and Hallward, *Badiou*, xxiii; Marty/Zarka, "Les manipulations," 170.
70 Alain Badiou, *Calme bloc ici-bas* (Paris: éd. P.O.L., 1997).
71 Badiou, *Polemics*, 184.
72 Badiou, *Saint Paul*, 15.

The Jewish site is not just a contingent, factual particularity, but the particularity as a matter of principle, i.e., the principle of particularity, law as the Law. The particular Jewish law is therefore formulated in Badiou's novel as the universal Law of Particularity: "In God's eye, you alone are who you are." What makes Jews exceptional is that "the Jewish discourse is a discourse of the exception" (41). The "Jew" names the paradigm, the very thought of particular identity as universal exception. "Jew" names the universal non-universal and as such is the name of the name, the particular, proper, the non-category of all proper names, and consequently, of all negative politics—all the way (can this conclusion be avoided?) to Nazism.

Jewish discourse thus recognizes and attests to universality as possible and at the same time precludes its reality. The "Jew" is, in other words, *virtual* universality, the site of universality's potential existence, actual inexistence—the site of universality's event. The Jews who *positively* identify themselves as such—who "only declare their identity"—are therefore "virtual Jews": "Because it must necessarily be there, that powerful and detestable identity, to enable a Jew who is more than the Jews to come."[73] The positive, "actual Jew" then perfects the Jewish identity precisely by breaking it: "What happens is that someone gets up who says: if I alone am who I am, that's because this 'myself' is nothing but all the others.... Let's call 'Jew' the one who...grasps his own being to brake the divisive law, and thereby exposes humanity to the universal" (168).

The "universal import" of the name "Jew" thus leads Badiou to an operation of renaming, strongly reminiscent of Paul: "For he is not a Jew, which is one outwardly; neither is circumcision that which is outward in the flesh. But he is a Jew who is one inwardly; and circumcision is that which is of the heart, in the spirit, and not in the letter" (Epistle to the Romans 2, 28–29). The negative element of this operation, as Badiou indicates, is not of "abolishing Jewish particularity."[74] The universality declared by Paul requires Jewish particularity as the site for its event, as its "principle of historicity." "Jew," designating community, law and book, names the absence of the subject as the universal singularity to come, the inexistence from which it is to emerge. Badiou expresses the same idea in respect of the relation between traditional Jewish communities and the State. The Jewish

---

73 Badiou, *Polemics*, 186.
74 Badiou, *Saint Paul*, 103.

people, he acknowledges, was "non statist, diasporic, transversal, and by this very fact, in its fundamental particularity, it was destined, convened to universality." It was thus the "localization for a possible universality, which, at its base, is homogenous to communism."[75] It follows that "being Jewish/the Jewish being (*l'être-juif*) in general, and the Book in particular, *can and must be resubjectivated*."[76] This "resubjectivation" abolishes neither book nor being. It rather renews: it transforms them into a new book, for example the New Testament, and a new subjective being, for example the Christian. The emergence of the actual Jew from the virtual Jew is less abolition than conversion.[77]

This operation is reflected in the list of proper names that make up Badiou's short history of the actual Jews: "from the apostle Paul to Trotsky, passing through Spinoza, Marx and Freud."[78] These people can only be defined as "Jews" by a radical criterion of particular identity: their mother.[79] Indeed, in the actuality of these persons, their Jewish particularity is for Badiou nothing but the *negative* condition of possibility, the "site," of their universal thinking. These "actual Jews" have been universal by converting their Jewish particularity into universality, thereby creating "new points of rupture" with Judaism: "They are people who enjoin the thought of all to the strictest universality, and, in memorable founding acts, enacted a rupture with any and every end of the law that was somehow exclusionary or identifying. They say 'no one is elected, otherwise everyone is.' And they can say it precisely because they were the supposed bearers of the most

---

75   Badiou and Finkielkraut, *L'explication*, 76–78.
76   Badiou, *Saint Paul*, 103.
77   For a critical reading of Badiou on this and other questions, see John M.G. Barclay, "Paul and the Philosophers: Alain Badiou and the Event," in *New Blackfriars* 91.1032 (2010): 171–184.
78   Badiou, *Polemics*, 162.
79   Luca Di Blasi, "Doppelte Nicht-Identität. Zur Gegenwartsrelevanz des Paulus," in *Dezentrierungen*, 89–110, thus observes: "Upon closer look, the presupposition whereby Jewish universalism would grow on a permanently identical basis of a 'powerful and detestable identity', a 'Jewish communitarianism', appears to be questionable. As suggested by the names Paul to Freud, this specific communitarianism would have to be a quasi timeless constant, which is however doubtful" (96).

radical election in the eye of God."[80] It is the same logic that ultimately leads Badiou to formulate his own announcement—personified perhaps, at least provisionally, by the proper name of Udi Aloni[81]—of the "Jew to come":[82] "It is clear that today's equivalent of Paul's religious rupture with established Judaism, of Spinoza's rationalist rupture with the Synagogue, or of Marx's political rupture with the bourgeois integration of a part of his community of origin, is a subjective rupture with the State of Israel" as a "Jewish State" (162–163).

The Jew of Study

A similar procedure of alleged reappropriation of the name "Jew" to the ultimate effect of negating it was deployed by Badiou in his response to the vehement critique against his collection on *The Uses of the Name 'Jew.'* In "The word 'Jew' and the Sycophant" (*Le mot 'Juif' et le Sycophante*),[83] a scathingly polemical reply to Éric Marty's own acrimonious anti-Badiou tract, accusing Badiou of "a hunt of the predicate 'Jewish,'"[84] Badiou stated once again that his intervention was not aimed at the name "Jew" itself, but at the specific political *uses* currently made of this name in France by a "small fraction that proclaimed itself proprietary of the word 'Jew' and its uses" (733). The precise political use that Badiou indicated as problematic was not primarily support of Israeli politics, but of *French* politics, namely the use of the name "Jew" for promoting "unprecedented reactionary offensive against workers of foreign origins, adolescents in housing projects (*cités*), universal schooling for children, the health of the poorest and

---

80 Badiou, *Polemics*, 185.
81 Maurice Samuels suggests other names: "[Cécile Winter, whose text was included in Badiou's book on the word "Jew"—E.L.], who proclaims her own Jewishness by disavowing it with what Badiou admiringly calls a 'rare violence', thus becomes another in the line of Jewish coauthors (along with Hazan and Ivan Segré) whose Jewish identity helps legitimate Badiou's attack on Jewish identity." See Samuels, *The Right to Difference*, 176.
82 Badiou, *Polemics*, 207.
83 Badiou, *Polemics*, 230–247.
84 Marty, *L'avenir d'une negation*, 25. See also Maurice Samuels, *The Right to Difference*, asserting that Badiou's "explicit goal is to abolish the 'name' of the Jews, which is to say, Jewish identity as such" (176).

weakest, women of different customs, worker households, the mentally ill..." (733). Against this use, Badiou suggested, as he will do again in 2011 in his coauthored *Anti-Semitism Everywhere*, that the name "Jew" and the predicate "Jewish" may also have *other* uses, in which "Jewish" will be the name of another kind of politics, "universalist and egalitarian," he argued, namely, for "a universalist and egalitarian meaning of this word" (733).

It may be asked what exactly it means, to have a word *have* a meaning, and what kind of *act* is required here. There seems to be here a matter of decision and one should ask of what nature and criteria, and of what domain such a decision on meanings and uses of words and names is. With respect to something like "Jews," it seems that what this name *means*, if it's not just a multitude of individuals, but a *political* concept, must somehow fundamentally arise from what Jews do and say—from Jewish political and intellectual history. In other words, the decision on the meaning of the name "Jew" is a decision on Jewish historiography. The historiography *rejected* by Badiou as the basis for the reactionary use of the name is formulated in a very summary, caricatural way, as "the triplet of Shoah, State of Israel and talmudic tradition," which he designates, as an ideological apparatus, with the acronym "SIT" (733). This highly symbolic formulation thus welds together and dismisses the two central political events of modern Jewish being, Shoah and the State of Israel, whose problematic role for the political meaning of the name "Jew" was analyzed by Badiou, with the "talmudic tradition," which stands here for and designates in fact the heart of non-Christian Jewish intellectual tradition since Paul's days: what Jews have been saying long before the Shoah—and after. Once again, Badiou identifies this entire tradition as "religious customs" and "fabled stories," which politically arise to "imperial particularities" and historiographically to a "substantialized and racialist interpretation" of Jewish history (735). Badiou thus reports in his reply how, to an interlocutor in the controversy around his texts on the word "Jew" who urged him to look at "the Hebraic texts," he replied that "all national and/or racial pretention makes a big deal about origins, foundational texts, immemorial laws etc." (744).

Having thus precluded proper Jewish intellectual tradition, the only Jewish history left as basis for deciding on the meaning of the name "Jew" is, once again, the negative history of intellectuals whose intellect meant a break with Jewish tradition: "These disparate Jews, these utterly singular Jews, these Jews for whom the predicate is at once unquestionable and completely floating. These Jews who want the universality of what they create to exceed the particularity, with which they may identify themselves or not. These Jews, finally, for whom the triplet SIT is a fatal injury to their freedom" (747). Whereas in earlier texts Badiou always identified these non-Jewish Jews only in Jews "in the flesh," who transcended carnal Jewishness in their spirit—Paul, Spinoza, Marx, Udi Aloni—his reply consummates the act of spiritualization, such that the meaning of "Jewish" based on *Jewish* negation of Jewish tradition is universalized into *any* negation of Jewish tradition, namely *anyone* who feels that "the triplet SIT," i.e., also Jewish intellectual tradition, whose paradigm is "talmudic tradition," "is a fatal injury to their freedom," for which the contemporary paradigm would be none by Badiou himself: "In this affair, and since everything that exists in the world, most of all names, is only thinkable in a situation, *le juif, c'est moi*" (747).

This negation of the *history* of the name or the meaning of the name "Jew" by way of self-appropriation "in a situation," *eo ipso*, however, opens a way to its opposite. In fact, if we take Badiou seriously, such that Badiou's naming himself "the Jew" is not just allegorical, not just rhetorical, it would mean that his use in fact instantiates a real *use* of the name "Jew," which in a specific situation does *not* operate as an "identity predicate," but as the name of the individual "Alain Badiou" *qua* the subject of a political truth, i.e., a subject who constitutes himself through the fidelity to the event of truth in the domain of politics. But if so, then this would mean, in a most consistent way with Badiou's conception of truth as "process" and "event," that also Jewish tradition and history, or at least some Jewish tradition, may in principle be read and written in its particularity, not only as "individual," but also as "subjective" in Badiouian terms, i.e., as the historical incorporation of a fidelity to a universal truth—not only by way of negation, but by way of affirmation, indeed, *fidelity*. Seeking this theoretical possibility in Badiou's *corpus* requires revisiting the site in which this possibility was precluded, namely the moment when universalism was, supposedly, historically founded by an act of fidelity to truth that meant *breaking* with Jewish tradition as "talmudic" or more precisely as *rabbinic*: the site of Paul.

Such a critical reexamination of Badiou's Paul has been in fact undertaken by two contemporary "talmudic" thinkers, who intervened precisely on the aforementioned question, both published in the same year, 2009. One of these thinkers, Daniel Boyarin, drew a distinction between Badiou and Jewish thought in Paul: he identified a Badiouian Platonic, Philosophical Paul and opposed to him a Jewish Sophist Paul. The second, Ivan Segré, drew a distinction in Badiou himself: he opposed Badiou's Paul to Badiou's Plato, whom he then aligned with Jewish thought. Segré's intervention, in other words, indicated how a coherent reading of Badiou's philosophy, against Badiou's own reading of Paul, rather than associating the process of truth with the *negation* of the "talmudic tradition," can and should on the contrary associate it with *acknowledging* the epistemo-political meaning of this tradition, as a non-reactionary meaning of the name "Jew." To conclude this chapter, I will now present these two interventions, and how the second one, Segré's internal critique of Badiou, with Badiou against Badiou, in fact led the philosopher beyond anti-anti-Semitism, to acknowledge "Jewish" as the name for a positive political epistemology.

Daniel Boyarin identified the basic merit of Badiou's reading of Paul in its non-Christian perspective, namely as asking, like Boyarin himself, "what can we learn from Paul if we *don't* believe Christian theological claims *per se*; don't accept the adoption of Jesus as son, the resurrection, nor even, for some of us, the apparent abrogation of Torah law?"[85] Boyarin's basic problem with Badiou's reading and more general intellectual project is defined as "dehistoricization." On Boyarin's reading of Badiou's philosophy, Badiou's Platonism entails the impossibility of seeing any truth in temporal, historical phenomena, such that the "event" or "process" of truth requires the negation of all such historical realities—"dehistoricization." For Boyarin, "dehistoricizing constitutes for Badiou the very structure of the event," such that truth "cannot be a matter of a particular time, place, historical circumstances, conflicts and possibilities. It has to be radically subtracted from anything 'communitarian'" (121). Badiou's reading of

---

85   Daniel Boyarin, "Paul among the Antiphilosophers; or, Saul among the Sophists," in *St. Paul among the Philosophers*, ed. John D. Caputo and Linda Martin Alcoff (Bloomington: Indiana University Press, 2009), 109–141, 110. See also Boyarin's own book on Paul, *A Radical Jew: Paul and the Politics of Identity* (Berkeley: University of California Press, 1994). For another reading engaged on the same question, with a critical discussion of Boyarin's position, see Elad Lapidot, "Paulus und die Grundlegung des Judentums," in *Täter und Opfer. Verbrechen und Stigma im europäischen-jüdischen Kontext*, ed. Claudia Simone Dorchain and Tommaso Speccher (Würzburg: Königshausen & Neumann, 2014), 19–41. For a recent critical discussion of Boyarin's, Badiou's, Agamben's and my own readings of Paul, see Luca Di Blasi, "Doppelte Nicht-Identität. Zur Gegenwartsrelevanz des Paulus," in *Dezentrierungen*, 89–110.

Paul would thus be a typical Badiouian operation, amounting to Platonic Paulinianism, which is, notwithstanding Badiou's own statements, nothing but pure Christology: "Having subtracted everything of the contingent, the historical, even the individual in his account of Paul, [Badiou] is left knowing nothing but Paul asserting Jesus Christ and him crucified (or resurrected)" (132). For Boyarin, this Platonic Christology would be the foundation of *Philosophy* itself, for whom historical collectives and collective names, like "Jewish," may never designate truth or thought, but always only a "particular identity." To "Philosophy," Boyarin then goes on and opposes another form of thinking or discourse, which he designates as "antiphilosophy" or "sophist" and "rhetoric" (121).

It is as a sophist, a "postcolonial sophist" (132), rather than a Platonist, that Boyarin in fact suggests reading Paul. Paul's basic universalizing operation, "there is neither Jew nor Greek," would thus consist not in negating these names, under the assumption that they designate nothing but "particular identities," but, on the exact contrary, *denying* that such names only designate particular identities, in fact calling into question the very notion of a "particular identity," rather indicating that "all identity is performative" (122)—both Greek and Jewish. One may say in other words, *Badiou's* words, that these names, these historical collectives, designate and constitute nothing but the performance, i.e., the subjective temporal and historical realization and "subjectivization" of some general, *generic* truth. *This* manner of perceiving truth, in multiple singular collective events emerging in history, this alleged antiphilosophical sophist epistemology, in Boyarin's eyes, would be a "challenge to any form of epistemological certainty, whether prophetic or philosophical" (128).⁸⁶

---

86   Sarah Hammerschlag draws the next conclusion from Boyarin's reading and shows how it is thus ultimately Badiou's Pauline universalism that features "the dynamics of exemplarity," i.e., universalism proclaimed by a particular group for legitimizing its particularity as "exemplary" of universalism: "The very act of locating and assigning Paul as the origin of this universalist project manages to set in place exactly what Badiou claims Paul set out to undo: it anchors the truth of universalism to a particular place, culture, empire and religion. In other words, it gets the dynamics of exemplarity up and running" (Hammerschlag, "Bad Jews," 232). Furthermore, by *denying* this necessary particularity, Badiou's universalism, Hammerschlag claims, is ultimately "far more divisive than the 'Judaic' modes of thought that Badiou maligns for their tribalism" (221). It seems to me that

That these words could indeed be Badiou's own—this is what Ivan Segré detected. In his essay of 2009, "Controversy on the Question of the Universal (Alain Badiou and Benny Lévy),"[87] he proposed readings of these two intellectual rivals—Badiou, who called Lévy a "sectarian Rabbi,"[88] and Lévy, who pointed at Badiou as "the core of the new anti-Semitism"[89]—as surprisingly close. To do so, Segré powerfully deploys the hermeneutics of "with-against": with Badiou/Lévy against Badiou/Lévy. Of main importance here is Segré's "with-against" intervention on Badiou's Paul. Similarly to Boyarin, Segré too deems Badiou's reading as "a gesture of great significance within Christianism, because [Badiou] disassociates Paulinian universalism from its theological and fideist gangue" (193). The problem that Segré diagnoses in Badiou's reading, however, is not, like Boyarin, too much "philosophy," but on the contrary, too much of the anti-philosophical medicine prescribed by Boyarin, "rhetoric": the "rhetoric of identifying Paul to a militant of a truth" (195). Accordingly, instead of distinguishing between the Platonic-Badiouian philosophical Paul from antiphilosophical/sophist Paul, Segré suggests an operation in Badiou's own textual body, "with Badiou against Badiou," with Badiou's philosophy against his rhetoric, which Segré understands as "distinguishing Badiou's Paulinism from his Platonism" (195).

One may ask about the ultimate appropriateness of this *naming*, first and foremost of the name "Platonism." It may even be suggested that the fundamental dispute here concerns the uses of the name "Plato." In fact, whereas Boyarin identified Badiou's Platonism in a notion of truth that "cannot be a matter of a particular time, place, historical circumstances,

---

the problem that Hammerschlag correctly identifies is nonetheless *internal* to Badiou's thought, a fundamental project of which, as I claimed above, is precisely to consider universal truth in its temporal and singular *event*. The problem of Badiou's Paul thus concerns the exact nature of the Pauline event, namely Christ, for Badiou. This is the center of Ivan Segré's critique.

87   Ivan Segré, «Controverse Sur La Question De L'universel (Alain Badiou et Benny Lévy),» *Lignes* 30 (2009): 169–200.
88   Alain Badiou, «Crime et châtiment de Jean-Paul Sartre. Le supplice de B.-H.L.Crime et châtiment de Jean-Paul Sartre. Le supplice de B.-H.L.,» *Libération*, 17 avril 2000.
89   Benny Lévy, *La Cérémonie de la naissance* (Paris: Verdier, 2005), 114.

conflicts and possibilities,"⁹⁰ so to speak exclusively eternal, non-temporal, and non-historical truth, Segré identifies at the center of Badiou's philosophy the exact opposite notion, of truth as a "procedure," as a process of "production" of universality, namely as a temporal occurrence, an "event." Badiouian truth exists not just in a supersensual world, but as "effective procedures of truth" in the domains of science, art, politics, and love, which take effect in the generation of a "subject." To speak in Boyarin's terminology, truth in Badiou's thought is "performance." If one must agree with Segré that this in fact is a cornerstone of Badiou's philosophy, one must also wonder with Boyarin whether this is Platonism or rather anti-Platonism.

It is in any case the Badiouian notion that Segré deploys against Badiou's own reading of Paul. As Segré states, Badiou's reading of Paul is "atheist or a-christological."⁹¹ This means that "the resurrection of Christ for him has no other status but of a 'pure mythological assertion'" (192), as Badiou in fact explicitly states (see above). This, however, means that the concrete appearance of truth in the world, the event or process of truth, which constitutes the basic occurrence to which the entire Paulinian discourse relates, for Badiou never took place, is no event at all, or is perhaps a "simulated" event only. It follows that the process of subjectivation that unfolds in Paul's discourse as the fidelity to this supposed truth event, Paul's "break" with the site in the name of this event, in Badiou's reading, is not founded, as in the case of effective procedures of truth (science, art, politics, love), on the production of a universal. Paul's is what Badiou calls a mere "theoretical break" (192). What Segré shows, one may suggest, is that Badiou's Paul, as Boyarin claims, is too Platonic: pure theory with no actual event. For Segré, however, thinking with Badiou, Paul without event is like Plato without idea: a figure of anti-philosophy, of *rhetoric*. Segré thus thinks with Badiou in order to criticize Badiou's "rhetoric of identifying Paul to a militant of a truth" (192), since "for founding universalism [in Paul], no truth (scientific, artistic, political, amorous) is any longer required for the philosopher" (197).

The epistemo-political consequences of this observation are twofold. First, concerning the universalism proclaimed by Paul, of which Paul

---

90   Boyarin, "Paul among the Antiphilosophers," 121.
91   Segré, "Controverse," 192.

is—so Badiou—a "militant." Segré points out the problem of universalist militancy that is not founded on any actual truth: "the laws of universality without truth, this is the Empire" (200). In other words, if Christ is but a fable, the only universalism actually founded by Paul is that of Rome.[92] Consequently, and this is the main point that interests our present investigation, Segré points out, secondly, that Badiou's reading of "the rabbinic reaction against Paul" as "a paradigm of anti-universalism, of the negation of universalism, i.e., a paradigm of denial that there are truths valid for all" (196), which leads Badiou, as shown above, to identify the 'talmudic tradition', i.e., the tradition of "Jewish literal Study, 'from generation to generation', to a 'sectarian' thinking" (196), all this, *in absentia christi*, is nothing but "anti-Jewish rhetoric" (196). In other words, Badiou's own philosophy delegitimizes Paul's break with his "site," rabbinic Judaism, who in the actual situation of Paulinian Christological militancy speaks Badiou's own truth: "The event proclaimed by Paul is precisely, in the eyes of the 'sectarian rabbi', a fable" (196). Badiou's event-Platonism sides with the rabbis against Paul.[93]

It is thus that Segré's surgical intervention in fact opens up in the Badiouian corpus a bridge toward rabbinic Judaism and the talmudic tradition of study, a bridge between "the philosopher and the Jew of study" (199). "The Jew of study," *le Juif de l'étude*, was offered to Badiou as a use of

---

92   For an analogous critique of Badiou's formalized Paulinian universalism as akin to *capitalism*, see Daniel Bell Jr., "Badiou's Faith and Paul's Gospel: The Politics of Indifference and the Overcoming of Capital," *Angelaki: Journal of the Theoretical Humanities* 12 (2007): 97–111. For a defense of Badiou, see Kyle Gingerich Hiebert, "Capitalism and Catholicity: Ecclesiological Reflections on Alain Badiou's Pauline Universalism," *New Blackfriars* 92.1041 (2011): 574–590.

93   A similar critique of "Badiou's militant equivocality" of "playing, on the one hand, on the proximity to, and on the other hand, on the distance from Christianism" was also made by Gérald Sfez, "L'antijudaïsme d'Alain Badiou. Le nom de vérité,» in *Le genre humain: L'antijudaïsme à l'épreuve de la philosophie et de la théologie*, ed. Danielle Cohen-Levinas et Antoine Guggenheim (Paris: Seuil, 2016), 474. Remaining, however, in contrast to Segré's (more talmudic?) intervention, in *external* polemics, Sfez's conclusion is that "Anti-Judaism is not a conjunctural or peripheral in Badiou's thought. It is central" (476). In other words, based on the same critical observation, Sfez proves to Badiou that he is anti-Jewish, whereas Segré proves to him that he is Jewish.

the word "Jew" so as to have it function not as a "particular identity predicate" for the sole politics of national statehood, but rather as importing "a universalist and egalitarian meaning of this word," which, on the other hand, would not only imply negation of the Jewish.

Badiou accepted this offer. In his reply to Segré, "Argued Discussion with Ivan Segré,"[94] a title that underlies the difference between this critical encounter and the more violent polemics around Badiou's texts on Jews, between two different types of polemics, which correspond perhaps to the two different types of uses of the word "Jew," Badiou in fact showed himself "pleased" by Segré's argument about "the relation between orthodox Jewish study and philosophy" (201). "Orthodox Jewish study," the same "Talmudic tradition" that has been a third pillar of the reactionary "SIT," is now acknowledged as somehow akin to philosophy, i.e., acknowledged as belonging to the sphere of truth, what I call the epistemic realm, and so susceptible to be perceived as embodying positive political epistemology:

> To the empirical definition according to which "Jewish" is a communitarian name that may without difficulties also be the name of a State, my interlocutor opposes a conception infinitely more profound and refined, i.e., that "Jewish" *is the name of a thought*.... As transmissible in the figure of study and maintenance of its achievements, particularity designates a spiritual place, in a certain respect trans-temporal, and whose formal characteristics are in any case comparable to those that my philosophy, this contemporary Platonism, designates as being those of truth.... It follows that this type of particularity is comparable to a process of localization of a possible universal. From this point of view, "Jewish" may be identified with no State. (201)

By identifying the conception of "Jewish" as "the name of thought," and thus indicating the possible perception of Jewish being as epistemo-political performance, Badiou takes a decisive step beyond anti-anti-Semitic discourse. This step requires a revised historiography, revised fidelity. It requires a re-reading of Paul, in which the philosopher's perspective, as suggested by Segré, is better articulated from the point of view of the Jews with whom

---

94   Alain Badiou, "Discussion argumentée avec Ivan Segré," *Lignes* 30 (2009): 201–206.

Paul broke—this time seen not as a anti-universal particularistic "sect," but as "a process of localization of a possible universal":

> In many places in my book on Paul, I speak of participation in a process of truth, or of a "truth of Paul." Considering the name Jewish conceived as thought, such statements are inadmissible. Since, if Paul preaches a break with the place of thought designated by this name, he cannot do it, according to my own criteria, but from the point of view of an event *that would affect this place in a real* (or ontological) *way*. However, I myself say that the Paulinian event (the resurrection of Christ) consists in a fable. A fable, as discursive elaboration of the imaginary, may well affect an empirical community and its representations, but it cannot affect a thought that is constituted as such. Consequently, Paul's alleged universalizing break, if conceived empirically as detachment from a community, does not have a proper value as the universality of a truth. (202)

Badiou's claims to the contrary in his Paul book were, the philosopher must accordingly admit, inconsistent with his philosophy, with philosophy *tout court*, were thus anti-philosophical or "rhetorical" (204). Once again, Boyarin in mind, one may ask whether Badiou's original reading of Paul was rather too philosophical, or too Platonic, in focusing exclusively on Paul's universalist "theory," disregarding the actual event and procedure of truth. Rereading Paul, an alleged *founder* of universalism, in fact shakes this foundation, and consequently leads Badiou to call into question the very category of "universalism": "It is true that this conception, which obscures the site of creation of eternal truths, which is always singular, lends itself to appropriation by imperialism.... And so, 'universalism' becomes a suspicious designation. In a recent debate with Etienne Balibar, I affirmed that *I was not a 'universalist'*.... Philosophy, for me, mustn't be a legitimization of universalism, but a theory of the processes of truth" (204).

Badiou concludes his text by suggesting the "continuation of the discussion between the Jewish place of study and the (Greek?) place of philosophy" (205). I will conclude this chapter by indicating one possible path of such continuation in Badiou's text. If philosophy is a theory of the processes of truth, "the Jew of study" would be an actual enactment of such a process, i.e., of the occurrence of truth as a process of its subjectivation—an epistemo-political truth emerging as the historical fidelity of a subjectivized collective. The concrete figure that Badiou perceives as such a

Jewish subject is not Benny Lévy, as Ivan Segré was trying to show, but Ivan Segré himself. In his preface to Segré's *Qu'appelle-t-on penser Auschwitz?*, "What Is Called to Think Auschwitz?," Segré's anti-anti-anti-Semitic collection of essays of the same year 2009,[95] Badiou writes: "Ivan Segré, in fact, inhabits this completely singular mental place that bears the name 'Jewish study.'"[96] It is in this text that Badiou further provides two observations pertaining to "the constitutive traits of Jewish study," pointing at two traits of this process of truth, this *thought*, which in fact presents it as performance of political epistemology. First, epistemologically, Badiou identifies in Segré's Jewish study—which, I recall, for the reader Badiou consisted to a considerable extent in a study of Badiou's own texts—"the priority of the letter and of its localized power over general interpretation" (9), in other words, "study" as a localized, situated, and performative *process* of truth, as *political* epistemology. Second, politically, Badiou identifies in Segré's Jewish orthopraxis, the observance of *mitzvos*, not particularistic sectarianism, but "the distance that it imposes with respect to the common world, its opinions, its prescriptions, its modes and its common wickedness" (12), i.e., a *philosophical* praxis, political *epistemology*.

This chapter presented and analyzed the second position of the anti-anti-Semitic discourse. Anti-anti-Semitism was characterized as critique of anti-Semitism by way of negating the epistemic value of Jewish being, thereby delegitimizing any possibility of making valid epistemic statements about Jewishness—either critique or affirmation. The first position, as analyzed in Chapter 2, carried out this epistemic negation of Jewishness by conceiving of any notion of (and judgment on) Jewish episteme as arising from anti-Semitism, whether as anti-Semitic hallucination of imaginary Judaism (Adorno and Horkheimer) or as anti-Semitic interpersonal production of real Jewish self-consciousness (Sartre). Either way, Jewish episteme is reduced to anti-Semitic episteme, or rather to anti-Semitic pseudo-epistemic or non-epistemic consciousness: psychology without knowledge.

---

95 Ivan Segré, *Qu'appelle-t-on penser Auschwitz?* (Paris: Lignes, 2009).
96 Alain Badiou, "Préface," 9–15, 11.

The second position, as analyzed in this chapter, restored anti-Semitic knowledge by acknowledging its object—Jewish episteme—as *real*. Jewish episteme is thus extracted from the anti-Semitic mind and posited as an independent collective historical agent, the Jews. The realm of the second anti-anti-Semitic position is not psychology, but political history—whether as factual (Arendt) or as theological-eventual (Badiou). The *negation* of Jewish episteme is now carried out not by reducing it to the anti-Semitic episteme, but on the contrary by interpreting it as the origin of anti-Semitism, such that Jewish episteme would hold the core elements of anti-Semitic thought. This ultimately means, once again, reducing Jewish episteme to anti-Semitic episteme—this time not psychologically (Jewish episteme is a figment of the anti-Semitic mind), but conceptually (Jewish episteme is based on the same fundamental notions—particularism, racism, identitarianism—as anti-Semitic thought).

A third, more recent anti-anti-Semitic position reaffirms the second position's acknowledgment of the reality of Jewish episteme as located in the domain of politico-theological history. It does not, however, like the second position, attribute the anti-Semitic conception of Jewishness to Jews themselves. Instead, the third anti-anti-Semitic position affirms the anti-Semitic origin of the anti-Semitic episteme, including its idea of Jewishness, while nonetheless tracing this anti-Semitic perception of Jewish being back, as a condition, to a real Jewish episteme. This Jewish episteme, however, is not identical to anti-Semitism but constitutes its *opposite*. Nevertheless, although it offers an opposition between anti-Semitic and Jewish knowledge, the third position remains within the anti-anti-Semitic discourse, or even paradigmatically performs it, since the Jewish knowledge that it posits is nothing but anti-anti-Semitism itself, i.e., the negation of any Jewish knowledge, which negation, for the third position, would paradoxically constitute the very essence of Jewishness.

4 The Anti-Anti-Semitic Jew

Jean-Luc Nancy

THIS THIRD ANTI-ANTI-SEMITIC POSITION, of the *anti-anti-Semitic Jew*, is the most potent. It possesses the potency of embodiment, in that it purports to articulate and accordingly generates a *Jewish* position or consciousness, a specific figure and performance of *Jewishness*. It in fact seems that the *anti-anti-Semitic Jew* functions as an archetype that is operative at the roots of various contemporary conceptions and *self*-conceptions of Jewish being. For this reason, this anti-anti-Semitic position, or elements thereof, are no doubt identifiable in works that shape the contemporary discourse not just on but *of* Jewishness. For the purpose of this chapter, however, I wish to focus on a text that remains within the boundaries of direct polemics against anti-Semitism, namely within primary anti-anti-Semitic discourse. To reconnect to my point of departure, I chose a text that intervened in the recent controversy on Heidegger and anti-Semitism: Jean-Luc Nancy's *Banalité de Heidegger*, "The Banality of Heidegger."[1] My analysis will also refer to Nancy's more recent *Exclu le juif en nous*, "The Excluded Jew in Us," which further develops his anti-anti-Semitic argument on some crucial points.[2]

---

1   Jean-Luc Nancy, *Banalité de Heidegger* (Paris: Galilée, 2015); translated by Jeff Fort as *The Banality of Heidegger* (New York: Fordham University Press, 2017).
2   Jean-Luc Nancy, *Exclu le juif en nous* (Paris: Galilée, 2018). See also Danielle Cohen-Levinas and Jean-Luc Nancy, *Inventions à deux voix: Entretiens* (Paris: Editions du Félin, 2015), 161–174.

Banalities

As its title "The Banality of Heidegger" suggests, the basic intervention of Nancy's essay on the question of Heidegger's anti-Semitism was to locate it in the realm of epistemological abnormality, pathology, or irrelevancy, diagnosing it as suffering from "banality." Nancy thereby inscribed his analysis in the anti-anti-Semitic tradition that reaches back at least to Adorno and Horkheimer's diagnosis of anti-Semitism as the epistemic pathology of "paranoia," the sick mind.[3] It should be nonetheless noted that "banality" is rather the abnormality of *over*-normality, the perversion of the too common or, as Nancy says, the "vulgar." Indeed, more than to Adorno and Horkheimer, *The Banality of Heidegger*'s explicit reference is of course to Hannah Arendt's *Banality of Evil*. In direct reference to Arendt, who understood banality as "thoughtlessness,"[4] Nancy too, by characterizing Heidegger's anti-Semitism as "banal," means to say it was "without thought by definition,"[5] asserting an "untenable link" between thought and anti-Semitism, which would thus lie outside of the—legitimate—epistemic realm.

There is, however, an important difference between Nancy's and Arendt's diagnosis of banality. Arendt uses this category within the context of a criminal trial in order to diagnose the mental disposition of the individual—Eichmann—who is operating as a cog in a bureaucratically organized machinery of mass murder. Her point was that even though Eichmann caused *evil*, his actions were not done with or predominantly determined by evil intentions; rather, he was operating as a bureaucrat, in the mode of banality. This was what in Arendt's eyes made his criminal conviction so difficult. Nancy's use of "banal" no doubt *also* applies to the intellectual disposition of the individual thinker Heidegger vis-à-vis the prevailing discourse of anti-Semitism, which the philosopher uncritically adopted. However, the main "banality" that Nancy's essay identifies is not only Heidegger's but the banality of anti-Semitism itself: "The most banal, vulgar, trivial and miry discourse that has been long moving around in Europe and that since about thirty years [prior to Heidegger's anti-

---

3   Cf. Nancy, *Exclu le juif*, 58.
4   *The Banality of Evil*, 287.
5   Nancy, *Banalité*, 15.

Semitic notes] has given itself the miserable publication of the *Protocols of the Elders of Zion*" (39).

There is no doubt a conceptual path in Arendt connecting Eichmann's thoughtless banality with the elimination of individual thought in twentieth century's totalitarian "ideology," one of whose constitutive components according to Arendt has been anti-Semitism. Nonetheless, it was precisely Arendt's refusal to see the Nazi crimes "in their utter banality," as Karl Jaspers suggested to her, which stood at the center of their 1946 correspondence, to which her later use of this concept can be traced.[6] The whole paradox for her was precisely that Eichmann's banality was the vehicle of "evil," which she on the other hand refused to demonize, and instead, and as an antidote to the perverse epistemology of this totalitarian evil itself ("ideology"), attempted to "comprehend'" by analyzing its intricate historical "origins." Arendt's analysis of *The Origins of Totalitarianism*, in particular her analysis of anti-Semitism, as discussed above, is in no way informed by the category of "banality."

For Nancy, in contrast, "banality," lack of thought, is the main concept for understanding—or rather for precluding the possibility of understanding—not only Heidegger's disposition regarding anti-Semitic discourse, but anti-Semitism itself or even any anti-Judaism. Indeed, where Arendt makes the distinction between (abstract) totalitarian anti-Semitism and (historically grounded) traditional hatred of Jews, for Nancy the banality of anti-Semitism lies in "the rejection of a supposed bad or false principle (or beginning) embodied or rather endured in a people, a race, a figure designated and destined (messianic, therefore, or in some way christic)" (83). In other words, the problem with anti-Semitism, its banality, is not that it speaks against Jews, but that it at all perceives "Jews"—a people, a race or most generally a historical "figure"—as embodying something that can legitimately be rejected or criticized, a "principle."[7] It is here that becomes visible the negative political epistemology underlying Nancy's anti-anti-Semitism, which nonetheless—and this paradox is constitutive as will be shown below—immediately proceeds to the operation of identifying and naming a historical figure or embodiment for the "bad or false principle"

---

6 Hannah Arend and Karl Jaspers, *Briefwechsel 1926–1969* (München/Zürich: Pieper, 1996), 98f.
7 Cf. Nancy, *Exclu le juif*, 13.

that it rejects, i.e., for the banality of historical figuration itself, namely the historical embodiment of embodiment: the "christic."

It should be insisted that Nancy's specific intervention in the Heidegger controversy in fact, in line with the basic anti-anti-Semitic nature of this debate as I analyzed it in Chapter 1, does not consist in refuting Heidegger's negative statements about the Jews but in refuting the very philosophical validity of *any* statements concerning Jews or any other historical collective of "people." Thus, Nancy's critique of Heidegger's anti-Semitic statements concerns the entire intellectual framework in which they arose, namely Heidegger's *Seinsgeschichte* of the early 1940s, the characteristic feature of which, according to Nancy, was the "necessity of a people" (27), namely the articulation of ontological moments and processes in the narrative form, as events of history, with beginnings and ends, performed and embodied by "peoples." In Heidegger's narrative, if the beginning or "first beginning" of the story of "the West" took place in the body of "the Greek," it is "the Jewish people" that is "the privileged actor of the decline of the West, or at least it constitutes its most characteristic figure" (26). It seems to me debatable to what extent this observation is supported by the handful of very brief notes concerning Jews in Heidegger's vast corpus on *Seinsgeschichte*. Be that as it may, Nancy subscribes here to Trawny's analysis of Heidegger's anti-Semitism as *seinsgeschichtlich*, as analyzed above, consisting in ascribing epistemic meaning to historical collectives, which for Trawny would transgress the realm of philosophy and arise instead from the world of myth.

At this point, Nancy's "banality" thesis immediately raises the same question as all attempts, anti-anti-Semitic or others, of discrediting thought as epistemic pathology by denying its relation to reality, namely the question pertaining to the undisputable historical reality of the discredited thought itself. The assertion that it has nothing to do with its object (here "the Jews") immediately raises the pressing question of why it has this object as its object, or more precisely what in this object makes it susceptible to this kind of thought. Why the Jews? Or as Nancy puts it, intervening in the controversy on Heidegger's anti-Jewish statements: "From where does Heidegger draw this figure?" (39).

It is noteworthy that Nancy rejects the *second* anti-anti-Semitic position, whereby the pathology of anti-Semitic episteme ultimately draws from and reproduces the pathology of Jewish episteme. It is this position that I indicated in Trawny and other voices in the current Heidegger debate, and articulated more meticulously in the work of Hannah Arendt and Alain Badiou. Indeed, as I already pointed out with respect to Nancy's use of the category "banality," notwithstanding the explicit Arendtian reference, his analysis of anti-Semitism diverges from hers. Not only does he consider "banal" more than just Heidegger's individual disposition, but, unlike Arendt, the entire anti-Semitic discourse; he also identifies and seems to be more attentive than Arendt to the danger of "transferring" anti-Semitic ideas to a Jewish origin. In fact, Nancy discerns an inherent feature of the "anti-anti" structure, the polemic against the polemic, namely that what anti-Semitism is accused of—in Nancy's case "banality"—can be easily turned into anti-Semitism's accusation against the Jews. "One can say that Heidegger shares the banality of a public spirit for whom the Jews incarnate the devouring banalization of the world—the loss of the spirit of peoples in the vulgar universal" (40).[8] The banality of anti-Semitism would be to accuse Jews of banality. However, and this is crucial, the "banalities" here are not identical but in fact contradictory. The banality, or thoughtlessness, that Nancy attributes to anti-Semitism consists in attributing the bad principle, i.e., "banality," to a people. In contrast, the banality that anti-Semitism attributes to the Jews, on Nancy's reading, is rather the "loss of the spirit of the peoples in the vulgar universal." In other words, anti-Semitism, as Nancy understands it, does not imitate but opposes the Jews.

Nancy is thus closer to the *first* anti-anti-Semitic position, inasmuch as his analysis of anti-Semitism focuses *mainly*—and this is a significant qualification—on the anti-Semitic episteme, as the paradigmatic epistemopolitical agent. In the current Heidegger debate, which opposed philosophy to anti-Semitism, Nancy has been one of the important voices to caution against a too quick dismissal of anti-Semitism from the epistemic realm, namely as a serious theme for the philosophical discussion. Against this dismissal, which I discussed in Chapter 1, *The Banality of Heidegger* calls for engaging thought on "the profound reasons for our condemnations [of Anti-Semitism]" (23). In *Exclu le juif en nous*, Nancy even warns against the "inverse banality" to Heidegger's anti-Semitic banality, namely "the banality of denunciation," a sort of vulgar anti-anti-Semitism, performed as

---

8   Nancy refers here to Heidegger's notes on Jewish "talent for calculation," as manifesting "empty rationality," thus so to speak "thoughtlessness"; and further on how this "race" leads to the deracination of all races; see Chapter 1.

a "guarantee of right-mindedness [*bien-pensance*]."[9] Nancy's—accordingly anti-anti-anti-Semitic—intervention thus explicitly announces a break "with all of the best analyses dedicated to anti-Semitism," such as "those of Adorno and Horkheimer, of Poliakov, of Arendt and of Milner" (21), and instead attempts to follow Philippe Lacoue-Labarth in thinking anti-Semitism as grounded in a profound "historical and spiritual complex" (20).

There is an apparent paradox, of course, in urging to invest thought in something that is from the outset declared to be "banal and without thought by definition."[10] Nevertheless, it is precisely this paradox of positing anti-Semitism within thought as non-thought, as the limit of thought inside of thought, which characterizes, as I tried to show, philosophy's post–World War II anti-anti-Semitism, to which Nancy thus connects the current Heidegger controversy. More precisely, Nancy, notwithstanding his declaration of going beyond Adorno and Horkheimer, similarly to them, attempts to identify the epistemic perversity of anti-Semitism as the very perverse *core* of mainstream epistemology, what Adorno and Horkheimer call "Enlightenment," and Nancy, among others, with Heidegger, "metaphysics." This pathologization or profound condemnation of thought immediately entails its relativization as a temporal-existential phenomenon, as a *certain*, problematic tradition or history of thought, namely thought as a (deficient) epistemic *project*, historical and collective, political, that is *epistemo-political*, which Adoro and Horkheimer call "civilization" and Nancy "the West" (*l'Occident*).

We, the West

It is noteworthy, and reveals a structural difficulty in a certain type of negative political epistemology, as well as in the "anti-anti-" discourse, that the condemnation of positive political epistemology, i.e., of the "banality" and "mythology" of perceiving and contemplating thought as embodied by collective historical figures, by "peoples," the paradigm of which would be anti-Semitism, veers, by the force of this condemnation, this "accusation," into the introduction of a collective historical figure that would embody the condemned episteme, i.e., anti-Semitism, as its factual-historical agent.

---

9   Nancy, *Exclu le juif*, 14–15.
10 Nancy, *Banalité*, 15.

It will shortly become clearer how this paradox reaches its culmination in the decisive act of *self*-accusation, i.e., self-affirmation through self-condemnation, performed by Nancy.

It is in fact by way of radical self-accusation, by accusation of a "we," of "us," that Nancy exhorts philosophy to take up the question of anti-Semitism, an exhortation that immediately entails the naming of this plural first person: the West, or "European humanity." "Two thirds of a century after the extermination, we still haven't sufficiently faced what happened to *us*, to *us* European humanity, which has become fully global [in modernity]."[11] One cannot avoid noting that the exhortation of Europe to self-reflection on its anti-Semitism and Nazism does not invoke it as the *agent*, as the *Täter*, but rather as the vehicle, object, and even target, almost *victim* of the events: "what happened to *us*" (*ce qui nous est arrivé*), what "happened to our civilization and through it" (87–88).[12] Putting aside the question of what role this configuration leaves to the Jews, it is crucial to indicate how accusing "our thought" of anti-Semitism, and by the radical force of this accusation, immediately entails or in fact demands most radically hypostasizing this thought in the historical image of "our culture," through the unrelenting penitent imperative of exposing its "roots" and "heart." The question of anti-Semitism, Nancy thus admonishes, "is addressed to us, all of us, to any exercise of thought, today as before. It is not enough to condemn the ignominy of anti-Semitism: one must expose its roots—and this means nothing less than intervening at the very heart of our culture" (85). As the title of his recent book suggests, the story of anti-Semitism is for him the story of "The Excluded Jew *in Us*."

That anti-anti-Semitism, condemning the figuration of the Jews, is a discursive apparatus for the self-imagination and self-figuration of "the West" as a historical collective—this already became visible in David Nirenberg's project *Anti-Judaism: A Western Tradition*, which I discussed above in the

---

11   Nancy, *Banalité*, 23, original emphases.
12   Note the remarkable similarity with the Stuttgarter Schulderklärung (*Stuttgart Declaration of Guilt*) of the Council of the Evangelical Church in Germany (EKD) of Oktober 19, 1945: "[Wir wissen] uns mit unserem Volk nicht nur in einer großen Gemeinschaft der Leiden …, sondern auch in einer Solidarität der Schuld. Mit großem Schmerz sagen wir: *Durch uns* ist unendliches Leid über viele Völker und Länder gebracht worden" (my emphasis). I am grateful to Luca Di Blasi for this reference.

context of Adorno and Horkheimer. Nonetheless, Nancy goes further, and indeed attempts to explicitly formulate the precise *locus* and function of anti-Semitism at the root of the West, or even as this root itself, so to speak not just as *a* but as *the* Western tradition. It is thus that the perception of anti-Semitism as an independent and self-referential, as "paranoid" *episteme*, is perfected by the upgrade of this *episteme* to feature as the very paradigm of Western self-consciousness. Indeed, in complete contrast to Arendt, who traces back anti-Semitism to Jew-hatred, and then to Jewish self-consciousness, Nancy strikingly explicates anti-Semitism not as hate of Jews, but—and this is his main thesis in the essay—as the "self-hate of the West" (54): "we do not like ourselves" (59).[13]

It is important to linger on this central point and to attempt to understand its meaning and implications for Nancy's analysis of anti-Semitism. According to Nancy, the "self-hate" that characterizes the West and is the root for its inherent anti-Semitism is intimately connected to "the most vehement will of self-affirmation" (61), both being manifestations of a fundamental desire or will that would constitute the essence of "the West": the will to "self"—*soi*. The concept of "self" and of a will to self is highly abstract and requires careful treatment and determination, which *The Banality of Heidegger*, as a local intervention in a current debate, provides only to a very limited extent. The critique of the category of the "self," in fact, as Nancy intends it, raises a polemic with an entire tradition of thought, the "Western," to speak with Nancy, for which, like in Hegel, the *selbst* is a fundamental category of thought itself, thought *tout court*. Consequently, in this tradition, and Nancy indeed locates himself within this tradition, putting in question the "self" amounts to putting in question thought itself, at the risk of—to remind of "banality"—sheer thoughtlessness.

Articulated in the Heideggerian context, Nancy's critique of the will to self presents a certain ambivalence. One central notion for Nancy is the "self" as "self-foundation" or "auto-foundation," the self that is the founda-

---

13 The—disturbingly biological—model to which Nancy, in his recent essay, refers to describe the essential dynamic of the phenomenon of anti-Semitism is "auto-immunity," i.e., of the West against itself; see Nancy, *Exclu le juif*, 22. What would make anti-Semitism a historically singular phenomenon of sociopolitical exclusion is—and this is Nancy's basic thesis—that Western exclusion of the Jews has been an "internal exclusion" to the "European organism" (24).

tion for itself, namely the self as the category for absolute being, which is entirely self-referential, having no relation but to itself, having no essence but its absolute identity with itself. As such, the "self" could be said to constitute the central category of the "subject," consummating the notion of being as substance, namely eternal, unchanging, and absolute presence, which for Heidegger has indeed been the foundational thought of the West, the *Abendland*, as "metaphysics." Heidegger's entire project, or at least considerable parts thereof, can be read, with Nancy, as articulating "the West" as the existential unfolding of this ontology from eternal substance to absolute subject, in the Western shapes of science, politics, and history, namely what Nancy describes as the "logical, political, truth-related and destinal auto-foundation" (89). For Heidegger, and this is the basis for his critique of Western tradition, these subject-oriented, self-oriented forms of logic, politics, truth, and history have in some fundamental way perverted or paralyzed logic, politics, truth, and history by disconnecting them from thought or from what Heidegger calls "the question of being." This critique of the West can be further read as criticizing the Western tendency to disconnect *polis* and *episteme*, namely as a critique of Western *negative* political epistemology.

Nonetheless, as should already be evident from the aforesaid, this is not Nancy's direction, rather the contrary. It is precisely in Heidegger's positive political epistemology, namely the perception of thought (i.e., the question or truth of being) in the existential-historical performance of a "people," that Nancy, in perfect coherence with the general discourse of the debate, identifies the basis for Heidegger's anti-Semitism, and thus, as has been now established, his complicity with the West and with the Western "self." Accordingly, what Nancy criticizes in "self-foundation" is not primarily the "self," namely as negation or oblivion of "foundation." On the contrary, his critique concerns "foundation" itself, and the "self" as the basis or foundation of foundation. It is in Heidegger's conception of thought in terms of "the initial, the foundation and the origin, the authentic and the proper" (62–63), in the figure of a "beginning" that holds the promise of "completion" (66), that Nancy perceives Heidegger's complicity with Western metaphysics of "self"—and accordingly with the "banality" of its anti-Semitism: "The motive of the beginning assembles all the values of authenticity, originality and propriety around which organizes itself what we can justly designate as a major banality of the most common metaphysician *doxa*" (80).

Foundation, origin, beginning, proper, end, destination. Nancy's critique of the "self" accuses the West and its metaphysics of a historical, evental, or destinal ontology, which implicates thought from the outset in the temporality of a project, of history, of politics. This ontology would be what Heidegger, notwithstanding his critique of the West, still shares with Western metaphysics. Disregarding the difficult questions that arise from the critique of historical or evental ontology *as such*, it should nonetheless be indicated that, as already visible in my brief summary of the Heideggerian project, this evental ontology that Nancy criticizes—far from being a discrete and marginal element in Heidegger's work, like for instance his anti-Jewish statements, which could be thus interpreted as an ossified remnant of metaphysical discourse—rather constitutes the heart of what Heidegger understands as the *overcoming* of metaphysics. It is precisely the *negation* of existence, of history, of temporality, of *being*, which for Heidegger makes up metaphysics. Consequently, it is not clear how much of Heidegger would be left, if any, after relieving his thought of the "banalities."

But Nancy's critique of historico-political epistemology is not only hard to reconcile with the Heideggerian project. In addition, as was already indicated, it appears to be undermined by its own articulation in Nancy's text. In fact, in order to explain the exact connection between the self-hate of the West, which would derive from a fundamental will to self, implicating thought in historical narration—*mythology*—of events and peoples, on the one hand, and on the other hand actual anti-Semitism, which has been as a matter of historical fact directed against Jews, Nancy is required to invest his own critical thought in history, "to turn to history" (51), albeit—Nancy is aware of the difficulty—"a history that is perhaps non-historial" (51), and to articulate his critique of historico-political epistemology in the form of a historico-political narrative: the "long provenance of anti-Semitism" (49).

This story has a central protagonist, a historical collective actor, a paradigmatic figure or "self": "Christianism." Christianism is not just a conceptual, ideal paradigm or type, but literally the *principle* of the self, its actual beginning and historical embodiment, so to speak the self of the self, inasmuch as the long provenance of anti-Semitism, i.e., Western self-hating self-assertion, goes back to "the birth of Christianism" (49) or the "Christian event" (81). It should be noted how Nancy's narrative of Christianism's birth echoes the same paradox as the Christian narrative of the birth of Christ, namely the paradox of succession as beginning, or the offspring as *Ursprung*. Indeed, Nancy's Christian "self" is born to at least two parents. First, insofar as the birth of Christianity can be described as "a mutation of the identity of the West" (52), "the West" itself, which nonetheless could only have become its "self" (and thus "the West") with the birth of the "self" as Christian. Second, "Judaism" or "Israel," insofar as the birth of Christianity can be also seen as "an internal transformation of the Judaism of Israel" (52). The identity of Christianity's Jewish parent is even more precarious than that of its Western parent, to the extent that Nancy—speaking from the constructed perspective of a pre-Christian West—can identify in the birth of Christianity the "apparition of *Judentum* in the history of the West" (49).[14]

Interestingly, Nancy's narrative of the Christian birth of the Western self also involves birth complications of a more Old Testament kind, namely that the same womb issues different children, who can become the enemies-brothers, the rival twins. Thus, referencing Daniel Boyarin, Nancy perceives in the birth of Christianity an event of double birth, namely also of "rabbinic Judaism of the diaspora," who would accordingly be the "twin brother" of Christianity (49).[15] It is therefore not just in the "Christian event," but in what should be designated more precisely as the "Judeo-Christian twin relations of the first centuries of our era" (52) that is located the birth or emergence of the West as will to self. Nevertheless, in conformity with mainstream historiography, which with Nancy may be called "Western" historiography or, if "history" is one of the categories that constitute the West, historiography *tout court*, Nancy's narrative tells only the story of the Christian twin, keeping total silence about its other, diasporic rabbinic Judaism.

Consequently, the story told by Nancy about the emergence of Western anti-Semitism in the Christian birth of the "self," whose constant desire for auto-foundation, to *create* itself, constantly generates self-hate, namely hate for what it always already *is*, reproduces more or less the narrative

---

14   These genealogical difficulties are to some extent attenuated or rather dislocated in the more complex historiographical narrative offered by Nancy in his more recent essay, by the introduction of the site or "hearth" (*foyer*) in which "the Christian event" took place, namely "the Roman hearth" (*Exclu le juif*, 32), which fused together "Greek logos, Latin technology and Jewish monotheism" (31).
15   The reference is to Daniel Boyarin, *Border Lines: The Partition of Judaeo-Christianity* (Philadelphia: University of Pennsylvania Press, 2004)

of Christian supersession, namely the supersession of Judaism, Israel of the flesh, by Christianity as *Verus Israel* (56), Israel of the spirit. Of course, Nancy's rendition of this narrative is done from a critical point of view, and thus offers a powerful philosophical problematization of the Christian story. Nancy's critique of Christianity to a large extent receives and conceptually develops Boyarin's critique of Badiou's celebration of Saint Paul as "the foundation of universalism," as discussed in the previous chapter. In contrast to Boyarin, however, it is not the idea of universalism, but more specifically the notion of its "foundation" that stands at the center of Nancy's critique. Thus, on Nancy's reading, the Christian "foundation of universalism" is the emergence of a radical "self," whose desire for radical self-foundation generates a radical negation of any preexistent, received being, identity or history of itself, down to its own body or "flesh," or as Badiou calls it, the "site" of its event, which for Christianity would be the Jewish. The Christian "self" founds itself by detaching "itself from its received identity (which is called 'Jewish people')" (52). The ensuing Christian Jew-hatred is "hate of that which evades self-foundation" (59).[16] And henceforth, Nancy's narrative continues, each time Christianity, who becomes the West, will redefine itself—anti-Judaism reappears. One may infer that the same mechanism was also at work in Heidegger's thought, generating the link between the vision of a "new beginning" to the *Black Notebooks*' anti-Jewish entries.

This is the story. I already indicated the paradox in the way that Nancy's critique of historical-political epistemology immediately generates or reproduces a historical-political narrative that is almost identical to the narrative it criticizes, only in the mode of condemnation. Interestingly, Nancy's own analysis seems to provide the conceptual structure for explicating this paradox. It is indeed hard not to discern in Nancy's discourse a performance of the very same dynamics that it identifies, articulates, and criticizes as the constitutive operation of "the West," namely self-foundation by self-condemnation.

In fact, having presented, by way of a confession, of a radical self-reflection and self-interrogation of "us" on the roots and heart of our

---

16   Cf. Nancy, *Exclu le juif*, where Christian anti-Judaism would be based on the two "passions" of "abolishing all distances" (49) (Christian love) and of auto-foundation (50).

culture, a powerful self-portrait of the Christian West, this confession turns into a radical self-condemnation and self-flagellation, a radical imperative of self-negation, commanding itself to renounce all "self." It is thus in the mode of self-imperative that Nancy concludes: "One must (*il faut*) learn to break with the model [adopted by our history], of a progress in the conquest of the world by man and of man by its own exponential ends" (85). Speaking in the terms of the Heideggerian self-critique of the West, Nancy stresses that it is not enough to subtract "being" (*Sein*) from traditional metaphysical "ontology": "one must also retract [being] from the naming of a *Seyn* as well as any other [naming], as well as from the destination that any name no doubt entails. In other words, one must learn to exist without being and without destination, not pretending to commence or re-commence anything—nor conclude either" (85).[17]

No beginning, no end, no destination, no being, no name—is this not negating pure and simple any project? Nonetheless, this negation of project is itself formulated as a paradoxical project of learning to have no project, as a "task": "Dissociating the 'question of being' or of the 'ontological difference' from the dispositive of the origin or the principality, this is the task, identical to the task of dissolving the haunting of the 'self' and of oneself" (63). It is hard not to detect here at least an echo of the call or even voice of the self-proclaiming self-lessness, Badiou would say "universality," which Nancy himself critically exposed as being precisely the seminal generation of the "self," bearing the specific names of "Christianity," "the West," and "Europe."

Interruption

Nevertheless, I do not think Nancy's operation is a simple reproduction of what he critically describes as the Western performance. This is a crucial point for my purpose, since it also means that I do not think that Nancy reproduces the anti-Semitism that he detects at the root of the West, nor any of the first two anti-anti-Semitic positions that I analyzed. To understand this point, a broader perspective on Nancy's work is required, which

---

17   Cf. Nancy, *Exclu le juif*, 68: "We must [*il faut*] stop with the principles, with the principle of relying on principles ('origins', 'natures', 'subjects'), because it is in principle exclusive, expulsive and exterminating."

I cannot hope to provide here in any degree of appropriateness. My focus here is on his reflections on Jewish being and *episteme*, in its conceptual nexus to his reflections on anti-Semitism, as presented above. It is therefore only as a passage from the latter to the former that I will hazard a general observation on the larger context of Nancy's oeuvre, more precisely on his epistemo-political critique of the West.[18]

In earlier works, Nancy has provided more detailed descriptions of this figure of "the West," situating his own intervention more accurately within this narrative. Next to the Christian event, as birth and beginning of the West, the central event that defines Nancy's discourse is "modernity," as a moment of culmination, completion, and perfection of the West, as a certain *end* of its history, or of history as such, in relation to which Nancy's intervention locates itself as a retrospect, namely existing already in a certain "contemporary" position beyond modernity, "postmodern." In a sense, it is precisely in giving effect to this position of postmodernity that Nancy's thought consists, its primal and constant task being accordingly the determination—and thus, termination—of "modernity" itself.

To use the conceptuality of *The Banality of Heidegger*, as I analyzed it above, modernity for Nancy, who in this inscribes himself in the intellectual lineage of Heidegger himself as well as already a tradition of postmodern thought, would indeed constitute the completion of the Western aspiration to "self." The modern perfection of the self would mean the abolishment of all relations to non-self, to alterity, exteriority, transcendence and difference, an abolishment of all relations, which would consequently constitute—as Nancy wrote in his earlier work—"the absolute," pure "immanentism," the philosophical paradigm of which Nancy identified in Hegel's work, and its sociopolitical manifestation, again echoing Arendt, in "totalitarianism."

Now, and this may seem trivial but is not, perhaps is even the heart of the matter, Nancy understands the *post*modern operation of his thought as articulating and generating opposition to the modern abolutization of

---

18   For a general introduction to Nancy's work, see Ian James, *The Fragmentary Demand: An Introduction to the Philosophy of Jean-Luc Nancy* (Stanford, CA: Stanford University Press, 2006); B. C. Hutchens, *Jean-Luc Nancy and the Future of Philosophy* (Montreal: McGill-Queen's University Press, 2005); more specifically for the question of politics and the community, see Ignaas Devisch, *Jean-Luc Nancy and the Question of Community* (London: Bloomsbury, 2013).

the Western self, as effecting a break, rupture, or interruption in its pure immanence. This operation is visible, for example, in Nancy's well-known early project on *La Communauté Désoeuvrée* (1983), translated "inoperative community," but perhaps better rendered as the "unemployed" or "out-of-work" community, whose significance for contemporary political epistemology demands a separate analysis, as well as in his historical-epistemological essay on *The Interrupted Myth* (1984).[19] Both follow the logic of postmodern interruption of modernity. Against what he perceives as the preclusion of communal being (*être-en-commun*) by modern totalitarianism of fascist communion, on the one hand, and radical individuality, on the other hand, Nancy proposes the community out-of-work (*désoeuvrée*), i.e., the community as "that which retreats from the work (*oeuvre*), that has nothing more to do with production or with completion, but that encounters interruption, fragmentation, suspense" (79). Similarly, presenting the myth as the "primordial language" of "self-foundation" (114), what Schelling called "tautagorie," such that "the idea of the myth presents perhaps by itself the very idea of the West" (117), and identifying in the modern "myth of the myth" the very completion of Western myth, embodied in the "Nazi myth" (116), it is the "interrupted myth" that Nancy suggests as a postmodern countermeasure.

The fundamental challenge of this undertaking, which already surfaced in the above-analyzed paradox of Nancy's Western critique against the West's self-foundation through self-critique ("self-hate"), lies in the nature of the "interruption" that it promotes, namely in the extent to which it is able to avoid reproducing or confirming and even absolutizing the very logic it seeks to interrupt. The question is, in other words, to what extent an "interruption" is *opposed* or rather on the contrary perfectly *complementary* to the continuum it interrupts. What relation or continuation subsists between the continuum and *its* interruption? More specifically to our context, what kind of relation is designated by the preposition "post"? By what logic is the "post"-modern breaking with the modern and by this very break defined by the modern, namely belongs to it and prolongs its "absolute"?

---

19   Both essays published in Jean Luc Nancy, *La communauté désoeuvrée* (Paris: Christian Bourgois Editeur, 1986, 1990), trans. Peter Connor, Lisa Garbus, Michael Holland, and Simona Sawhney as *The Inoperative Community* (Minneapolis: University of Minnesota Press, 1991).

Pending much more detailed and comprehensive consideration, which Nancy's work certainly deserves, I will point at only one recurrent motif in his analyses, which seems to exemplify or even to singularly express this ambivalence of the "interruption." What I mean is the *necessity* that Nancy attributes to interrupting the Western logic of the absolute immanence of the "self," a necessity that must therefore arise, and that Nancy indeed explicitly derives from the immanent order itself. Nancy thus seems to project a post-Hegelianism that prolongs Hegelianism: "The history of contemporary philosophy, by Marx, Nietzsche and Husserl up to Heidegger, Wittgenstein and Derrida, has operated on no other necessity than [the necessity of breaking the pure immanence], which turns the Hegelian necessity against itself" (213n.83). Hegelian necessity turned against itself remains Hegelian necessity. It is in fact in the internal logic of the absolute itself that Nancy identifies the necessity of its interruption—"the logic of the absolute does violence to the absolute" (18)—which is perhaps therefore no real violence or interruption, or ultimately such that makes no difference.

It is the same logic of necessary interruption that is at work in the out-of-work community and interrupted myth. "The ontology of community has no other task but to radicalize or to aggravate to the point of infringement, and via the thought of being and its differe/ance, the Hegelian thought of the Self" (205). The "being-in-common" that breaks and exposes the pure absolute immanence of the "self" is commanded, namely, by the same logic as the self itself. The community out-of-work, in other words, is still a part, consequence, or continuation of the totalitarian communal project of the West. Similarly, notwithstanding Nancy's insistence that "there is no myth of the interruption of the myth" (153), the crux of his analysis—once again echoing *The Dialectics of Enlightenment*—is the perceptive observation that the supposed modern, enlightened, scientific and rational break with mythology has rather *perfected* the myth by generating the "myth of the myth," namely an interruption of the myth that is inherent to the constitutive logic of the myth. Saying that "we no longer have anything to do with the myth" (117) is still defining "us"—"we—our community, if it is one, our modern, post-modern humanity" (132)—through the (negative) logical necessity of the myth.

The concrete effect that this ambivalent logic risks producing, by criticizing the Western myth as the perfect myth, Western communal work as the perfect work, and Western self as the absolute self, is rendering this self *de facto* absolute, since the only alternative is the interruption of myth, community, and self, which means that in fact there is no alternative. Consequently, the interruption of the Western myth, of "history," by breaking with the historical altogether, would be nothing but the actual performance of the modern notion of "the end of history," its completion. Renouncing the will to the self and the desire to the absolute would mean giving effect to the absolute self, which has in fact perfected itself, reconciled itself with itself, is absolutely present to itself, and no longer desires itself. Postmodernity would be the logical consequence and thus the effectuation and real *presence* of modernity, the nontemporal, nonfigural, anonymous, and universal *paroussia* of the Christian West.

As I said, all this requires a much more careful and detailed discussion, in general and specifically within the rich context of Nancy's oeuvre. If I nonetheless ventured here to formulate this broader observation pertaining to the epistemo-political ambivalence of the "postmodern" performance, as it is visible in some moments of Nancy's work, it was not just an excursion. Rather, the discussion that this observation opens is central for the question of political epistemology in the context and time of post-Heideggerian thought, in the controversy concerning which Nancy's *The Banality of Heidegger* intervenes. More specifically, it seems to me that awareness to the fundamental conceptual dynamics of Nancy's critique of the West is essential for better comprehending his analysis of anti-Semitism, which for him would constitute a seminal and radical manifestation of the West, and the specific type of anti-anti-Semitic position that I identify in it.

Dis-Figuration

In a nutshell, the specificity of this—already third—position, is that in view of anti-Semitism it does not, like the first anti-anti-Semitic position, deny any epistemic category of "Jewish," which would be a pure anti-Semitic projection, but does identify a Jewish episteme to which anti-Semitism reacts.[20] This Jewish episteme is understood as the origin of anti-Semitism, however, not by way of reproduction, as in the second anti-anti-Semitism position, but rather by way of opposition, contradiction, and difference.

---

20 Parts of this and the following section appeared in Elad Lapidot, "Disfigured Friends," *Jewish Studies Quarterly* 27 (2020): 1–21.

The third position thus already marks the limit of anti-anti-Semitism. If it nonetheless remains within anti-anti-Semitic discourse, and in a way constitutes its consummate figure, it is due to its exact understanding of Jewish epistemic being. It is my contention that what happens in the third and most recent anti-anti-Semitic position, of which I believe Nancy's text is a prominent expression, is that the "Jewish" emerges as the figure of the postmodern West. With all the ambivalence that this implies: the Jew becomes the figure of the non-figure, of the non-self. There would be Jewish knowledge whose Jewishness consists in the knowledge that there is no Jewish knowledge. This dis-figure of the Jew would thus constitute the figure of anti-anti-Semitism itself, as the epistemo-political essence of the contemporary West.

In fact, going back to Nancy's text, even though the expression does come up, the connection between Western self-hate and anti-Semitism, or more precisely between Christian Jew-hatred and Judaism, is actually not understood there as consisting in the utter and crude arbitrariness commonly designated as "scapegoat."[21] Rather, by the same paradox whereby Nancy's critique of the Western "self" is carried out through a powerful self-portrait of the West, so his critique of the anti-Semitic "banality" of asserting a Jewish principle or episteme in history nevertheless proceeds to acknowledge the counter-principle to this banality, i.e., to anti-Semitism, the West, and modernity, as historically "Jewish."

Already in the *Interrupted Myth*, Nancy—in a footnote—referred to Maurice Blanchot's anti-anti-Semitic remark, whereby "the Jews embody ... the rejection of myths, the renunciation of idols, the acknowledgment of an ethical order that manifests itself by the respect of the law. In the Jew, in the 'myth of the Jewish', which Hitler wants to annihilate, it is precisely man liberated from myths." Whereupon Nancy immediately performed the transfer from the Jewish to the postmodern by adding: "the 'man liberated from myths' belongs now to a community that we must let come and write itself."[22]

This nexus between the Jewish and the postmodern, in the strict sense that I articulated above, is now further developed and generalized in *The*

---

21   Nancy, *Banalité*, 63; Nancy, *Exclu le juif*, 60.
22   Blanchot, *Les intellectuels en question*, quoted in Nancy, *The Interrupted Myth*, 158n.69. See also Nancy, *Exclu le juif*, 40.

Banality of Heidegger. As a supposed countermovement to the modern absolutization of the Western "self," Nancy indicates a contemporary discourse, strongly influenced by Heidegger himself, which revolves around the concern of "alterity." Alterity would be a central category of resistance to or critique of the modern, a category of postmodernity. Nancy refers to a long list of authors, Sartre, Levinas, Foucault, Derrida, Lacan, Lyotard, Deleuze, who "in numerous ways all turned towards diverse motifs or figures of alterity or multiplicity."[23] Even though all these authors are French, their Frenchness plays no role in Nancy's analysis, is never even mentioned. It is rather by their decisive and absolute detachment from anti-Semitism and its banality (a somewhat striking decisiveness, considering that the banality of anti-Semitism is understood by Nancy to lie in the roots of the West) that the commonality of these French philosophers is characterized, even though only two of them ever identified themselves as Jewish, by their attachment to "a motif of Jewish alterity." "Not only did none of these bodies of thought pick up anything remotely resembling anti-Semitism from the always murmuring gutters of banality, but in various ways a motif of Jewish alterity was introduced—or else was brought to light—in the tradition that had supposed itself to be Greek" (70).

In the context of the Heidegger controversy, it is interesting to note that Nancy joins his voice to a scholarly conversation, which, complicating the debate on Heidegger's anti-Judaism, identifies common features between Heidegger's philosophy and Jewish thought.[24] Considering Nancy's reserves toward historicity, it is remarkable that he perceives this link in the form of a historical transmission, in which the nonetheless anti-Semitic Heidegger would play, despite himself, the role of introducing Jewish thought in postmodernity, or even, more consequently, introducing postmodernity by receiving Jewish alterity into the Western self. "By a paradoxical turn that is not without piquancy or (especially) bitterness, it was by way of Heidegger, although despite him—as well as thanks to a number of his contemporaries such as Cohen, Buber, Benjamin, and Rosenzweig—that this motif [of Jewish alterity] took on importance" (70).

It is thus in Heidegger's work that we can receive from Nancy a first indication of what exactly he understands under the "alterity" that would

---

23   Nancy, *Banalité*, 70.
24   See Lapidot and Brumlik, *Heidegger and Jewish Thought*.

characterize the Jewish. For sure, the recognition of "Jewish" motifs in Heidegger can have many and contradicting meanings, depending on what one understands as "Jewish," and what part of Heidegger one looks at. Nancy's choice is atypical. The Jewish motif of alterity that Nancy detects in the Heideggerian text, as a gateway to a new, different, non-Western manner of thinking, which "turns away from the foundational-destructive rage and from rancor" (71), is found in a concept that is quite—and not coincidentally—marginal in Heidegger's vocabulary, and which Nancy quotes from a rather random fragment of the *Black Notebooks*. It is the notion of "grace," *Gnade*, which Heidegger in the quoted passage offers as *one* meaning of the Greek *charis*, only to stress that "none of our words captures its essence." What Heidegger then says specifically about grace is terse and obscure: "The impossible is man's highest possibility: grace (*Gnade*) or fate/fatality/doom/calamity (*Verhängnis*)."[25]

Even though nothing in the original context of this quote suggests this, Nancy finds it nonetheless important here to indicate that the Greek word *charis*, for which *Gnade*, grace, would for Heidegger be one possible inaccurate translation, "this Greek word," and Heidegger "could not have been unaware of this," "translated—since the Septuagint to the Gospels—the Hebrew name (*chen*) for a thought that is indeed the one to which we refer when we use the word 'grace' in our modern language: the unjustifiable justification that can come from the wholly-outside, in particular when faced with catastrophe, as when *Noah found grace in the eyes of Yhwh*" (71). It would thus be none less than the Jewish God himself whom Heidegger, through the word "grace," introduces into Western thought as pure alterity that is the very principle of alterity, breaking with all immanence of self, grace that is justification beyond justice, given on the only condition "that nothing search for it or demand it," that "we cannot plan it or will it or even know if it will happen or not" (72).

Besides this venturesome hermeneutic feat in reading Heidegger, no less remarkable is Nancy's understanding of this notion of grace as a "Jewish" element in Heidegger and in Western thought. Indeed, it is not only different from the motifs more commonly identified as "Jewish" in Heidegger's thought, such as the attentiveness to language and hermeneutics, to history, to memory, peoplehood, and land. Grace as "the unjustifiable justification

---

25   GA 96, 273.

that can come from the wholly-outside" is precisely what an entire Pauline and later Lutheran tradition has preached as breaking with and liberating from Jewish justice of flesh, history, and law. It is the justification obtained not by works ("we cannot plan it or will it or even know if it will happen or not"), but by faith only, *sola fide sola gratia*. The grace of the loving god is what this same tradition has opposed to a judging god of "rancor," an old spirit of revenge from an old scripture. The translation of this Hebrew scripture to Greek, from *chen* to *charis*, has introduced the event of the New Testament, the event of Christianity, which is as such the event of the Old Testament. It is from a purely Christian perspective that translating back from Greek to the Hebrew of the Old Testament, to the story of Noah, a perfectly Christian canon, is "Jewish." Nancy's assertion of "Jewish alterity" in the seminal Christian notion of grace, a seminal notion of Christianity whose emergence according to him was the birth of the Western "self," is thus, to say the least, confusing. This confusion was attended to—but not resolved—in Nancy's more recent essay by retracing Jewish "alterity" to a Jewish project of "transcendence," which he anchored in the "call" to be heard by the more authentically Jewish *Shema Yisrael*.[26]

There is however in Nancy's text also a second, more precise characterization of what he understands as Jewish alterity, which could be perhaps described as the epistemo-political performance of grace, namely self-dispersion. Nancy indicates this motif not primarily in the Heideggerian text, but in Theodor Lessing's book, published in 1930, on assimilated Jews who become anti-Semitic, like Otto Weininger or Arthur Trebitsch, a phenomenon that Lessing claimed manifests a characteristic—as he titled his book—*Jewish Self-Hate*.[27] The resemblance to Nancy's own observation on Western self-hate is conspicuous, and the two theories actually seem to contradict. In contrast to Nancy's analysis of Western self-hate, however, Lessing's main argument did not consist in claiming that the Jewish was essentially constituted and defined by self-hate, even though it has historically become a central Jewish feature. Rather, for Lessing, Jewish self-hate is primarily the Jewish pathological reaction to centuries of non-Jewish

---

26 Nancy, *Exclu le juif*, 37.
27 Theodor Lessing, *Der jüdische Selbsthaß* (Berlin: Zionistischer Bücherbund, 1930; Nachdruck: München: Matthes and Seitz, 2004); see Nancy, *Banalité*, 44–45.

hate toward Jews: "Because, in order to turn men into dogs, all you need is to shout at them long enough: 'you dog!'"[28]

Nancy, in contrast, suggests another, stronger interpretation, which, necessarily calling into question his thesis on self-hate as an attribute of the West, and source for Western anti-Semitism, now perceives for Jewish self-hate an origin of "Jewish specificity." "The entirety of Europe (of the West), posited in its auto-affirmation ... repudiates in its midst an alien body that threatens it precisely by the fact that it disperses, dissolves or dissimulates its 'self'. Dispersion, dissolution or dissimulation of one's self, this is definitively that to which Jewish specificity comes down to" (45). *Exclu le juif* derives this self-dispersion from the "transcendence" on which the Jewish event would be founded, which has Jewish "autonomy" (self) built on a fundamental "heteronomy."[29] This formulation significantly complicates Nancy's aforementioned account of anti-Semitism as resulting from Western self-hate, which manifests Western will to self-foundation. Western self-hate, generated by Western desire for "auto-affirmation," is now described as addressed more specifically to an internal part of the West ("in its midst"), which is *essentially* "alien," inasmuch as it is constituted, paradoxically, in that it "disperses, dissolves or dissimulates its 'self,'" namely founded, exactly like the West itself, on "internal exclusion" (45). Would the West hate in itself precisely the part that hates itself? Would there be thus two kinds of self-hate, one original, and the second derivative, which hates its own self-hate for the sake of self-love?

Be that as it may, what Nancy suggests here is the Jewish as a figure of a specific episteme, a collective epistemic figure, namely a specifically Jewish epistemo-political figure, which is indeed the origin of anti-Semitism, not by way of reproduction, but by way of opposition. Anti-Semitism would be the opposing reaction ("hate") of the Western "will to self" to the Jewish as the collective figure of a "dispersion, dissolution or dissimulation of

---

28   Lessing, *Der jüdische Selbsthaß*, 17; however, Martine-Sophie Benoit, "Theodor Lessing et le concept de 'haine de soi juive,'" in *La haine de soi: Difficiles identités* (Brussels: Complexe, 2000), 27–46, to which Nancy refers, does point at an alternative account found in Lessing's work, which traces self-hate to a properly Jewish theology (33–34).

29   Nancy, *Exclu le juif*, 44.

one's self."[30] This figure is a paradoxical figure of resistance to the figure, to the coherent and integral shape, it is the form of negation of form, of disintegration, of disassembly, of dispersion, a disfigured figure, a dis-figure. This dis-figure is a paradoxical figuration of an epistemo-political paradox, namely of a Jewish being, which is a specific being, with its specific identity and name, specific self, whose specificity, and thus its "self," however, is constituted precisely by the resistance and negation, its 'hate' so to speak, to all "self."

The paradoxical character of this figuration of Jewish episteme, literally para-doxical, i.e., contrary to all *doxa*, to all appearance, is a significant feature that should be insisted on and contemplated carefully. As I noted above, this figure brings the anti-anti-Semitic discourse to its limit, precisely by pointing at a Jewish epistemic being that would not be only a moment of anti-Semitic logic, which for Nancy would be constitutive to Western-Christian logic. From a Western perspective, namely by means of the sole categories of Western logic, constituting its own horizon of visibility and of possible appearance, its own phenomenality, this Jewish figure, if it indeed constitutes something like radical "alterity," as Nancy claims, perforce cannot appear but through some aesthetical and logical transgression, as a paradox. Something, some self, which constitutes itself through the dispersion of all self. The entire question would be how to approach this dis-figure, this *diaspora*, by what phenomenology it may become visible, *known*—beyond its otherness and alterity *for* the West, if indeed, as postmodernity suggests, there is something beyond the West.[31]

If I nonetheless asserted that Nancy's text remains within the anti-anti-Semitic discourse and even consummates it, it is because, as I already noted above, it seems that it subscribes to a perception of Jewish alterity that is essentially negative. It signals nothing beyond the West, no alternative or alternatively "self," but draws its entire meaning not from overcoming or modifying but from *interrupting* the Western project, which

---

30 When Nancy, therefore, in contemplating the exclusion of the Jews by the West, notes that "Israel tended to separate itself from the *goyim*" (44) and draws the symmetry whereby "like the Jew separates himself from the 'nations', he is separated from them" (55), he should not be read, I think, as representing the second anti-anti-Semitic position, like Arendt.

31 Cf. Elad Lapidot, "Disfigured Friends," *Jewish Studies Quarterly* 27 (2020): 1–20.

for Nancy, as I interpreted him above, would mean interrupting the project of the project. Jewish being would be the project of no project. In *The Banality of Heidegger*, the most accurate conceptual formulation of this figure, in epistemo-political terms, is found not in an idea to which Nancy himself immediately subscribes, but in a thought that he rather attributes to Heidegger, namely the thought of the Jews as—the formulation is Nancy's, not Heidegger's—"a people of no-people" (*peuple du sans-peuple*).[32] For Heidegger, Nancy writes, "the Jew without land, without history, without a people and without identity" represents "the West, the metaphysics of being (*etant, Seiendes*), the no-history, the no-soil and the no-people" (47–48). Consequently, for Heidegger, overcoming the metaphysical, a-historical West would mean "to finish above all with this people of no-people" (48). For Nancy, in contrast, as I showed above, it is rather history, soil, and people, the desire thereto and the—also Heideggerian—lamentation on the loss thereof, that are the manifestations of the metaphysical-Christian-Western "will to self." Consequently, for Nancy, who is diametrically opposed to Heidegger on this point, the "people of no-people" readily suggests itself as the (negative) political epistemology of the diasporic self that constitutes, within the West, the principle of Jewish alterity. In *Exclu le juif*, Nancy formulates the principle of this negative alterity by using Derrida's description of his own Jewishness as "belonging without belonging."[33] In accordance with the dynamics already outlined and demonstrated above, Nancy immediately expresses this negative Jewish principle it the terms of his own conception of the postmodern "out-of-work" community, i.e., as "exposition to the exterior" (48), and suggests that it is already foundational to the Hegelian subject as being essentially "for the other" (48).

It should be emphasized again that Nancy is careful in his conceptual operations, or rather indications—his text features all the ambivalence and undecidability inherent to a discourse that purports to perform an end of discourse. If I do stress this specific reading, i.e., the negative anti-anti-Semitic political epistemology, it is because I contemplate Nancy's text in the context of a broader contemporary discourse, in which it partakes, in part explicitly. In Chapter 1, I already pointed at the fundamental anti-anti-

---

32 Nancy, *Banalité*, 48.
33 Nancy, *Exclu le juif*, 45, making also a reference to Freud.

Semitic operation of separating between real Jews and ideal (epistemic) "Jews" in Lyotard, to whom Nancy refers for the idea of "Jewish alterity" (70). I also suggested that in the recent Heidegger controversy this same operation is most visible in the work of Donatella Di Cesare, to which I now want to briefly refer more specifically as an articulate and clear expression of the third anti-anti-Semitic position, as I sketched it in Nancy's essay.

In fact, like Nancy, Di Cesare too, in her numerous contributions to the debate,[34] did not just identify (Heidegger's) anti-Semitism in the epistemization of the Jewish, namely in separating between the concrete, real, flesh-and-blood Jew, and a "metaphysical Jew," in the sense of a conceptual, figural, and abstract "Jew." Rather, like Nancy, Di Cesare too links anti-Semitism to a *specific* epistemology, not perverse, but rather the standard Western, which she, like Nancy, with Heidegger calls "metaphysics." In a recent essay she identified Western knowledge, which is the root of anti-Semitism, as dominated by "hierarchical oppositions" and "metaphysical dichotomies," which she describes as "secular oppositions," but also as "theological oppositions," such as "beginning/end, pure/impure, autochthonous/foreign, same/other, authentic/inauthentic, creative/reproductive, being/nothing."[35]

Many of the questions that I raised with respect to Nancy's conception and critique of Western "metaphysics" can be also raised with respect to Di Cesare's, not the least concerning its difficult relation to Heidegger, whose anti-Semitism Di Cesare too, like Nancy, understands as "metaphysical anti-Semitism," namely as the remnant in Heidegger's thought of the same metaphysical tradition that he himself criticizes. Similarly to Nancy, also Di Cesare, in her latest text, following Levinas, traces back Western metaphysics to a fundamental obsession with selfness, sameness, totality and ego, which would culminate, conceptually and historically, in anti-Semitism, namely in Auschwitz "as the logical conclusion of a philosophy in which knowledge is always identified with power—the power of an ego that simply persists in being" (83).

The relation between Western metaphysics and the Jews, as it is manifested in anti-Semitism, is for Di Cesare, like for Nancy, not just paranoid,

---

34 See references in Chapter 1, note 18.
35 Donatella Di Cesare, "Being and the Jew: Between Heidegger and Levinas," in Lapidot and Brumlik, *Heidegger and Jewish Thought*, 77.

but epistemic. Western anti-Semitic episteme refers to Jewish episteme not by way of reproduction (second anti-anti-Semitic position), but by way of opposition. Jews stand for non-Western epistemology, and "this is why National Socialism chose them as enemies" (79). It is in terms almost identical to Nancy's, namely of resistance or impossibility of "self," of insuperable otherness and resistance to auto-foundation, that Di Cesare consequently describes the principle of Jewish episteme: "The Jews are uncomfortable witnesses to the noncoincidence of the self with the self, to the immemorial expropriation, to insuperable otherness, to the impossibility of being with oneself. They hinder every project of appropriation, every foundation and self-foundation, every compulsion to completion" (79). Thus, Di Cesare reads in Levinas epistemic Jewishness or Judaism that is not only resisting "the parameters of Western philosophy," but constitutes a positive principle of "exit from the self towards the other," "exteriority," and "irreducible strangeness" (82).[36]

---

36 I will not critique here Di Cesare's reading of Levinas. The question concerning the relation between Levinas's thought and anti-anti-Semitic discourse, especially its third position, represented here by Nancy and Di Cesare, both building on Levinas, is complex and must be discussed separately. It seems to me that a critique of Levinasian political epistemology would echo many of the issues raised by Jacques Derrida's critical analysis of Levinas's work in "Violence et métaphysique: essai sur la pensée d'Emmanuel," in *l'Ecriture et la différence* (Paris: Seuil, 1967), 117–128.

I will nonetheless make a brief note concerning Levinas's 1947 essay *Être juif* [*Être juif: Suivi d'une lettre à Blanchot*, ed. D. Cohen-Levinas (Paris: Rivages, 2015)], "Being Jewish" or "Jewish Being," to which Di Cesare refers as paradigmatic for her reading in Levinas "the uprooting, the exteriority, the strangeness of the Jew" (81). I must admit that I have difficulties finding textual basis for Di Cesare's reading, which omits any concrete references. Levinas's essay begins by an explicit rejection of the anti-anti-Semitic discourse, à la Sartre, which understands Jewishness as reaction to anti-Semitism ("the Jewish question"). In clear Heideggerian terms, Levinas rather looks for the Jew's "place in the economy of being" (50). Levinas characterizes Jewish being in contrast to the basic "Christianism" of modern world. It is Christianism that Levinas describes as committed to the "present" and "everyday" and so lacking the dimension of history and origin, abandoning all salvation to "grace" (59).

Jewish being, in contrast, enacts "the past"—facticity, origin, history, creation, election, personality: "Jewish existence is thus the consummation of the human

It seems to me that the same dynamic that I identified and articulated in Nancy's text, whereby Jewish "alterity" operates as the no-self that does not negate but only "interrupts" and ultimately effects or perfects the Western "self," is also at work in Di Cesare's argument, which in fact leads to defining Judaism as "the exemplar of estrangement, of interruption, or rather of separation" (82). The interruption of Jewish otherness thus offers no alternative to the West, no other politics and political epistemology, but operates, quite on the contrary, as a guarantor and inner perfection mechanism of the West, namely as "the opening of the beyond that prevents Western civilization from drifting into a totalizing universalism" (82). This is the constellation in which I observed, in my analysis of Nancy, how Jewish episteme becomes the very figure of anti-anti-Semitism: Jewish epistemology as the negation of anti-Semitic epistemology that gives effect to "Jewish" epistemology; in other words, Jewish epistemology as the negation of "Jewish" epistemology.

It should be noted that Di Cesare, in her recent text, is aware of this difficulty in her essay and explicitly raises it as an epistemo-political question. She identifies the fundamental complicity between the apparently radical opposites of the "myth of a nation-state" or "statocentric order," i.e., the political epistemology of the modern Western self, and "endless diaspora," i.e., the alleged political epistemology of Jewish alterity. She thus concludes her essay with a series of questions that, without expounding here on their precise possible meanings, seem to inquire about what I would call a potentially *positive* Jewish political epistemology, which is neither Western nor absolute negative: "Can we dwell as strangers? Can we reside without being part and parcel of the earth, keeping our roots in the heavens? Can we stay separate from a land that is not claimed as a mother but welcomed as a bride? Can we be *gerim*, resident aliens, once we have returned? Can we preserve exile in return? And can an anarchic critique of the statocentric order of the world pass through Israel?" (85).

---

condition as fact, personality and liberty. And its whole originality consists in breaking with a world without origin and simply present" (65). In other words, it would seem that it is rather Christianity that for Levinas—very similarly to Heidegger—would represent modern "uprootedness" and alterity, which Nancy and Di Cesare attribute to the Jew, whereas for Levinas Jewish being would rather stand for historicity, which for Heidegger constitutes proper being, and that Nancy and Di Cesare decry as the Western root of Heidegger's anti-Semitism.

This series of questions corresponds, so it seems to me, to another series of question raised in Nancy's text, which I think equally suggests a horizon of thought beyond anti-anti-Semitism. Reflecting on the role of anti-Semitism in Heidegger's thought, Nancy at a certain point in fact observes in anti-Semitism not exactly the expression of political-historical epistemology as such, i.e., as principle of the Western self, but more precisely the expression of a *certain* epistemology, the opposite of which would therefore not be simply the negation of *all* but only of *one* history. *This* opposition to anti-Semitism would open the possibility "to speak of . . . another *Geschehen* that would arrive or that would be at least outlined here and there in the history of Europe."[37] In fact, Nancy moves to ask, "Hasn't there been already and differently—in an erratic manner—sometimes a re-commencement of (in) history? Hadn't there been more than one history? More and more or something else than '*one* history'? *The historial*, might it not be plural, scattered here and there along a path less ordered than the one that this thought assigns to the West?" (57–58).

This horizon of alternative history or alternative historiality, and I would add of an alternative political epistemology, which by its very nature is not purely theoretical or possible, but necessarily suggests an actual, already existent, namely *historical* alternative, in fact does not remain a mere formal indication. Rather, Nancy immediately points at a few concrete moments or locations where such alternative may be found, such as, in the Heideggerian oeuvre, Angelus Silesius or Augustine, or "many other possibilities . . . in philosophy, literature and art" (58), to which, in the Heideggerian context, one should no doubt and perhaps most prominently for Heidegger add the name Hölderlin. One possibility that Nancy does not mention in this context, and in fact would be hard (even if not impossible) to elicit from Heidegger's text, is the Jews. In the framework of the philosophical contemplation of anti-Semitism, this *topos* nonetheless seems called for, at least as a possibility to consider. In fact, Nancy's essay is not entirely silent about the possibility of the Jewish tradition as a location for alternative political epistemology. It contains at least one hint where the investigation in this direction could start. I mean what he calls

---

37 Nancy, *Banalité*, 57.

the "rabbinic Judaism of the diaspora," which would be the "twin brother" of Christianity, yet unavowed child of Western intellectual historiography.

Re-Figurations

To conclude the discussion of the third and last anti-anti-Semitic position, which I problematized as epistemo-political "dis-figuration" of the Jewish, I will mention and briefly discuss two other direct critical interventions on the same discourse that I analyzed above through Nancy's text. These two interventions did not specifically address the question of anti-Semitism but the notion of the Jewish. Both identified an issue of dis-figuration; both suggested different directions for what may be called "refiguration." I will now quickly examine these two forms of refiguration in view of the basic elements of the anti-anti-Semitic discourse that was analyzed in this chapter.

The first intervention is Sarah Hammerschlag's contemplation on the question of the postmodern figure of the Jew, *The Figural Jew*, of 2010.[38] Hammerschlag's book retraced in post–World War II French thought the process of revaluating anti-Semitic imagery of the deracinated Jew, namely an anti-anti-Semitic operation of positing "the Jewish" as a *positive* figure of deracination, dispersion, diaspora, and de-mythologization, what I characterized as dis-figuration. Similar to my own analysis, Hammerschlag too was concerned by the risk of this allegedly destabilizing figure actually serving self-affirmation. The potential self-affirmation Hammerschlag was mainly concerned about was, however, not the Western, but the Jewish. In other words, her concern was that what I perceive as dis-figuration of the Jew, in the sense of denying any positive Jewish episteme, idea, and image, is still suggesting *too much*. This, as long as this negative idea still suggests itself as an image or concept of some Jewish reality, namely, as long as this dis-figured "Jew" continues to operate, as Hammerschlag called it, following among others Jean-Luc Nancy, as a "myth" (11). It is in epistemo-political terms that Hammerschlag formulated the problem that she identified in this "mythically antimythic" (13) idea of the Jew, namely that it would lead to "a mere reengagement with a diasporic tradition

---

38   Sarah Hammerschlag, *The Figural Jew: Politics and Identity in Postwar French Thought* (Chicago: University of Chicago Press, 2010).

within Judaism, for that would only reconstruct Jewish communitarianism around this value" (266). This concern, which Hammerschlag mostly analyzed in Levinas, but which as immediately brings to mind Boyarin (see below), problematizes in the most general manner the very notion of positive political epistemology, namely of knowledge- and concept-oriented politics, of community built on idea or, to speak less Greek more rabbinic, *torah*. It means denying the collective project, such as Jewish being, any *episteme* and figure—what I call dis-*figuration*.

It is all the more confusing that "figure" is precisely what Hammerschlag suggests as a counter-notion to "myth." Against the "mythically antimythic" Jew, hers is *The Figural Jew*. What she means by "figure" is almost the exact opposite to what I do. Hammerschlag understands "figure" primarily as a linguistic phenomenon, a literary figure, a trope or "figurative language," the main feature of which is not its intimacy with reality, i.e., being idea or concept or form for the real, but on the contrary its *distance* from reality. The idea expressed as a figure of speech, a metaphor, "declares itself both to be and not to be what it represents" (14). Even more confusingly, in elucidating her concept of "figure" Hammerschlag refers to Philipp Lacoue-Labarth's notion of "*dé-figuration*."[39] What he calls the "'retreat' of the figure" (and to which I will return in the conclusion of this book), she explains as "figural language calling attention to itself, calling itself into question as representation and truth source" (14), namely something like self-conscious figural language, aware of the distance between its signs and their referents in reality, speech in the mode of "irony" (23, 266).

It seems to me that Hammerschlag ultimately performs precisely what I described as *dis-figuration*—raised to the second power. She does maintain a "figure" of the Jew; however, this figure is both, in its content, a figure of dis-figuration (deracination, disapora, de-mythologization, etc.), and also, in its form, a universal trope that is separated from Jewish reality, or as Hammerschlag says, "particularity" or "identity." Her *Figural Jew* would be dis-figured dis-figuration.

The two problems I see in this conception are accordingly two self-affirmations: first, self-affirmation of the particular identity of the

---

39   Philippe Lacoue-Labarthe, "Il faut,» *MLN* 107 (1992): 437–439. For my divergent reading, see the epilogue to this book.

non-figural, real Jew, which, purified of all *episteme*, *dis-figured*, would have to be understood, once again, in the category of the concrete individual "flesh and blood," of "life." It is thus that Hammerschlag's *Figural Jew* would converge with what seems and is proclaimed to be its exact opposite, the critique against any (most often postmodern, French) figuration, conceptualization, and categorization of the Jewish as supersessionist allegorization, replacing the Jew with "the Jew" (see below).

Second, self-affirmation of the West, which in Hammerschlag's account features as contemporary "politics of identity." Hammerschlag does explicitly put her "figural Jew" to the service of "politics of disidentification" (267), designed to "destabilize the politics of identity without resorting to the nostalgia of a universalizing humanism" (23). It is, however, hard to see how, in the absence of any such "nostalgia," which I earlier described as desire to the absolute, "irony" is able to lead to anything but reaffirmation of the status quo and, furthermore, to immunizing it against any change.

The second intervention I wish to mention was undertaken as one element of the much broader intellectual project of Jonathan and Daniel Boyarin. This project, no doubt one of the most significant and influential within contemporary academic discourse pertaining to "the Jewish," merits its own separate contemplation. The Boyarin project has a specific importance for the question of Jewish political epistemology, since it in fact sheds light on and accordingly intervenes in the research and historiography of Jewish intellectual tradition as a political performance. Particularly important for my own critical project of contemporary *negative* Jewish political epistemology, which I analyze under the title of "anti-anti-Semitism," are the Boyarins' engagements on *positive* historical instances of Jewish knowledge, most significantly Daniel Boyarin's work on rabbinic literature, which for this reason no longer falls within anti-anti-Semitism.

Nonetheless, I wish to point at a significant conceptual affinity between the Boyarins' project and Nancy's discourse, which pertains to the epistemo-political question. I will indicate this affinity in a couple of texts of the mid-1990s in which the Boyarins critically engaged on Nancy's earlier work.[40] Their critique concerned a basic operation that, according to

---

40   See Boyarin and Boyarin, "Diaspora"; Boyarin, *A Radical Jew*, 149–152; cf. Bennington, "Lyotard and 'the Jews'"; Silverman, "Re-Figuring 'the Jew.'"

them, has been carried out on the Jews in various forms by a Western tradition from Paul to contemporary French philosophy, a Christian tradition, an operation of "allegorization." Allegorization would consist in an act of generating a concept, figure, or idea of the "Jew," henceforth the *true* Jew, which would consequently substitute real, literal, non-allegorical Jews, who end up "being only a trope."[41] Besides in Paul, Lyotard, and Badiou, the Boyarins exemplified this operation also in Nancy's texts on *The Inoperative Community*, which they more generally criticized for presenting community as "nonbeing" by completely evacuating the dimensions of "history and memory" (698). As specifically allegorizing they found Nancy's reference to Blanchot, which I already mentioned above, asserting a Jewish "refusal of myths," thus generating "the Jewish" as the universal concept for anti-mythology, a concept subsequently available for postmodern reappropriation (698). The basic problem for the Boyarins was that this process of conceptualization entails the abolishment of Jewish "difference," in that it "deprives those who have historically grounded identities in those material signifiers of the power to speak for themselves and remain different" (697).

This critique of "allegorization" raises of course the basic question of conceptualization, and this entire book is dedicated to showing the problems arising from the objection *in principle* (i.e., in the name of anti-anti-Semitism) to any conceptualization or epistemization of Jewish being. All these problems are equally raised by the Boyarins' critique of the Jew as "trope" in the name of "real" or "living Jews" (720). Nonetheless, as I noted, the Boyarins explicitly engage on Jewish difference as *epistemic*. They thus *do* assert a basic episteme—a concept, idea, knowledge, or category—at the basis of what they read as the historical Jewish project, namely the rabbinic. In view of the Christian "genius" of universalism, which carries the risk of imperialism, they see "the genius of Judaism" in "its ability to leave other people alone" (712). Jewish particularism would not, however, simply be the opposite of Christian universalism. Rather, the relation between these two historical projects would be "dialectic" (720). If Christianity's challenge has been universalism without imperialism, the Jewish challenge has been particularism without nationalism or racism, or other evils represented for the Boyarins (and Badiou would surely agree) by the "Israeli

---

41   Boyarin/Boyarin, "Diaspora," 697.

General Security Services" (712). The historical project—"contribution" (720), "invention," or "model" (711)—that the Boyarins accordingly asserted in the rabbinic tradition, and which they have been further articulating and demonstrating in the quarter of a century since, is not anti-Christian, but anti-statist, namely *diaspora*.[42]

Indeed, it is only by identifying diaspora as the epistemo-political project, and thus something like the principle or essence or concept or idea of the real, living, historical Jewish being, that the Boyarins are able to criticize other conceptions of Jewish being, such as Zionism, not just as undesirable, but as "subversion" or "substitution" (712), i.e., of the true—rabbinic—meaning of historical Jewish existence. "To the extent that this diasporic existence is an actual historical entity," they note, "we ourselves are not prey to the charge of 'allegorizing' the Jews. It may be fairly suggested, however, that the model is so idealized as to be in itself an allegory" (711n.32). I note that the allegory of diaspora, inasmuch as it is an "antidote to racism" and to "the myth of autochthony," comes close to what early Nancy and Lacoue-Labarthe, with Blanchot, meant by the anti-mythical character of Judaism. Insofar as diaspora or "diasporic identity" means more specifically "disaggregated identity" and even "disrupts the very categories of identity" (721), one may further surmise that Nancy's later and recent dis-figuration of Jewish being as "dispersion, dissolution or dissimulation of one's self" is not only conceptually similar, but possibly draws directly from Boyarin, to whom Nancy in fact refers.

Anti-anti-Semitic discourse was analyzed in the previous chapters from the perspective of political epistemology. It was defined and articulated as a critique of anti-Semitism that is based on the rejection of any attribution of epistemic meaning to the Jewish collective historical existence, namely to any historical existence that may be designated as Jewish. In

---

42 Jonathan and Daniel Boyarin, *Powers of Diaspora: Two Essays on the Relevance of Jewish Culture* (Minneapolis: University of Minnesota Press, 2002); Daniel Boyarin, *A Traveling Homeland: The Babylonian Talmud as Diaspora* (Philadelphia: University of Pennsylvania Press, 2015). For my critique of the notion of diaspora, see Elad Lapidot, "Ger. Deterritorialized Immigrant in Talmudic Exile," *Jewish Culture and History* 20 (2019): 23–42.

other words, anti-anti-Semitism does not criticize anti-Semitism for judging Jews negatively, but for perceiving Jewish being—and any historical collective—as carrying any specific idea, concept, logic, or episteme, and thus as a possible object of judgment. From this perspective, the third anti-anti-Semitic position is also the last one, since, while further embracing negative political epistemology, it nonetheless identifies this negativity as the very—paradoxical—essence of a *Jewish* political episteme. The third position is an anti-anti-Semitic foundation of Jewish being. It was therefore crucial to show the conceptual solidarity between the last, accomplished form of anti-anti-Semitism and a contemporary positive, historiographical interpretation, even self-interpretation, of Jewishness, i.e., the affinity—and possible passage—between Nancy and Boyarin.

From here, there are two main directions for pursuing this contemplation. One direction is to make in fact this passage from negative to positive Jewish political epistemology. This would mean shifting the focus of the investigation from anti-anti-Semitism to something like Judaism or Jewishness or Jewish being et cetera, so *perceiving* some actual project of Jewish political knowledge, and then asking about its nature and principle or examining already existent attempt to do so. A good point of departure for this kind of questioning would in fact be the work of the Boyarins, as also other contemporary projects on Jewish or rabbinic political epistemology, such as of Sergey Dolgopolski and of Elliot Wolfson.[43] The central question of this direction of research would concern the exact nature of the alterity or otherness of the specifically *Jewish* political epistemology, in particular the exact nature of its *negativity* vis-à-vis non-Jewish political epistemology. The initial category to analyze would be the one suggested by both Nancy and Boyarin, i.e., *diaspora*, in contrast to other categories, such as, importantly, *exile*. It also requires calling into question the very name "Jew," as Daniel Boyarin has recently done with "Judaism."[44] This requires

---

43 Sergey Dolgopolski, *What Is Talmud? The Art of Disagreement* (New York: Fordham University Press, 2009); Dolgopolski, *Other Others: The Political after the Talmud* (New York: Fordham University Press, 2018); Elliot R. Wolfson, *Heidegger and Kabbalah: Hidden Gnosis and the Path of Poiesis* (Bloomington, Indiana: Indiana University Press, 2019).

44 Daniel Boyarin, *Judaism: The Genealogy of a Modern Notion* (New Brunswick, NJ: Rutgers University Press, 2018).

a new book.[45] The conclusion to this book offers an initial demonstration of this exercise with respect to the question of Heidegger's anti-Semitism, which opened this investigation.

Before that, however, the second part of this book will take another direction, which does not lead from negative to positive, but lingers in negativity, in the "anti." It moves from anti-anti-Semitism not to Judaism, but to anti-Semitism. The attempt will be to indicate and propose an initial articulation for a non-anti-anti-Semitic approach to anti-Semitism. The key, as I will now introduce and develop it in the latter part of this book, Part II, will be to approach anti-Semitism itself as an episteme, i.e., as a historical event, a political event—problematic, disturbing and outrageous, but nonetheless—of knowledge.

---

45 For a first attempt in this direction, see Elad Lapidot, "Jewish and Talmudic Logo-Politics," in Sergey Dolgopolski, ed., *Talmud, and, Philosophy* (Bloomington: Indiana University Press, forthcoming).

Part II

ANTI-SEMITISM

ANTI-SEMITISM AS TEXT

In the second part of this book, I would like to go beyond anti-anti-Semitism, the critique of anti-Semitism, and look directly at the object of this critique, at anti-Semitism itself. The basic question remains political epistemology. My aim is to see to what extent the basic dynamics made visible in the previous chapters in anti-anti-Semitic discourse, in its various permutations, which I characterized as post–World War II negative political epistemology, may also be observed in anti-Semitism. In other words, to what extent the various problems highlighted in anti-anti-Semitism, not the least the problematic, paradigmatic status of the Jews, may be traced back to anti-Semitism. Aiming beyond anti-anti-Semitism, my central question is whether and how anti-Semitism may be seen and analyzed not only sociologically and psychologically, but epistemologically, i.e., as an episteme, as a form of *knowledge*.

As I already noted with respect to my phenomenology of anti-anti-Semitism, all phenomenology, and all science, is predetermined by the choice of phenomenon, namely by the choice of the observable object or event that presumably manifests the analyzed conceptual constellation. I chose to observe the constellation of anti-anti-Semitism in its textual form, in philosophical writings that I claimed articulate it as a discourse, while emphasizing that anti-anti-Semitic phenomena may also have other forms, including contemporary performances of Jewishness or the West. This choice was facilitated by the fact that, even as I claim anti-anti-Semitism is a defining epistemo-political constellation of our time, "anti-anti-Semitism" is a new term, which, notwithstanding its conceptual power, hardly evokes any clear image of specific reality.

This is not the case with anti-Semitism. It was my own argument, that the importance of anti-anti-Semitic political epistemology lies precisely in the fact that after World War II "anti-Semitism" has become a name for political evil, immediately evoking the images of dystopia, of apocalypse, of the end of politics, knowledge, world, and discourse, the end of civilization. It would not seem unreasonable, and in some respects may be true, to say that the only object or event, the only entity, that constitutes the phenomenon of anti-Semitism is Auschwitz. And what more could words say?

Yet Auschwitz too is a name, is told. Its apocalyptic center, its raw immediacy, with a core of silence, has nonetheless produced, still produces or reveals—that is my argument concerning anti-anti-Semitism—meanings or fields of meaning, conceptual horizons, foundational discourses. One of the basic discourses in which our historiography has placed Auschwitz, as its eschatological *telos* and phenomenal avatar, is anti-Semitism. Unlike "Auschwitz," a proper name, "anti-Semitism" has the form of concept, and more specifically of scientific *terminus*: an attitudinal negation (*anti-*) of an attitudinal substantive (*-ism*) derived from a relatively marginal biblical name (*Sem*). In fact, as my analysis has shown, all analyzed anti-anti-Semitic positions were in agreement in considering anti-Semitism, most fundamentally, as an epistemic phenomenon, or actually as an epistemological constellation.

More precisely, the notion of anti-Semitic episteme presents a constitutive ambivalence. On the one hand, all anti-anti-Semitic writers consider anti-Semitism to be an epistemic pathology, distorting the very epistemic essence, namely the quality of being knowledge *of* something, a basic relation *to* some reality, i.e., Jews. On the other hand, for most accounts, this epistemological distortion is no exception to a historical norm, but is on the contrary symptomatic or even exemplary for a broader, indeed normative epistemo-political (dis)order. Thus, whereas Arendt saw anti-Semitism as an element of modern "totalitarianism," whose "ideological" epistemology should be enlightened with historical facts, Adorno and Horkheimer recognized in anti-Semitism the failure of enlightenment and civilization itself, what Nancy calls "the West."

Where, therefore, is anti-Semitism observable as this ambivalent epistemic being? Where is it to be found, to speak with Arendt, as a concrete historical fact? My contention is that the ambivalent anti-Semitic episteme is most immediately visible in the anti-Semitic text;[1] to begin with, the very notion or text of "anti-Semitic text." Text is episteme as historical being, i.e., knowledge that exists as a concrete, linguistically specific text.

---

1   My analysis and contention here is in direct—polemic—conversation first and foremost with the treatment of anti-Semitism by political philosophers, who, as I demonstrated in the introduction to this book, tend to posit anti-Semitism *outside* of philosophy and thought. I am unable here to properly discuss the question concerning the epistemology underlying the specific fields of academic knowledge that have been since World War II developed with respect to the specific object "anti-Semitism," so to speak the science of anti-Semitism, such as anti-Semitism studies or Holocaust studies. This would be a task in itself. I do believe, however, that my analysis here provides at least a basic question for this kind of inquiry. With respect to the question of the anti-Semitic *text*, it does seem that at least in some prominent historical studies, anti-Semitic writings function as the main site of anti-Semitism's historical appearance; see for instance Léon Poliakov, *Histoire de l'antisémitisme. tome I: Du Christ aux Juifs de Cour* (Paris: Calmann-Lévy, 1955); *tome II: De Mahomet aux Marranes* (Paris: Calmann-Lévy, 1961); *tome III: De Voltaire à Wagner* (Paris: Calmann-Lévy, 1968); *tome IV: L'Europe suicidaire* (1870–1933) (Paris: Calmann-Lévy, 1977); Jacob Katz, *From Prejudice to Destruction: Anti-Semitism, 1700–1933* (Cambridge, MA: Harvard University Press, 1980); Alex Bein, *The Jewish Question: Biography of a World Problem*, trans. Harry Zohn (Toronto: Associated University Presses, 1990). For a short review of main models offered by post–World War II scholarship for the historical analysis of anti-Semitism, see Shulamit Volkov, *German, Jews, and Antisemites: Trials in Emancipation* (Cambridge: Cambridge University Press, 2006), 67–81, 107–118. Volkov herself analyzes "The Language of Antisemitism" (82); Alex Bein suggested the notion of "the semantic of Jew-hatred" in "Der Moderne Antisemitismus und seine Bedeutung für die Judenfrage," *Vierteljahrshefte für Zeitgeschichte* 4 [1958]: 360). More recently, Alon Confino, *A World without Jews: The Nazi Imagination from Persecution to Genocide* (New Haven, CT: Yale University Press, 2014), spoke of a "world of anti-Semitic fantasies" and, in contrast to purely functional historiographies of the Holocaust, suggested an account of "what the Nazis *thought* was happening, [of] how they imagined their world" (17).

Accordingly, the historical existence of anti-Semitic episteme lies in the basic text that is the expression "anti-Semitism." "Anti-Semitism" would be the basic anti-Semitic text. Is, however, "anti-Semitism" in fact the basic concept of anti-Semitism, namely of what is perceived as anti-Semitism, and even as anti-Semitic *text*?

This hardly seems to be the case, rather, paradoxically, the opposite, a paradox or paranormality of language, inversion of or indifference to signification, which, as I shall show, seems constitutive to the anti-Semitic text and episteme. As one can read under the title *Anti-Semitismus* in Brunner, Conze, and Koselleck's *Geschichtliche Grundbegriffe*, "Historical Basic Concepts," having entered German political discourse in 1879, to feature in numerous polemics and political formations throughout the late nineteenth and early twentieth century, after 1933 the term *Anti-Semitismus* was "surprisingly discredited." The Nazi Propaganda Ministry even instructed the press "with respect to the Jewish Question to avoid the word anti-Semitic or anti-Semitism, since German politics is aimed only against Jews, but not against the Semites in general." Instead, the Nazi ministry advised to use the word "anti-Jewish."[2] In other words, the archetypical anti-Semites were terminologically anti-anti-Semites. In fact, the Nuremberg Laws do not speak of "Semites," but of "Jews." Similarly, Theodor Fritsch's canonic *Anti-Semiten-Katechismus*, the standard anti-Semitic handbook, first published in 1887 to see forty-nine editions until 1945, was in 1907 renamed *Handbuch der Judenfrage*, "Handbook to the Jewish Question"; in the last edition of 1944 it still sought to replace "the inadequate expression 'anti-Semitism' by the concept *anti-Judaism*."[3]

It is only after the war that *Anti-Semitismus* was reintroduced, such that, as the *Geschichtliche Grundbegriffe* reports, "the word *Anti-Semitismus* has been in Germany after 1945 without doubt more often used as in the previous twelve years" (152)—to primarily describe precisely these twelve years. "Anti-Semitism" has thus become a designation of a historical discourse, whose paradigmatic manifestation (Nazi language) explicitly rejected this

---

2   Thomas Nipperdy and Reinhard Rürup, "Anti-Semitismus," in *Geschichtliche Grundbegriffe. Historisches Lexikon zur politisch-sozialen Sprache in Deutschland*, hg. v. Otto Brunner, Werner Conze, Reinhart Koselleck, Bd. 1 (Stuttgart: Klett Verlag, 1972), 129–153, 151. See also Moshe Zimmermann, *Wilhelm Marr, the Patriarch of anti-Semitism* (Oxford: Oxford University Press, 1986), 114.
3   Quoted in the *Geschichtliche Grundbegriffe*, 152.

term as its self-designation. This means that "anti-Semitism" has detached itself from, if not properly negated, its own textuality, and thus its own historical existence, becoming the broadest "synonym for an unfriendly or hostile attitude towards the Jews" (153). Curiously, it is precisely in order to designate this meaning that the Nazis replaced "anti-Semitism" with "anti-Judaism," which is in fact more appropriate for designating anti-Judaism. The opposition to the Nazi *Sprachregelung*, "language rule," paradoxically has the more accentuated character of *Sprachregelung*, namely the conscious enactment of linguistic arbitrariness and detachment from historical contextuality. For instance, the monumental, still canonical work of Léon Poliakov, *Histoire de l'antisémitisme*, published in four volumes (1955–1977), begins the history of anti-Semitism "From Christ," classifying the proper "anti-Semitic" discourse of nineteenth-twentieth century as "modern anti-Semitism."[4] Would "anti-Semitism," as currently used, be an anti-anti-Semitic concept? A *Sprachregelung* to replace "anti-Judaism"?

A similar textual disturbance is also visible in more historically informed anti-anti-Semitic reflections on the concept "anti-Semitism," for example in the narrative of the *Geschichtliche Grundbegriffe* itself, concerning the historical origin and development of this fundamental concept of political-social language in Germany. Notwithstanding the post-1945 dehistorization of *Anti-Semitismus*, as well as the "indeterminateness" that according to this lexicon has characterized its usage and generates its power,[5] its origin is remarkably traceable, namely as an invention, an intentional event of language, an intentional statement.

Or rather two statements, separated by the hyphen of the epistemo-political. The first emergence of "anti-Semitism" or rather *Anti-Semitismus* would be political. The "creator" of this term is often considered to be the journalist and activist Wilhelm Marr, founder of the *Anti-Semiten-Liga*.[6] Although "no supporting document has been presented for this supposition" (129), and it would be "impossible to provide clear evidence" (138), the *Geschichtliche Grundbegriffe* nonetheless provides quite precise infor-

---

4   Léon Poliakov, *Histoire de l'antisémitisme. Tome III*, 321
5   *Geschichtliche Grundbegriffe* 141, quoting Salo Wittmayer Baron, *A Social and Religious History of the Jews*, vol. 2 (New York, 1937), 296n.3.
6   See *Geschichtliche Grundbegriffe*, 129; Poliakov, *tome III*, 432; "Anti-Semitism," in *Encylopaedia Judaica*, 2nd ed., ed. Skolnik and Berenbaum (Detroit: Thomson Gale, 2007), vol. 2, 206; Zimmermann, *Marr*, 112.

mation, situating the emergence of *Anti-Semitismus* in "early autumn 1879 in the circle of Marr in Berlin" (138). But the word has also a second documented origin and destiny, a scientific one. It is interesting to note how the *Geschictliche Grundbegriffe*, in pointing at this second, *epistemic* origin of *Anti-Semitismus*, transfers the fuzziness und uncertainty that naturally characterize the conceptual dynamics of political discourse into the realm of science. Having indicated the political origin of "anti-Semitism" in Marr, the lexicon briefly mentions a "sometimes asserted, but unevidenced early use of this word by Ernst Renan" (129), the French historian and philologist.[7] Another footnote refers to Ismar Elbogen's claim that it was the orientalist and bibliographer Moritz Steinschneider, who "in a personal letter," criticizing Ernst Renan, first used the word *Anti-Semitismus*, the historical lexicon immediately adding that "this information is probably based on oral tradition, it contains neither source information nor date" (153n.123).[8]

As I will show, both these "assertions" of early uses of *Anti-Semitismus* in mid-nineteenth century historical philology are actually correct and well documented. The point, however, is not that the *Geschichtliche Grundbegriffe* was not rigorous enough in its research. Rather, the dimming of the scientific origin of *Anti-Semitismus*—dated 1855—is based on its explicit dissociation from the political use, "since from a possible use of the word in Renan there is in any case no continuation to the concept that emerged in the political discussion around 1880" (129–130), precisely as "there is no identifiable connection between a possible use of the word by Steinschneider to the political concept formation of 1879" (153n.123). It is interesting to note that this same rupture between science and politics is equally asserted and so *effected* not only by contemporary historiography

---

7   Referring to *Jüdisches Lexikon*, ed. Georg Herlitz and Bruno Kirschner, Bd. 1 (Berlin 1927), 331; and Baron, *History of the Jews*, vol. 2 (New York, 1937), 287: "From here this assumption was adopted in numerous other works."

8   The reference is to Ismar Elbogen, *Ein Jahrhundert jüdischen Lebens. Die Geschichte des neuzeitlichen Judentums*, ed. Ellen Littmann (Frankfurt, 1967), 635. For another indication of Steinschneider as "the first known use of the word," which however does provide a precise source, see Alex Bein, *Jewish Question*, 594–595, reporting how Agnon—"in one of our numerous conversations"—drew his attention to this fact, or rather to the already existing statement and documentation of this source determination in the encyclopedia *Otzar Yisrael*, ed. Jehuda Eisentstadt (London, 1924), 2, 130ff.

of politics but also by contemporary historiography of science. Maurice Olender, in his important book on the conjunction of theology, race and language in nineteenth-century science, *Les langues du Paradis*, "Languages of Paradise," featuring centrally, among others, Ernst Renan, points out that "no one ignores that these two words, 'Semite' and 'Aryan', had become, in the 20th century, at the heart of Europe, terms deciding death and life . . . for millions of children, women and men."[9] However, Olender states, "Save exceptions, we will not find evidencing of the links that may have existed between this text or another and the odious use that was made sometimes only a few years later, if we think of the Dreyfus affair" (46–47).

What kind of "link" or "continuity" could one observe and demonstrate here, between scientific and political discourse? Obviously, no scientific link, such as the one that exists between one scientific text scientifically referencing another. As the historians of politics and of science tell us no such scientific link exists, nor, we can add, should we expect to find or even look for one. The epistemo-political event does not consist in political discourse referencing scientific discourse. The complicity is rather inherent and structural, science and politics and the distinction between them belonging to *the same epistemic system*. Olender is perfectly aware of this when he speaks, in another passage, of the "new ideological and political careers of the terms 'Semitic' and 'Aryan'" that begin in the 1870s "outside of the field of the philological and anthropological sciences, but often *drawing their legitimacy from them*" (37; emphasis mine). *Geschichtliche Grundbegriffe* equally recognizes the "pretended scientificity" of political anti-Semitism, a pretention that was also clearly recognizable for the immediate addressees of this discourse, such as the *Allgemeine Zeitung des Judentums*, in whose editorial of July 25, 1882, Ludwig Philippson decried the "appearance of scientificity" conveyed by the term *Anti-Semitismus*.[10] Indeed, the very expression "anti-Semitism" historically connects scientific text and political text, which, be that as pseudo-science or anti-science, and precisely as such, is intimately related to science.

---

9   Maurice Olender, *Les langues du Paradis* (Paris: Editions du Seuil, 1989), 47, trans. Arthur Goldhammer as *The Languages of Paradise: Race, Religion, and Philology in the Nineteenth Century* (Cambridge, MA: Harvard University Press, 1992).
10   Quoted in *Geschichtliche Grundbegriffe*, 142 and 140.

My own intervention here aims at shedding light on this intimacy of science and politics in the anti-Semitic text. The following is an attempt to make a few observations on how the so-called political discourse of historical anti-Semitism arises from and is embedded in the broader episteme and epistemology of modern science. My analyses offer a better understanding of the paradox that Jacob Katz observed as the basis for his own study of modern anti-Semitism, namely "how the anti-Jewish animosity grew in strength, paradoxically just when in the wake of the Enlightenment and modern rationality one might have expected it to disappear."[11] I will therefore look at how the term "anti-Semitism" emerges in nineteenth-century formulations of modern—and to an important extent

---

11   Katz, *From Prejudice*, v. For Katz, the exclusion of the Jews is inconsistent with the "rationalism, humanism, and universalism" of Enlightenment, such that anti-Semitism is for him "illogical" (8; "In ideological arguments, logic and consistency are hardly decisive; the train of thought is not guided by the quest for truth but by the need to justify prior beliefs") or "irrational" (320; "It was [the] composite nature of modern anti-Semitism—an absolute archaic image covered by a layer of justifications—that made it an irrational phenomenon inaccessible to overt, logically oriented argumentation"). My analysis, I think, shows a much greater consistency than Katz assumes, and so a much smaller "paradox." In this sense, my argument corresponds to the analysis offered by Michael Mack, *German Idealism and the Jew: The Inner Anti-Semitism of Philosophy and German Jewish Responses* (Chicago: University of Chicago Press, 2003), on "the relation between anti-Semitism, on one hand, and philosophy, aesthetics, and social theory, on the other" (1). See also Robert S. Wistrich, "Radical Antisemitism in France and Germany (1840–1880)," *Modern Judaism* 15 (1995): 109–135: "The same rationalist doctrines which triumphed in 1789 provided the ideological basis for the modern secular Jew-hatred of the nineteenth century" (109).

My analysis has some affinity to Paul Lawrence Rose's observation of the intimacy between German anti-Semitism and the German progressive politics that he calls "German revolution," an intimacy that he analytically conceptualizes with the category of "revolutionary anti-Semitism"; Rose, *German Question/Jewish Question. Revolutionary Antisemitism in Germany from Kant to Wagner* (Princeton, NJ: Princeton University Press, 1990), xv–xviii; cf. George L. Mosse, *The Crisis of German Ideology: Intellectual Origins of the Third Reich* (New York: Grosset and Dunlap, 1964). In contrast to Rose, I am not convinced of the analytical value of the categories "German" and "revolution" for understanding the conceptual foundations of anti-Semitic discourse, which I equally identify in French and non-revolutionary writers. Further in contrast to Rose ("To a large degree, the

still contemporary—human sciences, its role and signification in the epistemic system that conjoins spirit and race, language and people, philology and ethnography.[12] The main textual corpus for this exploration, a birthplace of "anti-Semitism," consists of both early and later works of Ernst Renan, an epistemo-politically ambivalent figure.[13] From this scientific discourse I will then move to the historical text of political anti-Semitism,

---

idea of race was but a late development that tied up some loose ends," xvii), I ascribe great importance to the emergence of race discourse—in France.

12   Arguably, it is as a reaction or response to the same configuration of the *Geisteswissenschaft*, lit. the "science of spirit" or "humanities," which emerged the new science of the human as society, "sociology." Amos Morris-Reich indicated "an interesting correspondence" in "the emergence of modern, academic social science and that of modern anti-Semitism," focusing on the early twentieth-century works of Georg Simmel, Franz Boas, and Arthur Ruppin—see Morris-Reich, "Argumentative Patterns and Epistemic Considerations: Responses to Anti-Semitism in the Conceptual History of Social Science," *Jewish Quarterly Review* 100, no. 3 (2010): 454–482. See also Marcel Stoetzler, ed., *Antisemitism and the Constitution of Sociology* (Lincoln: University of Nebraska Press, 2014). On the shift from *Geist* to *Gesellschaft* in the context of the Jewish Question, see my discussion of Marx in Chapter 6.

13   Renan is on the one hand a figure of scientific rationalism and a famous advocate of the civic notion of the "nation" (in contrast to what Paul Rose calls "German revolution"). He was, on the other hand, significantly influenced by such romantic German writers as Herder, of whom Renan wrote that he "is the German writer I know best"—quoted in Olender, *Langues*, 144. The figure of Renan thus complicates a common distinction between French "universal" nationalism versus a German "ethnic" nationalism; see for instance Saul Friedländer, *Nazi Germany and the Jews. Vol. I: The Years of Persecution, 1933–1939* (New York: HarperCollins, 1997), 85. Zeev Sternhell accordingly portrayed Renan as one of the protagonists of modern "anti-Enlightenment"; see Sternhell, *Les anti-Lumières. Du XVIII siècle à la guerre froide* (Paris: Fayard, 2006), trans. David Maisel as *The Anti-Enlightenment Tradition* (New Haven, CT: Yale University Press, 2009). Renan's ambivalence was noticed also by Hannah Arendt, who noted that Renan "was probably the first to oppose the 'Semites' to the 'Aryans' in a decisive '*division du genre humain*', although he held civilization to be the great superior force which destroys local originalities as well as original race differences" (Arendt, *Origins*, 174). The ambivalence in Renan is often explained away by a caesura in his work before and after the Franco-German war of 1870. My analysis below suggests that the ambivalence is inherent to Renan's epistemology.

interrogated in texts from Bruno Bauer and Karl Marx, through Wagner, Marr, von Treitschke and Fritsch, to Adolf Hitler. My intention is not to provide any kind of sufficient account and analysis of these texts, but only to indicate a few basic motifs, which I think are crucial for the epistemo-political question of anti-Semitism and anti-anti-Semitism.[14]

My analysis of anti-Semitism will go beyond or counter anti-anti-Semitic discourse in attempting to identify in anti-Semitism a trace of Jewish political epistemology. More specifically, in contrast to the first anti-anti-Semitic position, I analyze the anti-Semitic perception of "Jews" not as a mere psychological projection, but as an epistemic phenomenon, "knowledge" in the broadest sense of the notion, covering all kinds of relations to an object, including the negative: distortion, enmity, hate, destruction. In all these epistemic relations it is—also—the object itself that becomes visible: be that as a mere trace. It is only and strictly in this sense, of rendering visible historical Jewish being, that anti-Semitism may be said to hold some "truth."

The anti-Semitic truth that I will point at consists neither in reproducing an originally Jewish operation of (problematically) conjoining knowledge and collective, as argued by the second anti-anti-Semitic position, nor in negating an originally Jewish operation of (commendably) separating knowledge from the collective, as argued in the third kind of anti-anti-Semitism. Rather, my analysis identifies in anti-Semitism a trace, within modern political epistemology, of a *different* political epistemology, which in the language of modernity is called "Jewish" or "Semite." The basic requirement for this exercise is the willingness to engage in knowledge *in absentia* of its object, so to speak in the condition of epistemic exile, or perhaps even to perceive exile as the condition of knowledge.

---

14   Scholars have offered various historical accounts of anti-Semitism, with various periodizations. Whereas Bernard Lazare told of anti-Semitism from antiquity to Dreyfus (*L'Antisemitisme*), Poliakov (*Histoire de l'antisemitisme*) traced an anti-Semitic tradition from Christ to Hitler, while Robert Wistrich more recently spanned *A Lethal Obsession: Anti-Semitism from Antiquity to the Global Jihad* (New York: Random House, 2010). Accounts of *modern* anti-Semitism, closer to my own analysis, have varied as well: for instance, Jacob Katz (*From Prejudice*), even though stating the year 1879 as "the beginning of modern anti-Semitism" (245), told a story from Eisenmenger to Hitler, while Alex Bein ("Moderne Antisemitismus") identified the point of departure in Gobineau. My story, which begins with the emergence of the term "anti-Semitism" in Renan, is very similar to Bein's.

5 Renan's Anti-Semitic Science

AS ISMAR ELBOGEN STATED, in the passage referred to by the *Geschichtliche Grundbegriffe*, one of the first to use the expression "anti-Semitism" was Mortiz Steinschneider. This he did, however, not "in a personal letter," and the information about it is not only "oral tradition." Rather, the term appears in one of Steinschneider's periodic reviews of "new and older literature of Judaism," which he published in Berlin from 1859 to 1882 as *Hebräische Bibliographie*. One of the first issues, of January-February 1860, contains a short review of a text that was just published by the philologist Heymann Steinthal in Berlin, in the first issue of the new journal founded at the same year by Steinthal and Moritz Lazarus, *Zeitschrift für Völkerpsychologie und Sprachwissenschaft*, "Journal for Psychology of Peoples and Linguistics." Steinthal's text was also a review, a very polemic critique of another text, by Ernst Renan, published a few months earlier, in 1859, in Paris, *Nouvelles considérations sur le caractère général des peuples sémitiques, et en particulier sur leur tendance du monothéisme* ("New considerations of the general character of the Semitic peoples, and in particular on their tendency to monotheism"), originally published in the *Journal Asiatique*, the French Oriental studies journal.[1] It is this composi-

---

1 For Steinschneider's review, see Moritz Steinschneider, *Hebräische Bibliographie. Blätter für neuere und ältere Literatur des Judenthums* 3, no. 13 (January-February 1860): 16; for Steinthal's, see H. Steinthal, "Zur Characteristik der semit. Völker," *Zeitschrift für Völkerpsychologie etc.*, ed. M. Lazarus and H. Steinthal, Bd. I. Heft 4 (Berlin: Ferd. Dümmler's Verlagsbuchhandlung, 1860),

tion of Hebraism, *Wissenschaft des Judentums*, ethnography and philology, Semitism, monotheism, and Orientalism that makes out the basic plot of anti-Semitism's emergence in modern science.²

In Steinschneider's review of Steinthal's text, he reported that the latter had criticized "the contradictions in Renan's basic views and their unproductiveness for science and research," and exposed "the consequences, or rather inconsequences of his anti-Semitic prejudices [*antisemitischen Vorturtheile*]." Anti-Semitism thus emerges as an epistemological critique of science, namely a critique of the scientificity of science, or pretended science, a critique of its epistemic quality. The critique of Semitism, anti-Semitism, at least Renan's, would be pseudo-science, would only look like science, but in fact be a prejudice, an opinion before proper knowledge, before science. I will now turn to the Renanian text itself, where Steinschneider's use of "*antisemitisch*" points, to examine what exactly in Renan had given rise to this concept and to the critique that it expresses. Of particular interest will be to highlight and compare Renan's own, almost inverse, use of "anti-Semitic," which in fact appeared five years before Steinschneider's, in a prior work of 1855, *Histoire générale et système comparé des langues sémitiques*, "General History and Compared System of the Semitic Languages," in relation to which the 1859 essay on "New Considerations on the General Character of the Semitic Peoples" offered its new considerations.³

328–345; and finally, Ernest Renan, *Nouvelles considérations sur le caractère général des peuples sémitiques, et en particulier sur leur tendance du monothéisme* (Paris, 1859), extrait n. 3 de l'année 1859 du Journal Asiatique.

2   For general expositions of Renan's life and work, see David C.J. Lee, *Ernest Renan: In the Shadow of Faith* (London: Gerald Duckworth and Co., 1996); Richard M. Chadbourne, *Ernest Renan* (New York: Twayne, 1968); Charles Chauvin, *Renan* (Paris: Desclée de Brouwer, 2000).

3   Ernest Renan, *Histoire générale et système comparé des langues sémitiques* (Paris: Michel Lévy Frères, 1855). It is the same publishing house, since 1875 doing business as Calmann-Lévy, whose director will be interned as a Jew during France's Nazi occupation, that one hundred years after Renan's book will also publish Léon Poliakov's *Histoire de l'Antisémitisme*. See Jean-Yves Mollier, *Michel and Calmann Lévy, ou la naissance de l'édition moderne 1836–1891* (Paris: Calmann-Lévy, 1984).

There has been a long scholarly debate, still ongoing, on Renan's anti-Semitism and racism, as well as his reception by political anti-Semites in France

Race Spirit

One of the new perspectives that the sequel on "Semitic People," the first text in history to be called (by Steinschneider) "anti-Semitic," offers beyond the earlier "Semitic Languages" is a fundamental epistemological self-reflection of Renan's science on the meaning of science.[4] This self-reflection is formulated, in Renan's text, as an epistemo-political *apologia*. What Renan's science apologizes for is being a science of peoples, which ascribes epistemic value to ethnic collectives, speaking, for instance, of "the general character of the Semitic peoples." This ethnic science, he acknowledges, stands in blatant contradiction to the basic political project that is "modern civilization": "modern civilization, in particular of France, aspires to realize gradually the word of Saint Paul 'there is no longer a Jew, nor a Gentile, neither Greek, nor Barbarian.'"[5] Modern civilization would thus be the actual realization of the Pauline vision, as Renan understands it, of the disappearance, the undoing or unbeing ("there is no longer") of *ethnoi*. Already visible here is the complex, paradox conceptual dynamics that has this undoing of collective, ethnic identities—Jew, Gentile, Greek, Barbarian—operating as the generative principle of a collective identity,

---

and Germany, which without doubt existed. I reiterate that my purpose here is not to make any general claim about Renan and his reception, but only to indicate in his texts a basic conceptual configuration that has given rise to the notion and discourse of "anti-Semitism." My intervention in the more general conversation on Renan can therefore be no more than textually and conceptually limited and specific. For an excellent review of the historical and contemporary debate, see Robert D. Priest, "Ernest Renan's Race Problem," *Historical Journal* 58 (2015): 309–330. Priest asserts "two fundamentally incompatible 'Renans' in circulation by the turn of the twentieth century. The right's Renan was a racialist visionary behind the *Histoire générale* and anti-democratic ideologue of *La réforme intellectuelle et morale*; the left's Renan was a daring anti-clerical who wrote *Vie de Jésus* and valiant cosmopolitan of the 1880s lectures" (316). My following argument will undermine the alleged "incompatibility" between these two positions.

4 The most complete formulation of Renan's scientific vision may be found in his earlier written but only later published work, *l'Avenir der la science, pensées de 1848* (Paris: Calmann-Lévy, 1890). See Almog, "The Racial Motif," 179–184; Said, *Orientalism*, 130–148.

5 Renan, *Nouvelles considérations*, 102.

France, which thus stands for a different, new kind of collective, of polity, "a state of ethnic homogeneity": a nation.[6]

The articulation of this Pauline event of modernity, this transubstantiation of the body politic, calls forth two basic concepts, whose tension, i.e., solidarity in contradiction, is generative for central segments in modern political epistemology, of our age still: spirit and race.[7] Spirit, *esprit*, is indeed the name given by Renan to the basic being that constitutes the

---

6   I thus subscribe to and wish to further articulate Jonathan Boyarin's disagreement with Edward Said, for whom "for Renan … being a philologist meant the severance of any and all connections with the old Christian god" (quoted in Jonathan Boyarin, "The Missing Keyword: Reading Olender's Renan," *Qui Parle* 7, no. 2 [1994]: 48). It should be noted that Said, who indeed emphasized Renan's break with Christianity, nonetheless recognized that "in the new lay science," Renan retained "the historical world-view he had gained from religion"; Said, *Orientalism* (London: Penguin Books, 2003 [1978]), 135. This chapter follows Boyarin's suggestion of looking at Renan's "view of Christianity" as the "link between [Renan's] earlier notion of racial essences and his later obsession with the liberal state and individualism" (52). This is also one of the directions suggested by Priest, "Renan's Race Problem," 325. For a similar argument, see Hochberg, "Remembering Semitism," 208–210. Susannah Heschel has already argued that Renan introduced "racial categories into theological discussions," providing "an important religious legitimation for the rise of racial anti-Semitism in the 1880s"; see Heschel, *Abraham Geiger and the Jewish Jesus* (Chicago: University of Chicago Press, 1998), 30. On Renan's work on and intervention in Christianity, in particular his influential and controversial *Vie de Jésus*, "Life of Jesus," which made him famous in his lifetime, see Robert D. Priest, *The Gospel according to Renan: Reading, Writing and Religion in Nineteenth-Century France* (Oxford: Oxford University Press, 2015).

7   I refer to a growing body of scholarship that has observed and examined theological or Christological conceptions at play in the formation of the modern secular discourse, more specifically in the tension between enlightenment's universalism and European racism, between transcendental philosophy and race theory. See for example Theodore Vial, *Modern Religion, Modern Race* (Oxford: Oxford University Press, 2016) or J. Kameron Carter, *Race: A Theological Account* (Oxford: Oxford University Press, 2008). I find especially illuminating Denise Buell, *Why This New Race: Ethnic Reasoning in Early Christianity* (New York: Columbia University Press, 2005), arguing *inter alia* how resistance to the introduction of modern race categories into theology, her example being Ernest Renan, has led contemporary scholarship to ignore the specific, non-modern

principle and *telos* of modernity's event. "Spirit" is what unfolds and shows itself in the modern undoing of ethnic collectives, which Renan thus understands as the eschatological "progress of spiritualism." "A progress of spiritualism, because it is an effort to make men forget their earthly origin, and only keep the brotherhood resulting from their divine nature."[8] The "progress of spiritualism" for Renan explicitly signifies a process of de-epistemization, of unknowing or "forgetting," namely of the "earthly origin," the *ethnos*.[9]

I will indicate below how forgetting, namely of history, later becomes constitutive in Renan's account of the nation's emergence, here signaled still in theological terms as "brotherhood in divine nature." What is crucial at this point is how spiritualization entails forgetting of *ethnos* that leads to the disappearance of *ethnos*, un-knowing leading to un-being. This eschatology implies a specific perception of *ethnos* as somehow being already non-being, already a negative entity, the negative of spirit. *Ethnos* as negative spirit is *race*. Hence the exact formulation of Renan's vision, which could be read as the eschatological principle of modern political thought, the triumph of man over race, of humanism over racism: "There will come a day when races will no longer exist, which means when there will only be *man*."[10]

Placing race at the center of science hardly seems consistent with this vision, appears rather to simply contradict it: doesn't the spiritual progress of modern civilization require *forgetting* race? But spirit's relation to the flesh is more complicated than this: the life of spirit, even as it transcends flesh, needs and generates flesh, and so generates the distinction between spirit and flesh *within* flesh, namely requires and produces the figure of spirit in flesh, of embodied spirit, flesh spirit. This is already observable in Paul's retranslation or reconversion, by way of metaphor, of the spiritual

---

"ethnic reasoning" in early Christian canon. On my reading, this kind of scholarly *spiritualization* of Christianity precisely carries out the Renanian project.

8   Renan, *Nouvelles considérations*, 102.
9   Cf. Kameron Carter reading of the ancient Church father Irenaeus of Lyon's anti-Gnostic texts as objecting to "Gnosticism's denigration of Christ's flesh—indeed, its denigration of the material order of creation and embodiment" (Carter, *Race*, 7, 11–38). My reading of Renan presents similarities to Carter's reading—through Irenaeus—of the Gnostics.
10 Renan, *Nouvelles considérations*, 102.

belonging to Christ into the belonging to Abraham's "seed" (*sperma*) (Gal. 3:29). The same complex relation is revealed in Renan's *science*, which is a science of the flesh. It is the paradoxical science of what should be forgotten—science for the sake of forgetting. It has the task of knowing, i.e., perceiving and seeing all which is memorable, the task of remembering it, such that it would already have been constituted by forgetfulness, such that it would already exist as being-forgotten. Renan formulates this task of memory reconstruction in terms that could well describe the basic project of modern historiography, the project of writing history for those who are beyond history, the project of "history" as remembering to forget: "The complexity of human affairs will never be explainable if we do not go back to antique facts, which solely hold the secret of ideas, institutions and mores of those who have most completely lost all memory of them" (102).

The principle in history that undoes history, an ahistorical principle of history, that renders history reducible to a non-historical *origin*, or, in the language of historical epistemology, that renders history "explainable," and thus forgettable, is for Renan *race*. "The idea of race remains the great explanation of the past," such that ethnography is the "key to history" (101–102). This is a fundamental principle of all forms of racism and race logic: to have any consequences in the domain of spirit, in particular to *contradict* spirit, race must belong to the element of spirit, must, namely, be a figure, a negative figure of spirit, to which, in the "progress of spiritualism," history in its entirety would be reduced. Race is never pure biology, or biology is *eo ipso* a figure of *logos*. In Renan's terminology, race accordingly stands for "original impulses" (99) and *instincts*: "natural instincts" (2), "deepest instincts" (12), "essential instincts" (15).[11]

---

11   This point is my central contribution to the scholarly debate on Renan's racism. It undermines any dismissal of race as a foundational category in Renan's discourse with the argument that race for him was not "biological" but rather linguistic or "symbolic." See for instance Priest, "Ernest Renan's Race Problem," emphasizing that in "Renan's most rigid description of the Semitic race, he was keen to resist any biological explanation" (312). In contrast to the complexity of Renan's views on Semitism, Priest indicates however his more unequivocal racist disparagement of blacks and Chinese (315). For an attempt to distance Renan from race more specifically with respect to the question of anti-Semitism, see Paul Lawrence Rose, "Renan versus Gobineau: Semitism and Antisemitism, Ancient Races and Modern Liberal Nations," *History of European Ideas* 39, no. 4

The very idea of race accordingly functions as a localization of spirit and spiritualism, including the distinction between spirit and flesh, in the realm of flesh. Renan describes how in the course of history race splits into something like body and spirit. Whereas race-body disappears through the "enormous crossing of blood and ideas," race nonetheless remains as "impulses," or "intellectual and moral molds," "frames" and "types": "the originary impulses subsist, even though the races that contributed them disappeared or are unrecognizable."[12] "Races are permanent frames, of types of human life, which, once founded never again die, but are often refilled by individuals who have almost no link of physical kinship with the founders.... We do not know whether, originally, these great determinations in humanity have arisen from the condition of physiologically diverse birth, or whether they result from groupings posterior to the emergence of man and throughout the centuries became permanent divisions. What is certain, is that over time races have become nothing more than intellectual and moral molds" (101). And Renan immediately provides two opposite examples or paradigms, whose exemplarity for his science manifests, as I will immediately show, its specific, scientific, anti-Semitism: "The Turk,

---

(2013), writing that "for Renan, indeed, 'race' was not an anthropological or biological category, but a linguistic and cultural one" (530).

Rose's article, although mostly focused on Renan, at least in its title and intention raises the important question of Renan's conceptual relation to Gobineau. The latter's less scientific, more popular and accordingly more vulgar and physiologically determined race discourse has been a common comparative resource for the sake of highlighting Renan's "cultural" notion of race (see Rose, "Renan versus Gobineau"; Priest, "Renan's Race Problem," 312–313). My analysis calls into question the apologetic power of this difference, in fact shows the difference between "biological" and "spiritual" notions of race as being inherent to race discourse. It would be nonetheless important to look more closely—and comparatively—at the specific ways in which the basic dynamic of this discourse is deployed and articulated in Gobineau. I only note here that Gobineau's *Essai sur l'inégalité des races humaines* (Paris: Firmin-Didot, 1884 [1854]) features, albeit in a different composition, similar elements of race as "invisible base of history" (xi), which is expressed in basic human "instincts" (xx), predicated on the fundamental tension between "material" and "moral" (84), and valuated in its capacity to generate "civilization" (76), and which as a doctrine is not contradictory, but rather complementary to Catholicism (4, 62–75).

12   Renan, *Nouvelles considérations*, 99.

Muslim devotee, is nowadays a much more true Semite than the Israelite who became French, or better, European" (101).

It is crucial to note how race, once translated into the epistemic realm, namely as "instinct," signifies a primordial level of knowledge, or more precisely infrastructure or precondition of knowledge, which in itself is hardly knowledge, as it lacks almost any relationality to object and in fact describes a mental predisposition. It is in this sense that race "instincts" belong to animality, to organic "natural" life, which would be the primitive, nonhistorical origin of history. In its pre- or meta-historicity, in its nonrelationality, race, however, paradoxically, is akin to spirit, which transcends all historical differences. Indeed, race is precisely the negative figure of spirit as *embodied*, which is as such constituted for oblivion and unbeing in the "progress of spiritualism." This seemingly paradoxical but structurally coherent nexus of spirit and race finds its accurate expression in the basic concept by which Renan designates race as the object of the human science, namely race as the (negative) epistemic principle: "race spirit" (70–71).[13]

Philology as Science of Race Spirit

In what exactly consists the *science* of race spirit? This is the basic epistemological question raised by race as a fundamental epistemic category,

---

13   This affinity of spirit and race as categories beyond history may, I think, be brought into the conversation of the apparent contradiction between reason and race in Kant. The question would be to what extent both reason and race may be shown to function for Kant as conditions of experience, i.e., in some way as *transcendental*. Cf. Emmanuel Chukwudi Eze, "The Color of Reason: The Idea of 'Race' in Kant's Anthropology," in *Postcolonial African Philosophy: A Critical Reader*, ed. Emmanuel Chukwudi Eze (Cambridge, MA: Blackwell, 1997), 103–140. In the last three decades there has been an important discussion on Kant's role in the "invention of race"; see Robert Bernasconi, "Who Invented the Concept of Race? Kant's Role in the Enlightenment Construction of Race," in *Race*, ed. Bernasconi (Oxford: Blackwell, 2001), 11–36; Bernasconi, "Kant as un Unfamiliar Source of Racism," in *Philosophers on Race: Critical Essays*, ed. Julie K. Ward and Tommy I. Lott (Oxford: Blackwell, 2002), 145–166. For an excellent review of the discussion, see Jon Mikkelsen's introduction to the collection *Kant and the Concept of Race. Late Eighteen-Century Writings*, trans. and ed. J. M. Mikkelsen (Albany: State University of New York Press, 2013).

which, as it will later become clearer, touches the epistemo-political heart of the matter. What this question asks about is the precise entity or phenomenon in which race spirit is visible, such that it may be the object of the self-reflective knowledge that is science. Where is race spirit to be seen? The question is crucial, since the conceptual thrust of both spirit and race, as analyzed above, in its Renanian humanist sense, is to extract "man" from all historical differences, and so from all historical visibility. Accordingly, any science of race spirit has to confront the difficulty of one invisibility manifesting another invisibility.

To this difficulty, modern science, in projects like Renan's, found at least one seminal answer, which was crucial for the rise of scientific anti-Semitism. Renan begins his "anti-Semitic" essay on the "Semitic Peoples" by a declaration that sounds like an answer, but in fact formulates the above problem: "For judging the character of a nation and a race, one has to consider what it has done in the world, search by what it has left its trace in history, see in what it has succeeded" (1). Observing race in its "trace in history," namely in what Renan also calls "work" (*oeuvre*), or what is currently often called "culture," is paradoxical because race, as analyzed above, is precisely the nonhistorical element invoked for "explaining" history, as a "key to history." To speak with Nancy, and against Nancy, "race" is essentially a *communauté désoeuvrée*, a community "out-of-work."

This paradox, of looking in history for the non- or prehistorical, in fact reproduces itself in the notion of the work. It should be recalled that the entity to be observed by science is the "race spirit," which designates the negative or minimum epistemic condition of "instinct" or "intuition," namely by definition preceding or precluding any "work" in the sense of an intentional, self-aware, and historical project or invention, what Renan most often characterizes by the epistemic condition of "reflection" and "science." The "work" that would constitute the "trace in history" of the "race spirit," and thus serve as the concrete object for race science, is consequently less a work than an expression, product, or manifestation of instincts. Renan calls this kind of manifestations "popular manifestations," which simply restates his basic epistemo-political interpretation of *ethnos* as race: "The spirit of each race ... should be looked for above all in popular manifestations. The logic of the people is not the logic of the school" (71).

The paradigmatic work of race spirit, the "popular manifestation" in which it shows itself in history, for Renan, and an entire age of science, is *language*. Renan also speaks in this context about "religion"; however, a careful analysis would show that "religion" is less the concrete phenomenon of race science than an epistemic characterization of the race spirit that is manifested primarily in the concrete phenomenon of language. This role of language implies of course a specific understanding of language. This understanding, conceptually specific as it is, is in fact quite common, even banal, and stands at the basis of numerous modern theories and performances of language. In Renan's work this common understanding of language reveals its epistemo-political significance.

Renan formulates this common conception of language on the first page of his 1855 preface to his great early work on the "General History and Comparative System of the Semitic Languages." Language, he writes, is "the immediate product of human consciousness" (ix). This is a certain reformulation of Aristotle's canonic description of language: "Sounds are the symbols of mental experience and writings are the symbols of sounds" (*De Interpretatione*, 16a), which has already been criticized as anthropocentric (Heidegger) and logocentric (Derrida). In the present context, it is its epistemo-political consequence or use that should be highlighted in Renan's version. The first important point to be noticed is the difference between the exteriority of language to Aristotle's soul as a sign, and the exteriority of language to Renan's consciousness as a *product*. The first, Aristotelian exteriority, signifies the lack of inherent relation between thought and language, namely *arbitrariness*. The second, Renanian exteriority, signifies, on the contrary, a very inherent connection, "immediate" even—exteriority as externalized interiority, as expression. Language would be the paradigm of externalized interiority—of product, of work. It is pure exteriority, in the sense that it is the "immediate" product, the first product, the product whose essence is to be product, to constitute the dimension of production, of expression, of work. Language is in this sense the element of all history.

The "immediacy" of the language product, however, also refers to the immediacy of the human consciousness that produces it. Language would be, in Renan's conception, the product of the primordial level of consciousness, of "primitive intuition," and so the paradigm of the paradoxical "work" that nonetheless arises from no reflection and no invention. In other words, language would be the work of race spirit. Here lies the epistemo-political crux of Renan's conception. Indeed, in the Aristotelian understanding, the *arbitrary* exteriority of language means disconnection between language and thought, and therefore epistemic *indifference* for the most evident feature of linguistic exteriority, namely the *diversity* of tongues: "Just as all men have not the same writing, so all men have not the same speech sounds, but the mental experiences, which these directly symbolize, are the same for all, as also are those things of which our experiences are the images" (*De interpretatione*, 16a). For Renan, in contrast, the specificity of language as tongue is the precise expression of the specificity of instincts or "primitive intuition," namely of the specific *race* that produced it. In his "Semitic Peoples," speaking of the origin of Semitic monotheism (see below), he traces it back to "primitive intuition, analogous to the one that guided for each race the creation of language. In matters of religion and in matters of language, nothing is invented; all is the fruit of a direction taken [*un parti pris*] at the origin, once and for all."[14]

It is this conception of language that stands at the basis of Renan's foundation of the human sciences or humanities, i.e., the science of man, as a science of race whose primary object is language, namely as "comparative ethnography and philology" (100). It would be important to examine more closely how this conceptual intimacy of language and race informs modern science of language, both in the form of philology and in later forms, such as semiology and linguistics, which partly *react* to this conception.[15] At this point I only indicate how this conception of language is interconnected to a specific *perception* of language, namely a specific way of imagining and in fact seeing the concrete reality that one understands as "language," a reality that would thus constitute the objective field for scientific observation and knowledge-production. Understanding language as the work of race spirit means perceiving the most non-reflective, non-intentional, non-epistemic aspects of language as the paradigm of language. Language is not what is said, but the preliminary framework, so to speak the prehistory of saying: grammar and words. These, too, are not perceived and observed as saying or speaking, but rather as *expressing* or documenting prelinguistic, natural dispositions—or, as Renan says, "monuments" (*Semitic Languages* x, xvi). In fact, the unintentional linguistic expression serves even to *contradict* the actual statement. Thus, Renan demonstrates the alleged monotheism

---

14   Renan, *Nouvelles considérations*, 73.
15   For a broader discussion on the interplay between modern science of language and modern science of race, see Olender, *Langues de Paradis*; see also Christopher M. Hutton, *Linguistics and the Third Reich: Mother-Tongue Fascism, Race and the Science of Language* (London: Routledge, 1999).

of ancient, pre-biblical Semitic peoples, by looking at the proper names they give to the *multiple* gods they speak of (*Semitic Peoples*, x).

It is in this sense that language in fact operates as the manifestation or embodiment of race spirit, which in itself is *negative* spirit. As such—to evoke once again Pauline discourse—language is *dead* spirit. Or more accurately, pointing at the dead spirit in language is the task of science as philology, in preparing and facilitating the modern event of "spiritualism," the resurrection of spirit from race. It is in this radical sense that I suggest to understand Olender's observation whereby "Renan wants to found the Christical event in philology as irrefutable science."[16]

Semites

Olender's statement was taken here out of its context, in which it refers, more specifically, to the basic distinction organizing Renan's race-spirit science, its most basic perception or knowledge, for the sake of which it is analyzed here, namely the distinction between Aryans or Indo-Europeans and Semites. The main object of Renan's race science is the Semites, the "Semitic Peoples"; the object of his philology is the "Semitic Languages." Indeed, the Semitic operates in his work as a paradigm of race, in the specific configuration of race-spirit as manifested in language. I described earlier the inherent problem of *visibility* that race, like spirit, poses for science, and how language has become the very image of race, the visible figure of the invisible essence. This conceptual configuration itself is rendered by Renan exemplary visible in the image of the Semites, a race whose existence is so much dependent on language, that it may be said to be "created by philology": "The individuality of this Semitic race has not been revealed to us but by the analysis of language, singularly confirmed, indeed, by the study of the mores, literatures, religions, such that this race, somehow, was created by philology, and so there is actually only one criterion for recognizing the Semites: it is language."[17]

It is instructive to observe how the set of phenomena that Renan names "the Semitic languages" in fact embodies for him his notion of language as "trace" of race, as the dead figure of spirit. In the preface to his "Semitic

---

16   *Langues de Paradis*, 149.
17   Renan, *Semitic Languages*, 45.

Languages" he explains how the historical life of the Semitic languages, having completed "the series of its interior revolutions," has ended, such that in the present times, in the world of the living, this linguistic family is "no longer represented but by one idiom, the Arab" (xi). But also in itself, in contrast to the "Indo-European" family, featuring the ability of "self-reproduction and rebirth," the family of Semitic languages shows "little active interior life," "no profound revolutions, no development, no progress" (xii). All this, in addition to the lack of writing vowels, i.e., "the entire individuality of dialects," all this "reduces Semitic texts to a sort of skeleton, excellent for studying the anatomy of language, but unsuitable for studying movement and life" (xiii). Whereas Indo-European languages feature pure active life, breaking with all history, Semitic languages are the fossil of prehistory, having conserved their identity "since highest antiquity, maybe even since the first days of the appearance of language" (xiii). Renan's philological analyses of the Semitic languages lead him to the conclusion that, in contrast to the Indo-European language, the Semitic languages are poor in abstraction and syntax, and ill suited for metaphysics, philosophy, or purely intellectual speculation, but are rather of a "physical and sensual character" (18). If language in general is the "immediate product of human consciousness," the Semitic languages embody this notion in the realm of ethnographic narrative, in which the lower epistemic forms appear as the "childhood of human spirit," such that "it is permitted ... to think that the Semitic languages have conserved for us, more clearly than any other family, the memory of one of these languages that man must have spoken at the first awakening of his conscience" (24).[18]

---

18 It is in Renan's anatomical description of the Semitic languages that Edward Said identified the "paradox" that "stands ... at the very center of [Renan's] entire work, his style, and his archival existence in the culture of his time," namely "that even as he encourages us to see languages as in some way corresponding to 'être vivants de la natrure', he is everywhere else proving that his Oriental languages, the Semitic languages, are inorganic, arrested, totally ossified, incapable of self-regeneration; in other words, he proves that Semitic is not a live language, and for that matter, neither are Semites live creatures" (Said, *Orientalism*, 145). The paradox disappears, however, if the *negative* task of Renan's science becomes visible, i.e., carrying out the "progress of spiritualism." This element is however obfuscated in Said's account together with Renan's basic Paulinianism.

This Semitic state of language, which I claim constitutes the paradigm of language for Renan's philology, is visible in Renan's account of the designation "Semitic." This designation, Renan explains, has replaced for "modern scholars" the designation "oriental" (2). Maurice Olender in fact describes how "oriental" has become an inconvenient appellation for the Levant since the rise of the Far Orient, in particular India, in European science.[19] Why "Semites"? This term is taken from *Bereshit*, also known as the Book of Genesis. The role that this text, together with the entire corpus of the Bible, plays in the emergence and formation of modern science is a considerable issue, with special significance for any interrogation on modern Jewish and anti-Jewish epistemes. In the case of Renan, it would be instructive to examine more carefully how his contribution to the foundation of nineteenth century human sciences draws from Bible readings, and to characterize more closely the hermeneutics that serves him in this project. In his study on the "Semitic Languages," the biblical scriptures are characterized as the "written monument" (xvi) of the Semites, and the first chapters of Genesis as the "common archive of the Semitic race," which, due to its exemplary racial principle, namely genealogy, "has conserved the most distinct memory of its origins," such that "the origins told in Genesis have become, in the general opinion, the origins of the human kind" (27), the story of the origins of races.

Race theory would thus have at least one of its origins in modern biblical hermeneutics.[20] Renan's philological hermeneutics characteristically reads the biblical texts as "historical documents" (27). He has no hesitations writing, for instance, that Abraham is "a definitely real and historical figure" (30). The reading of the racial origin of humanity in Genesis, the book of origins, focuses on its first chapters, first and foremost chapter 10. This chapter tells a genealogy, the *toladot*, of Noah's sons after the flood

---

19   See Olender, *Langues de Paradis*, 35. While Renan mentions Eichhorn as having set the trend of using "Semitic,» Olender points at A. L. von Schlözer, "Von den Chaldäern,» *Repertorium für biblische und morgenländische Litteratur* 8 (1781): 161; and Herder's 1782 preface to his *Vom Geist der Ebräischen Poesie*, ed. B. Suphan (Berlin, 1879), 429, 442–444. See also Bernard Lewis, *Semites and Anti-Semite: An Inquiry into Conflict and Prejudice* (New York: W.W. Norton and Company: 1986), 44–45.

20   See Colin Kidd, *The Forging of Races: Race and Scripture in the Protestant Atlantic World, 1600–2000* (Cambridge: Cambridge University Press, 2006).

and how this one single family engendered the entire variety of postdiluvian peoples. Renan considers this genealogy a solid basis on which "the ethnographic and historical interpretation may proceed in complete confidence" (28). It is a reading of this text that generates both the Semites and, in Renan's interpretation, also the anti-Semites.

The "Semites," literally, are the descendants of Noah's son *Shem*, who are listed in 10:21–30. On Renan's reading, the story that immediately follows chapter 10's genealogy, the story of the Tower of Babel, in Genesis 11, which tells about the *separation* of the different peoples, their dispersion on earth and therewith the beginning of political history, is most fundamentally a story about the Semites' parting ways from the rest of humanity. It is due to the affair of the Tower of Babel that the Semites would leave the original dwelling of humanity, *Eden*, and move to the deserts of Arabia, to embark on—what Renan considers as—the characteristically Semitic destiny of nomadic life. What drives the Semites away from the origin is the project of the Tower of Babel, a Babylonian project, Renan reads. This "work of vanity, a rebellion against God ... gigantic constructions, this powerful organization of force, despotism, where the king usurped the place of God, must have been supremely antipathic to the simple mores, the pride, the tastes of independence, the elevated religion, which have distinguished pure Semites" (33). The Semites were repulsed by the deeds of the Babylonians, which Renan can therefore characterize as "anti-Semitic" (*anti-sémitiques*). "The great deeds to which attached themselves the names of Nimrod, Assur, Ninus, appear to us as anti-Semitic deeds, at least in relation to the Terachites, who remained loyal to the patriarchal customs, and we are inclined to see here the cause of the movement that carried the Semites away from Armenia and Kurdistan towards the Southern regions, more suitable for their nomadic life" (33). Five years before it is used as a reproach against him by Steinschneider, Renan thus uses "anti-Semitic" *positively*, to designate the original Babylonian force of culture and civilization, which is contrary to the simple nature of the Semites.

Before examining more closely Renan's anti-Semitism, there is still the question of the name, the designation. Following Renan's own documentary reading of Genesis 10, "Semitic" is, as Renan himself explains, a misnomer. The division of peoples born from Noah's sons, a story that would supposedly constitute for ethnography the sole and certain "memory" of the racial origins of human kind, is actually, Renan notes, not based on a racial-ethnographic but rather on a geographic-climatic criteria.

Not only not all of Sem's sons are racially "Semitic," but they also include *Elam*, which is identified with Airya or Iran, namely the paradigmatically Babylon-style, anti-Semitic *Aryans*. According to the sole existing record, *Shem* is therefore the father both of the Semites and of the Aryans, both of Semites and of anti-Semites. Here lies the basic problem of *Shem*, a proper name that in the Semitic language of this Semitic *ur*-memory is also a word that means "name." It is noteworthy that Renan designates the *Shemitic* problem by the same name on which semantically stands the Tower of Babel. For Renan this story is about the separation of the Semites from the anti-Semites, but the story more directly concerns the separation of tongues, or as the biblical text itself calls it, giving Semitic etymology to the Babylonian name *Bavel*, the story about "confusion."²¹ "We understand now," Renan writes, "how unfortunate was Eichorn's idea, when he gave the name *Semitic* to the family of Syro-Arab languages. This name, which custom obliges us to maintain, was and will be for a long time the cause of myriad confusions" (43).

To this "Semitic" problem, the problem of the name, the philologist Renan proposes a so-to-speak "anti-Semitic" solution. The philologist solution is based on acknowledging language for and treating it as what it is: dead letter. This is the passage from the exteriority of language as product to the exteriority of language as arbitrariness. To overcome the semantic problem of *Shem*, Renan thus proposes to disconnect the name from its flesh, in the text, in language, in history, in primitive "human consciousness," and sublimate it into an act of pure will, "pure convention" (43): "The denomination *Semitic* will not be inconvenient, from the moment we take it as a simple conventional designation" (2).²² The name "Semites" thus remains "Semitic" only in its body, in its race, where it confusingly

---

21   Cf. Jacques Derrida, «Des tours de Babel,» in *Psyché. Inventions de l'autre* (Paris: Galilee 1987), 203–235.
22   Cf. Georges Dumézil, *Leçon inaugurale à la chaire de civilisation indo-europeénne du Collège de France, faite le jeudi 1er décembre 1949*, Paris, 1950, pp. 6–7, on the designation "Semites": "This inadequacy of the etiquette to its object is precisely that which recommends it: it betrays what it should be, namely a *conventional* sign ... notifying that it is the hypothesis of an original community, a common heritage, which is the most probable explication of the correspondences that we notice between these so dispersed historical facts on the ground" (quoted in Olender, *Langues de Paradis*, 38).

mixes Semites with non- and anti-Semites, but henceforth, in its spirit, in its meaning, and in the mode of its signification (by convention), it is non-Semitic, or "anti-Semitic," and designates only the race of the Semites.

Monotheism

The Semitic languages are for Renan thus the paradigmatic language, the Semitic peoples are the paradigmatic race, which science has the mission of exposing as the negative being of spirit, to be transcended by modernity's progress of spiritualism. It is in this sense that Renan's epistemology, with all the ethnographic-philological science that it generates, is structurally "anti-Semitic," as Moritz Steinschneider accurately formulated it. In fact, the negativity of the Semites in Renan's text is unequivocal. "I am the first to acknowledge that the Semitic race, compared to the Indo-European race, represents in fact an inferior combination of human nature."[23]

Renan bases this Semitic inferiority on the two fundamental elements of "race spirit," namely language and religion. I have already discussed how the Semitic languages are for Renan the paradigm of language as dead spirit. His sequel essay, "General Character of the Semitic Peoples," focuses on the element of religion, which was already present in the earlier work on the Semitic languages. Like language, religion too, for Renan, is a product of immediate consciousness and primitive humanity, and thus not a work of reflective intention but the effect of instincts. The essay on the "Semitic Peoples" is dedicated in large part to the claim that the specific Semitic form of religion, "*monotheism*," is indeed paradigmatically "religious," insofar as it is not the work of reflection, not based on the rational progress of science and philosophy, but emerges from instincts and intuition.

It is thought provoking to see how a critique of monotheism becomes a pillar in such a Christological project as Renan's, as shall be further clarified below. And yet, it is indeed in monotheism that Renan identifies the manifestation of the more general negative epistemic principle of the Semitic race-spirit, namely the "lack of fecundity in imagination and language" (78). Indeed, and here appears one of the many "contradictions," of which Steinthal, as reviewed by Steinschneider, accused Renan. Monotheism is for Renan the paradigmatically religious, i.e., primitive, form of race spirit.

---

23   Renan, *Semitic Languages*, 4.

Nonetheless, he characterizes monotheism, compared to Indo-Europeans, *polytheistic* religions, as a poor form of religion, a reduced and rudimentary form, a "minimum of religion" (78), with only one God. Monotheism would reduce all beings to the single principle of the one God and would therefore constitute, as minimum of religion, a minimum of knowledge, a "a great disdain to knowledge" (86), lacking all curiosity and tolerance: "God is, God created the world; this said, all is said" (10).

The epistemic deficiency goes hand in hand with a political deficiency. The Semites for Renan are essentially "nomadic," organized by tent, family, and tribe, by a principle of patriarchs and blood (13), such that they have developed no political civilization, being too sensual and physical and at the same time—this is another of Renan's anti-Semitic "contradictions"—too religious to separate the secular from the spiritual, and so acknowledging "only spiritual power," their leaders are all prophets (95). No knowledge, no polity, no joy: the monotheistic and nomadic Semites have developed no plastic art, and Renan even identifies the lack of all "ability to laugh" (12). To sum it up: "The Semitic race features almost exclusively negative characters: it has no mythology, no epos, no science, no philosophy, no fiction, no plastic arts, no civil life; in sum, absence of complexity, of nuance, exclusive sentiment of unity. There is no variety in monotheism" (16).

Renan's anti-Semitism is thus open and very literal. Nevertheless, and this is one of the greatest paradoxes of race epistemology, as I already indicated, race spirit as such is invisible—it does not appear *as such* in history. This means that "Semites" too do not appear as such in history. By categorical necessity, and not by some empirical contingence, there is no historical collective or culture that has identified itself or been known to other historical, pre-nineteenth-century European cultures as "Semite," which is a term and entity "created by philology." Indeed, as Hegel has recognized, it is the very logic of bio-logical categories, that the genus never exists as such, but always in an individualized form: in Hegelian terms, the biological category is essentially *abstract*.[24] The crucial question, and the most fundamental operation, of the concept "Semites," as paradigmatic to all race discourse, pertains to perception, to an ability to see the invisible be-

---

24 See G.W.F. Hegel, *Phänomenologie des Geistes* (Frankfurt am Main: Suhrkamp, 1986), "Beobachtung der Nature," 187–225.

hind the visible—to a certain intuition beyond seeing, certainty beyond knowledge: an instinct or faith. Who in history are "the Semites"?

Thinking back from post–World War II anti-anti-Semitism, the answer may seem trivial: anti-Semitism is anti-Jewish, which means that the Semites are paradigmatically the Jews. I already indicated how the Nazis rejected this identification. Neither does it simply apply to Renan's science. In fact, "Jews" for Renan is already a religious category, a type of monotheism. As noted above, religion is a primary historical phenomenon, product or expression, of race-spirit. It is however only a product of race, not race itself. Race is articulated in different kind of categories, non- or rather pre-religious, signifying pre-religious ethnic collectives, prehistorical "peoples," indeed *races*. What is the specificity of these racial categories? How are races *named*? How is anything named or known, which is before history? The names used by Renan, like many others, are paradoxical at least insofar as they are taken not just from history, but from the seminal Semitic religious historiography (according to Renan), namely the biblical *Genesis*, telling its own origins. Based on these readings, in a text that speaks of no "Jews," Renan determines that the paradigmatic Semites are the two main peoples of the "nomadic brunch" of the Semitic race, who are the "Arabs" and the "Hebrews."

Renan is an exemplary *topos* for the ongoing reflection over the last decades concerning the ways in which the configuration of Jew/Israeli/Hebrew versus Muslim/Arab, under the surface of one of the most paradigmatic current geo-political and theo-political conflicts, is in fact a performance of Christian political theology in its modern secular dispensation.[25] In the Renanian, philological-racial variant, the pair "Hebrews"/"Arabs" features as the basic embodiment of the "Semites," and so as the basic body of race *überhaupt*. The binary structure is crucial: it is precisely the ethnic duality, namely the duality or variety of ethnic forms that the Semitic race has developed in the course of its existence, which provides the conceptual counterpart to the original unity of the race. It is the same bio-logy that generates the interrelations between the genus and the species, as articulated by Hegel. Of course, in Renan's science, this conceptual constellation is expressed in positivist terms, dressed as an empirical proof, whereby the

---

25   See Anidjar, *Semites*; Hochberg, "Remembering Semitism," as well as my discussions of them in the introduction to this book.

similarity of the Hebrews and the Arabs demonstrates the original singularity of the Semitic race—and of the original racial diversity of humankind in general. The Hebrews and the Arabs are "these two great individualities, whose astonishing resemblance, throughout the centuries, is the surest indication of a primitive psychological variety of humanity" (85).

Be that as it may, the same set of questions concerning the visibility of the race, of the Semites, could be equally raised with respect to the species, the peoples—who are the Arabs and the Hebrews? The first criterion for answering this question seems to be already evident, as it underlies the entire epistemological structure of Renan's ethnographic philology, namely language. As we saw, language is the "immediate product" and so the original "popular manifestation" of race-spirit. Arabs and Hebrews would thus be simply the names of the collectives whose languages are, respectively, Arab and Hebrew. This statement is of course already far from simple. My above notes on the specific understanding of language at work in race philology already indicated some of the fundamental difficulties raised by any science of Semitic languages, and by extension of the Arab and Hebrew species. What interests me here is the shift, surely no contingent, but structurally conditioned, from the phenomenon of language, governing Renan's earlier "On the Semitic Languages," to the phenomenon around which revolves Renan's later essay "On the Semitic Peoples and their Tendency to Monotheism," the first text ever to be designated as "anti-Semitic," namely the phenomenon of *religion*.

This movement of race science from language to religion no doubt manifests its theological underpinnings, as I indicated them above with respect to the categories race and spirit. Within the anti-spiritual realm of race, which is in its turn divided into biological race, "body"-race, and epistemic race, i.e., race spirit, both language and religion are primary products of race spirit. By virtue of the constant polarization between flesh and spirit, once again, so it seems, this dichotomy operates within the realm of race-spirit to the effect of generating the distinction between its bodily side, language, and its spiritual side, religion. And so, notwithstanding language as the "immediate product of human consciousness," when Renan attempts to discern "the general character of the Semitic peoples" by observing the Semitic race's "trace in history," the "popular manifestation" that serves as primary phenomenon for observation and analysis, "the work (*oeuvre*) of the Semitic race," is indeed *monotheism*. The dual linguistic-ethnic figure of the pair Hebrews/Arabs is counterposed by the monotheistic trinity of "Judaism, Christianism and Islamism" (73).

This movement from the binary to the trinitary follows the basic dynamics of supersession, of the specific form that generates the event of modernity as it is coded in Renan's ethno-philology, indeed a "Christical event," as noted by Olender. "Jewish, Muslim and Christian" designate the different moments within this event.

Muslim Race

The point of departure for Renan's account is indeed binary, the two "pure forms" of monotheism, based on the dual Hebrew-Arab figure of the Semitic race, being "the Hebrew form or Mosaism, and the Arab form or Islamism."[26] Nevertheless, the flesh-spirit dichotomy is once again at work within the already spiritualized realm of race-based religion. Notwithstanding the identical point of departure of the Hebrew and the Arab religions, "the Hebrew form has so quickly mixed and surpassed so astonishingly in some aspects the limits of the particular race spirit, that it is really Arabia that should be taken as the measure of the Semitic spirit" (14). The underlying configuration of race epistemology should be highlighted. Semitism, the paradigmatic race spirit, in its very spirit (religion), is divided into a racial and spiritual part, so to speak a race spirit of race (Muslim), which affirms race, and a race spirit of spirit (Jewish), which surpasses race. It is precisely this distinction that Renan uses as the example for illustrating the meaning of the notion "race spirit" as the central category of race science. Originally biological, "what is certain," according to Renan, "is that over time races have become nothing more than intellectual and moral molds. The Turk, Muslim devotee, is nowadays a much more true Semite than the Israelite who became French, or better, European."[27]

For Renan, in fact, it is not Judaism, but Islam that presents the "ideal of monotheism" (38). To be sure, the historically relatively late appearance of Islam, compared to Judaism and Christianity, is not a problem. Religion being expression of race, Renan traces Islam back to pre-Islamic Arabic monotheism arising from the "deepest instincts of Arabia" (37).

---

26   Renan, *Semitic Languages*, 14.
27   Renan, *Semitic Peoples*, 101.

The seventh-century event of Muhammad thus represents no revolution but a reform that goes back to the roots of Arabic monotheism (37). The paradigmatic historical phenomenon of Islam for Renan, however, is not Muhammad, nor any other form of Arabic Islam, but, as the above quote shows, Turkey.[28] This choice is no doubt influenced by the geo-politics of Renan's day, the Imperial Ottoman Caliphate embodying in his eyes the "Semitic establishment" (93). Nevertheless, the signification of this choice for Renan is more than geo-political. Turkey is the epitome of the Semitic spirit and establishment insofar as the Turkish peoples are *not* originally, namely *racially* Semitic. In other words, Islam would be the paradigmatic Semitic race spirit insofar as it is a *racial* race spirit, a race spirit of race, which is capable of subjecting the bodies of other, non-Semitic races, such as the Turks, "violently folding the most diverse races to its own measures" (93), and thus so to speak of *converting* them to Semitism. "Islamism, in fact, is such an imperial mold for the nations that are subjected to it that all peoples who become Muslim become, somehow, Semites" (93).[29]

Christian Nation

What, then, would the Hebrew form of monotheism, Judaism, be, in comparison to Islam? The answer is complex. It is not simply the *opposite* principle. Before looking more closely at Renan's perception of Judaism, it will therefore be crucial to point at the precise phenomenon that would embody in history the opposite principle to Islam, namely *Christianity*. In fact, if Islam is the monotheistic form, and thus epitome of racial race spirit, Christianity is the embodiment of *spiritual* race spirit. Whereas Islam is the race spirit that affirms race, which converts non-Semitic races into Semitism, into the very principle and spirit of race, Christianity is the exact contrast: it is the element of Semitic race spirit that has *transcended* Semitism. Christianity is the spiritual, namely non-racial race spirit of Semitism, which detached itself from this race of races, and surrendered

---

28 Renan also refers to the Algerian leader of the struggle against French colonialism in the mid-nineteenth century, Emir Abdelkader (15).

29 For more on Renan and Islam, see Priest, "Renan's Race Problem," 328–329.

itself completely to the paradigmatic *other* of the Semites—the Aryans or Indo-Europeans.

Renan provides no detailed account of what is exactly meant by these designations, and in what "traces of history" they can be observed. As mentioned above, his text operates within an already existing and to an important extent established epistemic field, in which "Aryans" and "Indo-Europeans" prevail as evident entities.[30] Important for my purposes is the structural role that these categories assume in his discourse. The binary tension Aryans/Indo-Europeans vs. Semites is the hypostasis of the tension spirit vs. race in the realm of races, analogous to the tension Hebrew vs. Arab within the Semitic race itself. Whereas the Semites are the paradigmatic race insofar as the Semitic race spirit is the spirit of race, as attested by the Semitic language and religion, the Aryans or Indo-Europeans are the race of spirit, namely the race of no-race. In contrast to Semitic monotheism, enslaved to necessity and authority, the Indo-European religion—whatever it may be, and Renan, as aforesaid, provides no specifics—is polytheistic, liberated, and open to the complex and diversified play of "free causes." "The Aryan understands nature as multiple and animated in each one of its parts; he saw in all the phenomena of this world the action of free causes."[31] Similarly, Indo-European languages, in opposition to the "skeleton" of the Semitic ones, are characterized by "self reproducing and rebirth."[32] On the whole, therefore, in contrast to the Semitic spirit of primitive, racial instincts, i.e., the Semitic *racial* race spirit, the Indo-European race spirit is the high-end, spiritual spirit, "the very spirit of philosophy of science,"[33] where Renan's project situates itself. His anti-Semitic finding whereby "the Semitic race features almost exclusively negative characters" receives its full meaning in light of the contrasting indication concerning "the much more essential gifts that the Indo-European race has given to the world, [and] which form ... the *substratum* of all civilization" (85).

In contrast to the Semitic race, the paradigmatic race, the race with the spirit of race, the Indo-European race is the race of spirit, the race that

---

30 See Olender, *Langues de Paradis*.
31 Renan, *Semitic Peoples*, 44.
32 Renan, *Semitic Languages*, xii.
33 Renan, *Semitic Peoples*, 13.

transcends and ultimately negates race, a figure that reminds of Nancy's description of the Jews as the "people of no-people," or, of Marx's proletariat as the class whose vocation is to abolish classes. Indo-Europeans or Aryans as race beyond race feature centrally also in political anti-Semitism, as I will show below. At this point, in the context of Renan's science, it is crucial to see how the Indo-European race of spirit is the exact match, the perfect body, for Christianity, as the spiritual permutation of the Semitic race spirit, which transcends Semitism, in contrast to Islamic spirit, which converts to Semitism. "The wall of separation that nowadays so profoundly separates the Muslim peoples and the Christian peoples represents in reality the division between the Semitic spirit and the Indo-European spirit, Christianism having completely transcended the limits of the Semitic spirit, conforming to the spirit of the peoples that adopted it, while Islamism, in contrast, violently folded the most diverse races to its own measures" (93).

In the context of the epistemo-political question, it will not be superfluous, to further point at how this Christo-Indo-European constellation underlies the epistemo-political formation that Renan's work posits against the essentially Semitic formation of "race." I mean the very political figure of enlightened modern humanity, of which Renan has been one of the most prominent advocates and early theorists—the *nation*. His seminal text of 1882, *Qu'est-ce qu'une nation?*, "What Is a Nation?," narrates the birth of the modern nation from the marriage of Germanic national principle with Christianity.[34] The essence of Renan's concept of the nation lies in a principle of spirit emerging, through the "progress of spiritualism," from the negation of race, "the ethnographic principle." The bulk of Renan's definition of the nation consists in *negating* all worldly "popular manifestations," all 'works.' A nation is defined neither by ethnicity, nor language, nor religion, nor soil, nor culture (13–25). Nation is indeed not race, but "a soul, a spiritual principle"—a "spiritual family" (26).

The notion of "spiritual family," easily translatable to "spiritual race," conveys the ambivalent kinship of spirit and race, race itself already signifying in fact, as shown above, "race spirit." Similar to race, nation too is a collective principle that transcends all historical and cultural realities.

---

[34] Ernest Renan, *Qu'est-ce qu'une nation? Conférence faite en Sorbonne, Le 11 Mars 1882* (Paris: Calmann-Lévy, 1882), 4–5.

It is true that Renan does assert, in the second, positive part of his definition, that a nation requires a common past, "a rich heritage of memories," of "great things," sacrifice and glory (27). Nevertheless, Renan's emphasis is not on history but on memory, namely not on historical reality but on a common historiographical narrative. National memory, Renan in fact declares, essentially requires *forgetting* history: "Forgetfulness, and I would even say the historical error, are an essential factor for the formation of a nation" (7–8).[35] Accordingly, in the national narrative constructed by Renan himself, the primitive, racial origin of the national principle in the Germanic peoples is mentioned only to be forgotten and superseded by a national memory of French great things: "It is the glory of France of having, by the French revolution, proclaimed that a nation exists by itself. . . . The principle of the nations is ours" (10).

The actual and sole element of national being, which could be said to represent the essence both of spirit and of race, is not common past, but the absolute common presence, an absolute presence of the nation to itself, beyond or before any exteriority, any objectivity, any world or history, beyond or before any *knowledge*, a collective self-foundation, which Renan calls "will." Nation is the collective *will* to be a nation, or as Renan's famous formulation goes: "A nation is a plebiscite of every day." I wish to indicate the negative political epistemology that thus seems to govern the notion of the nation, in its canonic Renanian articulation, tying together race science and Christian spirit.[36] The rise of the modern European nation is the very event of spirit transcending (and perfecting) race, by negating history and science, negating the epistemic domain of knowledge, of "metaphysical or theological abstractions," for the sake of pure presence of man to himself. "We chased away from politics the metaphysical or theological abstractions. What remains after this? What remains is man, his desires, his needs" (28). Hence Renan's no less famous image of ideal human civ-

---

35 On the central motif of forgetfulness in Renan's conception of the nation, see Benedict Anderson, *Imagined Communities* (New York: Verso, 2006 [1983]), 199–201.
36 Cf. Boyarin, "The Missing Keyword," 52; Anidjar, *Semites*, 45–53. For the opinion that Renan's concept of the "nation" clearly dissociates him from race thinking, see Bierer, "Renan and His Interpreters," 378; Rose, "Renan versus Gobineau," 535–536.

ilization under national conditions as humanity's making itself heard to itself: "Nations serve for the common work (*oeuvre*) of civilization; each contributes one note to this great concert of humanity, which, ultimately, is the highest ideal reality that we achieve" (29).[37]

Modernity as Jewish Conversion from Race to Spirit

What about the Jews, this third, Hebrew form of Semitic monotheism? I already indicated the affinity, in Renan's eyes, between Judaism and Islam as the two "pure forms" of monotheism, and how it is rather Islam that has come to represent the "ideal of monotheism," which for Renan in his time was embodied by Turkey. Nonetheless, in his essay on the "Semitic Peoples," Renan raises the obvious question, at least from the point of view of Christian historiography, of whether monotheism was not after all "the special work (*oeuvre*) of the Jewish people."[38] Isn't the common Semitic archive and *urtext* of monotheism, the Book of *Genesis*, again, at least from a Christian perspective, the first book of Moses, of the Hebrew, Jewish Bible? Renan does not deny this special, exemplary role of the Jews in the emergence of Semitic monotheism. He acknowledges the "chosenness" of the Jews and interprets it in Greek terms as a Jewish "aristocracy" within the broader mass of the Semites: "Greece plays in the Indo-European race a role highly analogous to the role of the Jewish nation in the Semitic race" (3). The crucial difference between the Greeks and the Jews would of course be that monotheism, essentially Semitic and thus essentially belonging to the more primitive, racial part of race spirit, is not a feat of "discovery and an accomplished scientific progress" (16), like Greek philosophy and science, but rather "the result of a certain disposition of race" (16). The Jewish religion is "rather negative than positive," its "principle goal" being "to avoid superstitious practices" (14). The "chosen," aristo-

---

37 Cf. Derrida's notion of the consummation of the metaphysical subject's presence to itself as "s'entendre parler," "to hear oneself speak," in *De la Grammatologie* (Paris: Les Editions de Minuit, 1967), 136; Derrida, *La voix et le phenomena* (Paris: PUF, 2012 [1967]), 16. Derrida further points at the political figure of this category in Rousseau's description of the paradigmatic polity as the assembly where each person can hear the others; see Derrida, *De la Grammatologie*, 429–435.
38 Renan, *Semitic Peoples*, 14.

cratic status of Jews among the Semites therefore signifies no intellectual, political, moral, or any other cultural "superiority," but is purely a matter of instincts: "I thus submit that, since an antiquity that surpasses all memory, the Hebrew people has possessed the essential instincts that constitute monotheism" (15).

Nevertheless, this original, prehistoric acuity of Jewish monotheistic instinct has found its expression, so Renan's observations, also within history. There would be a sort of historical Jewish form of "Semitic establishment," which, in contradistinction to the Islamic form, focuses not on expansion but on self-preservation. "The Israelites," Renan explains, "managed to build for themselves a system of precautions sufficient for victoriously maintaining their patriarchal cult" (18). Referring no doubt to the rabbinic tradition, he notes how the "intellectual aristocracy of the nation" has set up "around the people a strict fence for keeping them from any contact with the foreign" (18). Once again, as Semitic, Renan does not consider this form of collective organization to be properly *political*, but purely "religious." Jewish historical identity is understood as a form of organic self-preservation, indeed a racial, biological instinct. This instinct is not only foreign to civilization—"the Jewish people never had a political life, and the Jewish institutions, which have served so much the religious progress of humanity, have served so little the progress of public life"—but even has anti-civilizatory, destructive effects: "by disseminating everywhere a people detached of any homeland, and too much inclined...to provide the sovereigns with docile servants against their subjects" (92).

It is thus that in Renan's historiography the Jews, who have preserved Semitism not just in spirit but in their proper bodies, become the very site of the modern event, the abolishment of flesh in spirit, of race in the nation—of the Jew in the French. "The Turk, Muslim devotee, is nowadays a much more true Semite than the Israelite who became French, or better, European" (101). This is the main point, which builds the passage from scientific to political anti-Semitism: the conversion of the Jews, not to Christianity, but to Europe, namely the events of *emancipation* and *assimilation*, constitute the consummation of civilization in the modern European, the supersession of Semitic race spirit *in the Semitic body*: "How many Israelites today, who descend directly from the ancient habitants of Palestine, possess nothing of the Semitic character, and are no more than modern men, driven and assimilated by this great force, superior to races and destructive of local origins, called civilization!" (xv–xvi). The Jewish body is the site for the epistemo-political event of modernity.[39]

---

39 I therefore disagree with Jonathan Boyarin that "for Renan the Jews seem to be politically irrelevant in the present"; "The Missing Keyword," 47.

6 Aphenomenology of the Jewish Question

Bauer and Marx

IT IS THIS EVENT, MODERNITY, in this body, the Jewish, that stands at the basis of political anti-Semitism. "Political" anti-Semitism is what today, in retrospect, is most commonly understood to constitute, both conceptually and historically, the essence of anti-Semitism, i.e., the modern discourse and practice aimed against Jews, which culminated in the National Socialist anti-Jewish politics. This discourse is indeed the only historical discourse that, in some of its key moments, has named itself "anti-Semitism," even though, as already indicated above, its most accomplished form, Nazism, explicitly rejected this designation. To what extent it is justified to call this discourse "political," and to talk about anti-Jewish "politics"—this question refers back to the fundamental epistemo-political question. It may and is said to be "political" in contrast to Renan's "scientific" anti-Semitism. This statement is true not simply in the sense that political anti-Semitism takes place and effect in a different dimension than science, is not theoretical, academic, or scholarly, but *practical*. For such a description already supposes a very specific understanding of praxis, namely that *excludes* science. The distinction between "scientific" and "political" anti-Semitism, as I will show below, more specifically arises from the discourse of political anti-Semitism itself, which has an essential *anti-scientific* component. In this, however, and this goes back to my basic claim, political anti-Semitism is in no way nonepistemic or separated from science or epistemology. Rather, it is precisely in its anti-scientificity that anti-Semitic politics embodies anti-Semitic science.

In its political form, anti-Semitism is a part of the political event of modernity, insofar as this event manifests itself paradigmatically by Jews becoming an integral part of the non-Jewish polity, or, to repeat Renan's words, by Jews becoming "modern men, driven and assimilated by this great force, superior to races and destructive of local origins, called civilization!"[1] From this perspective, the assimilation of the Jews is a fundamental phenomenon of the modern European polity, of modernity as a polity, namely of the modern state. Accordingly, the question of the modern state is the question underlying all anti-Semitism, the Jewish Question.[2]

To access the meaning of this question, it is helpful to recall the nature of the modern state as a nation-state, a state that exists in the body of a nation. Becoming a part of the state thus means *assimilation* into the national body, means therefore, fundamentally, that Jews become, politically, socially, bodily, like others, like non-Jews. The Israelite becomes French. As Renan explained, the modern nation is based on the principle of will, of pure will, of living, present, and permanent will that breaks with all history, with all political history, first and foremost with all "ethnicity." There would be consequently a fundamental principle of modern political epistemology whereby the appearance of modernity entails the disappearance of the Jews.[3]

---

1   Renan, *Semitic Peoples*, xv–xvi.
2   On the semantic history of the "Jewish Question," see Jacob Toury, "'The Jewish Question': A Semantic Approach," *Leo Baeck Institute Year Book* 11 (1966): 85–106. Toury's general conclusion was that "the catchword *Judenfrage* emerged at the crossroads between old and new Jewry and between traditional Jew-hatred and new extreme antisemitism. In its anti-Jewish context it denied the feasibility of emancipation, or—where emancipation had been granted—its capability of solving the problem of Jewish integration" (106). Emancipation is also posited as the crucial condition for the emergence of political anti-Semitism by Jacob Katz, *From Prejudice*, 1.
3   Cf. J. Katz's account of Voltaire's anti-Judaism, which Katz posits as a precursor of modern anti-Semitism: "[Voltaire] is no longer speaking in terms of the Christian concept of absorption of the Jews through conversion, but rather of gradual assimilation.... Lacking an ideology of justification, Jewry and Judaism were laid bare to crushing criticism and were judged totally worthless—lost remnants of ancient times that had no place in new circumstances. The prophecy

This is a complex and difficult statement. Both appearance and disappearance have many forms, which for a philosopher like Edmund Husserl, for instance, himself an "ethnic" Jew who converted to modern Christianity, constituted the object of philosophy as a science of phenomena, as phenomenology. Would there be, at the origins of phenomenology, an act of assimilation? The phenomenology of modern spirit in any case entails an a-phenomenology (from the Greek ἀφανίζει, "to disappear") of the Jew. At the center of this aphenomenology would stand the modern designation "Jew" as the name of dis-appearance, of the essentially invisible, of the hidden difference. "Jew"—like *Sein* for Heidegger—would designate not an object, but a question. The modern performance would be the positing of the Jewish question. This performance too has many forms. Not the least of them is the appearance of *modern* Judaism, i.e., of Judaism as a figure of modernity, not the least in the shape of the modern nation-state. The form of the Jewish Question that is of primary interest here, however, is anti-Semitism.

Anti-Semitism may be traced back *textually* to the Jewish Question. In 1882, three years after the emergence in Germany, around Wilhelm Marr, of a political movement that explicitly defined itself as "anti-Semitic," Ludwig Philippson, founder and editor-in-chief of the *Allgemeine Zeitung des Judentums*, looking back, identified as "the real father of anti-Semitism" the ex-theologian, intellectual, and publicist Bruno Bauer, who had just passed away. This was due, according to Philippson, to Bauer's "essay *Die Judenfrage* [that] contained *in nuce* everything inimical to the Jews that has developed from then on in Germany."[4] Bauer's text on "The Jewish Question" (JQ), first published in 1842, together with his further essay, a year later, on "The Capacity of Present-Day Jews and Christians to Become Free" (CPJC),[5] did constitute one of the first explicit formulations of this

---

seemed evident, and it held that they were destined and deservedly doomed to disappear from the world" (*From Prejudice*, 47).

4   AZdJ, 1882, 282. Quoted in Toury, "The Jewish Question," 99–100.
5   Bruno Bauer, "Die Judenfrage," *Deutsche Jahrbücher für Wissenschaft und Kunst* v (1842), and later as a pamphlet, *Die Juden Frage* (Braunschweig, 1843); Bauer, "Die Fähigkeit der heutigen Juden und Christen, frei zu werden," in *Einundzwanzig Bogen aus der Schweiz*, Herausgegeben von Georg Herwegh (Zürich und Winterthur, 1843), 56–71.

question, and molded a discourse that a few decades later will develop, among others through later texts of Bauer himself, into anti-Semitism.[6] From a contemporary perspective, one of the most significant responses to Bauer's essays was penned by a young Karl Marx, a son of Jewish assimilation, who in 1843 published *Zur Judenfrage, On the Jewish Question*, which itself has been the object of a long controversy due to the harsh anti-Jewish language that it contains.[7]

Both Bauer and Marx on the Jewish Question could be and have been seen as anti-Semitic *avant la lettre*.[8] Nonetheless, the explicitly hermeneu-

---

[6] Toury confirms that "Bauer's arguments seem to have played a most important part in the diffusion of the anti-Jewish slogan and its new contents," and may be thus considered as "a decisive contribution to the concept of the modern *Judenfrage*" ("'The Jewish Question,'" 97). See also Paul Lawrence Rose, *German Question*, 263: "[Bauer] developed the concept of a coherent 'political antisemitism' that would implement the insights of critical revolutionary antisemitism in the real world."

[7] Karl Marx, "Zur Judenfrage," in Karl Marx and Friedrich Engels, *Werke*, Band I (Berlin: Dietz Verlag, 1981), 347–377; originally published in "Deutsch-Französische Jahrbücher," Paris 1844. Yoav Peled showed to what extent a long reception of Marx's essay systematically failed to read him in light of Bauer's texts; see Peled, "From Theology to Sociology: Bruno Bauer and Karl Marx on the Question of Jewish Emancipation," *History of Political Thought* 13 (1992): 463–485. For other Jewish and non-Jewish, objecting and supportive responses to Bauer's text, see Nathan Rotenstreich, "For and against Emancipation: The Bruno Bauer Controversy," *Leo Baeck Institute Year Book* 4 (1959): 3–36. Marx's relation to his Jewish background has been a concern of an ongoing scholarly debate. Sander I. Gilman, "Karl Marx and the Secret Language of Jews," *Modern Judaism* 4 (1984): 275–294, analyzed Marx's relation to language as arising from structural tensions of assimilationist identity logic. For a study arguing for "structural affinities between Marx's thought and the worldview of the Jewish tradition" (9), focusing on "the plotline of the biblical narrative, with its themes of exile and return" (9), see Dennis K. Fischman, *Political Discourse in Exile: Karl Marx and the Jewish Question* (Amherst: University of Massachusetts Press, 1991).

[8] For Bauer, see Philippson above; for Marx, the classic is Dagobert D. Runes in his introduction to the English translation of Marx's "*Zur Judenfrage*" as Karl Marx, *A World without Jews* (New York: Philosophical Library, 1959), v–xi; Sven-Eric Liedman, *A World to Win: The Life and Works of Karl Marx*, trans. Jeffrey N. Skinner (London: Verso, 2018), 99; Rose, *German Question*, 302–304.

tical methodology that guides the present investigation, which has so far revealed the significance of language on various levels of the "Jewish" question, is particularly sensitive to the paradox of reading a text *avant la lettre*. My aim in this chapter is to shed light on the epistemo-political drama that animates this preparatory discourse to anti-Semitism. The conceptual drama will be presented, with a comparative view to Renan, through the polemic between Bauer and Marx. If Bauer, in affinity with Renan, may indeed be read as proto-anti-Semitic, I will show how Marx's anti-Judaism as formulated in *On the Jewish Question* should be rather read as *pre*-anti-Semitic, i.e., as a precursor, prehistory, preparation, or, as Arendt would say, an "origin" of anti-Semitism, but at the same time as *non*-anti-Semitic, i.e., as distinguished from anti-Semitism. My reading of Marx, in contrast to Bauer, will accordingly serve to delineate the conceptual outline of anti-Semitic political epistemology, which will be discussed in the next chapter.

But first, Bauer.

The Question according to Bauer

Bruno Bauer's "Jewish Question" did not purport to *raise* the question. The question was already there.[9] The task that Bauer set for himself was rather "the correct posing of the question" [*Die richtige Stellung der Frage*].[10] Having in mind the recent controversy on Heidegger's anti-Semitism, Bauer's treatment of the *Judenfrage* reminds of Heidegger's project of the *Seinsfrage*, the Question of Being, the initial task of which as formulated in the first page of *Sein und Zeit* was: "to pose anew [*erneut stellen*] the question on the meaning of being."[11] The analogy is, formally, instructive. Like the

---

9   For an introduction to Bauer, see Douglas Moggach, *The Philosophy and Politics of Bruno Bauer* (Cambridge: Cambridge University Press, 2003); E. Barnikol, *Bruno Bauer. Studien und Materialien* (Assen: Van Gorcum, 1972); more specifically for the relations between Bauer and Marx, see Zvi Rosen, *Bruno Bauer and Karl Marx: The Influence of Bruno Bauer on Marx's Thought* (Den Haag: Martinus Nijhoff, 1977).
10 Bauer, *The Jewish Question*, 4.
11 *Sein und Zeit*, 1, emphasis in the original. For a discussion on the possible link between the *Judenfrage* and the *Seinsfrage*, see Di Cesare, *Heidegger, die Juden, die Shoah*, 111.

Question of Being for Heidegger, also the Question of the Jews for Bauer had already been posed. It was precisely the presence of this question, in its precise position, that fundamentally characterized what Bauer perceived as the existing situation, the situation of existence, in which this question was posed. Like Heidegger's Question of Being, also Bauer's Question of the Jews was seen as fundamental for the factual, historical condition of human existence in general: "If the cause of the Jews has become popular, it is not due to the merit of its advocates, but can only be explained thus, that the people sense [*das Volk ahnet*] the connection between the emancipation of the Jews and the development of our overall conditions."[12]

This foundation of knowledge ("can be explained") on "sensation" whose agent is the "people" will become a central element in anti-Semitic epistemology, as I show below, and already echoes some basic elements from my analysis above of Renan's science. The central common element, however, is the insertion, inclusion, or integration of the Jews into the European polity, the "emancipation of the Jews," as a paradigm or symbol for the historical situation in general: "The question of emancipation is a general question, the question of our time in general. Not only the Jews, we too want to be emancipated" (61).

The communality with Renan goes further. The "time" of Bauer is, like Renan's time, a *kairos*, a moment of event. This event of modernity, a political event, which Renan refers to as the rise of "modern civilization" and Bauer as "emancipation," is the beginning of "a new era in human history."[13] Both acknowledge the epistemic event at the basis of the political one, which is therefore an epistemo-political event of, as Renan says, "spiritualization," or, for Bauer, "enlightenment" (*Aufklärung*). Like Renan, Bauer too perceives this epistemo-political event eschatologically, the "new era of human history" being in fact the *end* of history, insofar as it signifies the disappearance or dissolution of "the historical traditions."[14] The disappearance of "historical traditions" has a clear political significance insofar as it means, for Renan as for Bauer, the disappearance, or forgetfulness, of all collective, political differences, all distinctions between peoples, for the

---

12   Bauer, *The Jewish Question*, 1.
13   Bauer, *The Capacity of Present-Day Jews*, 184.
14   Bauer, *The Jewish Question*, 19.

sake of the common "human essence," as the sole principle of the modern European polity, the state (20).[15]

The answer or solution to the Jewish Question is therefore obvious. The solution to the Jewish Question is the dissolution of the Jewish Question, which means the disappearance of the Jews. Emancipation, the emergence of the modern state, means that the Jews "may stop being Jews" and—here the deep ambivalence of freedom in the form of "emancipation" clearly shows itself—"*must* stop being Jews" (22; my emphasis). The radicality of Bauer's answer to the actual political question of the Jewish emancipation, i.e., the radical rejection of emancipation to Jews as long as they continue being Jews, must be noted, since it goes beyond Hegelianism.[16] The solution proposed by Bauer, the "Robespierre of Theology,"[17] to the Jewish question opens up the entire question of Being. What does "stop being Jews" mean? What is the meaning of "Jewish-being"? What kind of being is it? Paraphrasing Heidegger's *Being and Time*, we can say that the preliminary question of Jewish-(non-)being concerns the "understanding of the meaning of this question."[18]

Obviously, it is a *negative* kind of being, which is destined to disappear with and as a condition for the rise of the fully emancipated human being. Renan called this kind of negative being "race," which would disappear in the "progress of spiritualization." Bauer at this point does not use the category "race," which he will use a decade later.[19] In his writing on the Jewish

---

15   Moggach (*Bauer*, 1) underlies more specifically Bauer's "republicanism," which highlights further his conceptual affinity to Renan. Paul L. Rose, *German Question*, emphasizes Bauer's "revolutionism" (263).
16   As David Leopold noted, Hegel himself supported Jewish emancipation, for example in the *Grundlinien der Philosophie des Rechts*; see David Leopold, "The Hegelian Antisemitism of Bruno Bauer," *History of European Ideas* 25 (1999): 189.
17   Rotenstreich, "Bauer Controversy," 11.
18   *Sein und Zeit*, 1.
19   See Leopold, "Hegelian Antisemitism," 188; Rotenstreich, "Bauer Controsrsry," 32–36, referring to Bauer's contribution in Hermann Wagner's *Staats- und Gesellschafts-Lexicon* of 1859, "Das Judentum in der Fremde," where he wrote, for instance: "Being able to exist only in connection to fermenting organism, only through the intrusive interference in the inner struggle of other spirits, and at the same time, as an independent, as a dominating race, who alone remains intact, wishing to consume these organisms (the seat of its only

Question, Bauer's basic category for understanding the being of "historical traditions," such as, paradigmatically, the Jewish-being, is not race but *religion*. And so, for Bauer, the Jewish Question is not the race question but the question of religion. The Jewish Question, the question concerning the dissolution of the Jews, is the question concerning the dissolution of religion.[20] The fundamental thrust of Bauer's intervention on the Jewish Question lies precisely in "correctly posing" this question, such that—to the supposed great shock of Christian ears—it is no longer understood as the traditional religious problem that Jews represent for Christians; rather, it now means the problem that religion altogether (as arche-category for historical difference) represents for the enlightened and emancipated human.

It is highly significant that the Jewish Question is, for Bauer, not formulated as the question of race, like for Renan, but as the question of religion. Placing the question of religion at the center of sociopolitical critique was in fact a constitutive feature of the Young Hegelian discourse from which both Bauer and Marx arose.[21] "Religion," in Hegelian language a form of consciousness, of knowledge, of *spirit*, would seem to stand in stark opposition to "race." Nonetheless, my above analysis of Renan's discourse has already revealed some intimate links between these notions within the

---

possible existence)—this chimeric intention, this hubris constitutes the misfortune [*Unglück*] of the Jews, but also naturally provokes the reaction of other races, which do not agree to be consumed" (reprint; Berlin: Heinicke, 1863, iii). According to Rotenstreich, the racialization of the Jewish Question was the "innovation of Bauer," which "heralded the next stage of anti-Semitism in the modern world" (35). See also Rose, *German Question*, 276: "Bauer's *Judaism Abroad* signaled the arrival of a new phase of revolutionary antisemitism where nearly all future discussion of the Jewish Question was established on a racial basis." Rose characterized Bauer's intellectual trajectory as moving "from philosophical to racial antisemitims" (277).

20   Bauer, *The Capacity of Present-Day Jews*, 184.
21   It is within this discourse that actual textual relations may be traced between Bauer and Renan. Zvi Rosen (*Bauer and Marx*, 17–44) described how the literary beginning of the Young Hegelian movement can be located in David Friedrich Strauß' *Das Leben Jesu* (1835), an important inspiration for Renan and his *Vie de Jésus* (1863). It is in his harsh critic against Strauß' book that the young Bauer first made his name. Later on, in the 1870s, Bauer published critical essays against both Strauß and Renan; see Bruno Bauer, *Philo, Strauß und Renan und das Urchristenthum* (Berlin: Hempel, 1874).

purview of a certain Pauline logic, or a modern permutation thereof. My reading of Bauer attempts to render this intimacy visible from the perspective of the Jewish question.

There is of course much to be said—as Marx will do—about the understanding of the basic epistemo-political question of history through the category of "religion" as already operating within a theological framework. A constitutive observation for the critique of secularism will be that a very similar logic underlies both the religious question and the question of religion.[22] In Bauer's contemplation of the Jewish Question, this ambivalence of "religion" is articulated through the basic difference that organizes his discourse, a basic *religious* difference, namely the difference between Jews and Christians—no role given to Muslims, who remain outsiders to the question of emancipation and the constitution of the European republic.

The ambivalence of "religion" surfaces in the tension between Bauer's two basic and famous contentions. The first contention results directly from his effort to correctly formulate the Jewish Question. Since the question is *not* religious, the solution of the Jewish Question through the dissolution of the Jews does not mean a religious dissolution of Judaism, namely does not mean that Jews should become Christians. Rather, emancipation requires that both Jews and Christians, religion altogether, be dissolved: "The solution of the opposition is that it completely vanishes, and the Jews may stop being Jews, without having to become Christian, or rather must stop being Jews, and may not become Christian."[23] Nevertheless, Bauer's analysis of the Jewish Question is critically determined by another question, concerning, as the title of his second text on the subject reads, "The Capacity of Present-Day Jews and Christians to Become Free." The question concerning the dissolution of religion is epitomized in the specifically *Jewish* question and is therefore nonetheless determined through a religious difference, an interreligious or rather an inner-religious question. For this question too, Bauer has an unequivocal answer: "Christianity ... stands far above Judaism, the Christian far above the Jew, and his capacity to become free is

---

22 For a conceptual-historical problematization of the application of the category "religion" to Judaism, see Leora Batnitzky, *How Judaism Became a Religion: An Introduction to Modern Jewish Thought* (Princeton, NJ: Princeton University Press, 2011).

23 Bauer, *The Jewish Question*, 22.

by far greater than that of the Jew."[24] The question of emancipation as the question of religion raises both a Jewish and a Christian question. But the questions are different, and so are the solutions—and dissolutions. It is this Jewish-Christian difference that gives its meaning to the Jewish Question.[25]

To understand this meaning, it is crucial to look more closely at Bauer's understanding of religion.[26] "Religion," as noted above, is Bauer's basic category for the historical human being, which is basically a negative being, destined to be negated by the eschatological event of modernity, enlightenment, and emancipation. "Religion" thus features the basic ambivalence of the *process*—it is already animated by its goal, its end, which, however, exists in the process itself only as absent, as not yet there. The process is both the presence and the absence of its end. Religion is for Bauer the process of enlightenment. He expresses the ambivalence of this process by saying that religion is enlightenment that remains "illusion,"[27] an idea central also for Marx's critique of religion,[28] and more generally inherent to all historical phenomenology, where appearance—or truth—is temporal, i.e., understood as a process or an event, as history.

In religion, i.e., the history of enlightenment in the mode of negative appearance, of illusion, Bauer identifies two main moments: the Jewish and the Christian. These two moments appear as chrono-logically or-

---

24   Bauer, *The Capacity of Present-Day Jews*, 192.
25   Accordingly, against Peled's claim that "Christianity did not fare any better than Judaism in Bauer's two essays" ("Bauer and Marx," 469), I concur with David Leopold (and Marx—see below) that "in his discussion of 'the Jewish question', Bauer does not typically propound a homogeneous and negative view of religion but differentiates, in a striking and provocative manner, between the relative merits of Judaism and Christianity" ("Hegelian Antisemitism," 181).
26   Moggach (*Bauer*, 140–146) shows how the argument of *The Jewish Question* (1843) arises from the broader conceptual framework formulated by Bauer earlier in the same year in *Das entdeckte Christenthum. Eine Erinnerung an das achzehnte Jahrhundert und ein Beitrag zur Krisis des neunzehnten* (Zürich and Winterthur: Verlag des literarischen Comptoirs, 1843). Leopold notes ("Hegelian Antisemitism," 181) how *Das entdeckte Christentum* is another expression of Bauer's intellectual debt to the anti-Jewish classic of Johann Andreas Eisenmenger, *Entdecktes Judentum* (Königsberg, 1700), which Bauer in *The Jewish Question* refers to as a "work of solid theological scholarship" (86).
27   Bauer, *The Capacity of Present-Day Jews*, 185.
28   Cf. Rosen, *Marx and Bauer*, 139–140.

dered, however this chronology is phenomenology, i.e., unfolds according to the logic of manifestation, here of enlightenment. The first moment is Judaism. Bauer identifies in Judaism a basic drive of enlightenment, i.e., of transcending historical differences for the sake of the one united "human essence": "All states and peoples are unjustified and have no right to exist before the One, before Jehova."[29] In the epistemo-political context, it is important to note how the negative historical being, destined to be dissolved in enlightenment, is characterized as an ethnic-political ("states and peoples") principle, a supposedly prehistorical, natural principle, i.e., what Renan called "race."

Apparently, in contrast to Renan, for whom Hebrew Semitic monotheism constitutes a paradigm of race, for Bauer, monotheistic Judaism would be the first antiracial movement. Nevertheless, by the inherent ambivalence of religion, Judaism would also be the first moment of illusion. The Jewish illusion is built on exception. According to Bauer, Judaism transcended all peoples *except* one—the Jewish people itself, the "chosen people": "only against itself, against its own people, was Judaism unwilling to take this enlightenment seriously" (189). Accordingly, Judaism remained an "illusion" of religion, an ethnically limited transcendence of ethnicity. This notion raises questions, first and foremost about the exact nature of this "exception" and the ways in which it would, could, and must be something other than a simple contradiction. The difficulty shows itself in Bauer's description of the Jewish religion as built on the absolute difference between Jews and non-Jews. Bauer recognizes the possibility of *becoming* Jewish. He nonetheless insists that non-Jews, even if they join the Jewish people, will always remain foreign.[30]

---

29   Bauer, *The Capacity of Present-Day Jews*, 189.
30   Bauer, *The Jewish Question*, 31. See Bauer's discussion of the proselyte in Judaism, the *ger*, who according to him forever *remains* foreign even after joining the Jewish people. This for Bauer is the ultimate proof of the absolute Jewish separation between Jews and non-Jews. For a recent confirmation of Bauer's analysis with respect to early rabbinic Judaism, see Adi Ophir and Ishay Rosen-Zvi, *Goy: Israel's Multiple Others and the Birth of the Gentile* (Oxford: Oxford University Press, 2018). See my critique in Elad Lapidot, "The Goyish Goy," *Political Theology* 21.1–2 (2020): 151–156, and my diverging analysis, Elad Lapidot, "Deterritorialized Immigrant."

It seems that all difficulties ultimately arise from Bauer's perception of Judaism as the first moment in the history of religion, which is the history of enlightenment's absence, or empty presence, i.e., as mere illusion. By transcending the original, prehistorical—racial—ethnic diversity for the sake of the one people, Judaism has replaced a simply *given*, natural ethnic difference with a religious, i.e., historical *principle* of ethnicity, an ethnic institution or *constitution*: "It permitted one people to exist, as the only one justified, and precisely by this constituted [*stiftete*] the most limited and singular popular and political life."[31] In other words, the Jewish religion would be the religion of non-religion, the religion of *ethnos*, or, to go back to Renan, the religion of race. Judaism, the first moment in the process of enlightenment, would—in Hegelian terms—negate the immediate ethnic reality only to preserve and elevate (*aufheben*) it to the level of an ethnic principle, such that this first moment of enlightenment dialectically becomes the principle of anti-enlightenment. This is a similar logic to Badiou's conception of Judaism as the universal principle of particularity, as I analyzed it in Chapter 3. Bauer's characterization of Judaism, which he among others traces back to the mentality of "the Orient,"[32] is consequently almost identical to Renan's characterization of Semitism: a spirit of resistance to the progress of history, to art and science, to freedom and reason (10–15), a spirit of—to highlight one of the key terms of theological anti-Judaism—"stubbornness."[33] Judaism is the spirit of anti-spirituality, the "mere cleverness of sensual egoism."[34]

It is within this dialectics that Christianity appears as the second moment of enlightenment: "The Christian religion is the *Aufhebung* of Judaism."[35] Christianity represents the reemergence of enlightenment from its own self-negation. By repeating the movement of transcendence of ethnicity, which was initiated by Judaism, on the Jewish people itself,[36] Christianity has completed the process of religious enlightenment, arriving at the post-ethnic "general concept of the human essence" (179), and thus of "freedom and equality of all men" (190). Within the historical pro-

---

31 Bauer, *The Capacity of Present-Day Jews*, 189.
32 Bauer, *The Jewish Question*, 11.
33 Rose, *German Question*, 267.
34 Bauer, *The Capacity of Present-Day Jews*, 180.
35 Bauer, *The Jewish Question*, 17.
36 Bauer, *The Capacity of Present-Day Jews*, 189.

cess of enlightenment, i.e., within the history of religion, Judaism would accordingly represent the principle of anti-enlightenment, whereas "enlightenment has . . . its true seat in Christianity" (183). Indeed, Christianity too is still a moment of history, is still religion. However, Christianity is the *completion* of religion, i.e., both summit and end, what Bauer calls "pure religion" (183). As religion, Christianity remains a "fantasy" (191) or illusion of emancipation; however, in particular in the form of Protestantism, it becomes "complete and omnipotent illusion," which "takes hold of man in his entirety, and dominates him not externally, through priestly, hierarchical or church power, but by his own inner self" (185). We may say that in Protestant Christianity, which transcends not only the Jewish people but also the historical being of Christianity, the Church, the illusion of enlightenment, religion, becomes something like the pure thought of enlightenment.

The two basic forms of illusory enlightenment—Judaism and Christianity—require two different forms of dissolution for accomplishing the event of emancipation. Both religions or historical traditions indeed must dissolve, cease to be: emancipation is the negation of both. But the nature of this negation is different. Christianity constitutes the appearance of emancipation, the rise of human essence, in its negative form, as pure illusion: "Christianity is the religion that promised humanity the most, i.e., everything, but has also failed the most, i.e., in everything. It is therefore the birth place of the highest freedom, just like it was the power of the greatest enslavement" (192). Emancipation is accordingly the direct negation of Christianity by inversion, by revolution: "The Christian, when he dissolves his Christian essence, gives to humanity everything it can take: he gives it itself: he brings it back to itself" (186); "humanity, where it finds itself as Christian, has reached the point where a comprehensive revolution will heal all damage caused by religion in general" (192). However, this revolutionary negation of Christianity is nothing but its *Aufhebung*, i.e., the application of the Christian principle, originally applied to Judaism, to Christianity itself. In other words, the negation of Christianity for the sake of enlightenment is nothing but the enactment of the Christian principle itself: "The obligation of the Christian is to correctly recognize the result of Christianity's development, its dissolution and the elevation of man above the Christian, i.e., cease from being Christian, in order to become man and free" (194). The Christian should acknowledge political emancipation, i.e., the citizenship in the modern nation-state, as the true accomplishment of Christianity. The negation of Christianity is therefore for Bauer something like *secularization*.

The emancipatory negation of Judaism is different. I recall that the historical *Aufhebung* of Judaism, i.e., the dialectical, negating-preserving-elevating negation of Judaism, was and is Christianity. One could therefore play with the thought that the Jews, to become free, must first convert to Christianity and then secularize their Christian love to human rights. Bauer however, as I said, rejects this idea: "If they wish to be free, the Jews should not convert to Christianity, but to dissolved Christianity, to dissolved religion in general, i.e., to enlightenment, critique and its result—free humanity" (193). If conversion to Christianity is *Aufhebung* of Judaism, the kind of negation that emancipation requires with respect to Judaism is of a graver kind, "more and harder than just to change one religion with another" (195). What is required of the Jew? As Bauer describes it, "The Jew . . . must sacrifice the chimerical privilege of his nationality, his fantastical, detached [*bodenlos*] law—as hard as this sacrifice may be to him, since he must completely renounce himself and negate [*verneinen*] Judaism—for humanity, for the result of the development and dissolution of Christianity" (194). There is here an interesting problem in Hegelian dialectics: there would be a way, so it seems, to "jump" from an earlier moment in the dialectical process directly to the end of the process, without passing through the intermediary stages, so to speak to circumvent dialectics—and history. Be the formal logical explanation of this possibility as it may, what it seems to imply, at least with respect to the Jews, is a negation that is no longer dialectical, no longer negation-preservation-elevation, no longer *Aufhebung*, but a non-dialectical negation, an utter *Verneinung*. Judaism should not be converted but negated. In other words, Jewish emancipation would not lie in Christianity, but in *secular anti-Judaism*, which could be at least one description of anti-Semitism.

This formulation goes beyond Bauer's explicit statements. His text does provide, however, some indication for the epistemo-political significance of emancipation's anti-Judaism. I already pointed at how, like Renan, Bauer too perceives the positive reality of emancipation and enlightenment, of "dissolved Christianity," of liberated human essence, in the political existence of the modern civil state. The liberated human is the *Staatsbürger*, the citizen of the state. It is in fact the modern state that Bauer identifies as standing in fundamental and utter contradiction to Jewish being: "Only by way of sophistry, of seeming, would the Jew be able to remain in state life; if he wishes to remain Jew, the mere seeming would prevail and become the essence, i.e., his life in the state would be only a seeming or a momentary exception to the essence and rule" (176–177). A Jewish citizen is a figure of "hypocrisy" (177–178).

It is crucial to highlight here two points. First, Jewish being, be it an "illusion," namely the illusion of religion, is at the same time an illusion of *religion*, which is the illusion of emancipation. Judaism is the illusion of illusion, and so, unlike Christianity, the "pure illusion," Jewish being is *real*, and so manifests itself as a polity, as a people and state, which accordingly, unlike Christianity, stands in direct confrontation with the modern, secular state: the one negates the other. This explicitly *political* understanding of Jewish being, and thus the understanding of the "Jewish Question" not as a religious question, not as a question of faith, not primarily concerning the question of God, but as a political question, primarily concerning the question of the State, is where Bauer's discourse no longer approaches Judaism from a religious, Christian, perspective. The political conception of Jewish being, which Bauer draws, among others, explicitly from Mendelssohn, constitutes the trace of *actual* Jewish political epistemology in Bauer's thought.[37] This conception will be constitutive to the entire "Jewish Question" discourse, including, as will be shown in the next chapter, anti-Semitism.

The second crucial point, the more specifically *epistemo*-political, is the specific form of contradiction that Bauer identifies between Jewish being and modern "state life," namely the form of "seeming" or "hypocrisy." Jews *can* seem to live as citizens of the state. The contradiction is not on the visible level: Jews can behave and act and look and be in the world like

---

37 Cf. Peled, "Bauer and Marx," 467–468. In the framework of my aphenomenology of the modern Jewish, of which anti-Semitism constitutes just one significant but in no way the only manifestation, I find noteworthy Rotenstreich's remark whereby "Bauer could find all his arguments against the stubbornness of the Jewish religion in the writings of those Jewish Reformers themselves who, though they polemized against him in their struggle for Jewish emancipation, yet agreed with him in their verdict on Jewish orthodoxy.... The similarities of argument are too striking to be explained by anything but the common ideological and sociopolitical background" ("Bauer Controversy," 12). See Toury ("'The Jewish Question," 100–105) for an analysis of early Jewish uses made of the phrase "*Judenfrage*."

everyone else. The problem concerns being beyond or in contrast to seeming, appearing, and seeing, a political element, I suggest, of non-worldly and anti-epistemic being. My above analysis of Renan has revealed two such elements, seemingly contradictory, but actually interrelated: *race*, the ethnographic principle, and *will*, the principle of the nation. The state of which Bauer speaks is the nation-state. The political emancipation of the Jews, by way of their disappearance, should take place through their assimilation into the "nations of our time."[38] The modern nation-state, as my analysis of both Renan and Bauer showed, dissolves all historical differences. This polity is thus governed by the principle of will, i.e., the will to be a nation, which liberates, "emancipates," from all historical and worldly attachments: "a nation is a plebiscite of every day." It is this unworldly, invisible element of will, which stands in contradiction to Jewish being as the anti-historical and unworldly principle of exclusive and absolute peoplehood, which Renan calls "race."

The unique epistemo-political power of this contradiction is that it takes place between two essentially invisible elements: will and race. This essentially indeterminable contradiction sets the realm of social appearance, of concrete political existence, constantly in the mode of potential "mere seeming": one invisible entity (national will) may always conceal another invisibility (Jewish race). There is however one way of demonstrating, attesting to, or witnessing attachment to the unworldly invisible, a very old way, namely by way of martyrdom, of self-sacrifice. In the nation-state, this self-sacrifice is performed institutionally through the generalized military service. Conscription, in particular in wartime, has played and still plays a central role in the emergence and life of modern nations—a much stronger form of "plebiscite" than the elections. Military service has played an equally central role also in the history of Jewish emancipation, being the main symbolic element constantly raised by and against Jews as proof of loyalty to the nation-state. "Front-line soldiers" featured as the sole and constant exception even in the Nazi anti-Jewish legislation.[39] It is the military "sacrifice for the state" that Bauer too evokes as the sole concrete

---

38 Bauer, *The Jewish Question*, 61.
39 See Raul Hilberg, *The Destruction of the European Jews, Volume I* (New York: Holmes and Meier, 1985), 87–89.

example for the "hypocrisy" of Jewish state life. Interestingly, he evokes this martyrdom to show that even this ultimate act of self-sacrifice is still *no* proof of Jewish loyalty to the state, since "sacrifice for the state on Shabbat is allowed exceptionally only this time."[40]

Marx and the State Question

If the Jews have historically been for Christianity the living potential of *becoming* Christian and so the living, embodied resource of Christian being, in modernity they became the paradigmatic site of emancipation as the living source of the nation-state. That the Question of the Jews is the Question of the State—this was the basic observation underlying young Karl Marx's famous reply to Bruno Bauer, *On the Jewish Question*, which was reformulated a year later in *The Holy Family*.[41] It would be possible to trace a conceptual line leading from early Marx's contemplation on the Jewish Question to later developments of Marxist political thought.[42] Such a reading would constitute an important chapter in any broader reflection on modern political epistemology. In the present context I will point only at several central motifs in Marx's anti-Judaism.

First and foremost, it is important to note how Marx simultaneously shared and completely turned on its head the basic framework of Bauer's discourse—and of Renan's. Marx's thought too circled around the perception or imagination of modern emancipation. Like Bauer, Marx too

---

40   Bauer, *The Capacity of Present-Day Jews*, 177.
41   Friedrich Engels and Karl Marx, *Die heilige Familie oder Kritik der kritischen Kritik. Gegen Bruno Bauer und Konsorten*, in Karl Marx and Friedrich Engels, *Werke*, Band II (Berlin: Dietz Verlag, 1962), 3–223. For an excellent and comprehensive discussion of Marx's texts, in their sociopolitical as well as intellectual context, and of the diverse forms of its reception, see Julius Carlebach, *Karl Marx and the Radical Critique of Judaism* (London: Routledge and Kegan Paul, 1978).
42   See Rose (*German Question*, 298–299), who also refers to diverging opinions, such as J. Katz's assertion that, as Rose formulates it, "anyone interested in the development of Marx's socialist doctrine can dispense with his original linkage of it to the Jewish Question"; Rose refers to Katz, *From Prejudice to Destruction: Anti-Semitism 1700–1933* (Cambridge, MA: Harvard University Press, 1980), 170ff.

identified, as the basic epistemo-political condition of emancipation, the critique of religion. As he wrote around the same time of writing *On the Jewish Question*, in the first line of his *Introduction to the Critique of Hegel's Philosophy of Right* of 1844, "the critique of religion is the condition for all critique."[43] For Marx too, like Bauer, religion occupies this crucial place since it embodies the counter-emancipatory condition of *illusion*. Religion is pseudo-emancipation. Famously, in this same introduction to his critique of Hegel, Marx describes religion as "opium of the people" (378).[44]

However, and this is the crucial point, Marx's understanding of the "illusion," is diametrically opposed to Bauer's—and to Renan's. For Marx, the illusion of religion consists precisely in the motif that for Bauer and Renan constitutes emancipation: the transcendence of all historical differences by the "progress of spiritualization," or in more political terms, the dissolution of the historical peoples in the imagined nation. For Marx, religion is illusion not because it is still too attached to the concrete, worldly, historical human condition, what he calls society (*Gesellschaft*), but on the contrary because it disregards concrete social conditions. It is not the people who are the opium of religion—religion is the opium of the people.

Marx therefore contests the very perception of the entity "religion." If religion is illusion, then any attempt to contemplate religion beyond illusion may not contemplate religion from inner religious perspective, from the sole perspective of *theology*. Herein lies his critique of Bauer. "Where the question stops being *theological*," he writes, "Bauer's critique stops being critical."[45] The truth of religion cannot be assessed in religious standards. On the contrary: the truth of religion is the exact opposite of what religion says. And the dimension where both truth and illusion exist is not the realm of religion and theology, but the realm of the world as society, which will become the element of Marx's science. Religion is "a perverse world consciousness" of a "perverse world": "the fantastic realization of

---

43 Karl Marx, "Zur Kritik der Hegelschen Rechtsphilosophie. Einleitung," in Karl Marx and Friedrich Engels, *Werke*, Band I (Berlin: Dietz Verlag, 1981), 378–391.
44 On the complex question of religion in Marx's thought, see Carlebach, *Radical Critique*, 148–150; more recently, John Brentlinger, "Revolutionizing Spirituality: Reflections on Marxism and Religion," *Science and Society* 64 (2000): 171–193.
45 Marx, *On the Jewish Question*, 351.

human being, because human being possesses no true reality."[46] The more religion claims to be spiritual and unworldly, the more it is illusory unworldliness that truly manifests "worldly limitedness."[47]

Interestingly, Marx thus agrees with Bauer that the paradigm of "pure religion" is Christianity. Spirit's transcendence of body, world, and history is "the fantasy, dream and postulate of Christianity" (360). The problem or illusion, for Marx, does not however lie in Christianity's continuous attachment to its own historical and worldly existence, which would contradict its aspiration to surpass world history. Rather, the problem lies in this aspiration itself, which counters the human social condition and is thus "the expression of the separation and alienation of man to man" (360).

Consequently, and this is the major thrust of Marx's critique of Bauer—and of Renan—the dissolution of Christianity in the modern nation-state, which for all of them constitutes the actual *realization* of the Christian principle, is not the end of religion, but on the contrary the culmination of religion and religious illusion, which becomes the very structure of the world. Bruno Bauer's "faith in Jehovah," Marx writes in *The Holy Family*, "transformed into faith in the Prussian State."[48] According to Marx, the separation between heaven and earth, spirit and flesh that governs Christian fantasy has metamorphosed into the real separation between politics and society, between the bourgeois, civil nation-state and actual social conditions: "Political democracy is Christian insofar as in it man ... is deemed as sovereign, supreme entity, but man in his uncultivated, unsocial appearance, man in his random existence."[49] "The "disintegration [*Zersetzung*] of man" would be the very principle of "political emancipation" (357), to which Marx—it is apropos the Jewish Question that he does so for the first time[50]—opposes "human emancipation" that would reintegrate the individual in the social world (370).

Social *disintegration* in the modern state, i.e., the reality of universalized religion beyond Christianity, manifests itself, according to Marx, precisely in the universalization of the Christian notion of religion, as worldless faith

---

46   Marx, *Critique of Hegel*, 378.
47   Marx, *On the Jewish Question*, 360.
48   Marx and Engels, *Holy Family*, 118.
49   Marx, *On the Jewish Question*, 360.
50   See Peled, "Bauer and Marx," 482–483; Jonathan Sperber, *Karl Marx. A Nineteenth-Century Life* (New York: Liveright Publishing, 2013), 107.

or confession. The modern notion of faith no longer designates specifically Christianity, but a general realm of plural and multiple "religions," what is called today "world religions":[51] "The religious consciousness indulges in the abundance of the religious opposition and religious multiplicity."[52] In other words, the perfect phenomenon of religious illusion is secularism, in which religion, the very principle of nation-state politics, is classified as a private matter that belongs to the realm of "unpolitical differences." To the condition of 'hypocrisy,' which for Bauer characterized the split between Jewish and state life, Marx thus opposes the graver split of *indifference* between social world and bourgeois state. Consequently, Marx's position on the concrete question of the emancipation of the Jews in Prussia is that this emancipation does not contradict modern state logic, as Bauer claimed, but is in perfect harmony with it.[53]

It is against illusion, against the empty phenomenology of religion, of spirit, that Marx will deploy his real knowledge, the knowledge of non-illusory being, or science. Marxist science is an explicit project of modern political epistemology. For Marx, the ultimate form of being, both substance, medium, and subject of knowledge, is not the Hegelian *Geist*, not spirit, but, as aforesaid, *Gesellschaft*, society. Marx's phenomenology is socio-logy. And so, a guiding motif in the development of Marxist theory will be the translation, visualization, or incarnation of Hegelian dialectics in the body of social oppositions, *Gegensätze*, that exist as concrete *Kämpfe*, as struggles between social classes. As the first line of the *The*

---

51   Cf. Tomoko Masuzawa, *The Invention of World Religions, Or, How European Universalism Was Preserved in the Language of Pluralism* (Chicago: University of Chicago Press, 2005).

52   Marx, *On the Jewish Question*, 361.

53   Which is not to say Marx was an advocate of Jewish emancipation, as correctly noted by Carlebach, *Radical Critique*, 165, 266. Cf. Shlomo Avineri, "Marx and Jewish Emancipation," *Journal of the History of Ideas* 25 (1964): 445–450. For the claim that in the *Jewish Question* Marx's "aim was to defend the right of Jews to full civil and political emancipation," see more recently Robert Fine, "Karl Marx and the Radical Critique of Anti-Semitism," *Engage* 2 (2006); in response, see Larry Ray, "Marx and the Radical Critique of Difference," *Engage* 3 (2006), who pointed out that "Marx's position is essentially an assimilationist one in which there is no room within emancipated humanity for Jews as a separate ethnic or cultural identity."

Communist Manifesto, after the preamble, will state five years after *On the Jewish Question*, in 1848: "The history of all society so far is the history of class struggles."[54]

In 1843, however, in the framework of his polemic against Bauer's "Question of the Jews," the concrete sociological phenomenon that Marx posits as the object of observation against Bauer's theological reflections is *the Jews*. The possible shift from theology to sociology, and so their paradoxical (*malgré* Marx) inseparability, at least in the context of the Jewish question, is signaled by the ambivalence of the German category of *Judentum*, which can mean both the Jewish religion, Judaism, and the Jewish people, Jewry. When Marx defines the precise object of his contemplation of the Jewish Question as "the specific position of the *Judentum*"[55] in the world, he means not Jewish theology but Jewish society. The object of his contemplation is not Judaism but the Jews, "the real [*wirklich*] worldly Jews," "the real [*wirklich*] Jew" (372).

There is here a clear early instance or prototype of the later *anti*-anti-Semitic notion of the "real," "living," "flesh and blood" Jews, contrasted to the "figural" or "ideal" Jews, a notion I criticized throughout this book as de-epistemizing the Jewish. Nonetheless, it is essential to note the solidarity, in Marx's text, between social reality and theological ideality. His distinction between social and theological Jewishness does not simply separate (real) Jews from (ideal) Judaism, but differentiates *within* social, worldly Jewish being.[56] The way Marx distinguished between his epistemology and Bauer's is as follows: "Let us look at the real [*wirklich*] worldly Jews, not the *Shabbat-Jew*, as Bauer does, but the *Everyday-Jew*. Let us not look for the secret of the Jew in his religion, but rather let us look for the secret of religion in the real [*wirklich*] Jew."[57] In other words, Jewish theology is not entirely unworldly, but has a worldly existence, namely the

---

54 Karl Marx and Friedrich Engels, "Manifest der Kommunistischen Partei," in Karl Marx and Friedrich Engels, *Werke*, Band IV (Berlin: Institut für Marxismus-Leninismus Beim ZK der SED, Dietz Verlag, 1977), 462.
55 Marx, *On the Jewish Question*, 372.
56 This is my response to Paul Rose's critique of "the ambiguity of the term *Judentum*" by Marx, who "fluctuates constantly between *Judentum* as a purely allegorical depiction of civil society and as the term for actual Jewry" (*German Question*, 301).
57 Marx, *On the Jewish Question*, 372.

Jews in their socio-religious performance, which in bourgeois society is a *private* performance, a weekend practice: the Jew on *Shabbat*.[58]

Complementarily, the everyday, worldly, nontheological Jew is for Marx not simply "real," but *wirklich*. It would be hardly trivial to understand this category as *excluding* any epistemic significance from its object, here the Jew, in any direct conversation with Hegel's *Philosophy of Right*, which Marx's text—as Bauer's—no doubt was. "*Was vernünftig ist, das ist wirklich; und was wirklich ist, das ist vernünftig*," "That, which is rational [i.e., pertains to the realm of reason and sense, of *Vernunft*], is real/actual [i.e., pertains to the realm of effectiveness, of actual existence, 'acts', *wirkt*]; and that, which is actual, is rational." These are among Hegel's most famous words.[59] They are also among Hegel's most controversial words and most open for interpretation, specifically concerning the exact nature and concrete manifestation of this alleged link between rationality and actuality. Marx solves the riddle with the category of *society*: the social—and the political—is rationality, *Vernunft*, in its effective existence, and vice versa, the social is reality, *Wirklichkeit*, as epistemically founded. The paradigmatic *episteme* would not be theology but politics. In this sense, if the *wirkliche* Jew is distinguished from the theological Jew, it is not by denying but on the contrary by asserting Jewish being as a constellation of *Vernunft*, or, as I formulate it, as an *epistemo-political* constellation. The *wirklich* Jewish is "the specific position of *Judentum*" in the social world, both as a social reality, people, and, as a social idea, politics.

Marx's Anti-Judaism

It is here, as a description of this constellation, that Marx formulates his infamous anti-Jewish statements, his supposed anti-Semitism *avant la lettre*, which deploys what will become some decades later central motifs

---

58   Sander Gilman, "Karl Marx and the Secret Language of Jews," suggested that Marx's epistemological response to Bauer is also, and perhaps primarily, linguistic, Marx shifting from Bauer's abstract text of philosophy and theology to the language of reality, and thereby, so Gilman, he "chooses a language which is Jewish" (282). For a more general argument in this direction, see Dennis Fischman, *Political Discourse in Exile*.

59   G.W.F. Hegel, *Grundlinien der Philosophie des Rechts* (Frankfurt am Main: Suhrkamp, 1986), 24.

of anti-Semitic discourse. In reading this passage, which presents what Marx's asserts as a description of socially real in contrast to theologically illusory Jews, one question that presents itself is what actual social reality Marx historically experienced and perceived as paradigmatically manifesting Jewish being, what Jews exactly he had in mind. It seems that these are the same Jews that both anti-Semites and many anti-anti-Semites will keep seeing. Noteworthy is the strong intimacy between social and theological observations, so strong that it is not clear which determines which, whether social insights are the basis for the theological ones or the other way around. Ultimately Marx's perception of the Jews seems to keep drawing on Christian theology.

"What is the worldly basis of Judaism? Practical need, self-interest [*Eigennutz*]. What is the worldly cult of the Jew? Haggling [*Schacher*]. What is his worldly God? Money."[60] Marx's rhetoric has a Shakespearean echo.[61] Many possible sources of inspiration for Marx's associating Jews with money have been suggested by scholars, mainly Ludwig Feuerbach and Moses Hess.[62] For the future author of the *Kapital* this *topos* became the focus. It is instructive to see how key elements in Marx's later critique of capitalism emerge here as economic glosses on theology. Like Renan, Marx's also highlights Jewish monotheism: "Money is the jealous God of Israel."[63] The important aspect for Marx, however, is more specifically informed by the theological notion of the *alien* God, which was important already for Hegel, and for Bauer.[64] The religion of the alien God corresponds for Marx

---

60 Marx, *On the Jewish Question*, 372.
61 See Stephen Jay Greenblatt, "Marlowe, Marx and anti-Semitism," *Critical Inquiry* 5 (1978): 291–307.
62 Cf. Ludwig Feuerbach, *Das Wesen des Christenthums* (Leipzig: Otto Wigand, 1841), trans. Marian Evans as *The Essence of Christianity* (London: Kegan Paul, Trench, Trübner and Co., 1893); Moses Hess, "Über das Geldwesen," *Rheinische Jahrbücher zur gesellschaftlichen Reform* 1 (1845) 1–34; Carlebach, *Radical Critique*, 110–125. Jacob Katz (*From Prejudice*, 161) indicates this motif even earlier, in the work of the Hegelian historian Heinrich Leo.
63 Marx, *On the Jewish Question*, 374.
64 G.W.F. Hegel, *Der Geist des Christentums und sein Schicksal* (1799/1800), in *Frühe Schriften*, Werke 1 (Frankfurt am Main: Suhrkamp, 1986), 274–418; for a discussion of Hegel's and Bauer's influence on Marx's notion of alienation, see Rosen, *Marx and Bauer*, 162–179.

to the sociopolitical human condition of *alienation*, which will become a central characteristic of capitalism in Marxist theory: "Money is the essence of man's work and existence as alienated from him, and this alien essence dominates him, and he worships it" (375).

There are many ambiguities here, first and foremost concerning the different theological significations of alienation, not the least in both Christian and Jewish discourse on idolatry. Arguably, the notion of God as alien and radically unworldly plays a critical role not only in Jewish but perhaps even more importantly in Christian theologies, most obviously in the more Gnostic ones such as Marcionism.[65] It is also not entirely clear whether for Marx the alienated essence of money means that it is too worldly or too unworldly. Be that as it may, Marx links "money" specifically to the Jewish religion, with all of its supposed shortcomings, which are very similar to the Semitic deficiencies according to Renan: "What lies in Jewish religion in abstract form, the contempt for theory, art, history, man as self-purpose, this is the *actual conscious* position, the virtue of the moneyman."[66] Accordingly, the political performance of Judaism, the Jewish people, would constitute a "nationality of merchants, of moneyman in general" (375). Marx thus depicts Judaism as the sociopolitical regime governed by the principle of "egoism" (374), which accordingly represents the purely *negative* social order, anti-social politics, "a general *present* antisocial element" (372). Marx's eschatological vision of Jewish emancipation therefore goes beyond Bauer's. Where Bauer conditions the emancipation of the Jews on the disappearance of Judaism, Marx concludes his text by declaring—in anticipation of all future anti-Semitism—the disappearance of Judaism as the condition for *general* emancipation of all humanity: "The social emancipation of the Jew is the emancipation of society from Judaism" (377).[67]

Nonetheless, there is a fundamental difference between Marx, on the one hand, and on the other Bauer, as well as later anti-Semitism. This difference concerns the basic perception of "the Jews." Marx's text is so theologically charged that rather than being a description of empirically

---

65 See, for instance, Hans Jonas, *The Gnostic Religion: The Message of the Alien God and the Beginnings of Christianity* (Boston: Beacon Press, 1958).
66 Marx, *On the Jewish Question*, 375.
67 See also "The emancipation of the Jews is in its last signification the emancipation of humanity from Judaism" (373).

given "real" Jews, it can be more appropriately read as *positing* the theological, Christian *concept* of "the Jews," and then suggesting a corresponding *social* phenomenon. For Marx, the reality, the *Wirklichkeit* that is designated by the concept "Jew," is neither religion (Bauer) nor race (Renan), both ultimately *individual* categories; rather, "Jewish" is for Marx a sociopolitical order: "It is not only in the Pentateuch or in the Talmud that we find the essence of today's Jew, but in today's society, not as an abstract, but as a highly empirical essence" (377).

Accordingly, Marx accepts Bauer's negative concept of "the Jew," of theological origin. He also subscribes to the notion that the problem with the Jewish lies in that it represents some *limitation* in the sociopolitical order. However, in direct refutation of Bauer, Marx emphasizes that the Jewish limitation is not the particularism of an individual group but a universal social configuration: "the Jewish" exists "not only as the limitedness of the Jew, but as the Jewish limitedness of society" (377). Instead of "particularism," Marx identifies Jewish sociopolitical limitation as "egoism" or "self-interest."[68] This limitation manifests itself not in the particular group that calls itself or being referred to, on religious or racial basis, as "the Jews," but in the phenomenon of the "moneyman." This phenomenon, far from being particular and exceptional, has according to Marx—and here lies the main thrust of his entire argument—become *the norm of bourgeois society*, which means that the concrete, real, and actual *wirkliche* Jews are nothing but bourgeois society itself: "Judaism reached its summit with the consummation of bourgeois society" (376).

Marx thus also redefines the relations between Judaism and Christianity. In response to Bauer's linear story of progress, from Judaism to Christianity to the State, Marx suggests a fundamental complicity and simultaneity of Jewish and Christian limitedness. Their genealogical relationship progresses not only from Jewish to Christian, but also in a circle back from Christian to Jewish: "Christian egoism of beatitude turns in its consummated practice necessarily into the Jew's egoism of flesh, heavenly need in earthly, subjectivism in self-interest" (377). Jewish economic egoism would be the practical application of Christian spiritual individualism, both forms of anti-social disposition: "sale [*Veräußerung*] is the practice of alienation [*Entäusserung*]" (376). Similarly, Jewish bourgeois society

---

68   Cf. Feuerbach, *The Essence*, 121; see Carlebach, *Radical Critique*, 106–109.

would be the practical side of Christian bourgeois state: "Only under the rule of Christianity, which *alienates all* national, natural, ethical, theoretical human relations, could bourgeois society separate itself entirely from state life, cut all binds of the human kind and instead install egoism, self-interested need, dissolve human world in a world of atomistic, mutually hostile individuals. Christianity originated in Judaism. It re-dissolved in Judaism" (376).

It is here that transpires an idea that will become foundational for all anti-Semitic discourse. This idea is linked to the logic of modern Jewish disappearance. According to this idea, the disappearance of the Jews in the process of assimilation does not mean that Jews ceased to exist, but that they ceased to be *perceptible*. This imperceptibility or invisibility means that the *distinction* between Jews and non-Jews disappeared, which is the precise meaning of assimilation. The abolishment of difference and the consequent disappearance of the Jews do not however necessarily mean that the Jews are no longer there, but, quite on the contrary, could also mean that they have become *omnipresent*. In 1843, Marx describes it, in contrast to the "social" emancipation of the Jews (i.e., the emancipation of society from Judaism), as the "Jewish" emancipation of the Jews, in which "the practical spirit of the Jews [*Judengeist*] has become the practical spirit of the Christian nations. The Jews have emancipated themselves worldwide, insofar as the Christians have become Jewish" (373). Three and a half decades later, in 1879, Wilhelm Marr will call this supposed Jewish omnipresence in modernity the "triumph" of the Jews.

But before moving from Marx to Marr, it is important to insist once again on Marx's basic conception of Jewish being not in terms of race or faith, but in terms of sociopolitical performance. This, I think, separates Marx from later anti-Semitic discourse. It is not that Jewish people tend to be moneymen, but the moneymen *are* the modern Jewish people, i.e., people who observe the allegedly Jewish principle of self-interest in their sociopolitical performance, regardless of their racial or confessional identity. As I will discuss in the conclusion to this chapter, "Jews" will never become a significant social category in Marx's thought.[69]

---

69 For the few exceptional mentions of Jews at all in Marx's later writings, see for instance Solomon Bloom, "Karl Marx and the Jews," *Jewish Social Studies* 4 (1942): 3–16.

But why Jews? Why does Marx identify the historical collective known as the Jews with self-interest, egoism, and money? I already explained how I read Marx's anti-Jewish text as responding to Bauer's text and therefore explicitly engaging in Bauer's *theological* discourse, primarily the category of "the Jew," with the intention of deconstructing or dislocating it, from theology to sociology. And yet, when Marx speaks of the *wirkliche* Jew, even as he ultimately argues that this is none other than the Christian bourgeois, his discourse necessarily implies some *image* of the people who are historically identified as "the Jews," as the underlying paradigm of the modern moneymen.[70] Marx even seems to subscribe to Bauer's Christian perspective, whereby the historical Jews are the people who have been adhering to Jewish theology, which for Bauer would be based on particularism and for Marx on egoism. And yet, in contrast to Bauer, Marx cannot accept theology as constitutive for social *Wirklichkeit*: this is the central point of his polemic against Bauer. "Let us not look for the secret of the Jew in his religion, but rather let us look for the secret of religion in the real [*wirklich*] Jew" (372). It is social reality that gives rise to religion and not vice versa.

What sociopolitical reality has given rise to Judaism, with its alleged antisocial principle of self-interest and money worship? Obviously, this must be the sociopolitical reality that Marx criticizes in *On the Jewish Question*, namely the bourgeois world, split between bourgeois state and bourgeois society. In our specific context, Marx characterizes the sociopolitical condition of this world of alienation as "enslaved" (*geknechet*). Indeed, his alleged

---

70   Against authors such as David McLellan, *Marx before Marxism* (London: Macmillan, 1970), who argued that for Marx the German word *Judentum* simply meant "commerce," such that his anti-Jewish passage could be seen as a "pun on Bauer's expense" (142), I tend to agree with Carlebach that Marx "confirms and supports Feuerbach and Bauer's criticisms of the Jewish religion and Jewish history and adds some comments of his own, which are even more contemptuous and certainly less informed than those of his predecessors" (*Radical Critique*, 172–173). Paul Rose described Marx's use of "the Jews" in this context as a "moral myth" (*German Question*, 296ff.). Carlebach spoke of "mystification," which is precisely what Marx accused Hegel of doing (152). He further points out that Feuerbach's contribution to the same collection of the *Deutsch-Französischen Jahrbücher*, "Umrisse zu einer Krilik der Nationalökonomie," formulated a very similar critique of capitalism as Marx's, without however making any mention of "the Jews" (161).

observation of the *wirkliche* Jew does not take place in a neutral horizon. Rather, the Jewish is conceptualized by Marx as a "specific position" within the sociopolitical matrix of an "enslaved world." His anti-Judaism refers to "the specific position of Judaism within today's enslaved world" (372). We saw that, in contrast to Bauer's theology of Jewish particularism, according to Marx Judaism has become the universal practice of this social world, i.e., human (anti-)social practice under the condition of enslavement. Judaism would be the egoism of slaves.[71] This reading of Marx, i.e., money-worshipping Judaism as anti-social politics of slaves, calls to mind the still very prevalent anti-anti-Semitic *apologetics* of alleged Jewish money culture, explained by historical anti-Jewish persecution.[72] Marx could thus be read as a source of inspiration for both anti-Semitism and anti-anti-Semitism.

To conclude this discussion of Marx, I wish to suggest that he can be also read as a source of inspiration for anti-anti-anti-Semitism—in the sense of identifying positive Jewish political epistemology. Whether of theological or sociological foundation, the Jewish constellation identified by Marx in *On the Jewish Question* is clearly negative: not only politically negative, also epistemically negative. Judaism is pure practice: whether in its religious "contempt for theory" or the same contempt as "the *actual conscious* position, the virtue of the moneyman" (375). Accordingly, the Jews would be the negative epistemo-political paradigm of the ignorant slaves. Nonetheless, as I already mentioned, Marx's sociopolitical anti-Judaism responds to Bauer's theological anti-Judaism, and as such it contains a critical element for the epistemo-political perception of Judaism and for political epistemology in general. What I refer to is Marx's rejection of Bauer's theologically informed conceptualization of Jewish historical specificity as *anti-universal* particularity. This conceptualization is intimately related to

---

71 This calls to mind the "slave morality," which Nietzsche's 1887 *On the Genealogy of Morality* will equally trace back to Judaism, however, arguably with the exact opposite sense, not of egoism but of altruism; see Friedrich Nietzsche, *On the Genealogy of Morality*, ed. Keith Ansell-Pearson, trans. Carol Diethe (Cambridge: Cambridge University Press, 2007), 20.

72 Cf. Dennis Fischman's reading: "What Marx chooses to call 'Jewish' is nothing less than the driving force of his social and political theory: the reality of human need, as expressed in the contradictions of capitalist society" (*Political Discourse*, 24).

the kind of epistemology that has been constantly the object of my analyses in this book, namely the epistemology that *negates* the epistemic significance of historical collectives, of "peoples." Marx's counterinterpretation of Judaism not only as a general social order, but as such that has *de facto* become the universal order in the world of capitalism, is advanced by Marx explicitly in refutation of this epistemology. In other words, Marx's anti-Judaism contains a response to one of the central elements in the negative political epistemology underlying traditional anti-Judaism, and it seems to me also both anti-Semitism and anti-anti-Semitism.[73]

In a nutshell, this response constitutes the core of Marx's critique of religion as the illusion of emancipation—which is the illusion of universalism: freedom in heaven that dissimulates and enables enslavement on earth. I already indicated how Marx in *On the Jewish Question*, against Bauer, diagnoses bourgeois politics not as overcoming but as consummating this illusion through the split between state and society. In the *Introduction to the Critique of Hegel's Philosophy of Right*, Marx applies this critique to what he perceives as the most advanced existing forms of emancipatory, critical literature, namely Hegel's philosophy, and later in *The Communist Manifesto* also to what he calls the "Critical-Utopian Socialism and Communism" of Saint-Simon, Fourier, and Owen. "Critical-utopian" is indeed what Marx accuses this literature of being, namely offering a purely theoretical freedom, an idea of universality that has no concrete *location* in social reality. What Marx demands in contrast, and here lies one of the most powerful and historically effective elements of his thought, is to think of freedom in terms of *liberation*, i.e., not as a state but as a process or event, a temporal happening, which thus must be located in history. The historical localization and thus abolishment of "utopian" emancipation means that it needs to exist within history, as an element of history, of *Wirklichkeit*, and this means as represented, practiced, and performed by some historically concrete and existing, some *particular* historical collective, a people.

---

73 My reading is here close to that of Carlebach, who, in refuting readings of Marx's call to *auflösen* (abolish, dissolve) Judaism as a precursor to later National Socialist extermination politics, argued that "Marx was determined to elevate Judaism into an abstract element like labour and that he no more intended personal harm to individual Jews by calling for the dissolution of Judaism than he would have wanted workers to be attacked when he called for the abolition of labour" (*Radical Critique*, 178).

It is the identification and exposition, the *manifestation* of such a particular collective agent of universal social liberation that will become the heart of Marx's own historical intervention in the form of *The Communist Manifesto*, which would, in this sense, be the completion of his critique of religion. It would require a separate analysis to reflect on the precise nature of history, a *material* history, and accordingly of the historical collectives and polities that are operative in Marxist political epistemology. Clearly, the main historical protagonists of the *Manifesto* are not those of the *Jewish Question*, *wirkliche* history for Marx being not theological but socioeconomical, "the history of class struggles." A central question in the investigation of modern political epistemology would be the conceptual relations between the specificity of the particular historical collective that is the "people" and that of the "class." I recall that the two important classes in the narrative of the *Manifesto* are the two last classes in the history of class struggles, which is the last struggle in history, the last split in society, the bourgeoisie and the proletariat: the universally, world ruling class versus the universally oppressed and therefore revolutionary class. In a way, since the proletariat is the total negativity and nothingness of the existing bourgeois world—it is "without property"—in its class *particularity* it is already the manifestation of the *universally* emancipated world to come—it "holds the future in its hand."[74] However, the task of the proletarian class is to abolish all classes—including itself. The proletariat is still a figure of this world, of enslavement.

The true figure and imperfect, partial presence of the world to come, of the future "communist society," in this world, are the communists themselves, who, so *The Communist Manifesto*, originally *The Manifesto of the Communist Party*, "represent in the present movement the future of the movement" (492). What distinguishes the communists from the rest of the revolutionary class is *knowledge*: they possess "*Einsicht*" (474) insight, clarity and understanding of the situation and the movement.[75] Communist knowledge is radically different from the illusory universal consciousness of religion, philosophy, and utopian theory. It is a disillusioned conscious-

---

74   Marx and Engels, *Manifest*, 472.
75   A *Gnosis* perhaps received from this "portion of bourgeois ideologists, who raised themselves to the level of theoretical understanding of the historical movement as a whole," like Marx himself, and who then "went over to the Proletariat."

ness of absent redemption, absent emancipation; an absence, nonetheless, that doesn't signify nonexistence but rather a presence in coming: future. Communist *episteme*, as paradigmatically revealed in *The Manifesto*, is thus universal knowledge historically situated in a particular collective, which, as representing yet absent future, must *necessarily* maintain its particularity, its situatedness, namely its identity, must remain a *party*, which means it must exist as the collective practice of *struggle*. The Communist Party belongs to an *anti*-communist world. This constellation of knowledge and collective being, this Communist epistemo-politics, which Marx developed out of the critique of religion, is a key element in any positive political epistemology, and in any anti-anti-anti-Semitic approach to the Jewish Question.

7 Triumph of Judaism

From Marr to Hitler

MARX'S REFORMULATION OF THE *Judenfrage*, the Jewish Question that is the Question of the Jews, provides a conceptual gateway into the historical discourse that can be most properly referred to as "anti-Semitism." The propriety of this designation arises partly from the fact that at important moments and in considerable circles this discourse has referred to itself explicitly, declaratively, as anti-Semitism; and partly because this is how it has been and still is referred to without exception from the perspective of historical reflection, mostly critical, largely anti-anti-Semitic. It should be reiterated, however, that "anti-Semitism" has in no way been the sole or even dominant or most characteristic self-designation of this discourse. In its most crucial moments this term is absent or, as in Nazi Germany after 1935, even explicitly rejected. Referring to this discourse as "anti-Semitism," and thus positing this name as the assembling center around which the perception and comprehension of this discourse are organized, this operation is a central feature of anti-anti-Semitism, the central tendency of which is to dissociate anti-Semitism from the Jews. Accordingly, a basic effort of the anti-anti-anti-Semitic analysis of anti-Semitism is to *suspend* the very designation "anti-Semitism," at least as a defining term for the conceptual unity of this discourse, i.e., for what constitutes it as *one*, as *this specific* discourse. Instead, as an initial attempt, I will indicate a few elements that, so it seems to me, constitute the specificity of so-called anti-Semitism as a reaction to and reformulation of the Jewish Question, and so, fundamentally, as a modern perception and, most broadly speaking, *knowledge* of Jewish being.

Anti-Semitic Discourse

It may sound trivial, but I hope that by now I have been able to show how much it is not: anti-Semitism's central concern has indeed been the Question of the Jews. The Question of the Jews, or Jewish Question, is not an abstract question, but a concrete historical discourse, some basic features of which I attempted to highlight above in Bruno Bauer and Karl Marx. The Jewish Question has arisen from and concerns what is known as the emancipation of the Jews, the event in which Jews were to become part of the modern European polity. A central, perhaps *the* central motif of anti-Semitism, a motif that connects together Renan's "scientific" anti-Semitism, as I analyzed it, with all "political" anti-Semitism, is the notion of Jewish emancipation and assimilation as a *defining* event of modernity, and so of the Jewish Question as the decisive question of modern politics. This radical *significance* given to Jews by anti-Semitism, in manifold expressions, from early programmatic manifestos to the global politics of the Third Reich, in which the Jews feature as a cornerstone for the entire structure of worldview and agenda, this radical significance is the great mystery posed by anti-Semitism to anti-anti-Semitism.

In contrast to Renan, however, and similarly to Marx, anti-Semitic discourse is defined by a fundamental *skepsis* regarding the precise nature and meaning of the Jewish event of modernity. The emancipation and assimilation of the Jews, in this discourse, rather than signifying the ultimate triumph of human civilization, signifies its downfall. At work is a critical aphenomenology, a phenomenology of disappearance, similar to the one I indicated in Marx's response to Bauer: the disappearance of the Jews by the effect of assimilation would not arise from the absence of the Jews but rather from their omnipresence: "The Judaism of bourgeois society."[1] It is this basic observation that has guided the thought of Wilhelm Marr, "the Patriarch of anti-Semitism," who was greatly influenced by Bauer and Marx.[2] I have already mentioned the notion of "The Triumph of Judaism"

---

1   Marx, *On the Jewish Question*, 374. An earlier version of Chapter 7 was originally published as "Invisible Concealment of Invisibility: Crypto-Judaism as a Theological Paradigm of Racial Anti-Semitism," *Religions* 9 (2018): 339.
2   "The Patriarch of anti-Semitism" is how Marr reportedly called himself; see Zimmermann, *Wilhelm Marr, the Patriarch of anti-Semitism*, vii. On Bauer's influence on Marr, see Rose, *German Question*, 279–280; for Marx's influence on Marr,

that was at the center of Marr's best known work, published in 1879, under the title *The Triumph of Judaism over Germanism: Considered from a Non-Confessional Standpoint*.³ This text is deemed as one of the first anti-Semitic manifests, "the first anti-Semitic best-seller,"⁴ though it makes no mention of the term "anti-Semitism" (it does occasionally use "Semitic"). Marr's concise manifesto: "I hereby loudly proclaim, with no ironic intention, the triumph of Judaism in world history" (4). The same self-conscious spirit of paradox and social critique ("with no ironic intention") seems to characterize all proclamations on the *Verjudung*, the "Jewification" of modern society, such as another of Marr's sources of inspiration, Richard Wagner,⁵ and "the founder of modern French anti-Semitism,"⁶ Edouard Droumond, who a few years after Marr exposed "The Jewish France."⁷

---

see Zimmermann, *Marr*, 73. Alex Bein, "Der Moderne Antisemitismus," noted that it was upon Marr's founding of the *Antisemitenliga* that "the concept of 'anti-Semitism' emerged in the *political reality*" (347).

3   Wilhelm Marr, *Der Sieg des Judentums über das Germanentum. Vom nicht konfessionellen Standpunkt aus betrachtet* (Bern: Rudolph Costenoble, 1879). Jacob Katz (*From Prejudice*, 94–96) points at the appearance of the notion of a threat to Germans by the growing and excessive power of the Jews already in the 1810s, in writers such as Garlieb Helwig Merkel.

4   J. Katz, *From Prejudice*, 260. According to Katz's assessment, Marr's book added no ideological content to earlier modern anti-Judaism, its significance being in extracting anti-Judaism from any other discussion and positing it as an independent issue: "Marr's pamphlet was the first, since the reemergence of the Jewish question in the 1870s, to clearly announce its anti-Jewish tendency in its title. Anti-Semitism was now sailing under its own steam" (260).

5   Richard Wagner, *Das Judentum in der Musik* (Leipzig: Weber, 1869 [1850]), 12, writing on the *Verjudung* of modern art. According to J. Katz (*From Prejudice*, 186), it is in this text, "the consummation of the anti-Jewish trend" of its time, which Wager introduced this term for the first time.

6   Bein, "Moderne Antisemitismus,» 550.

7   Edouard Drumont, *La France Juive. Essai d'Histoire Contemporaine* (Paris: C. Marpon et E. Flammarion, 1886 [1883]). The motif of Jewish domination and oppression of Christians can be found also in earlier sources. Raul Hilberg, for instance, indicates it in a statement by Emperor Frederick II of 1237; see Hilberg, *Destruction*, 17. Hilberg also indicates this motif in Nazi discourse, such as Hitler's speech of 1940, where he spoke of how "all-powerful Jewry declared war on us" (19), and a Julius Streicher speech of 1935: "Only one people remained victorious

The title of Marr's book reveals, however, another basic feature of anti-Semitic discourse. The alleged "Triumph of Judaism" is over *Germanentum*, "Germanism." The paradigmatic rivalry and difference of Judaism, the paradigmatic difference that *constitutes* "Judaism," is not vis-à-vis Christianity. As Marr's subtitle asserts, anti-Semitism deploys the Jewish Question "from a non-confessional standpoint." This is a crucial point. Anti-Semitism seems to fully subscribe to Marx's critique of Bauer, namely his critique of the religious-theological, the basically Christian framing of the Jewish Question. Indeed, one of the central solidarities between anti-Semitism and its anti-anti-Semitic critique is the assertion of a fundamental break between "modern" non-religious anti-Semitism and "traditional" religious anti-Judaism. Marr in fact sounds almost like he is quoting Marx when he declares that the Question of the Jews is not confessional but "a social-political question."[8] That the phenomenon of Judaism is not primarily religious, and therefore should not be primarily interpreted in "confessional" categories, is also what Adolf Hitler will later describe as his personal formative realization, namely that the Jews are "not German of a special confession, but a different people."[9] This proclaimed non-Christian perception of Judaism will manifest itself in the Nazi refusal to recognize Jewish converts to Christianity as non-Jews.[10] Anti-Semitism may be said to have gone even beyond Marx in de-Christianizing Judaism. Seemingly, anti-Semitic discourse departs from Christian theology so radically, that, unlike Marx, it no longer even *names* the object of its antagonism by the Christian category of "the Jews," but rather reverts to the scientifically sounding term "Semitism."

---

in [the Great War], a people of whom Christ said its father is the devil. That people had ruined the German nation in body and soul" (20).

8   Marr, *Sieg*, 41.

9   Hitler, *Mein Kampf. Eine kritische Edition*, hg. v. Christian Hartmann et al. (München and Berlin: Institut für Zeitgeschichte, 2016), 211. On Hitler's infamous book, "the Bible of National Socialism," see 13–53. Among the "intellectual-historical roots" of *Mein Kampf*, the critical edition mentions Gottfried Feder, Alfred Rosenberg, Houston Stewart Chamberlain, Theodor Fritsch, Henry Ford, and Gobineau (56–58).

10 J. Katz (*From Prejudice*, 269) indicated this motif already in early anti-Semitism.

For the purpose of the current study, it is important to indicate once again, as I did in relation to Marx, the intellectual potential in critiquing the dominance of Christian theological perception of the Jews, down to the very category "Jew." Indeed, due to the dialogical nature of thought in history, anti-Semitic discourse too, even in its worst, contains elements of enhanced clarity. And so, be that in distorted forms and to sinister effects, it may strangely enable the appearance of a non-Christian image of the Jews, which might be closer to Jewish self-understanding. I will develop this insight in the Epilog in the context of the recent Heidegger debate. In the context of political anti-Semitism, the Nazi non-recognition of Jews' conversion to Christianity as expunging their Jewishness, which was motivated racially and justly condemned as such, nonetheless *de facto* dismissed a Christian principle, i.e., faith, as defining Jewish being, which in this sense is consistent with historically dominant inner Jewish perspectives. Obviously, *not* believing in Christ has not been the foundational principle of historical Jewish self-understanding.

And yet, on a closer look, the contrast between anti-Semitism and theological anti-Judaism is less radical than both anti-Semitism and anti-anti-Semitism would have it seem. On the level of naming, as already mentioned, the "Semitic" terminology has scarcely ever replaced the "Jewish." Interestingly, as Moshe Zimmermann showed, Marr's partner in founding the *Anti-Semiten-Liga*, the "League of Anti-Semites," in the same year that Marr's book was published, 1879, Hector De Grousillier, understood "Semitism" to designate a specifically Jewish mindset, expressed in Jewish *religion*, to the exclusion of non-religious "Jewish Germans."[11] In this sense, the term "anti-Semitism," with its "appearance of scientificity," served to designate the spirit of Judaism, in contrast to Jewish being merely in the flesh. In other words, the term "anti-Semitism" may be even said to have had an *anti-racist* intention. The continuity with Christian anti-Judaism manifests itself, however, most clearly in the fact that anti-Semites, in contrast to Marx, never ceased from speaking of Jews. Whereas Marx, after the polemic with Bauer "On the Jewish Question," will scarcely ever again write about "Jews," will indeed replace the theological categories of Christians and Jews with socioeconomico-political categories such

---

11   Zimmermann, *Marr*, 91.

as Bourgeois and Proletariats, Jews—and not "Semites"—are the constant center of anti-Semitism. Long before the Nazis declined the use of the term "anti-Semitism" for describing their anti-Jewish politics, already in 1907, one of the canonic anti-Semitic texts of the time, the title of which asserted its canonicity in theological terms, *Anti-Semiten-Katechismus*, "the Catechism of the Anti-Semites," changed its title to *Handbuch der Judenfrage*, the "Handbook of the Jewish Question." The "Catechism" had been published by Theodor Fritsch since 1887, and from the very beginning defined "anti-Semites" as "anti-Jewish" (*Judengegner*).[12] Eight years earlier, the League of Anti-Semites, in its bylaws, defines its objective as "saving our German fatherland from the complete *Verjudung*."[13]

In fact, considered from the point of view of political epistemology, "modern" anti-Semitism is intimately connected to "religious" anti-Judaism.[14] In epistemo-political terms, its "anti-confessional" standpoint does not as radically break with theology as Marx. Rather, it remains within the same discourse and only *deploys* it from a different standpoint. This standpoint, so my basic claim, the standpoint of "political" anti-Semitism within the theological discourse, is conceptually identical to Renan's "scientific" anti-Semitism, as I analyzed it above. Its organizing concept is "race." Epistemo-politically, "race" stands in a fundamentally different kind of opposition to "spirit" as "class." As I argued above, the force of Marx's notion of "class" is the localization of political agency in social history, in explicit polemics with the utopian unworldliness—the "illusion"—of

---

12   Theodor Fritsch, *Anti-Semiten-Katechismus. Eine Zusammenfassung des wichtigsten Materials zum Verständnis der Judenfrage* (Leipzig: Verlag von Herm. Beher, 1893) (25. Aufl.; 1887). J. Katz described Fritsch, who was active on the cause of anti-Semitism from 1881 to his death in 1933, as "the living bridge between the inception of the movement and its disastrous culmination" (*From Prejudice*, 304).

13   Statuten des Vereins "Anti-Semiten-Liga," Berlin, 1879.

14   Cf. J. Katz (*From Prejudice*, 319): "Modern anti-Semitism turned out to be a continuation of the premodern rejection of Judaism by Christianity, even when it renounced any claim to be legitimized by it or even professed to be antagonistic to Christianity." Friedländer, *Nazi Germany*, found Katz's interpretation "excessive," but nonetheless noted that "the impact of religious anti-Judaism on other modern forms of anti-Semitism is apparent" (83). More precisely with respect to Nazi discourse, see Confino, *World without Jews*, arguing "for an intimate link between Nazism and Christianity" (19); cf. Hilberg, *Destruction*, 21.

Christian spirit as consummated in the bourgeois state. In contrast, the force of Renan's notion of "race" is the scientific *grounding* of Christianity's consummation in the nation-state. Race is *negative* Spirit: it is the nonhistorical ground of history as the gradual negation of race in the "progress of spiritualism."

Racial Epistemology of the Invisible

The category of "race" shapes anti-Semitic politics from Marr to Hitler.[15] My claim, however, is that "political" anti-Semitism does not just adopt Renan's "scientific" standpoint, but that it radicalizes it, by drawing the most extreme consequences from this category. I already noted how for both Renan and the anti-Semites the emancipation and assimilation, and so the *disappearance* of the Jews in the modern polity, constitutes the critical political event of modernity. I also noted how, on the other hand, their interpretations of this event are exactly opposite: Renan considers this disappearance as the triumph of Aryan civilization, whereas the anti-Semites, like Marx, see in this disappearance "the triumph of Judaism." Both Marx and the anti-Semites interpret the disappearance of the Jews not as the dissolution but on the contrary as the full realization of Jewish being. They understand this realization, however, in two fundamentally different ways. For Marx, "Judaism" is a sociopolitical form that "disappeared" only insofar as it has become all too visible, in the omnipresent form of the "moneymen." For the anti-Semites, in contrast, the disappearance of the Jews means literally that the Jews have become invisible, imperceptible in any social and cultural phenomena, and it is this very invisibility that constitutes the consummation of Jewish being, namely as a "Semitic race."[16] In contrast to Renan, who identifies the contemporary paradigm of

---

15   Cf. Alexander Bein, "Moderne Antisemitismus," 342. Whereas I analyzed the emergence of race discourse in Renan's work, Bein focuses on Gobineau; see above Chapter 5. See also Hilberg, *Destruction*, 21.

16   Marr, *Sieg*, 23. It should be noted that precisely here lies the crucial shift between Marr's earlier anti-Jewish position, as expressed for instance in his *Der Judenspiegel* (Hamburg, 1862), where he called for the "the ennoblement of the Jews" through "a concrete fleshly interbreeding" (47), and his later, properly anti-Semitic discourse in the *Sieg des Judentums*, which precluded assimilation—quoted in Paul Lawrence Rose, *German Question*, 284.

Semitic race-spirit in Muslim Turkey, the most *visible* Other of Christian Europe, for the anti-Semites, the paradigmatic phenomenon of Semitism is the *invisibility* of the assimilated European Jews.

This fundamental anti-Semitic position is in fact more consistent with the category of "race" than Renan's. Race, as the negative of spirit and just like spirit, lies outside of history. It is the "key to history" inasmuch as history is the manifestation, the phenomenon of race. But history remains mere phenomenon of race—it is not race itself. The force of the race category is that it transcends history. Accordingly, inasmuch as historical, social, political, and cultural phenomena can be traced back to race, race itself cannot be traced back to such phenomena. It is rather its independence and difference from historical and cultural phenomena that constitutes the essence of race. It follows that inasmuch as history manifests race, race presents itself most purely in detachment from history, namely as non-manifest or *invisible* in the historical and cultural medium. It is in its social invisibility that race is most present.

It is possible, based on this principle, to sketch a general outline of anti-Semitic—as a paradigmatic racist—political epistemology. This epistemology, far from being naïve or unreflective, possesses central features of *critical* thought, namely—to recall Adorno and Horkheimer—of enlightenment, insofar as it is based on doubt vis-à-vis phenomenal and received knowledge. However, since the object of anti-Semitic knowledge, "race," presents itself in invisibility, anti-Semitic epistemology is not just suspicious in face of phenomena, it does not just look for better or more certain evidence, but looks beyond or before evidence—looks *against* evidence. Whereas, therefore, Renan posited race as the foundation of *science*—philology and ethnography—"political"' anti-Semitic epistemology is, as noted above, pronouncedly *anti-scientific*.

The anti-phenomenal relation that anti-Semitism asserts to its object, Jewish being, as race, challenges the limits of what can be called "knowledge." A basic operation of anti-Semitic epistemology is to discredit and consequently to deactivate all epistemic spaces, all *media*, in which its object may become visible, known. Anti-Semitism is anti-media. More specifically, it disqualifies the spaces of intersubjective communication, where knowledge is generated as a collective process, as epistemo-polity, and within which the assimilation of Jews was to take place by way of *disappearance*. Anti-Semitism discredits the sociopolitical media in which Jews were to become invisible: intellectual discourse, literature, press, economy.¹⁷ It does so by qualifying all these media as "Jewish," which is structurally the same proceeding as in Marx, i.e., of explaining the invisibility of the Jews by their omnipresence. In contrast to Marx, however, for whom the media—"society"—*is* reality, which means that bourgeois society *is* Jewish, for the anti-Semites "Jewish" media is a *lie*, which conceals reality, i.e., the unassimilated and unassimilable Jewish race.

I once again wish to underline the conceptual solidarity or at least commensurability that this anti-Semitic epistemology entertains with religious discourse. There is a statement of Hitler that provides a radical formulation of this affinity, when he writes about the Jews, that "their entire existence is already built on one big lie, namely that what they are is a religious congregation, while [in fact] it is a race."¹⁸ Sociopolitical media provides the phenomenal space for the apparition of Jewish assimilation, which means the apparition of Jewish invisibility in the sociopolitical sphere. Apparent sociopolitical invisibility (i.e., the Jewishness of persons has no relevancy for their political function) signifies that Jewishness is allegedly a nonpolitical existence, that it is or became a mere "religious congregation" of faith. This sociopolitical invisibility, the appearance of Judaism as religion, however, would be a lie, is *the* lie: it is a fake invisibility that conceals a true invisibility, namely that of race. Race is the invisible behind the invisible, a real invisible concealed by a fake invisible.¹⁹

I will shortly discuss the political implications of this epistemology of double invisibility. But first I wish to indicate, next to its negative, antimedial aspect, also its affirmative aspect, whereby anti-Semitism *does* assert knowledge of Jews. This knowledge can only be *immediate* knowl-

---

17   See Fritsch, *Katechismus*, 17–18; Drumond, *France*, xv; Eugen Dühring, *Die Judenfrage als Frage der Racenschädlichkeite für Existenz, Sitte und Cultur der Völker. Mit einer weltgeschichtlichen, religionsbezüglich, social und politisch freiheitlichen Antwort* (Berlin: H. Reuther's Verlagsbuchhandlung, 1892 [1880]), 13, 55.

18   Hitler, *Mein Kampf*, 617.

19   This motif can be already found in Martin Luther: "Now behold what a nice, thick, fat lie it is when they complain about being captives among us. Jerusalem was destroyed more than 1400 years ago and during that time we Christians have been tortured and persecuted by the Jews in all the world. For nearly 300 years (as stated above) we might well complain that during that time they captured and killed the Christians, which is the clear truth." See Luther, *The Jews and Their Lies* (Los Angeles: Christian Nationalist Crusade, 1948), 36.

edge, a paradoxical notion, which, as noted above, in fact seems to abolish the fundamental condition of the knowledge relation. Anti-Semitic discourse articulates itself in fact most frequently in an epistemically critical and reflective manner, its negation of media always entailing the invocation of immediate knowledge, most often "instinct" or "intuition." I recall how already in Renan "instinct" was invoked as the liminal epistemic faculty, the proto-cognitive dimension, in which "race"—as "race spirit"—is present. "Instinct" is the faculty through which anti-Semitism asserts immediate relation to and knowledge of Jewish racial being. It is noteworthy how the immediacy of instinct, which explicitly operates as subversive to sociopolitical media, is nonetheless embodied in anti-Semitic discourse in a collective figure: "the people."

In contrast to the press and literature that corrupt the intellectual, the educated, the cultivated, *gebildete* mind, the philosopher Eugen Dühring—"the first and most significant theoretician of racial anti-Semitism,"[20] for grounding his view on "The Jewish Question as a Question of Racial Detriment [*Racenschändlichkeit*] for the Existence, Morals and Culture of the Peoples" (1880)—thus invoked the "natural instincts and feeling" and the "immediate impressions" of "the low people and the common citizen."[21] Similarly, the historian Heinrich von Treitschke summoned "the instinct of the masses," the alleged generator of popular anti-Semitism, as the truth-sensor for his famous pronouncement of the same anti-Semitic year 1879 that "the Jews are our misfortune!"[22] Houston Stewart Chamberlain, in his

---

20   Bein, "Moderene Antisemitismus," 341. According to Bein, Dühring's text "already contained everything that later literature discussed and popularized more broadly. It can be designated as the classic foundation of modern anti-Semitism" (550). As Bein notes, "In his Zionist diary, Herzl stated that it was upon reading this text that his inner transformation had begun, which led to Zionism. The *Judenstaat* contains statements of Herzl, which sound like an echo of and response to Dühring" (n. 22). Katz (*From Prejudice*, 265) indicted how Dühring was influenced by Voltaire and Renan.

21   Dühring, *Die Judenfrage*, 3, 55.

22   Heinrich von Treitschke, "Unsere Ansichten," in *Preußische Jahrbücher*, Band 44, Berlin, 1879, S. 559–576, 572, 575. According to Shulamit Volkov, it was Treitschke "who first achieved the intergration of all [earlier] elements [of anti-Semitism] into one influential context.... He made antisemitism *salonfähig*, that is, worthy of the elegant salons of the affluent and the educated in German bourgeois society" (Volkov, *Germans, Jews, Antisemites*, 98).

Foundations of the Nineteenth Century, claimed to speak from "intuition": "I approached these subjects not as a scholar, but as a child of the present time who wishes to understand his living present."[23] In France, too, for removing the veil of press and literature and seeing *the Jewish* France, wrote Drumond, "*C'est dans la rue que je vous propose de regarder*," "I suggest that you look at the street," using "the patriot's common sense."[24] Another one of Marr's sources of inspiration, Richard Wagner, in his *Judentum in der Musik* (1850), already appealed to the "instinct-like," "natural," and "unconscious sensation, which emerges in the people as innermost repulsion against the Jewish essence."[25] Whereas Wagner went ahead to explore this "unconscious sensation" of repulsion in the auditory realm, "in music," it is rather the olfactory sensation, "smell," that will reveal to young Hitler the essence of Jews: "I often grew sick to my stomach from the smell of these caftan wearers."[26]

It is illustrative to indicate how this radical anti-scientific race epistemology related more specifically to the realm of *language*. As discussed in Chapter 5, based on the traditional conception of "language as expression of the soul," language was for Renan the primary medium of race's "manifestation" and consequently the primary object for his race science, as philology. Language has in fact been one of the most important media of Jewish assimilation. It is as German or as French writers that the

---

23   Houston Stewart Chamberlain, *Die Grundlage des 19. Jahrhunderts*, I. Hälfte (München: Bruckmann, 1903 [1899]), 17. On Chamberlain's book, which Jacob Katz described as "the most renowned anti-Semitic treatise of the age," see Katz, *From Prejudice*, 306–310. Katz (315) mentions Chamberlain as a major source of influence for Alfred Rosenberg, *Der Mythos des 20. Jahrhunderts* (Munich: Hohenreichen-Verlag, 1934).

24   Drumond, *La France Juive*, xx.

25   Richard Wagner, *Das Judentum*, 9–11. This observation undermines J. Katz's finding, whereby "radical and venomous as [Wagner's] rejection of the Jew may have been, it was not based on racial notions" (Katz, *From Prejudice*, 191). Contra Katz, see Rose, *German Question*, 365. For more on Wagner's anti-Semitism, see Paul Lawrence Rose, *Wagner: Race and Revolution* (New Haven, CT: Yale University Press, 1992); Jacob Katz, *The Darker Side of Genius: Richard Wagner's Anti-Semitism* (Hanover, NH: University Press of New England, 1986); H. Zelinsky, *Richard Wagner—Ein deutsches Thema. Eine Dokumentation der Wirkungsgeschichte Richard Wagners 1876–1976* (Vienna/Berlin: Medusa, 1983).

26   Hitler, *Mein Kampf*, 213.

Jewishness of Jewish authors could disappear, accomplishing Renan's "progress of spiritualism." Language has thus become one of the main fronts of anti-Semitism. It is a complex front, since, anti-Semitism itself operating in language, it could not simply discredit this medium as "Jewish." Accordingly, discussion on language has given rise to radicalized expression of anti-Semitism's race epistemology, in which, as stated above, the expression or manifestation of race (language) is *eo ipso* the concealment of race.

It is against this concealment, this pseudo-assimilation that conceals crypto-difference, that Wagner wrote on "The Jews in Music." According to him, it is indeed not on the manifest level of language, but rather on the latent, subliminal, "unconscious" level that the essence of language would lie. If language constitutes a "historical communality," nonetheless "only he who grew up unconsciously in this communality also takes part in its creation."[27] Against all appearance, therefore, the Jew, who has been "standing outside of this communality," necessarily speaks "modern European languages" always "as a foreigner" (14), a radical foreignness that Wagner extends by the power of metaphor to "our entire European civilization and art," which "remained for the Jews a foreign language" (15). Echoing native or mother tongue ideologies (such as Schleiermacher's: "one [produces originally] only in one's mother tongue"),[28] Wagner thus proclaims that the foreigner, the Jew, may only imitate or reproduce, never "really speak, make poems or create works of art" (15). The *evidence* for this latent foreignness, which Wagner paradoxically still insists on providing, he locates not in the semantics of language, but, as already noted above, in language as sensation, as sound. It is in the *music* of language, in *singing*, that Wagner identifies "the liveliest and irrefutably truest expression of the person's essential sensation" (17). Jewish foreignness would manifest itself acoustically in the "Semitic pronunciation," i.e., "the hissing, shrilling, humming and flawed sound expression" (15).

This last paradoxical piece of evidence for the invisible Jewish foreignness behind the invisible Jewish sameness in language is rendered

---

27   Wagner, *Das Judentum*, 15.
28   "Jeder [producire ursprünglich] nur in seiner Muttersprache"; see Wagner, *Das Judentum*,60. *Über die verschiedenen Methoden des Übersetzens* ("On the Various Methods of Translating"), written in 1813, in *Das Problem des Übersetzens*, ed. Hans Joachim Störig (Darmstadt: Wissenschaftliche Buchgesellschaft, 1963), 38–70.

unnecessary and in fact impossible by the ever-radicalizing discourse of Hitler, who draws the last consequences from the understanding of language as "expression" of thought: "A person can simply change the language, that is to say he can use a different language; in the new language, however, he will express the old thoughts; his inner essence will not change."[29] Race, the "inner essence," is only expressed by language, but *is* not language. Language still belongs to media, to society, to history—to exteriority, to "works." It is at this point that the intimacy of race and spirit becomes visible, as "race spirit" is embodied in one phenomenon of "inner essence"—the essence, the spirit, the liquid of life: blood:[30] "Race does not lie in language, but only in blood, something that no one knows better than the Jew, who in fact places only very little value on preserving his language, and rather all value on keeping his blood pure."[31]

The Secret Race State

I will shortly discuss this anti-Semitic motif, already encountered in Renan, of identifying the Semite, here the Jew, as the paradigm of race, an identification that seemed perfectly coherent with Renan's spiritual anti-Semitism and may seem contradictory in Hitler's affirmatively racist politics. Before that, I wish to point at the latter's politically crucial conclusion regarding language, which stands in opposition to Renanian philology. If, for Renan's science, language manifests race, for Hitler—who on this point, as I indicated, is more consistent with the logic of race—language *conceals* race. "The language of the Jew," he writes, "is for him not the means to express his thoughts, but the means to conceal them. Speaking French, he thinks Jewish" (337). This is the logic that will later guide the "12 Theses against the Un-German Spirit," a flyer formulating the platform of the Nazi students' *Aktion* that culminated in the book burnings of May 1933, in demanding that "Jewish works shall be published in the Hebrew language. If they are published in German, they shall be designated as translations."[32]

---

29 Hitler, *Mein Kampf*, 813. The editors' commentary refers to this idea as recurring in Theodor Fritsch's publication *Hammer* since 1903 (814–815n.158).
30 Anidjar, *Blood*, viii.
31 Hitler, *Mein Kampf*, 813.
32 On the book burnings, see Werner Treß, *Wider den undeutschen Geist. Bücherverbrennung 1933* (Berlin: Parthas, 2003); Treß, ed., *Verbrannte Bücher 1933*.

The anti-epistemic epistemology of anti-Semitism, the epistemology of double invisibility, in fact carries inherent political implications, is political epistemology. It is after all for a certain *politics* that anti-Semitism has primarily become the name. I already indicated the formally similar assertions of both Marx and the anti-Semites about shifting the Jewish Question from religion to politics, and their formally similar underlying anti-religious or anti-Christian critique. For Marx, this shift initially meant reinterpreting Jewish particularity as the specificity of a certain sociopolitical practice, i.e., egoism, which subsequently meant abandoning "Jews" as a political category altogether. Anti-Semitism, in contrast, turns the de-Christianized Jews into a paradigm of politics. One of the fundamental operations of anti-Semitic discourse has been to assert the political essence of Judaism against its religious interpretation. Marr's basic observation from his "non-confessional standpoint" was that "The Jewish 'confession' was nothing more than the statutes of a people."[33] Judaism is not a religion but "the particular Jewish state" (9). I already mentioned Hitler's constitutive realization that Jews are "not German of a special confession, but a different people [*ein Volk für sich*]."[34] In support of this claim he refers, among others, as Eichmann will too in Jerusalem, to Zionism,[35] and to the "factual" nature of the Talmud: "the Talmud too is not a book of preparation for the hereafter, but only for practical and tolerable life in this world."[36]

Mit Feuer gegen die Freiheit des Geistes. Eine Anthologie (Bonn: Bundeszentrale für politische Bildung, 2009); Confino, *World without Jews*, chap. 1.

33   Marr, *Sieg*, 20.
34   Hitler, *Mein Kampf*, 211.
35   On Eichmann, see Arendt, *Eichmann*, 40–41.
36   Hitler, *Mein Kampf*, 795. The editors' critical commentary notes that, in contrast to the more common references to the Talmud by anti-Semitic authors such as Fritsch and Rosenberg, this one here is the sole reference of Hitler to the Talmud in *Mein Kampf*. They suggest that "Hitler was probably aware of the contradiction that arises when one defines Judaism, on the one hand, as 'race' and not as a religious community, but on the other hand constantly makes arguments using the Talmud—one of the main texts of the Jewish religion" (n. 119). This suggestion is obviously problematic, since Hitler's claim here is that the Talmud is not religious ("preparation for the hereafter") but political ("practical and tolerable life in this world").

Visible here is the assertion of "the people" *against* "confession": the Jews are not confession *but* a people; the Talmud is not about the hereafter *but* about this world. I already indicated how this allegedly anti-confessional position is in fact an anti-confessional position within the confessional discourse: it asserts the political as the non-confessional *versus* the confessional, "the people" *versus* faith.[37] The political, "the people," draws its meaning from faith in the "hereafter," as its *negative*: "race." The Talmud is not about the hereafter, but about collective life in this world, namely, Hitler explains, it provides "instructions for ensuring the purity of blood of the Jewry [*Judentum*]." (9) "Not . . . but." This is the structure of the formally critical quality of anti-Semitic discourse, unveiling truth behind seeming. For understanding the political implications of this claim it is crucial to recall the paradox of unveiling race behind confession, a true invisible behind a seeming invisible. It is by virtue of this logic that anti-Semitism considers assimilated, invisible Jews as the most accomplished form of the Jewish polity, an invisible state that would constitute—rather than Renan's Turkey—the accomplished form of race state.

The political significance of this conception becomes clearer in the—paradoxical—anti-Semitic imagination of the invisible Jewish polity. Once again, the comparison with Marx is illustrative. Marx interprets the disappearance of the Jews, Bauer's particularistic "chosen people," in the process of emancipation as the universalization of Jewish "egoism," such that the new Jewish figure is bourgeois society or the common "moneymen." Anti-Semitic discourse, in contrast, interprets the disappearance of the Jews in the imagery of *conspiracy*. Jewish disappearance signifies Jewish triumph not because Jewish politics has become universally visible, but, on the contrary, because Jewish particularistic politics has become so powerful as to control all media, all social conditions of possible experience, and so to make itself invisible, which is the consummation of race politics.

The motif of secret, crypto-Judaism has a history that reaches further back into the theological tradition. It no doubt structurally arises from or is closely related to the epistemo-political challenges posed by the un-

---

37 Thus, already the twenty-five-point program drawn up by the founders of the Nazi Party after World War I, of February 1920, provided that a member of the people's community [*Volksgenosse*] must be "a person with German blood, *regardless of his religious adherence*" [my emphasis]; see Hilberg, *Destruction*, 32, 65.

worldliness and absolutely inner being of *faith*, which in the political or inter-subjective dimension immediately raises the question of *evidence*. The question of evidence, i.e., for the invisible faith, becomes acute in the case of conversion, where the basic premise is the initial *absence* of faith. Paradoxically, conversion is consequently the establishment of the convert's fundamental faithlessness, which the convert, in the very act of conversion, claims to have overcome. It is easy to see the conceptual constellation that thus presents conversion as structural deception. At the Iberian threshold of modernity, in the face of mass Jewish conversion and assimilation, this paradox appeared in the image of the "new Christians," the *marranos*, structurally suspected of being crypto-Jews, to the effect that the ultimate evidence of faith (for eligibility to high office) was a certificate of *limpieza de sangre*, "purity of blood." According to historian Yosef Hayim Yerushalmi, the *limpieza de sangre* statutes obtained the highest level of official recognition, by both pope and king, in 1555, "as the last vestiges of active crypto-Judaism seemed to be disappearing and there was no basis for doubting the attachment of most of the New Christians to the Catholic religion."[38] In other words, *blood*, socially invisible element of life, emerges

---

38   On the question of the relation between premodern Iberian *limpieza de sangre* and modern racial anti-Semitism, see Yosef Hayim Yerushalmi, "L'antisémitisme racial est-il apparu au XXe siècle? De la limpieza de sangre espagnol au nazisme: continuités et ruptures," trans. Jacqueline Carnaud, in *Esprit* 190 (3/4) (1993): 5–35, 18.

Pointing at "common traits" and "morphological affinities" (8), Yerushalmi called into question the scholarly maxim of "radical rupture" (25) between premodern religious anti-Judaism and modern racial anti-Semitism, and more specifically "the never questioned postulate of incompatibility in principle between Christianism and racial conceptions" (27). He speaks instead of "latent *racial* anti-Semitism in premodern Christian Europe" (27), "actualized" in Spain and Portugal. The difference to modern "organized forms of political anti-Semitism" arises according to Yerushalmi mainly from "the totalizing pretentions of modern ideologies" (29), i.e., not from any fundamental conceptual difference.

In the present context of the discussion of the anti-Semitic trope of Jewish invisible "conspiracy," it is remarkable how the main motifs are already present in fifteenth-sixteenth century Iberia, as described by Yerushalmi: the "historical irony" (14) that precisely the fulfilling of the Christian hope of Jewish conversion (assimilation) generates the fear of the "inner enemy" (14) explicitly invoking

as a political marker with the complete *disappearance* of its alleged socially visible manifestations.[39] This could be described as the political emergence of race in the Jewish body.

This logic is pushed to greater extremes in modernity, when the transformation of Jewish being is carried out not as *conversion*, i.e., not as a change of inner essence, transubstantiation, but as *assimilation*, i.e., as a change of appearance, a phenomenal change, whereby Jews remain Jews—ever more so in face of the disappearance of all sociocultural manifestations of Jewishness. The ensuing structural deception was already invoked by Bruno Bauer: "Only by way of sophistry, of seeming, would the Jew be able to remain in state life; if he wishes to remain Jew, the mere seeming would prevail and become the essence."[40] Essence as seeming becomes

---

the "existence of an international Jewish plot that almost anticipates the modern *Protocols of the Sages of Zion*" (15).

The identification of the laws of *limpieza de sangre* as antecedent of racial anti-Semitism was already proposed by Bernard Lewis, *Semites and Anti-Semites*, 82–84. For an analysis of the *marrano* as a paradigm of modern Jewish philosophy, focusing on the question of language, see Agata Bielik-Robson, *Jewish Cryptologies of Late Modernity: Philosophical Marranos* (New York: Routledge, 2014).

39   See Gil Anidjar, *Blood: A Critique of Christianity* (New York: Columbia University Press, 2014), asserting "blood is the *element* of Christianity," such that "a consideration of what blood reflects, produces, and sustains, what it engenders, must take—as one adopts—the form of a critique of Christianity" (ix). See in particular Anidjar's discussion of the *limpieza de sangre*, which he inscribes in a broader theological context under the title "Eucharist and Inquisition," asserting the medieval and early modern rise of "a new theologico-political thought and form," when "Christians were becoming a community of blood" (59): "For with this new material and rhetorical link unifying it, the community no longer depends on a transcendental condition or external, indeed expropriating, order. Grounded in its own materiality, in its own unified existence qua community, the community no longer awaits unification, no longer needs to *perform* its unity. It no longer gives itself away, nor does it need to be gathered (from above or from below). It *is* already one in blood; it is the general kinship of blood" (68).

In his earlier work, Anidjar pointed at a further analogy or precursor to modern, racist, anti-Semite race politics in the early American "war on witches," which was waged under the motto "The Reality of Invisibles" (Anidjar, *Semites*, 1).

40   Bauer, *The Capacity of Present-Day Jews and Christians*, 176–178.

in anti-Semitism the very operative definition of the Jewish race, of the Jewish as race, the paradigmatic political performance of which would be the "secret society."[41]

Herein lies the suggestive power of the canonic document of twentieth-century anti-Semitism, *The Protocols of the Elders of Zion*, or as titled in the Marsden translation, *The Protocols of the Meetings of the Learned Elders of Zion*.[42] "The Protocols" are in fact a document and not a text. They are an artifact, a piece of evidence that *presents* the invisible. Their exact content is less significant than their material existence, which attests to the existence and actual presence (the "meetings") of the invisible Jewish polity. *The Protocols* do not just attest to the presence of the secret Jewish state, but re-present it, in the image of the "Elders of Zion": they *embody* the disappearing Jews. *The Protocols* in fact speak in the first-person plural of the "we"—they demand to be read as a recording of the authentic Jewish voice.

This is why the main question raised by *The Protocols* concerns not their veracity but their authenticity. This question reflects the paradox of evidenced invisibility: the authenticity of *The Protocols* means they make visible the invisible Jews *as invisible*, whose evidenced invisibility would be the proof for their omnipotence and omnipresence. The connection

---

41 Katz notes the emergence of the notion of secret Jewish politics in post-Napoleonic Germany and the subsequent "repression of social and political aspirations, which were not satisfied under the new regime" (Katz, *From Prejudice*, 89). On the motif of Jewish conspiracy see Friedländer, *Nazi Germany*, 83–85, who described it as a "Christian phantasm" (84). However, Friedländer attributes the rise of the Jewish conspiracy phantasm in *modern* anti-Semitism to the "increasing visibility" of Jews (82), in contrast to the *invisibility* asserted as a crucial element by my own analysis.

42 This pamphlet was distributed in different versions with various titles in numerous languages. I use here the following version: *The Protocols of the Meetings of the Learned Elders of Zion*, with preface and explanatory notes, trans. Victor E. Marsden (former Russia correspondent of *The Morning Post*) (n.p., 1934). On the protocols, see Friedländer, *Nazi Germany*, 94–95; Norman Cohn, *Warrant for Genocide: The Myth of the Jewish World-Conspiracy and the Protocols of the Elders of Zion* (New York: Harper and Row, 1966); Stephen Eric Broner, *A Rumor about the Jews: Reflections on Antisemitism and the Protocols of the Learned Elders of Zion* (New York: St. Martin's Press, 2000); Richard Landes and Steven T. Katz, eds., *The Paranoid Apocalypse: A Hundred-Year Retrospective on The Protocols of the Elders of Zion* (New York: New York University Press, 2012).

of power and invisibility is a precept confessed to by *The Protocols* "themselves," stating as their main principle: "Force and Make-Believe. Only force conquers in political affairs, especially if it be concealed in the talents essential to statesmen" (147). Under these conditions, any positive evidence of Jewish conspiracy would *eo ipso* constitute evidence *against* its power. Accordingly, evidence to Jewish power is provided paradoxically by the powerful *opposition* to it, i.e., by anti-Semitism, to which in *The Protocols* the "Elders of Zion" take credit: "Nowadays, if any States raise a protest against us it is only *pro forma*, at our discretion and by our direction, for *their anti-Semitism is indispensable to us for the management of our lesser brethren*" (169). Anti-Semitism itself would be the ultimate living evidence for the Jewish conspiracy, which is so powerful as to generate the appearance of anti-Jewish power. Similarly, the authenticity of *The Protocols* is structurally proven by everything that *speaks against it*. Jewish authorship is evidenced by the lack of evidence of Jewish authorship, as Henry Ford's *The International Jew* (1920) argued: "If these documents were the forgeries which Jewish apologists claim them to be, the forgers would probably have taken pains to make Jewish authorship so clear that their anti-Semitic purpose could easily have been detected."[43] Jewish authorship is proven by the *denial* of Jewish authorship: "The claim of the Jews that the Protocols are forgeries is in itself an admission of their genuineness."[44]

---

43   *The International Jew: The World's Foremost Problem: Being a Reprint of a Series of Articles Appearing in The Dearborn Independent from May 22 to October 2, 1920*, November 1920, p. 110. The publication states no author, place of publication, or publisher, and has in its turn raised an authorship dispute resembling the one pertaining to *The Protocols*. See Victoria Saker Woeste, *Henry Ford's War on Jews and the Legal Battle against Hate Speech* (Stanford, CA: Stanford University Press, 2012); see also Max Wallace, *The American Axis: Henry Ford, Charles Lindbergh, and the Rise of the Third Reich* (New York: St. Martin's Griffin, 2003).

44   As stated in the introduction to Marsden's translation, p. 137. The text nonetheless continues to explain the argument by criticizing the forgery allegations of evading answer to "the facts": "for they *never attempt to answer the facts* corresponding to the *threats* which the Protocols contain, and, indeed, the correspondence between the prophecy and the fulfillment is too glaring to be set aside or obscured" (137). Hitler, who radically asserts the epistemo-political power of paradox, typically uses the openly and intentionally paradoxical formulation: "[*The Protocols*] are based on a forgery, the 'Frankfurter Zeitung' moans every

There is still much to be asked about the epistemo-political presuppositions that underlie the notion of Jewish politics as "world conspiracy." In the framework of this explicitly epistemic study of anti-Semitism, i.e., the study of anti-Semitism as a constellation of *knowledge*, it would be important to examine more closely how *The Protocols* and their anti-Semitic readings reflect actual, self-affirming performances of Jewishness. One such obvious event was the First Zionist Congress of 1897, which the Marsden translation mentions as the answer to the question, "When did the Meetings take place and by whom were the Protocols promulgated?"[45] There is paradox in pointing at the Zionist Congress as the location of Jewish world conspiracy, of course, due to the *patent* nature of the Zionist Congress: both its own constitutive visibility as a public event and the specific visibility it claimed for the Jews: a formally distinguished and separate state. In the logic of crypto-Judaism, however, the Zionist Congress, very much like *The Protocols* themselves, was not so much a text as a *document*, which demonstrated the existence, behind or beyond the visible event, of an invisible Jewish society, a secret, *international* Jewish polity, whose purpose is not really a nation-state, but a world-state, a *cosmo-polis*.

In this sense, *The Protocols* may be more cogently considered as an anti-Semitic imagination of the Talmud. The talmudic texts could indeed be described and read as minutes, transcripts, or "protocols" of discussions between ancient Jewish scholars, "learned elders." These meetings, not only the ones of late antiquity and the Middle Ages, but also in contemporary rabbinic academies, in contrast to Zionist Congresses, have in fact remained invisible for the European public. The only evidence for their existence is their protocols, the Talmud. It is noteworthy to what extent the Talmud, rarely mentioned by anti-anti-Semitic authors, plays a significant role in anti-Semitic texts.[46] Much more than Zionist discourse,

---

week to the world: the best proof that they are authentic" (Hitler, *Mein Kampf*, 799).

45   *Protocols*, 137.

46   There is in fact a motif of "exposing" the Talmud as the secret, anti-Christian and later anti-Gentile book of the Jews, as a constitutive act of modern anti-Judaism and later anti-Semitism. The history of this motif can be traced, in German literature, from Johann Andreas Eisenmenger's *Entdecktes Judentum* ("Judaism Revealed") of 1700, exposing Jews' contempt of Christianity as stated in their "own books," "so far completely or partly unknown among the

talmudic discourse in fact contains innumerable elements of a *universal* vision, which may be very reasonably characterized as worldly-political rather than unworldly-religious. An unlikely designation for the Zionist nation-state paradigm, "world rule" could be used much more sensibly for describing the proclaimed talmudic adhesion to the project of *ribono shel olam*, "The Sovereign of the World."

In the anti-Semitic representation of the Talmud, the universal is subjugated to the particular: the main point made by all anti-Semitic accounts is the talmudic political and legal, *normative* distinction between Jews and non-Jews. It has been a traditional anti-Jewish trope, as visible in Bauer, or Kant, for instance, to criticize Judaism for being basically a *nomos*—law, institution, and culture—of particularism.[47] The unique feature of anti-Semitism is the notion that this particularistic *nomos* is nothing but the expression of a particularistic *physis*, race. Jewish law would be the expression of the Semitic race spirit. The primary feature of this *nomos* is that it is—like race—hidden beneath the surface of historical phenomena: it is a secret racial law of an invisible race state that is most powerful when nowhere to be seen.

In these conditions, the talmudic or Jewish universal claim can only be interpreted as a Jewish conspiracy for world domination, the basic principle of which is Jewish *exploitation* of non-Jews. Here lies the sense of acute menace arising from anti-Semitic imagination of the invisible Jewish polity and the modern process of *Verjudung*. In political terminology, the Jews are imagined, in contrast to Muslims, the *external* enemy, as the *inner* enemy,[48] which always means a secret, invisible, and hidden enemy, an enemy that

---

Christians," to the 1893 edition (Dresden: Otto Brander), which presents itself as "literal translation of the most important passages of the Talmud and other Hebrew-rabbinic literature, to a large extent still completely unknown to the Christians," passing through August Rohling, *Der Talmudjude* (Münster: Adolph Russells Verlag, 1871), and featuring in works such as Fritsch's *Anti-Semiten-Katechismus* (12ff.).

47   Emmanuel Kant, *Die Religion innerhalb der Grenzen der bloßen Vernunft*, mit einer Einleitung und Anmerkungen herausgegeben von Bettina Stangneth (Hamburg: Meiner, 2003 [1793]), 125: "Jewish faith, in its original setting, is a compendium (*Inbegriff*) of mere (*bloß*) statutory laws, on which a state constitution was founded."

48   Cf. Gil Anidjar, *The Jew, The Arab*, passim.

does not *look like* an enemy, but rather as a friend or better—that has no visible distinction at all. This internal political rivalry is paradigmatically described as "a state within the state," which exploits the state and does so under the false pretense of being a religion. As Marr put it: "The Jewish confession was nothing more than the statutes of a people, which constitutes a state within the state and this by-state or counter-state [*Nebenstaat, resp. Gegenstaat*] demanded very specific material advantages for its members."[49] Emancipation would mean admitting the enemies of the state to be its citizens and potential *rulers*, "equal political participation in legislation and administration of the very state they theocratically negate" (21), which evokes the image of political suicide.

The more extreme anti-Semitic language, asserting more radically the logic of race, does not describe the invisible Jewish state in political but in biological terms. The internal malignant Jewish agent is neither a state nor an enemy but "a foreign element"[50] or "a parasite,"[51] whose harmfulness arises from its foreignness to the organic system, something for which Hitler had many names, such as "poison," "spiritual pestilence," "germ carriers."[52] The inner destruction that they signify is not death by suicide, but death by disease. It is noteworthy that the biological semantics detaches its object—and thus itself—from any moral or more generally from any *normative* aspects. The phenomena it describes are not in the order of the political but in the order of the natural. The death and destruction associated with Jewish emancipation arise in a process that involves no real guilt or responsibility, but is moved by organic necessity. In this sense, the Jews are not even real agents or causes, but an epiphenomenon of the inner downfall, parasites not of life, but of death: "like maggot in the rotting flesh."[53]

---

49   Marr, *Sieg*, 20. Katz points out that this notion goes back to anti-Jewish discourse of the 1780s, by authors such as Johann Heinrich Schulz, and was famously used by Fichte (Katz, *From Prejudice*, 58–60).
50   Wagner, *Das Judentum*, 31.
51   Dühring, 8; Hitler, *Mein Kampf*, 791; Katz notes the description of Jews as parasites already in Herder (*From Prejudice*, 60).
52   Hitler, *Mein Kampf*, 216–217.
53   Fritsch, *Kathechismus*, 155; Hitler, *Mein Kampf*, 217; see already Wagner: "the flesh dissolves in the swarming multiplicity of worms" (*Das Judentum*, 31).

The powerfulness of these strong images, namely what makes them strong *images*, what constitutes and intensifies their specific operation of making visible, lies no doubt in their insistence not only on the death of the body, but on the body of death, on the body as death. The flesh appears there not as the matter or substrate of spirit and form, not quite as *body*, but as the formless, decaying biomass, which above all provokes disgust and horror. Disgust is the relation to the invisible not as the unseen visible, such as the Platonic ideas, which, invisible to the sensual eye, are nonetheless the intellectual *forms* of all visibility, and so shine forth in beauty.[54] Disgust, nausea, repulsion, is the relation to the invisible in the mode of formlessness, to the invisible as de-formed, monstrous, *ugly*—it does not evade the eye, but repulses the *will* to see. Jews, racial beings, embody the ugliness of the invisible real, the appalling flesh and blood beneath the skin of appearance. The horror of their image arises from their essential concealedness. The less they are seen the more horrific their image gets.[55] Like Baudelaire's devil, their finest trick was to convince the world, by "the progress of enlightenment," that they didn't exist.[56] Or as Hitler put it: "It is one of the most ingenious tricks that were ever devised, to make [the Jewish racial] State sail under the flag of 'religion.'"[57] Jewish politics of race is at its peak when the Jew—together with the Marxists—*denies* race: "While he seems to overflow of 'enlightenment', 'progress', 'freedom', 'humanity' etc., he himself exercises the strongest locking-up of his race. . . .

---

54   Plato, *Phaedrus*, 250d, as discussed by Martin Heidegger, *Nietzsche I* (Frankfurt am Main: Vittorio Klostermann, 1996 [1961]), 190–202.

55   Cf. Friedländer, *Nazi Germany*, 100: "The all-pervasive Jewish threat becomes in fact formless and unrepresentable."

56   Charles Baudelaire, *Petits Poèmes en prose*, Œuvres complètes de Charles Baudelaire (Paris: Michel Lévy frères, 1869), IV. Petits Poèmes en prose, Les Paradis artificiels, 90, where the devil states that the only moment when he was concerned about his power was when he heard a preacher shouting: "Mes chers frères, n'oubliez jamais, quand vous entendrez vanter le progrès des lumières, que la plus belle des ruses du diable est de vous persuader qu'il n'existe pas!»

57   Hitler, *Mein Kampf*, 427. For a discussion of affinities between Baudelaire and Hitler on the question of "evil," see Claire Ortiz Hill, *The Roots and Flowers of Evil in Baudelaire, Nietzsche, and Hitler* (Chicago: Open Court, 2006).

In order to mask his activity and lull his victims, however, he talks more and more of the equality of all men without regard to race and color" (825).

Kampf

The anti-Semitic *struggle* against the Jews, an agenda that immediately arises from the anti-Semitic representation of the Jews and that becomes ever more urgent as Jews continue to assimilate and disappear, consists initially in a multifaceted operation of *discerning* and rendering the Jews *visible*.[58] The Jews must be displayed as the invisible being concealed by the invisible being they claim to be: race and not confession.[59] Against Jewish denial of race, anti-Semitism asserts race, is in this sense *racist*. This may seem to contradict Renan's "progress of spiritualization," in which, for the sake of the nation, race is to be *forgotten*. Nonetheless, it is for the sake of forgetting race that Renan too asserts race and race-based science. Race is produced as the sacrifice demanded by spirit, a sacrifice that seemingly represents the opposite of racist politics. Racism rather affirms political power on the basis of race, and this affirmation is a fundamental feature of all political anti-Semitism as well as Nazism.

This is not the place for a thorough analysis of Hitler's race theory, but *Mein Kampf* no doubt asserts race, the "drive of self-preservation of the race," as the basic principle of politics. "The drive of preservation of the species is the first cause for the formation of human communities" (427); "all events of world history are only the manifestation of the self-preservation drive of the race" (769). Like Marx's "class," Hitler's "race" is the collective agent of history; Marxist history is animated by class struggle, Hitler's by race struggle. However, whereas the *telos* of Marx's history, the end of class struggle, is to end class, and Renan's history progresses to end race,

---

58 The methods used for this purpose, such as requiring Jews to wear a yellow star, were very often retrieved from medieval church policies; see Bernard Lewis, *Semite and Anti-Semites*, 91; Hilberg, *Destruction*, 10–15.

59 It is noteworthy that, as Raul Hilberg pointed out, to *evidence* the essentially invisible Jewish race, the Nazi laws, in the preparatory stage to the enactment of anti-Jewish measures that Hilberg called "definition," i.e., the creation of the legal category of the "Jew," did not resort to biological criteria, but to the *religious* affiliation of a person's grandparents, which would presumably be, to recall Renan, a "manifestation" of race; see Hilberg, *Destruction*, 66–67.

Hitler's race struggle does not work to end race but to *preserve* race. Race struggle is the "means for promoting the health and force of resistance of the species" (741). Forgetting race, which for Renan is the event of the modern nation, is proclaimed by Hitler to be the cause for the downfall of all great cultures in history (753). It is in properly theological terms that he preaches the principle of race: "The sin against blood and race is the original sin of this world and the end of humanity that commits it" (657).

This terminology, however, simultaneously asserts and undermines the anti-religiosity of the race principle. The proximity to Renan is in fact greater than it first seems. It shows itself most clearly in Hitler's and general anti-Semitic narrative of the actual history of race struggle, as articulated most fundamentally by the struggle between Aryans and Semites. As in all race theory, its theology manifests itself in teleology. Aryans and Semites are not just two competing races, like all races. Rather, they represent different stages in the principle of race—as Renan called it, different "race spirits"—and so articulate the logic of race as the principle of human history. The Aryan race stands for the end of this history as accomplished civilization, is the *superior* race, the paradigm of humanity. According to Hitler, human culture is "almost exclusively the creative product of the Aryan," such that "he alone was the founder of superior humanity in general, and is thus the paradigm of what we understand by the word 'man'" (755). What precise quality does the Aryan race possess, which qualifies it for this role? The foundation of superior humanity, of "culture," is "the capacity to form a broader commonwealth [Gemeinwesen]," namely beyond the natural family, which requires "the readiness to put back purely personal interests" (771). Culture demands, so Hitler, a "will to sacrifice," a sense of "duty," or "idealism" (775), which means the will to transcend self-preservation and therewith to transcend the principle race. The Aryan, superior race of culture, would be the race that transcends race, the idealistic, spiritual race. There is here a perfect analogy to Renan's Aryans as the race of spirit, and "the nation," will beyond race, as the principle of the Germanic race.

Now, "the most radical opposition to the Aryan is the Jew" (777). In contrast to the spiritual Aryan race-spirit stands the racial Semitic race-spirit, which for Renan was embodied by the Turks and for Hitler by the Jews. Just as the Semitic languages served for Renan as a paradigmatic object for his race science, so for Hitler the Jews paradoxically appear as the paradigm of race politics, the politics based on "self-preservation drive":

"Hardly any people in the world have a more developed self-preservation drive than the so-called chosen ones. The best evidence for this should be already provided by the simple fact of the mere existence of this race" (777). "What an infinitely tenacious will to life, to preserve the species arises from these facts!" (777), Hitler wrote in admiration.[60] The problem of the Jews is that they are too much race, namely lack "the most essential condition for a people of culture, the idealistic mentality" (783).

Accordingly, in *Mein Kampf*, Hitler can describe his "struggle" in the name of the Aryan race not just as a mere biological, natural necessity, but as a historical event of a religious mission: "What we have to fight for is securing the existence and multiplication of our race and our people, nurturing our children and maintaining the purity of blood, the freedom and independence of our fatherland, so that our people may grow to fulfill the mission that it too was allotted by the creator of the universe" (576–577). The casual "too," *auch*, is dramatic here. It shows how easily and conveniently, in what familiar and obvious way, the bluntest race discourse draws on the tradition of theology. The theological notion of a collective "mission," a collective chosenness, election, and calling, a collective historical predestination and destiny, provides the epistemo-political meaning of the category "race." The spirit of race, race-spirit, is a divine calling. The "too" invokes of course the other, better known, *exemplary* chosen people, the Jews, Israel in the flesh, the race of Israel. The chosen race of Israel serves as the paradigm for the chosen German race—but not only as paradigm: both as a proto-type and as adversary, namely as an inferior version of itself. Aryan Israel is chosen to fight Jewish Israel: "And so I believe today to act as intended by the almighty creator: by fending off the Jews, I fight for the work of the Lord" (231).[61] Anti-Semitism shows itself to be a modern

---

60 Cf. Chamberlain, *Die Grundlage*: "The Jews deserve admiration, because they conducted themselves with absolute confidence according to the logic and truth of their specific kind, and never had the silliness of humanity ... made them forget the holiness of the physical law" (324). On Hitler and Chamberlain, see also Friedländer, *Nazi Germany*, 89–90; Hitler, *Mein Kampf*, 57–58.

61 The editors of the critical edition of *Mein Kampf* note here: "This phrase was in the Third Reich one of the most quoted phrases from *Mein Kampf*" (231n.228).

operation of supersession and *Aufhebung*—of the race of Israel in flesh by the race of Israel in spirit.[62]

It is in accordance with this political epistemology that the anti-Semitic agenda, its plan of action, its operative *anti*, namely its anti-Jewish war, has taken its shape, eventually amounting to what will be called the "Final Solution" of the Jewish Question, and later the Destruction of the Jews, the Holocaust or the Shoah.[63] I am aware of the temptation and risk of reading history from Auschwitz backward—but there is also a risk in avoiding such a reading, which is the risk of avoiding history, namely as a dimension where ideas become real and reality visible, i.e., history as a dimension of positive political epistemology. Of course, it is only to a very

---

62 This theological component of substitution or transubstantiation complements Alon Confino's analysis of "the Nazis' dream of a clean historical slate," such that "by persecuting and exterminating the Jews, the Nazis eliminated the shackles of a past tradition and its morality, thus making it possible to liberate their imagination, to open up a new emotional, historical, and moral horizons" (Confino, *World without Jews*, 24–25). Quoting Renan's "What Is a Nation?" Confino does however identify in Nazism also the national motif of "the search for origins" (33). I believe that my analysis accounts for this seeming contradiction. I further note the affinity of my readings to Saul Friedländer's observation of what he called Hitler's "redemptive anti-Semitism" (*Nazi Germany*, chap. 3), inspired by "the spirit of Bayreuth" (87), which Friedländer describes as "a German (or Aryan) Christianity." Friedländer refers, among others, to Hitler's speech of 1926, where he was reported by the police to have said that "National Socialism was nothing but a practical fulfillment of the teachings of Christ" (102). See also Hitler, *Mein Kampf*, 52–53.
63 Cf. Bein, "Moderne Antisemitismus," 360: "The Hitler era in fact added ideologically nothing to the theoreticians of racial anti-Semitism. It actualized with gruesome systematic the teachings of modern anti-Semitism that emerged around 1880." Similarly, J. Katz: "Ideologically, Nazi anti-Semitism added nothing new to the prewar variety.... The basic principle of racial anti-Semitism, the denial to Jews of the right to exist, came here as a wholly unexpected, but not inconsistent, fruition as the policy of a government" (*From Prejudice*, 315–317). Raul Hilberg too considered the destruction to be "the final product of an earlier age" (*Destruction*, 5). For a critique of the "continuity thesis," see Shulamit Volkov, *Germans, Jews, Antisemites*, 81.

limited extent that Hitler's text can be considered as *theory*: not only due to the strong anti-scientific, anti-epistemic intentionality of anti-Semitism, and not only due to the ensuing operative, militant, and *sermonic* nature of anti-Semitic discourse, pushed to extremes in Hitler's text and speeches. Hitler's text, of course, is more than that: it is one of the closest things to a universally accessible blueprint and conceptual matrix for the actual politics carried out by both Nazi German state and society.[64] It is therefore a manifest epistemo-political location, a strong link between a central, and even constitutive modern political epistemology, as I tried to present it, and a paradigmatic catastrophe of modern politics.

What was conceived, planned, organized, coordinated, and carried out on a world scale as "The Final Solution of the Jewish Question" was directly conditioned through the interrelated conceptions and perceptions that were named "The Jewish Question" or "The Question of the Jews," the conception and perception of the Jews as the Question. A fundamental anti-anti-Semitic tendency, as I analyzed it in Part I of this book, endeavors to neutralize the epistemic nature of anti-Semitism by denying its Jewish Question any epistemic relation to the Jews—anti-Semitism would constitute no knowledge, neither bad nor good knowledge, *of* Jews. The Jewish Question would have nothing to do with Jews. This tendency is one significant motivation for the very current use of the term "anti-Semitism," a modern phenomenon, supposedly separated from traditional, religious "anti-Judaism," which, presumably, *would* know about Jews. Against this anti-anti-Semitic tendency, my analysis shows that the anti-Semitic discourse of the Jewish Question, first, constitutes a reaction to, and thus a perspective on and a *perception* of the defining modern Jewish event, i.e., emancipation; and second, *conceptually* draws, through race discourse, from the theological tradition. Looking closer at this anti-Semitic knowledge of Jews, I do, however, concede to anti-anti-Semitism that anti-Semitic

---

64 See the discussion in the scientific introduction to Hitler, *Mein Kampf*, 10, referring among others to Eberhard Jäckel, who wrote: "Rarely or perhaps indeed never in history had a ruler, before he came to power, outlined in writing as accurately as Adolf Hitler what he later did." Further quoted is Victor Klemperer, describing as "the greatest enigma of the Third Reich," how *Mein Kampf* "was able, or rather had to be distributed utterly publicly, and how nonetheless Hitler's rule was possible as well as the twelve years of this rule, although the bible of National Socialism had been available for years before the taking of power" (44).

knowledge of Jews is epistemologically *negative*, which also invokes its similarity to anti-anti-Semitic knowledge of Jews. Whereas the paradigmatic anti-anti-Semitic perception of Jews is the negative perception of the Jew "flesh and blood," a Jew without any concept, form and figure, a Jew behind the "Jew," the anti-Semitic perception of the Jews is the double negative of the invisible race behind the invisible confession, the crypto-Jew.

The Final Solution of the anti-Semitic Jewish Question, namely the question, problem, or issue posed by the Jews to the modern polity as a different political entity or a different political being, could have been neither conversion nor assimilation. Conversion and assimilation were rather the problem, since *it is precisely by disappearance that the invisible comes into being*. The less Jewish Jews seemed, the Jewisher they became.[65] The race state, a human base state, prehistorical origin of history, reemerged from beneath the cover of all its historical manifestations, purely present in its invisible glory. Transcending this origin, this root and race, progressing from race to spirit, to nation, to culture, namely consummating modernity by solving once and for all the question of the Jews, can no longer take place in the dimension of sociohistorical phenomena, but must proceed at the root itself, in the dimension of real being, of the individual "flesh and blood." The ultimate conversion from race to spirit is not the disappearance but the extinction of race, the termination of its racial being, its organic life. The final conversion of the Jews into modernity, as the ultimate moment in the European "progress of spiritualization," was to be their conversion from life to death, their physical, bodily, individual extermination. It is through a striking fidelity to this theopolitical epistemology that the official post-World War II memory of Auschwitz, i.e., its existence as anti-anti-Semitic state knowledge, will in fact conceive and make sense of it by the category of ultimate sacrifice, will name and know it to be *The Holocaust*.[66]

---

65   Cf. Bein, "Moderne Antisemitismus," 357.
66   On the history and semantics of the term "holocaust" as designation of the Jewish destruction by the Nazis, see Zev Garber and Bruce Zuckerman, "Why Do We Call the Holocaust 'the Holocaust'? An Inquiry into the Psychology of Labels," *Modern Judaism* 9 (1989): 197–211. The authors trace the introduction of this term back in particular to a Jewish personality, Elie Wiesel: "It was a particular scene of sacrifice that Wiesel had in mind—the *Akedah*, i.e., the story in Genesis 22 where God orders Abraham to offer his son as an *olah* sacrifice" (203).

Epilogue

*The End of Anti-Anti-Semitism
as Introduction to Talmud*

WHAT IF—anti-Semitism has been, after Jewish assimilation, one of the only remaining traces that there ever has been an actual Jewish question, a question posed by Jews as Jews, a Jewish being, namely, that subsists not in the realm of pure substance, but in the realm of questions, of answers, of debates, of *pro* and also *anti*, the realm of thought? Anti-Semitism fought Jewish thought not in thought, not by refuting it, but by denying it the status of thought, by treating it as race, which is only refuted by extermination. Anti-Semitism is the perception of Jewish thought by the sole form of extermination. Rejecting, condemning, fighting the extermination, anti-anti-Semitism does not open new ways for perceiving or receiving Jewish thought, but wipes out one of the only remaining traces that there ever has been Jewish thought, by denying anti-Semitism itself the status of thought. The wiping out of Jewish thought is itself wiped out—the effacement effaced, a forgetting of the forgetting. More radical oblivion than the name of Amalek, whose blotting out from under heaven was prescribed for eternal memory. What remains from Jewish thought after Auschwitz is race murder, genocide.

Effacement has many shapes, oblivion being only one, and not always the worst. There are dangers lurking in remembrance. A recent project of commemoration reminds of this. In 2016, the *Institut für Zeitgeschichte*

München-Berlin published a critical edition of *Mein Kampf*.[1] The edition is highly self-reflective. A long, pensive introduction, which begins with the question "Why this edition?" (9), carefully presents and discusses the difficulties, problems, and risks in this republication of Hitler, balancing them against the benefits of producing a scientifically informed, critical "edition with a position" (*Edition mit Standpunkt*) (53). This project, with its provocative aim of turning *Mein Kampf* into a "huge museum" (67) of Nazi semantics, merits a careful reading.

There is, however, one immediately peculiar aspect of this edition, namely the aspect of its immediate aspect—its appearance. A last section of the introduction, "Typography and Visual Designing," alleges the "high complexity" of critically editing of Hitler's book, "with dense commenting, chapter introductions and text comparison," which would—so one is led to understand—surpass all comparable critical editions. The need for preserving "graphic clarity" required, so was the editors' conviction, an "unconventional layout" (75). So exceptional the hermeneutical situation was deemed to be, so much beyond any contemporary example, that the graphic designers had to look further away for a suitable model. It comes as quite a surprise to read in the introduction that the main "prominent precursors" (75) identified by the editors of *Mein Kampf*'s critical commentary for its graphic design were the early printed editions of the commented Jewish Bible and the Talmud (75). The choice is illustrated with little photos of the 1546 Venice Jewish Bible and the 1979 Jerusalem Talmud (as well as Erasmus's 1515 *Moriae Encomium*) at the bottom of the page (75) and is clearly visible in the edition's layout. The most striking is that this highly self-reflective and dense commented edition provides no comment on the use of the Jewish Bible as the template for the bible of National Socialism. It does provide a—caricaturesque—illustration of a possible passage from anti-anti-Semitism to Talmud.

In the following pages I would like to propose a more serious demonstration of how moving away from anti-anti-Semitic discourse may open a way to engage on anti-Semitism not as the negation of Jewish thought but as a gateway to it. What could such a gateway look like? And, perhaps most crucially, what is exactly meant here—and throughout this book—

---

1   Hitler, *Mein Kampf. Eine kritische Edition*, hg. v. Christian Hartmann et al. (München and Berlin: Institut für Zeitgeschichte, 2016)

by "Jewish thought" or "Jewish knowledge" or the "epistemic value" of the Jewish? To suggest a preliminary direction for answering these questions, which the present book, by overcoming anti-anti-Semitism, only permits to ask, I now return to Heidegger, whose anti-Semitism stands at the center of the debate that gave rise to this investigation and was discussed in its first chapter.

In the first chapter I explicitly avoided offering any analysis of Heidegger's anti-Semitic passages and focused instead on demonstrating the elements and mechanisms of the anti-anti-Semitism that dominated the recent debate concerning these passages. Having discussed in length anti-anti-Semitism, I now wish to offer an alternative analysis that will indicate, precisely in Heidegger's anti-Semitism, a gateway to Jewish thought, and more specifically to the Talmud.

"Talmud" or "talmudic literature," also known as "rabbinic literature," means here, in the broadest sense, the tradition that is based on a corpus of texts known as the Talmud,[2] whose most canonic version is believed to have been redacted in Babylonia around the seventh century CE, and which is currently still active and developing.[3] The proposition that Heidegger may be considered as introducing to Talmud is odd, because Heidegger, like virtually all Western philosophers, never mentioned the Talmud. If Heidegger's work contains any indirect reference to the Talmud, it is his notes on the Jewish, namely his anti-Semitism. Accordingly, if Heidegger's work provides any perspective on the Talmud, there is a good reason to situate it rather in the tradition of anti-Semitic introductions to the Talmud.[4]

Without denying both facts, Heidegger's ignorance of Talmud and his anti-Semitism, both unexceptional in the history of modern philosophy, I nonetheless wish to claim that Heidegger's thought, unlike modern philosophy before him, opened, within contemporary thought, a path toward talmudic literature, an introduction of sorts. This claim not only does not ignore or disregard Heidegger's anti-Semitism and Nazism, but

---

2   I follow Sergey Dolgopolski in differentiating between "the Talmud" as a textual corpus (like "the Bible" or "the Odyssey") and "Talmud" as a system of thought, a discourse or an episteme (like "Philosophy," "Modern Historiography," etc.); see Sergey Dolgopolski, *Other Others*.
3   For a recent accessible exposition, see Barry Wimpfheimer, *The Talmud: A Biography* (Princeton, NJ: Princeton University Press, 2018).
4   See Chapter 7, note 46.

it sets out from them. Heidegger, like the entire tradition of philosophy, ignored Talmud, however, more than any other modern philosopher it was Heidegger who sought for thought beyond philosophy, for "another" thought. Heidegger's thought was embedded in the discourse, world, and time, in the *being* of Nazi anti-Semitism, and so of the Holocaust. But it is also Heidegger who portrayed the encounter with philosophy's Other and so with the otherness of the West, not as a peaceful academic exchange but as an end of the world. It is in Heidegger's thought, as it was deployed in the immediate proximity to the end of the world that were World War II and the Holocaust, which I wish to point at a door to Talmud.

The Jewish-Christian Jew of the Bible

The site at which this apocalyptic event of contemporary thought's encounter with Talmud takes place, or in which a space is opened for such a place to be taken, is *the Jewish*. The Jewish is the site, figure, or configuration through which the Talmud obtained some kind of presence in Western thought, and in Heidegger, that is a presence of absence, a trace. As this book shows, the Jewish has been and still is a very unstable and ambivalent site. In the case of Heidegger, long before the appearance of the *Black Notebooks*, Emmanuel Levinas, for instance, portrayed Heideggerian thought as the contemporary epitome of Western philosophy of Being, of Greek origin, to be contrasted to a Jewish—and talmudic—wisdom of the Other.[5] In 1990, simultaneous with the debate following Victor Farias's book on Heidegger's involvement in National Socialism, albeit in pronounced detachment from this debate and from any *political* question, Marlène Zarader, against Levinas, revaluated Heidegger's own quest for otherness, i.e., for a non-Greek way of thinking. Zarader's provocative

---

5   See, for instance, Emmanuel Levinas, *Totalité et Infini: Essai sur l'extériorité* (Paris: Kluwer Academic, 1991 [1961]), trans. Alphonso Lingis as *Totality and Infinity: An Essay on Exteriority* (Boston: Martinus Nijhoff, 1979), where on the first page Levinas writes, clearly with Heidegger in mind: "We do not need obscure fragments of Heraclitus to prove that being reveals itself as war to philosophical thought" (11). On the nonetheless much more complex relation of Levinas's to Heidegger's philosophy, see Michael Fagenblat, "Levinas and Heidegger: The Elemental Confrontation," in *The Oxford Handbook of Levinas*, ed. Michael L. Morgan (Oxford: Oxford University Press, 2019), 103–133.

claim was that Heidegger's portrayal of non-Greek thought—centered on language, memory, faithfulness, and prophetic poetry—not only sounded Jewish but was in fact indebted to the "Hebraic heritage." Zarader identified this heritage with the *Hebrew Bible* and the Jewish tradition of its Hebrew exegesis, from early Midrash to medieval Kabbalah.[6]

This was prior to the *Black Notebooks*, on the background of an almost total silence of Heidegger on the Jewish. The explicit anti-Judaism found in the published *Black Notebooks* could be asserted now as evidence against Zarader's thesis, even though she was well aware that the Jewishness she identified in Heidegger's thought was and would be never acknowledged but only *denied* by Heidegger himself. This denial, a self-denial, was in fact a central element in Zarader's analysis. Nonetheless, the actual debate that has unfolded regarding Heidegger's anti-Semitism did not so much refute Zarader's claim of Heideggerian Jewishness as exposed the ambivalence of its epistemo-political meaning, which Zarader carefully avoided discussing. As I showed in Chapter 1, already in the context of the debate on Heidegger's National Socialism, and now also in the context of the debate on Heidegger's anti-Semitism, various scholars have indicated that both Heidegger's National Socialism and anti-Semitism arise from a political metaphysics or theology, which is very Old Testamentary and thus Hebraic-Jewish. In 2000, John Caputo pointed at the "Jewish *Urquell*" of the "murderous twin myth of the people of God and of the people of being," both myths of "the originary language, the originary people, the original land," arising from "the narratives of the Jews and their God in the Tanach."[7] And in 2015, reflecting on the anti-Semitic passages in the *Black Notebooks*, Françoise Dastur was reminded of the "Old Testament," where, inherent to "Jewish self-conscience," appeared notions of "blood" and "soil," rooted in "the principle of separation, founded on the biblical doctrine of election."[8]

According to this kind of reading, which I analyze in this book as arising from anti-anti-Semitic discourse, not only are there Jewish elements in Heidegger's thought, it is precisely in this unavowed Jewishness that

---

6   Marlène Zarader, *La Dette impensée. Heidegger et l'héritage hébraïque* (Paris: Seuil, 1990), trans. Bettina Bergo as *The Unthought Debt: Heidegger and the Hebraic Heritage* (Stanford, CA: Stanford University Press, 2006).

7   John Caputo, "People of God, People of Being," 90–96.

8   Dastur, "Y a-t-il une 'essence' de l'antisémitisme?," 79, 87 and 88n.30.

Heidegger was still too connected to the problematic intellectual and political heritage of the West, including nationalism and anti-Judaism. If there is a promise of "other thinking" in Heidegger, of non-Greek, non-Western thought, it would have to be just as much non-Jewish. In fact, also in Zarader's reading, "the Hebraic"—as the unavowed source of Heidegger's other, non-Greek thinking—is not brought to light through Heidegger's work as radically other, as lying *beyond* the West, but, on the contrary, as the "unthought" *origin* of the West. Zarader's reproach to Heidegger is of having radically *effaced* the West's Hebraic origin by attributing it to the— pre-philosophical, pre-Socratic—Greek. It is accordingly a deeply Western "Jewish" that Zarader renders visible through Heidegger, a deeply familiar Jewishness, which requires no "specific erudition in the domain of Jewish Studies," since it is a rather evident, obvious Jewishness, which "marked our culture."[9] Zarader followed Ricoeur and is in agreement with Caputo and Dastur when she identified the textual source and paradigm of this Western Jewishness, this "Hebraic heritage," in the Hebrew Bible.

For the purpose of the following analysis, I wish to suggest that this biblical, Hebraic, Western Jewishness is the Christian Jewishness, the Judeo-Christian. It is the "Jewish" as has been seen and constructed by the Christian and post-Christian West, traditionally as the *negative* origin, from which the West emerges by an act of supersession. Accordingly, identifying in "the Jewish" in Heidegger a potential access to talmudic literature as other to Western thought, would require identifying in Heidegger an opposition to "the Jewish" as Judeo-Christian, as biblical; this opposition may not, however, itself be Christian and biblical (New Testament instead of Old). I suggest that such a position may be found in Heidegger's opposition to National Socialism. My claim is therefore that it was not so much from Heidegger's pro-Nazi as from his anti-Nazi position that his anti-Semitism arose.

Heidegger's Anti-Nazi Anti-Judaism

Heidegger claimed to have developed his opposition to National Socialism, during the Nazi era, after his *Rektorat* period, in his work on Nietzsche and Hölderlin. My demonstration will focus on the Hölderlin lectures, which

---

9   Zarader, *La Dette*, 31.

concentrate less on polemics with Western tradition of metaphysics and more on a positive attempt to indicate its otherness, a non-metaphysical thought, which would be *eo ipso* an other to National Socialism. Heidegger's lectures on Hölderlin mark and analyze the otherness of thought paradigmatically as otherness of language. The radical other of philosophical thought is thought as *Dichtung*. This site of poeto-political opposition to National Socialism is also a site, so I claim, of Heidegger's critique against the Jewish-Christian, against the Jewish as Old Testament.

The basic figure around which Heidegger's discourse is built, the figure that bears the name Hölderlin, is the *Dichter*, the poet. The *Dichter* is the founder, who lays the ground for human existence, for being and dwelling in the world. The *dichterische* foundation of human dwelling is "*wortfahte Stiftung*,"[10] an act of words, a linguistic operation—*the* foundational operation of language. The *Dichter* is therefore not exactly a poet, not engaged in *poiesis*, in "making" or "producing." Heidegger more precisely explains the verb *dichten* as akin to the Latin verb *dicere*, "to say," and Greek *deiknumi*, "to show": *Dichtung*, foundational language, is "Sagen in der Art des *weisenden Offenbarmachung*."[11] I translate:[12] "saying in the manner of indicative revelation," namely making something manifest by pointing at it. The basic operation of *Dichten* is indicating, which is paradigmatically done in language through naming.

This "wordly foundation" of the world by the *Dichter* may be deemed as profoundly theo-logical—and biblical. The speech act of *dichten*, as Heidegger reads in Hölderlin, is inherently related to the "gods." It responds to the gods, it names the gods. In *Dichtung*, Heidegger says, "gods come into word and world appears" (GA 4: 40), *Dichterich wohnen*, "to dwell poetically," means "standing in the presence of the gods" (GA 4: 42). *Dichtung*, and so *Stiftung*, "foundation," arises from the union, the wed-

---

10   Martin Heidegger, *Erläuterungen zu Hölderlins Dichtung*, ed. Friedrich-Wilhelm von Herrmann (Frankfurt am Main: Vittorio Klostermann: 1981, 1996 [1944]) (GA 4), 41; trans. Keith Hoeller as *Elucidations of Hölderlin's Poetry* (Amherst, MA: Humanity Books, 2000).
11   Martin Heidegger, *Hölderlins Hymnen "Germanien" und "Der Rhein,"* ed. Susanne Ziegler (Frankfurt am Main: Vittorio Klostermann: 1980) (GA 39), 30; trans. William McNeill and Julia Ireland as *Hölderlin's Hymn "Germanien" and "Der Rhein"* (Bloomington: Indiana University Press, 2014).
12   All the translations in this chapter are mine unless otherwise indicated.

ding of gods with men. Hölderlin's poems that Heidegger focuses on are his *Hymnen*, namely, he explains, "praise of the gods,"[13] Psalms. It should be noted, as a first sign of distance from Jewish-Christian theology, that Heidegger, with Hölderlin, speaks of *gods*, not of God. The plural does not signify rejection of monotheism in favor of polytheism but rather signifies a *distance* from theological certainty.

The second main feature to highlight in Heidegger's conception of the *dichterische* theological foundation is its political nature. "Gods," he says in 1935, "are always gods of the people (*Volk*)" (GA 39: 170). This explosive word, *Volk*, must be handled with care. Heidegger's *Volk* does not arise from race but from history. *Volk* is collective human existence not as abstract "human race" but under historical conditions, in the course of *Geschichte*, namely a collective that is specific, temporal, and diverse: generated and corresponding to a shared lot, a *Geschick*. *Volk* is a "*geschichtliche Menschentum*," a "historical mankind" (GA 4: 106). This means that, as Heidegger says, "*Dichtung* is the *Ursprache*, the original language of a people" (GA 39: 74). The *Dichter*'s gods are the people's gods, and so are his words. Accordingly, the *dichterische*, poetic dwelling is the dwelling of a people, it is a *polis*.

One may therefore say that what Heidegger offered his students during the Nazi time in his Hölderlin lectures is a political theology, which is not dogmatic but *poetic*, less new and more old testamentary, more prophetic and "Hebraic," a Jewish kind of Bible. I remind of Caputo's claim, whereby Heidegger's support of Nazism was a turn to Jewish myth. Nevertheless, what Heidegger claimed to have formulated in these lectures is rather his opposition to National Socialism, and he explicitly addressed this opposition against Jewish-Christian prophetic political theology. At least structurally, Heidegger's Hölderlin thus purports to offer an *internal* break within scriptural theo-logo-politics.

Let us begin with Heidegger's basic understanding of politics: of the *polis*, and of what it means to found and inhabit it. In Heidegger's lectures on Hölderlin's poem "The Ister" of 1942, he elucidates politics in contrast to

---

13   Martin Heidegger, *Hölderlins Hymne "Der Ister,"* ed. Walter Biemel (Frankfurt am Main: Vittorio Klostermann, 1984) (GA 53), 1; trans. William McNeill and Julia Davis as *Hölderlin's Hymn "The Ister"* (Bloomington: Indiana University Press, 1996).

National Socialism. The essence of *polis*, he says, is not the modern State, as unquestionable, *fraglos*, as the absolute and totalitarian apparatus of domination technology. Rather, *polis* is the *site*, *Stätte*, of "human historical dwelling in the midst of beings" (GA 53: 101), *Polis* is the site of the *Volk*: homeland, *Heimat*, which is, I recall, dwelling in the nearness of the gods. Politics thus means acquiring *Heimat*, "*Heimischwerden*, coming to be at home in the midst of beings" (GA 53:101).

However, a basic thrust of Heidegger's Hölderlin readings is that *Heimischwerden* in the midst of beings, of *Seiende*, requires a more fundamental *distance* from beings, what he calls relation to or understanding of or truth of Being, *Sein*, which accordingly features the human as profoundly *unheimlich*—uncanny—and *unheimisch*—"homelandless." As a site of *becoming heimisch*, the *polis* is more fundamentally the site of the *Unheimische*: not "State," but the site of homelessness and questionability, *das Fragwürdige*. *Dichterisch* foundation of home therefore implies not clinging to national identity but, in contrast, *Unheimischwerden*, turning away from homeland and *Ausfahrt in die Fremde*, going in exile. The *Dichter* are not farmers but seamen.

This is the most explicit statement of political opposition that Heidegger's lectures on Hölderlin offer. In this explicitness, they no doubt challenge common understandings of nationalistic patriotism, and under Nazi regime, during wartime, they could very well have been intended, felt, and heard as political critique. At the same time, however, and certainly with the great advantage of retrospect, there are many difficulties in reading this as anti-Nazi resistance. The *Fremde* (foreignness) Heidegger speaks of is very specific and very German, namely the German *Greek*, i.e., "the Greek" as a constitutive figure in the constitutive texts of "the German," not the least in Hölderlin. It is in a German, not in a Greek *Dichter* that Heidegger looks for the Foreign. Accordingly, his *Ausfahrt*, "emigration," cannot but sound very allegoric, almost pure symbol for return, which in its turn is almost pure symbol for staying, *bleiben*, which Heidegger in fact did. Heidegger could be thus said to use the language of foreignness only allegorically or metaphorically, not literally enough.

Yet there is here a more fundamental difficulty in the status and state of foreignness *in language*. Heidegger himself is aware of this difficulty when he distinguishes between poetic and prophetic language, between *Dichtung* and the (Christian-)Jewish Bible. At a certain point in his essay on Hölderlin's *Andenken* (Remembrance) of 1943, commenting on the *Dichter*'s "golden dreams," Heidegger describes the *dichterische* act of foundation as giving words to something unreal—a "dream"—that is however not *less* existent than the real, but more existent, because foundational to reality, something like a *vision*. The poets are the visionary, they say not what is real, but what is in coming. This means that "their word is the *foretelling* [*voraussagende*] word in the strict sense of *propheteuein*. *Dichter* are 'prophetic'" (GA 4: 114). This literal kinship, however, serves Heidegger to mark a decisive difference. If *Dichter* are "prophetic," he immediately explains, it is not in "the Jewish-Christian meaning of this name" (GA 4: 114). What characterizes Jewish-Christian prophets, according to Heidegger, is that "they immediately foretell the God, on whom the confidence of salvation in the celestial beatitude relies" (GA 4: 114). Jewish-Christian prophecy immediately foretells, immediately speaks *of* God—its words have certainty, nearness, *Heimat*. In other words, Heidegger does not criticize here the Bible for its theo-logo-political concern. Zarader is right to point out that Heidegger basically shares this "Hebraic" concern. Nonetheless, precisely because of this affinity, Heidegger more fundamentally criticizes the mode of relation *to* god that constitutes language as biblical prophecy, namely the mode of immediate, direct speech, the word in the immediacy of God; and—perhaps—the word that *is* immediately God.

The *Dichter*'s words, in contrast, are godly, but do not speak of God or the gods. The word of the *Dichter*, Hölderlin's word, as Heidegger keeps saying, is not God, but *das Heilige*, the Holy. The Holy, Heidegger explains, is not God, but "the time-space of the appearance of the gods" (GA 4: 114), the dimension in which something like "gods" may be encountered and so "the dwelling of historical man on this earth" (GA 4: 114) may be founded. The *Dichter* is in this sense more foundational than the prophet. This means that the *Dichter* does not dwell in the nearness and certainty of god, his words are not "powerfully sounding" (GA 4: 138) as the prophet's. His site is not the *Heimat*, but *Wanderschaft*, a wandering *Dichter*, close to the *Fremde*: not in the sense of a different place than his birth place or home, but in the sense of the place of no-place, of words that speak the absence of what they signify. Consequently, the *Dichter*'s discourse, *Dichtung*, even as it ultimately means god, i.e., aims at an encounter with the godly, is not exactly a discourse of God, *theo-logos*. As Heidegger notes: "The Holy may not at all be accounted for 'theologically', because all 'Theology' already presupposes the *theos*, the God."¹⁴ *Dichtung* is not theology, but, literally, *hierology*, discourse of holiness.

All this is highly conceptual. Heidegger's thought, however, insists on being *geschichtlich*, historical. In fact, the distinction between prophets and *Dichter*, theology and hierology, is not just conceptual but inherently temporal. Prophecy and *Dichtung* are discourses of different times. One might say that the *Dichter* precedes and prepares the Prophet, by opening the space in which the coming gods may appear. However, what Heidegger insists on is that the *Dichter* belongs to the time of the absence of gods, which not only precedes presence but also follows presence. Heidegger's focus is on the *Dichter* that comes *after* the gods, namely after the gods' disappearance or departure, what Heidegger calls the "flight" of the gods, *die Flucht der Götter*. "What does Hölderlin's *Dichtung* say? Its word is: the Holy. This word speaks of the flight of the gods" (GA 4: 195).

Heidegger's Hölderlin, and so Heidegger himself, the *Denker* of the *Dichter*, belong to a historical time that Heidegger describes as a "spacetime of the god-lessness," of "*Gott ist tot*," of holiness that is a "Holy *Night*" (GA 4: 109). In Hölderlin's words, Heidegger calls this time a *dürftige Zeit*, a "desolate time." Hölderlin is a *Dichter* in a *dürftige Zeit*. It is a time of double absence, double "no": the "no-longer" of the gods who have flown, and the "not-yet" of the gods to come. Furthermore, Hölderlin's time, our time, is so desolate, so *dürftig*, that the very absence of the gods is unnoticed, is an absent absence. The gods' absence becomes invisible inasmuch as the very dimension of godly appearance, *the Holy*, disappears: "*Das Heile entzieht sich. Die Welt wird heil-los*," "What is whole [*das Heile*] withdraws. The world is being emptied of what is whole and heals [heil-los]. As a result, not only does the holy [*das Heilige*] remain hidden as the track to the godhead, but even what is whole, the track to the holy, appears to be extinguished."¹⁵

---

14   Martin Heidegger, *Hölderlins Hymne "Andenken,"* ed. Walter Biemel (Frankfurt am Main: Vittorio Klostermann, 1982) (GA 52), 132–133; trans. William McNeill and Julia Ireland as *Hölderlin's Hymn "Andenken"* (Bloomington: Indiana University Press, 2018).

15   Martin Heidegger, *Holzwege*, ed. Friedrich-Wilhelm von Herrmann (Frankfurt am Main: Vittorio Klostermann, 1977, 2003 [1950]) (GA 5), 295; trans. Julian Young and Kenneth Haynes, *Off the Beaten Track* (New York: Cambridge University Press, 2002).

What Heidegger means with this is not secularization, insofar as this term means the disappearance of God, namely the Jewish-Christian one. On the contrary: against Christian readings of Hölderlin, Heidegger asserts that it is upon the death of Christ, i.e., with the beginning of Christianity, that "the end of the day of the gods began. Evening falls [*Es wird Abend*]" (GA 5: 269). Christianity is the absence of gods. Christian nearness to God, knowledge and discourse of God, *Theology*, Heidegger says, "already presupposes the *theos*, the god, and with such certainty, that whenever theology arises, the god already began the *flight*" (GA 52: 132–133). Theology is gods' absence that appears as the presence of God, the God of what Heidegger also calls "onto-theology."[16] The era of (onto-)theology, the Christian era, would be the time of the absent absence, the *dürftige Zeit*. The Christian era is, however, also the Jewish-Christian era, and Christian theology presupposes and regenerates the prophets of the Jewish Bible. A *Black Notebooks* entry of the mid-1940s names, beyond Christian theology, Jewish prophecy as discourse of the desolate time. "Prophecy," Heidegger writes there, in one of his strongest anti-Jewish notes, is "forward-looking history," arising from technology, thus being "an instrument of the will to power" and—we may add—the modern, total, also National Socialist State (GA 97: 159).

It is in this way that Heidegger's critique of National Socialism can be read as based on a critique of biblical Judaism, insofar as it has operated, through Christianity, as an origin of the West.[17] On this reading, the Jewish Bible is understood as an alleged nearness of the word to God, to *Heimat*, which conceals actual godlessness and *Heimatlosigkeit*, homelessness. It is

---

16   On "ontotheology," see Iain Thomson, "Technology, Ontotheology," in *Heidegger on Technology*, ed. Aaron James Wendland et al. (New York: Taylor & Francis, 2018), 174–193; see also Laurence Paul Hemming, "Heidegger's God," in *Heidegger Reexamined. Vol. 3: Art, Poetry, Technology*, ed. Hubert Dreyfus and Mark Wrathall (New York: Routledge, 2002), 249–294; for a broader recent discussion, see the various contributions in, *Heidegger's Black Notebooks and the Future of Theology*, ed. Mårten Björk and Jayne Svenungsson (Switzerland: Palgrave Macmillan, 2017).

17   For an analysis of Heidegger's conception of Judaism as a component of Western Christianity in the context of his critique of technology, see Elad Lapidot, "Is Technology Jewish? A Conversation with Heidegger," *Journal of Jewish Thought & Philosophy* 28 (2020): 90–125.

crucial to insist once again that this is a critique not of what the Bible says, but of the constitutive biblical mode of saying: the immediacy of the biblical word of god, paradigmatically in the very word God. For this reason, against the Jewish Bible, Heidegger does not propose the Christian Bible, which is all the more biblical, but the words of Hölderlin, *Dichter in dürftiger Zeit*, the poet in desolate times, which reveal neither God nor gods, but their absence, and this by revealing, or unconcealing, the time-space of the godless Holy Night. This would be the hiero-political act performed by Hölderlin's *Dichtung*, foundational accordingly of a specific historical dwelling, an alternative site and *polis*, a land of the night, *Abend-land*, which will not be a State, but a *Heimat* of *Unheimischkeit*, whose citizens would have to be themselves the dweller of the *Unheimische*: poets and thinkers, *Dichter und Denker*.

Jews Interrupted

I now wish to indicate how Heidegger's critique of the Jewish-Christian logos, as logos of presence, even as it posits the Jewish-Christian as origin of National Socialism (in a similar way to anti-anti-Semitism), nonetheless opens a horizon for the emergence, within contemporary thought, of a different notion of the Jewish, a non-Judeo-Christian Jewishness, which in its turn, so I claim, opens access to the nonbiblical Jewish, perhaps even non-Jewish Jewish, namely to the Talmud. I will indicate this horizon within the reception of Heidegger in postwar French thought, focusing on Phillipe Lacoue-Labarthe's critical reflections on the relations between politics and literature.[18]

Lacoue-Labarthe, characteristically to postwar French reception of Heidegger, subscribes to Heidegger's basic observation and pronouncement of the end, limit, or closure (*clôture*) of philosophy, meaning the hegemonic tradition of Western thought, and adopts the ensuing intentionality toward non-philosophical otherness. A central element of Lacoue-Labarthe's

---

18   Philippe Lacoue-Labarthe, *La Fiction du politique. Heidegger, l'art et la politique* (Paris: Christian Bourgois Editeur, 1998 [1987]), trans. Chris Turner as *Heidegger, Art and Politics: The Fiction of the Political* (Oxford: Blackwell, 1990); Philippe Lacoue-Labarthe, *Heidegger. La politique du poème* (Paris: Galilée, 2002), trans. Jeff Fort as *Heidegger and the Politics of Poetry* (Urbana: University of Illinois Press, 2007).

argument is the insistence that the pronouncement of philosophy's end still takes place *within* philosophy. This means that the operation of this discourse can be only negative or reflective, i.e., its sole object can be philosophy, but it cannot have an image, idea, notion, or figure of philosophy's otherness, i.e., it cannot "see" the nonphilosophical thought that lies beyond or after philosophy. "Seen from here, namely from philosophy itself, this beyond, always suspected, remains undetectable (*indécelable*)."[19]

The concept of the figure stands at the center of Lacoue-Labarthe's general characterization of Western thought, which is at the same time epistemological, poetological, and political. In a nutshell, Lacoue-Labarthe argued that Western thought and praxis, from Plato to National Socialism, consisted in what he called "onto-typology," i.e., a mode of conceptualization and construction of existence, of "being," which is oriented by the notion of the "type"—the model, paradigm, ideal, idea, or figure. The idea generated by Western philosophy has been operating as the ideal for Western politics, which consists in the mimetic self-modeling of the collective subject in light of its ideal: politics as self-fabrication and self-fabulation—as fiction.[20] "The City (*la Cité*) arises from plastics, formation and information, fiction in the strict sense."[21] Western politics is a self-producing artwork. The paradigm for Western philosophy and politics, the paradigm of the paradigm, has therefore been the paradigm that has no paradigm, a figure without a model, i.e., entirely original, independent and immanent, entirely self-sustaining—absolute. The literary form of this paradigmatic figure of the West, Lacoue-Labarthe argues, has been the myth, whose most powerful modern deployment was the "Nazi myth."[22]

The affinity between Lacoue-Labarthe's critique of Western self-presence in myth and Heidegger's critique of Western God's presence in biblical prophecy is visible, but neither obvious nor clearly articulated by Lacoue-Labarthe. He rather highlights in Heidegger's work on

---

19   Lacoue-Labarthe, *La Fiction*, 16.
20   Cf. Jean-Luc Nancy's critique of the conception of the community as *œuvre*, "work," in *La communauté désoeuvrée*, to which Lacoue-Labarthe explicitly refers and subscribes in *La Fiction*, 111.
21   Lacoue-Labarthe, *La Fiction*, 102.
22   Lacoue-Labarthe, 134–139; cf. Phillipe Lacoue-Labarthe and Jean-Luc Nancy, *Le mythe nazi* (La Tour d'Aigues: Editions de l'Aube, 1991); Jean-Luc Nancy, "Le mythe interrompu," in *La communauté*, 110–174.

Hölderlin Heidegger's falling back into Western philosophy. This fall, or *fault*, would consist, first, in Heidegger's very attempt to present a *figure* for non-philosophical thought, i.e., Hölderlin's poetry. Second, on Lacoue-Labarthe's reading, the notion of *Dichtung* that Heidegger develops from Hölderlin's text conceives of poetry essentially as myth, as *Sage*, which consolidates the self-presence of the historical people in its historical language. Heidegger opposed factual National Socialism, so Lacoue-Labarthe's famous claim, for the sake of the truth underlying National Socialism (and dissimilated by it), which is the accomplished form of Western politics of fiction as modern "national aestheticism."[23]

In the terms of my above analysis, Lacoue-Labarthe's critique could be said to expose Heidegger's Hölderlin, notwithstanding Heidegger's own critique of the prophetic logos of presence, as still too prophetic, too biblical, too Judeo-Christian. The *Dichter* word is still revelation, still foundation and dwelling. *Dichtung*, "indicative revelation," is still *Sage*, and the *Dichter*, if godless, is nonetheless holy, a *Halbgott*, "demigod" (GA 4: 103, 147)—divine Author. To be sure, Lacoue-Labarthe's initial analysis traces back national aestheticism rather to Plato, not to the Bible. Yet in later texts he characterizes the problem in Heidegger's poeto-politics as "religiosity" and "piety,"[24] and problematizes Heideggerian and National Socialist national aestheticism as theo-politics of "deploring 'existential' loss, calling to recommencement, hearing the 'evangelical' poem," and so of "messianic" hope for the "restoration (which is only profane with respect to Christianism) of political religion."[25] It is a small step to Caputo's critique of Heidegger's nationalism as Old Testamentary, Jewish myth.

Nonetheless, it is in the horizon that Lacoue-Labarthe, following Heidegger's quest of the other thought, attempted to indicate beyond or in contrast to Platonic-biblical mythology, in which another, anti-mythical, and in this sense anti-biblical Jewish figure emerges. In fact, in resistance to Western and specifically Heideggerian *figuration*, Lacoue-Labarthe explicitly avoided presenting or representing Western philosophy's otherness in any narrative, history, or figure. His indication of otherness consisted rather in conceptualizing the negative need to "interrupt": in-

---

23   Lacoue-Labarthe, *La Fiction*, 83.
24   Lacoue-Labarthe, *Heidegger*, 40–41.
25   Lacoue-Labarthe, 174.

terruption of philosophy, of myth, of the absolute subject, interruption of theo-politics, of the people, of history, of language. Interestingly, very similarly to Heidegger, it was, however, less through abstract conceptualization than through the identification and analysis of a *positive* trace that Lacoue-Labarthe articulated the antimythical interruption of the West. Like Heidegger, he found this trace primarily in the *Denker's Dichter*, i.e., in Hölderlin, this time read by Walter Benjamin. It is in Benjamin's Hölderlin that Lacoue-Labarthe identified a modern conception of poetry not as myth and figuration, but on the contrary as *dis-figuration*, literalization, and "rupture of the name."[26] This rupture would be "holy sobriety," such that modern poetry would manifest itself paradigmatically in prose and even more radically in literary theory and critique. The dis-figurative rupture of the name is at the same time interruption of poeto-politics: "The life of a pure work of art can never be the life of a people, or the life of an individual, or anything else than this pure element that we find in the *dictamen*."[27]

But there is another positive trace, another figure, that Lacoue-Labarthe's earlier text had rendered visible, and which vanished in his later essays. Lacoue-Labarthe initially identified the rupture of Western myth not only in the "pure element" of poetics, be it Heidegger's philosophy, Hölderlin's *Dichtung* or Benjamin's theory, but also in "life," in an event of post-modern revelation, around which the entire debate and *topos* of Heidegger may be deemed to revolve, and which Lacoue-Labarthe named "the apocalypse of Auschwitz": "In the apocalypse of Auschwitz, it is not more and not less than the West, in its essence, that revealed itself—and that, since, does not cease from revealing itself."[28] Auschwitz is the caesura, the break and interruption of history and of History, of Western figuration and myth: it interrupts all representation and thereby makes the regime or history of representation and aesthetics, i.e., the West itself, visible. But at the same time, by the same event, the apocalypse of Auschwitz, by its very exterminatory blaze, renders visible also the *other* of the West, namely as that which the West, by the inherent force of its mytho-political presence, as it culminated in Nazism, negated: the Jews. "God in fact died in Auschwitz—the God of the Greco-Christian [in the English translation:

---

26   Lacoue-Labarthe, 110.
27   Lacoue-Labarthe, 104.
28   Lacoue-Labarthe, *La Fiction*, 59.

Judaeo-Christian] West at least. And it is by no sort of chance that those who were sought to be exterminated were the witnesses, in this same West, of another origin of God who was venerated and thought of there—if it's not, maybe, another God, who remained free of the Hellenistic and Roman rendition."[29]

Beyond the Jewish-Christian, another Jewish figure appears, or better *signaled*, because it is the paradoxical figure of dis-figuration (see Chapter 4). As Lacoue-Labarthe quotes Blanchot: "The Jews incarnate... the rejection of the myths, the renouncement of idols, the recognition of an ethical order that manifests itself by the respect of the law."[30] Jewish aniconism, a biblical topos, emerges here as renouncement of figuration itself—renouncement or resistance to the figure, the idea, image, and form. This is a rejection of the myth that does not transcend all discourse of God, people, and language. On the contrary, it consists in their inner dis-figuration: the imageless god has a formless people, "an unformed, unaesthetic 'people,'"[31] whose text generates no work, no *oeuvre*, or rather the *désoeuvre*, the no-work, the no-Bible.

Talmud Unthought

This non-Judeo-Christian Jewish, signaled by French reworking of Heidegger's indication toward non-philosophical, *other* mode of thinking, marks a contemporary access, so my claim, to Talmud. In these concluding words, I can provide only a few concise indications of how this signal was and may be concretely understood, and to what extent it may give access to Talmud. In the context of my own analysis, the crucial question to ask is how Lacoue-Labarthe's Jewish figure of *dis-figuration* may *not* lead to the dissolution of all Jewish thought (as I demonstrated in the last anti-anti-Semitic position, such as recently deployed by Nancy—see Chapter 4); how, instead, the disfiguration of the Judeo-Christian Jewish may lead to a *refiguration* of Jewish thought.
As already noted, Lacoue-Labarthe himself, in his later texts, follows the signal of otherness away from Jewish intellectual tradition, toward the es-

---

29   Lacoue-Labarthe, 62.
30   Lacoue-Labarthe, 138.
31   Lacoue-Labarthe, 139.

sence of "modern literature" as *prose*. Closer to Jewish textual tradition, the same modern category of literature may guide and has guided, within literary theory, a revision or rereading of the Old Testament, which could be characterized as anti-mythical, prosaic, and dis-figurative, i.e., suspending and interrupting the text's immediate power of indication, of re-presentation—and incarnation. Already Erich Auerbach noted how, in contrast to the Homeric gods, God in the Bible "is not comprehensible in his presence, as is Zeus; it is always only 'something' of him that appears, he always extends into depths."[32] A reading of the Hebrew Bible in the mode of nonpresence was recently proposed by Michael Fagenblat, critiquing Heidegger's German through Scholem's Jewish Hölderlin.[33]

Taking a step further away from from the biblical presence, contemporary thought indicated the non-Judeo-Christian Jewish in the figure of post-biblical *rabbinic* literature. In 1982, Sarah Handelman identified the emergence of elements from "rabbinic hermeneutics" in contemporary literary theory, such as Freud, Lacan, Derrida, and Harold Bloom, noting among others a "debt to the thought of Heidegger."[34] Handelman characterized rabbinic hermeneutics with the term "Slayers of Moses," namely through an anti-prophetic, anti-Bible disposition, while nonetheless, similarly to Zarader, maintained the Bible as the central point of reference, such that the paradigmatic rabbinic text and genre was presented as *midrash*, i.e., classic rabbinic biblical exegesis, as well as later, medieval rabbinic exegesis in *kabbalah* literature.[35]

---

32   Erich Auerbrach, *Mimesis. Dargestellte Wirklichkeit in der abendländischen Literatur* (Bern: Francke, 1994 [1946]), trans. Willard Trask as *Mimesis: The Representation of Reality in Western Literature* (Princeton, NJ: Princeton University Press, 2003 [1953]).

33   Michael Fagenblat, "On Dwelling Prophetically: On Heidegger and Jewish Political Theology," in *Heidegger and Jewish Thought*, 245–268.

34   Sarah Handelman, *The Slayers of Moses: The Emergence of Rabbinic Interpretation in Modern Literary Theory* (Albany: State University of New York Press, 1982), 16.

35   For a different, critical approach to Kabbalah, see the extensive work of Elliot Wolfson, for instance in *Language, Eros, and Being: Kabbalistic Hermeneutics and the Poetic Imagination* (New York: Fordham University Press, 2005); *Alef, Mem, Tau: Kabbalistic Musings on Time, Truth, and Death* (Berkeley: University of California Press, 2006); *Giving Beyond the Gift: Apophasis and Overcoming Theomania* (New York: Fordham University Press, 2014); *The Duplicity of*

It would be an illuminating exercise to show how the biblical paradigm has been configuring and regulating the various discourses through which "the Jewish" and even the non-Christian Jewish, i.e., the rabbinic, appeared for modern and contemporary knowledge, science, and thought. The "biblical paradigm" does not only or not exactly refer to the specific textual corpus of the Old Testament; rather, it refers to this corpus inasmuch as it has been constructed, represented, and developed as the prototype for the *biblios*, the Book, and so as the paradigmatic logos of theo-poeto-political presence. The most critical place to observe and examine the workings of this biblical paradigm in the contemporary epistemological construction of "the Jewish" is the academic study of Talmud. The talmudic text is not based on the biblical text, is not biblical exegesis. The references that are made to the biblical text in the Talmud, in the form of occasional quotes, sometimes of just one word, do not portray a book, but something like an archive of discrete acts of signification, of textual and verbal fragments. In fact, the Talmud is to a constitutive extent generated by a non- or anti-biblical paradigm, which—to use the terminology of Lacoue-Labarthe and Nancy—"interrupts" the basic signifying function of the text, of the name, of the *Sage*, of "indicative revelation."

One guiding question for any future reflection on the Talmud's potential to open within Western thought an access to non-Western epistemic otherness is therefore to what extent the *biblios* is still at work in any attempt to access Talmud through the sole category of *literature*.[36] In the horizon of political epistemology, I suggest, any attempt to think Talmud beyond Greco-Judeo-Christian thought, would have to contemplate just as fundamentally the performative mode of language that we call *law*.

Philosophy's Shadow: Heidegger, Nazism, and the Jewish Other (New York: Columbia University Press, 2018); *Heidegger and Kabbalah: Hidden Gnosis and the Path of Poiēsis* (Bloomington: Indiana University Press, 2020). Wolfson's work focuses not on the biblical but on the uniquely kabbalistic, *Lurianic* myth, which Wolfson deconstructs to poetics. For a discussion, see Elad Lapidot, "Ethnocentrism in Esoteric Circles: On Political Gnoseology," *Comparative and Continental Philosophy* (2020).

36   This includes such current projects as Daniel Boyarin's and Sergey Dolgopolski's, mentioned above, which have gone the furthest in critically exploring the potential significance of the Talmud for contemporary thought.

Bibliography

Adorno, Theodor. *Minima Moralia. Reflexionen aus dem beschädigten Leben*. Frankfurt am Main: Suhrkamp Taschenbuch Wissenschaft, 2003 [1951].
Adorno, Theodor, Else Frenkel-Brunswik, Daniel J. Levinson, and R. Nevitt Sanford. *The Authoritarian Personality*. New York: Harper and Row, 1950.
Anderson, Benedict. *Imagined Communities*. New York: Verso, 2006 [1983].
Anidjar, Gil. "Antisemitism and Its Critics." In *Antisemitism and Islamophobia in Europe: A Shared Story?*, edited by James Renton and Ben Gidley, 187–214. London: Palgrave Macmillan, 2017.
Anidjar, Gil. *Blood. A Critique of Christianity*. New York: Columbia University Press, 2014.
Anidjar, Gil. *The Jew, The Arab: A History of the Enemy*. Stanford, CA: Stanford University Press, 2003.
Anidjar, Gil. *Semites. Race, Religion, Literature*. Stanford, CA: Stanford University Press, 2008.
Anidjar, Gil. "When Killers Become Victims: Anti-Semitism and Its Critics." *Cosmopolis: A Review of Cosmopolitics* 3 (2007). http://agora.qc.ca/cosmopolis.
Arendt, Hannah. *Elemente und Ursprünge totaler Herrschaft. Antisemitismus, Imperialismus, totale Herrschaft*. Munich: Piper, 2008 [1986].
Arendt, Hannah. "Anti-Semitism." In *The Jewish Writings*, edited by Jerome Kohn and Ron Feldman, 46–124. New York: Schocken Books, 2007.
Arendt, Hannah. *Between Past and Future: Six Exercises in Political Thought*. New York: Viking Press, 1961.
Arendt, Hannah. *The Burden of Our Times*. London: Secker and Warburg, 1951.
Arendt, Hannah. *Denktagebuch. 1950 bis 1973*. Band 1, edited by Ursula Ludz und Ingeborg Nordmann. Munich: Piper, 2002.
Arendt, Hannah. *Eichmann in Jerusalem: A Report on the Banality of Evil*. New York: Penguin Books, 2006 [1963].

Arendt, Hannah. *The Human Condition*. Chicago: University of Chicago Press, 1958.
Arendt, Hannah. *The Life of the Mind*, vol. 1. *Thinking*. New York: Harcourt Brace Jovanovich, 1978.
Arendt, Hannah. *Men in Dark Times*. New York: Harcourt, Brace, 1968.
Arendt, Hannah. *The Origins of Totalitarianism*. New York: Harcourt Brace and Co., 1979.
Arendt, Hannah. "Philosophy and Politics." *Social Research* 71, no. 3 (2004): 427–454.
Arendt, Hannah. "A Reply." *Review of Politics* 15, no. 1 (1953): 68–85.
Arendt, Hannah, and Karl Jaspers. *Briefwechsel 1926–1969*. Munich: Pieper, 1996.
Arendt, Hannah, and Gershom Scholem. *Der Briefwechsel*, edited by Marie Luise Knott. Frankfurt am Main: Juedischer Verlag, 2010.
Aschheim, Steven. "Nazism, Culture and the Origins of Totalitarianism: Hannah Arendt and the Discourse of Evil." *New German Critique* 70 (1997): 117–139.
Auerbach, Erich. *Mimesis. Dargestellte Wirklichkeit in der abendländischen Literatur*. Bern: Francke, 1994 [1946]. Translated by Willard Trask as *Mimesis: The Representation of Reality in Western Literature*. Princeton, NJ: Princeton University Press, 2003.
Avineri, Shlomo. "Marx and Jewish Emancipation." *Journal of the History of Ideas* 25 (1964): 445–450.
Babich, Babette. "Heidegger's Black Night: The Nachlass and Its Wirkungsgeschichte." In *Reading Heidegger's Black Notebooks 1931–1941*, edited by Ingo Farin and Jeff Malpas, 77–78. Cambridge, MA: MIT Press, 2016.
Badiou, Alain. *Circonstances, 3. Portées du mot «juif.»* Paris: Lignes and Manifeste, 2005. Translated by Steven Corcoran. *Polemics*. New York: Verso, 2011.
Badiou, Alain. «Crime et châtiment de Jean-Paul Sartre. Le supplice de B.-H.L.» *Libération*, April 17, 2000.
Badiou, Alain. "Discussion argumentée avec Ivan Segré.» *Lignes* 30 (2009): 201–206.
Badiou, Alain. *L'éthique, essai sur la conscience du mal*. Paris: Hatier, 1993. Translated by Peter Hallward as *Ethics: An Essay on the Understanding of Evil*. New York: Verso, 2012.
Badiou, Alain. *The Incident at Antioch / L'Incident d'Antioche. A Tragedy in Three Acts / Tragédie en trois actes*. Translated by Susan Spitzer. New York: Columbia University Press, 2013.
Badiou, Alain. "Le mot 'Juif' et le sychophante.» *Les temps moderns* 637/638/639, no. 3 (2006): 733–747.
Badiou, Alain. *Saint Paul. La fondation de l'universalisme*. Paris: PUF, 1997. Translated by Ray Brassier as *Saint Paul: The Foundation of Universalism*. Stanford, CA: Stanford University Press, 2003.
Badiou, Alain, and Eric Hazan. *L'antisémitisme partout: Aujourd'hui en France*. Paris: La fabrique, 2011.
Badiou, Alain, Eric Hazan, and Ivan Segré. *Reflections on anti-Semitism*. Translated by David Fernbach. London: Verso, 2013.

Badiou, Alain, and Alain Finkielkraut. *L'explication. Conversation avec Aude Lancelin*. Paris: Lignes, 2010.

Baehr, Peter. "Identifying the Unprecedented: Hannah Arendt, Totalitarianism and the Critique of Sociology." In *Hannah Arendt: Critical Assessments of Leading Political Philosophers*. Vol. I, *Arendt and Political Events*, edited by Garrath Williams, 224–264. New York: Routledge, 2006.

Baron, Salo Wittmayer. *A Social and Religious History of the Jews*, vol. 2. New York: Columbia University Press, 1937.

Barclay, John M.G. "Paul and the Philosophers: Alain Badiou and the Event." *New Blackfriars* 91.1032 (2010): 171–184.

Barnikol, Ernst. *Bruno Bauer: Studien und Materialien*. Assen: Van Gorcum, 1972.

Batnitzky, Leora. *How Judaism Became a Religion: An Introduction to Modern Jewish Thought*. Princeton, NJ: Princeton University Press, 2011.

Baudelaire, Charles. *Petits Poèmes en prose*, Œuvres complètes de Charles Baudelaire. Paris: Michel Lévy frères, 1869.

Bauer, Bruno. *Das entdeckte Christenthum. Eine Erinnerung an das achzehnte Jahrhundert und ein Beitrag zur Krisis des neunzehnten*. Zurich: Verlag des literarischen Comptoirs, 1843.

Bauer, Bruno. "Die Fähigkeit der heutigen Juden und Christen, frei zu werden." In *Einundzwanzig Bogen aus der Schweiz*, edited by Georg Herwegh, 56–71. Zurich: 1843.

Bauer, Bruno. *Die Juden Frage*. Braunschweig, 1843.

Bauer, Bruno. "Das Judentum in der Fremde." In *Staats- und Gesellschafts-Lexicon*, edited by Hermann Wagner. Berlin: Heinicke, 1863 [1859].

Bauer, Bruno. *Philo, Strauß und Renan und das Urchristenthum*. Berlin: Hempel, 1874.

Bauman, Zygmunt. "Allosemitism: Premodern, Modern, Postmodern." In *Modernity, Culture, and 'the Jew,'* edited by Bryan Cheyette and Laura Marcus, 143–156. Stanford, CA: Stanford University Press, 1998.

Bein, Alex. *The Jewish Question: Biography of a World Problem*. Translated by Harry Zohn. Toronto: Associated University Presses, 1990.

Bell, Daniel Jr. "Badiou's Faith and Paul's Gospel: The Politics of Indifference and the Overcoming of Capital." *Angelaki: Journal of the Theoretical Humanities* 12 (2007): 97–111.

Bell, Linda A. "Different Oppressions: A Feminist Exploration of Sartre's 'Anti-Semite and Jew.'" *Sartre Studies International* 3, no. 2 (1997): 1–20.

Benhabib, Seyla. "Identity, Perspective and Narrative in Hannah Arendt's 'Eichmann in Jerusalem.'" *History and Memory* 8, no. 2 (1996): 35–59.

Benhabib, Seyla. *The Reluctant Modernism of Hannah Arendt*. Lanham, MD: Rowman and Littlefield, 2000.

Bennington, Geoffrey. "Lyotard and 'the Jews.'" In *Modernity, Culture, and 'the Jew,'* edited by Bryan Cheyette and Laura Marcus, 188–196. Stanford, CA: Stanford University Press, 1998.

Benoit, Martine-Sophie. "Theodor Lessing et le concept de 'haine de soi juive.'" In *La haine de soi: Difficiles identités*, 27–46. Brussels: Complexe, 2000.
Benz, Wolfgang. *Was ist Anti-Semitismus?* Munich: C.H. Beck, 2004.
Bergen, Bernard. *The Banality of Evil: Hannah Arendt and "The Final Solution."* Lanham, MD: Rowman and Littlefield, 1998.
Berkowitz, Roger, Jeffrey Katz, and Thomas Keenan, eds. *Thinking in Dark Times: Hannah Arendt on Ethics and Politics.* New York: Fordham University Press, 2010.
Bernasconi, Robert. "Kant as un Unfamiliar Source of Racism." In *Philosophers on Race. Critical Essays,* edited by Julie K. Ward and Tommy I. Lott, 145–166. Oxford: Blackwell, 2002.
Bernasconi, Robert. "Who Invented the Concept of Race? Kant's Role in the Enlightenment Construction of Race." In *Race,* edited by Robert Bernasconi, 11–36. Oxford: Blackwell, 2001.
Bernstein, Richard. *Hannah Arendt and the Jewish Question.* Cambridge, MA: MIT Press, 1996.
Bielik-Robson, Agata. *Jewish Cryptologies of Late Modernity: Philosophical Marranos.* New York: Routledge, 2014.
Björk, Mårten, and Jayne Svenungsson, eds. *Heidegger's Black Notebooks and the Future of Theology.* New York: Palgrave Macmillan, 2017.
Bloom, Solomon. "Karl Marx and the Jews." *Jewish Social Studies* 4 (1942): 3–16.
Bowie, Andrew. "Philosophy, Science and Politics in the Black Notebooks." In *Reading Heidegger's Black Notebooks 1931–1941,* edited by Ingo Farin and Jeff Malpas, 253–268. Cambridge, MA: MIT Press, 2016.
Boyarin, Daniel. *Border Lines: The Partition of Judaeo-Christianity.* Philadelphia: University of Pennsylvania Press, 2004.
Boyarin, Daniel. *Judaism: The Genealogy of a Modern Notion.* New Brunswick, NJ: Rutgers University Press, [2018].
Boyarin, Daniel. "Paul among the Antiphilosophers; or, Saul among the Sophists." In *St. Paul among the Philosophers,* edited by John D. Caputo and Linda Martin Alcoff, 109–141. Bloomington: Indiana University Press, 2009.
Boyarin, Daniel. *A Radical Jew. Paul and the Politics of Identity.* Berkeley: University of California Press, 1994.
Boyarin, Daniel. *A Traveling Homeland: The Babylonian Talmud as Diaspora.* Philadelphia: University of Pennsylvania Press, 2015.
Boyarin, Jonathan. "The Missing Keyword: Reading Olender's Renan." *Qui Parle* 7, no. 2 (1994): 43–56.
Boyarin, Jonathan, and Daniel Boyarin. "Diaspora: Generation and the Ground of Jewish Identity." *Critical Inquiry* 19, no. 4 (1993): 693–725.
Boyarin, Jonathan, and Daniel Boyarin. *Powers of Diaspora: Two Essays on the Relevance of Jewish Culture.* Minneapolis: University of Minnesota Press, 2002.
Brentlinger, John. "Revolutionizing Spirituality: Reflections on Marxism and Religion." *Science and Society* 64 (2000): 171–193.
Broner, Stephen Eric. *A Rumor about the Jews. Reflections on Antisemitism and the Protocols of the Learned Elders of Zion.* New York: St. Martin's Press, 2000.

Brumlik, Micha. "Die Alltäglichkeit des Judenhasses—Heideggers Verfallenheit an den Anti-Semitismus." In *Heidegger und der Anti-Semitismus. Positionen im Widerstreit*, edited by Walter Homolka and Arnulf Heidegger, 202–211. Freiburg: Herder, 2016.

Buell, Denise. *Why This New Race: Ethnic Reasoning in Early Christianity*. New York: Columbia University Press, 2005.

Canovan, Margaret. *Hannah Arendt: A Reinterpretation of Her Political Thought*. Cambridge: Cambridge University Press, 1992.

Caputo, John. "People of God, People of Being: The Theological Presuppositions of Heidegger's Path of Thought." In *Appropriating Heidegger*, edited by James E. Falconer and Mark A. Wrathall, 85–100. Cambridge: Cambridge University Press, 2000.

Carlebach, Julius. *Karl Marx and the Radical Critique of Judaism*. Boston: Routledge and Kegan Paul, 1978.

Carter, J. Kameron. *Race: A Theological Account*. Oxford: Oxford University Press, 2008.

Chadbourne, Richard M. *Ernest Renan*. New York: Twayne, 1968.

Chamberlain, Houston Stewart. *Die Grundlage des 19. Jahrhunderts*, I. Hälfte. Munich: Bruckmann, 1903 [1899].

Chauvin, Charles. *Renan*. Paris: Desclée de Brouwer, 2000.

Cheyette, Bryan, and Laura Marcus, eds. *Modernity, Culture, and 'the Jew.'* Stanford, CA: Stanford University Press, 1998.

Cohen, Joseph, and Raphael Zagury-Orly, eds. *Heidegger et "les juifs."* La Règle du Jeu no. 58–59. Paris: Grasset, 2015.

Cohen, Richard I. "Breaking the Code: Hannah Arendt's 'Eichmann in Jerusalem' and the Public Polemic: Myth Memory and Historical Imagination." *Michael: On the History of the Jews in the Diaspora* 13 (1993): 29–85.

Cohen-Halimi, Michèle, and Francis Cohen. *Le cas Trawny. À propos des 'Cahiers Noirs' de Heidegger*. Paris: Sens and Tonka, 2015.

Cohen-Levinas, Danielle, and Jean-Luc Nancy. *Inventions à deux voix. Entretiens*. Paris: Editions du Félin, 2015.

Cohn, Norman. *Warrant for Genocide: The Myth of the Jewish World-Conspiracy and the Protocols of the Elders of Zion*. New York: Harper and Row, 1966.

Confino, Alon. *A World without Jews: The Nazi Imagination from Persecution to Genocide*. New Haven, CT: Yale University Press, 2014.

David, Alain. "Die Abwesenheit von Antisemitismus genügt keineswegs." In *Heidegger, die Juden, noch einmal*, edited by Peter Trawny and Andrew J. Mitchell, 215–232. Frankfurt am Main: Vittorio Klostermann, 2015.

David, Alain. *Racisme et Antisémitisme. Essai de philosophie sur l'envers des concepts*. Paris: Ellipses, 2001.

Dastur, Françoise. «Y a-t-il une 'essence' de l'antisémitisme?» In *Heidegger, die Juden, noch einmal*, edited by Peter Trawny and Andrew J. Mitchell, 75–96. Frankfurt am Main: Vittorio Klostermann, 2015.

Derrida, Jacques. *L'Ecriture et la différence*. Paris: Seuil, 1967.

Derrida, Jacques. *De la Grammatologie*. Paris: Les Editions de Minuit, 1967.
Derrida, Jacques. *Psyché. Inventions de l'autre*. Paris: Galilee, 1987.
Derrida, Jacques. *La voix et le phenomena*. Paris: PUF, 2012 [1967].
Devisch, Ignaas. *Jean-Luc Nancy and the Question of Community*. London: Bloomsbury, 2013.
Di Blasi, Luca. *Dezentrierungen. Beiträge zur Religion der Philosophie im 20. Jahrhundert*. Wien/Berlin: Turia + Kant, 2018.
Di Cesare, Donatella. "Being and the Jew: Between Heidegger and Levinas." In *Heidegger and Jewish Thought: Difficult Others*, edited by Elad Lapidot and Micha Brumlik, 75–86. London: Rowman and Littlefield, 2018.
Di Cesare, Donatella. *Heidegger, die Juden, die Shoah*. Frankfurt am Main: Klostermann, 2015.
Di Cesare, Donatella. "Heidegger's Metaphysical Anti-Semitism." In *Reading Heidegger's Black Notebooks 1931–1941*, edited by Ingo Farin and Jeff Malpas, 181–194. Cambridge: MIT Press, 2016.
Di Cesare, Donatella. "Heideggers metaphysischer Anti-Semitismus." In *Heidegger und der Anti-Semitismus. Positionen im Widerstreit*, edited by Walter Homolka and Arnulft Heidegger, 212–219. Freiburg: Herder, 2016.
Di Cesare, Donatella. "Das Sein und der Jude. Heideggers metaphysischer Anti-Semitismus." In *Heidegger, die Juden, noch einmal*, edited by Peter Trawny and Andrew J. Mitchell, 55–74. Frankfurt am Main: Vittorio Klostermann, 2015.
Diner, Dan. "Hannah Arendt Reconsidered: On the Banal and the Evil in Her Holocaust Narrative." *New German Critique* 71 (1997): 177–190.
Dolgopolski, Sergey. *Other Others: The Political after the Talmud*. New York: Fordham University Press, 2018.
Dolgopolski, Sergey. *What Is Talmud? The Art of Disagreement*. New York: Fordham University Press, 2009.
Dossa, Shiraz. "Lethal Fantasy: Hannah Arendt on Political Zionism." *Arab Studies Quarterly* 8, no. 3 (1986): 219–230.
Drumont, Edouard. *La France Juive. Essai d'Histoire Contemporaine*. Paris: C. Marpon et E. Flammarion, 1886 [1883].
Dühring, Eugen. *Die Judenfrage als Frage der Racenschädlichkeite für Existenz, Sitte und Cultur der Völker. Mit einer weltgeschichtlichen, religionsbezüglich, social und politisch freiheitlichen Antwort*. Berlin: H. Reuther's Verlagsbuchhandlung, 1892 [1880].
Dumézil, Georges. *Leçon inaugurale à la chaire de civilisation indo-europeénne du Collège de France, faite le jeudi 1er décembre 1949*. Paris, 1950.
Dunkhase, Jan Eike. "Beiträge zur neuen Heidegger-Debatte" (book review). *H-Soz-Kult*, March 13, 2017. http://www.hsozkult.de/publicationreview/id/rezbuecher-27447.
Eisenmenger, Johann Andreas. *Entdecktes Judentum*. Königsberg: 1700.
Eisentstadt, Jehuda, ed. *Otzar Yisrael*. London: 1924.
Elbogen, Ismar. *Ein Jahrhundert jüdischen Lebens. Die Geschichte des neuzeitlichen Judentums*, edited by Ellen Littmann. Frankfurt: Europäische Verlagsanstalt, 1967.

Elon, Amos. "The Excommunication of Hannah Arendt." *World Policy Journal* 23, no. 4 (2006/7): 93–102.
Engels, Friedrich, and Karl Marx. *Werke*, Band II. Berlin: Dietz Verlag, 1962.
Eze, Emmanuel Chukwudi. "The Color of Reason: The Idea of 'Race' in Kant's Anthropology." In *Postcolonial African Philosophy: A Critical Reader*, edited by Emmanuel Chukwudi Eze, 103–140. Cambridge, MA: Blackwell, 1997.
Fagenblat, Michael. "Levinas and Heidegger: The Elemental Confrontation." In *The Oxford Handbook of Levinas*, edited by Michael L. Morgan, 103–133. Oxford: Oxford University Press, 2019.
Fagenblat, Michael. "On Dwelling Prophetically: On Heidegger and Jewish Political Theology." In *Heidegger and Jewish Thought: Difficult Others*, edited by Elad Lapidot and Micha Brumlik, 245–268. London: Rowman and Littlefield, 2017.
Fanon, Frantz. *Les damnés de la terre*. Paris: François Maspero, 1961. Translated by Richard Philcox as *The Wretched of the Earth*. New York: Grove Press, 2004.
Fanon, Frantz. *Peau Noire, Masques Blanc*. Paris: Seuil, 1952. Translated by Charles Lam Markmann. *Black Skin, White Masks*. New York: Grove Press, 1967.
Farin, Ingo, and Jeff Malpas, eds. *Reading Heidegger's Black Notebooks 1931–1941*. Cambridge, MA: MIT Press, 2016.
Faye, Emmanuel. *Arendt et Heidegger. Extermination nazie et destruction de la pensée*. Paris: Albin Michel, 2106.
Faye, Emmanuel. *Heidegger, l'introduction du nazisme dans la philosophie*. Paris: Albin Michel, 2005.
Feuerbach, Ludwig. *Das Wesen des Christenthums*. Leipzig: Otto Wigand, 1841. Translated by Marian Evans. *The Essence of Christianity*. London: Kegan Paul, Trench, Trübner and Co., 1893.
Fine, Robert. "Karl Marx and the Radical Critique of Anti-Semitism." *Engage* 2 (2006). https://engageonline.wordpress.com/2015/11/04/karl-marx-and-the-radical-critique-of-anti-semitism-robert-fine-engage-journal-issue-2-may-2006.
Fischman, Dennis K. *Political Discourse in Exile: Karl Marx and the Jewish Question*. Amherst: University of Massachusetts Press, 1991.
Freud, Sigmund. *Der Mann Moses und die monotheistische Religion*. Frankfurt am Main: Fischer, 1999 [1939]. Translated by James Strachey as *Moses and Monotheism*. London: Hogarth, 1939.
Friedländer, Saul. *Nazi Germany and the Jews. Vol. I: The Years of Persecution, 1933–1939*. New York: HarperCollins, 1997.
Fritsch, Theodor. *Anti-Semiten-Katechismus. Eine Zusammenfassung des wichtigsten Materials zum Verständnis der Judenfrage*. Leipzig: Verlag von Herm. Beher, 1893; 25. Aufl.; 1887.
Gabriel, Markus. "Heideggers antisemitische Stereotypen." In *Heidegger und der Anti-Semitismus. Positionen im Widerstreit*, edited by Walter Homolka and Arnulf Heidegger, 220–231. Freiburg: Herder, 2016.
Gander, Hans-Helmuth, and Magnus Striet, eds. *Heideggers Weg in die Moderne. Eine Verortung der «Schwarzen Hefte»*. Frankfurt am Main: Vittorio Klostermann, 2017.

Garber, Zev, and Bruce Zuckerman. "Why Do We Call the Holocaust 'the Holocaust'? An Inquiry into the Psychology of Labels." *Modern Judaism* 9 (1989): 197–211.

Geulen, Christian. "Gewollt willenlos. Heideggers Schwarze Hefte als historisches Dokument." In *Martin Heideggers "Schwarze Hefte". Eine philosophische-politische Debatte*, edited by Marion Heinz and Sidonie Kellerer, 275–287. Berlin: Suhrkamp, 2016.

Gilman, Sander I. "Karl Marx and the Secret Language of Jews." *Modern Judaism* 4 (1984): 275-294.

Gobineau, Arthur de. *Essai sur l'inégalité des races humaines*. Paris: Firmin-Didot, 1884 [1854].

Greenblatt, Stephen Jay. "Marlowe, Marx and anti-Semitism." *Critical Inquiry* 5 (1978): 291–307.

Grondin, Jean. "Warum ich Heidegger in schwieriger Zeit treu bleibe." In *Heidegger und der Anti-Semitismus. Positionen im Widerstreit*, edited by Walter Homolka and Arnulf Heidegger, 232–241. Freiburg: Herder, 2016.

Habermas, Jürgen. *Der philosophische Diskurs der Moderne. Zwölf Vorlesungen*. Frankfurt am Main: Suhrkamp, 1985.

Hallward, Peter. *Badiou: A Subject to Truth*. Minneapolis: University of Minnesota Press, 2003.

Hammerschlag, Sarah. "Bad Jews, Authentic Jews, Figural Jews." In *Judaism, Liberalism, and Political Theology*, edited by Randi Rashkover and Martin Kavka, 221–240. Bloomington: Indiana University Press, 2014.

Hammerschlag, Sarah. *The Figural Jew: Politics and Identity in Postwar French Thought*. Chicago: University of Chicago Press, 2010.

Handelman, Sarah. *The Slayers of Moses. The Emergence of Rabbinic Interpretation in Modern Literary Theory*. Albany: State University of New York Press, 1982.

Harries, Karsten. "Nostalgia, Spite, and the Truth of Being." In *Reading Heidegger's Black Notebooks 1931–1941*, edited by Ingo Farin and Jeff Malpas, 207–222. Cambridge, MA: MIT Press, 2016.

Hartmann, Christian et al., eds. *Hitler, Mein Kampf. Eine kritische Edition*. Munich and Berlin: Institut für Zeitgeschichte, 2016.

Hegel, Georg Wilhelm Friedrich. *Frühe Schriften*, Werke 1. Frankfurt am Main: Suhrkamp, 1986.

Hegel, Georg Wilhelm Friedrich. *Grundlinien der Philosophie des Rechts*. Frankfurt am Main: Suhrkamp, 1986.

Hegel, Georg Wilhelm Friedrich. *Phänomenologie des Geistes*. Frankfurt am Main: Suhrkamp, 1986.

Hegel, Georg Wilhelm Friedrich. *Wissenschaft der Logik. Erster Band. Die objektive Logik* (1812/13), Werke 5. Frankfurt am Main: Suhrkamp Taschenbuch Wissenschaft, 1969.

Heidegger, Gertrud, ed. *Briefe Martin Heidegger an seine Frau Elfriede 1915–1970*. Munich: Deutsche Verlags-Anstalt, 2005.

Heidegger, Martin. *Anmerkungen I–V (Schwarze Hefte 1942–1948)*, edited by Peter Trawny. Frankfurt am Main: Klostermann Verlag, 2015.
Heidegger, Martin. *Bremer und Freiburger Vorträge*, edited by P. Jaeger. Frankfurt am Main: Vittorio Klostermann: 1994; 2. Auflage 2005.
Heidegger, Martin. *Erlaüterungen zu Hölderlins Dichtung*, edited by Friedrich-Wilhelm von Herrmann. Frankfurt am Main: Vittorio Klostermann, 1981, 1996 [1944]. Translated by Keith Hoeller as *Elucidations of Hölderlin's Poetry*. Amherst: Humanity Books, 2000.
Heidegger, Martin. *Hölderlins Hymne "Andenken,"* edited by Walter Biemel. Frankfurt am Main: Vittorio Klostermann, 1982. Translated by William McNeill and Julia Ireland as *Hölderlin's Hymn "Andenken."* Bloomington: Indiana University Press, 2018.
Heidegger, Martin. *Hölderlins Hymne "Der Ister,"* edited by Walter Biemel. Frankfurt am Main: Vittorio Klostermann, 1984. Translated by William McNeill and Julia Davis as *Hölderlin's Hymn "The Ister."* Bloomington: Indiana University Press, 1996.
Heidegger, Martin. *Hölderlins Hymnen "Germanien" und "Der Rhein."* Edited by Susanne Ziegler. Frankfurt am Main: Vittorio Klostermann, 1980. Translated by William McNeill and Julia Ireland as *Hölderlin's Hymn "Germanien" and "Der Rhein."* Bloomington: Indiana University Press, 2014.
Heidegger, Martin. *Holzwege*. Edited by Friedrich-Wilhelm von Herrmann. Frankfurt am Main: Vittorio Klostermann, 1977, 2003 [1950]. Translated by Julian Young and Kenneth Haynes as *Off the Beaten Track*. New York: Cambridge University Press, 2002.
Heidegger, Martin. *Nietzsche I*. Frankfurt am Main: Vittorio Klostermann, 1996 [1961].
Heidegger, Martin. *Sein und Zeit*. Edited by Friedrich-Wilhelm von Herrmann. Frankfurt am Main: Vittorio Klostermann, 1977. Translated by John Macquarrie and Edward Robinson as *Being and Time*. Oxford: Blackwell, 1962. Translated by Joan Stambaugh as *Being and Time*. Albany: State University of New York, 1996.
Heidegger, Martin. *Überlegungen II–VI (Schwarze Hefte 1931–1938)*, edited by Peter Trawny. Frankfurt am Main: Klostermann, 2014. Translated by Richard Rojcewicz as *Ponderings II–VI: Black Notebooks, 1931–1938*. Bloomington: Indiana University Press, 2016.
Heidegger, Martin. *Überlegungen VII-XI (Schwarze Hefte 1938–1939*, edited by Peter Trawny. Frankfurt/Main: Klostermann, 2014. Translated by Richard Rojcewicz as *Ponderings VII–XI: Black Notebooks, 1938–1939*. Bloomington: Indiana University Press, 2017.
Heidegger, Martin. *Überlegungen XII–XV (Schwarze Hefte 1939–1941)*, edited by Peter Trawny. Frankfurt/Main: Klostermann, 2014. Translated by Richard Rojcewicz as *Ponderings XII–XV: Black Notebooks, 1939–1941*. Bloomington: Indiana University Press, 2017.
Heinz, Marion, and Sidonie Kellerer, eds. *Martin Heideggers "Schwarze Hefte." Eine philosophische-politische Debatte*. Berlin: Suhrkamp, 2016.

Held, Klaus. "Heidegger und das ‚Politische.'" In *Heidegger und der Anti-Semitismus. Positionen im Widerstreit*, edited by Walter Homolka and Arnulf Heidegger, 257–268. Freiburg: Herder, 2016.

Hemming, Laurence Paul. "Heidegger's God." In *Heidegger Reexamined. Vol. 3: Art, Poetry, Technology*, edited by Hubert Dreyfus and Mark Wrathall, 249–294. New York: Routledge, 2002.

Herder, Johann Gottfried. *Vom Geist der Ebräischen Poesie*. Edited by Bernhard Suphan. Berlin, 1879.

Herf, Jeffery. "*Dialectic of Enlightenment* Reconsidered." *New German Critique* 117 (2012): 81–89.

Herlitz, Georg, and Bruno Kirschner, eds. *Jüdisches Lexikon*, Bd. 1. Berlin 1927.

Herrmann, Friedrich-Wilhelm von. "The Role of Martin Heidegger's Notebooks within the Context of His Oeuvre." In *Martin Heideggers "Schwarze Hefte." Eine philosophische-politische Debatte*, edited by Marion Heinz and Sidonie Kellerer, 89–94. Berlin: Suhrkamp, 2016.

Herrmann, Friedrich-Wilhelm von, and Francesco Alfieri. *Martin Heidegger. Die Wahrheit über die Schwarzen Hefte*. Translated by Pascal David. Berlin: Duncker and Humbolt, 2017.

Heschel, Susannah. *Abraham Geiger and the Jewish Jesus*. Chicago: University of Chicago Press, 1998.

Hess, Moses. "Über das Geldwesen." *Rheinische Jahrbücher zur gesellschaftlichen Reform* 1 (1845): 1–34.

Hiebert, Kyle Gingerich. "Capitalism and Catholicity: Ecclesiological Reflections on Alain Badiou's Pauline Universalism." *New Blackfriars* 92.1041 (2011): 574–590.

Hilberg, Raul. *The Destruction of the European Jews. Volume I*. New York: Holmes and Meier, 1985.

Hill, Claire Ortiz. *The Roots and Flowers of Evil in Baudelaire, Nietzsche, and Hitler*. Chicago: Open Court, 2006.

Hochberg, Gil. "Remembering Semitism" or "On the Prospect of Re-Membering the Semites." *ReOrient* 1 (2016): 192–223.

Homolka, Walter, and Arnulf Heidegger, eds. *Heidegger und der Anti-Semitismus. Positionen im Widerstreit*. Freiburg/Basel/Wien: Herder, 2016.

Horkheimer, Max. *Gesammelte Schriften*, Bd. 4. Frankfurt am Main: Fischer Verlag, 1988.

Horkheimer, Max. *Gesammelte Schriften*, Bd. 7. Frankfurt am Main: Fischer Verlag, 1985.

Horkheimer, Max, and Theodor Adorno. *Dialektik der Aufklärung. Philosophische Fragmente*. Frankfurt am Main: Fischer, 1988; New York: Social Studies Association, Inc., 1944. Translated by Edmund Jephcott. *Dialectic of Enlightenment*. Stanford, CA: Stanford University Press, 2002.

Husserl, Edmund. *Ideen zu einer reinen Phänomenologie und phänomenologischen Philosophie. Erstes Buch. Allgemeine Einführung in die reine Phänomenologie*. Den Haag: Martinus Nijhoff, 1976.

Husserl, Edmund. *Logische Untersuchungen. Zweiter Band. Untersuchungen zur Phänomenologie und Theorie der Erkenntnis*. Den Haag: Martinus Nijhoff, 1984.

Hutchens, B. C. *Jean-Luc Nancy and the Future of Philosophy*. Montreal: McGill-Queen's University Press, 2005.

Hutton, Christopher M. *Linguistics and the Third Reich: Mother-Tongue Fascism, Race and the Science of Language*. London: Routledge, 1999.

James, Ian. *The Fragmentary Demand: An Introduction to the Philosophy of Jean-Luc Nancy*. Stanford, CA: Stanford University Press, 2006.

Jay, Martin. "The Jews and the Frankfurt School: Critical Theory's Analysis of Anti-Semitism." *New German Critique* 19 (1980): 137–149.

Jonas, Hans. *The Gnostic Religion. The Message of the Alien God and the Beginnings of Christianity*. Boston: Beacon Press, 1958.

Judaken, Jonathan. "Blindness and Insight: The Conceptual Jew in Adorno and Arendt's Post-Holocaust Reflections on the Antisemitic Question." In *Arendt and Adorno: Political and Philosophical Investigations*, edited by Lars Rensmann and Samir Gandesha, 173–196. Stanford, CA: Stanford University Press, 2012.

Judaken, Jonathan. *Jean-Paul Sartre and the Jewish Question: Anti-antisemitism and the Politics of the French Intellectual*. Lincoln: University of Nebraska Press, 2006.

Jules-Rosette, Bennetta. "Jean-Paul Sartre and the Philosophy of Négritude: Race, Self, and Society." *Theory and Society* 36, no. 3 (2007): 265–285.

Kant, Emmanuel. *Die Religion innerhalb der Grenzen der bloßen Vernunft*, edited by Bettina Stangneth. Hamburg: Meiner, 2003 [1793].

Katz, Jacob. *The Darker Side of Genius: Richard Wagner's Anti-Semitism*. Hanover, NH: University Press of New England, 1986.

Katz, Jacob. *Exclusiveness and Tolerance: Jewish-Gentile Relations in Medieval and Modern Times*. London: Oxford University Press, 1961.

Katz, Jacob. *From Prejudice to Destruction. Anti-Semitism, 1700–1933*. Cambridge, MA: Harvard University Press, 1980.

Kennedy, Duncan. "Knowledge and the Political: Bruno Latour's Political Epistemology." *Cultural Critique* 74 (2010): 83–97.

Kidd, Colin. *The Forging of Races: Race and Scripture in the Protestant Atlantic World, 1600–2000*. Cambridge: Cambridge University Press, 2006.

König, Helmut. *Elemente des Antisemitismus. Kommentare und Interpretationen zu einem Kapitel der Dialektik der Aufklärung von Max Horkheimer und Theodor W. Adorno*. Weilerswist: Velbrück Wissenschaft, 2016.

Lacoue-Labarthe, Philippe. *La Fiction du politique. Heidegger, l'art et la politique*. Paris: Christian Bourgois Editeur, 1998 [1987]. Translated by Chris Turner as *Heidegger, Art and Politics: The Fiction of the Political*. Oxford: Blackwell, 1990.

Lacoue-Labarthe, Philippe. *Heidegger. La politique du poème*. Paris: Galilée, 2002. Translated by Jeff Fort as *Heidegger and the Politics of Poetry*. Urbana: University of Illinois Press, 2007.

Lacoue-Labarthe, Philippe. "Il faut." *MLN* 107 (1992): 437–453.

Lacoue-Labarthe, Phillipe, and Jean-Luc Nancy. *Le mythe nazi*. La Tour d'Aigues: Editions de l'Aube, 1991.
Landes, Richard, and Steven T. Katz, eds. *The Paranoid Apocalypse: A Hundred-Year Retrospective on The Protocols of the Elders of Zion*. New York: New York University Press, 2012.
Lapidot, Elad. "Disfigured Friends." *Jewish Studies Quarterly* 27 (2020): 1–21.
Lapidot, Elad. "Ethnocentrism in Esoteric Circles: On Political Gnoseology." *Comparative and Continental Philosophy* (2020): forthcoming.
Lapidot, Elad. "Ger: Deterritorialized Immigrant in Talmudic Exile." *Jewish Culture and History* 20 (2019): 23–42.
Lapidot, Elad. "The Goyish Goy." *Political Theology* 21, no. 1–2 (2020): 151–156.
Lapidot, Elad. "Invisible Concealment of Invisibility: Crypto-Judaism as a Theological Paradigm of Racial Anti-Semitism." *Religions* 9 (2018): 339.
Lapidot, Elad. "Is Technology Jewish? A Conversation with Heidegger." *Journal of Jewish Thought and Philosophy* 28 (2020): 90–125.
Lapidot, Elad. "Jewish and Talmudic Logo-Politics." In *Talmud, And, Philosophy*, edited by Sergey Dolgopolski. Bloomington: Indiana University Press, forthcoming.
Lapidot, Elad. "Schmitt's Warring Wars: On the Political Epistemology of Political Theology." *Philosophical Journal for Conflict and Violence* (2020): 36–53.
Lapidot, Elad. "The Word 'Jew.'" In *The Badiou Dictionary*, edited by Steve Corcoran, 230–240. Edinburgh: Edinburgh University Press, 2015.
Lapidot, Elad. "Paulus und die Grundlegung des Judentums." In *Täter und Opfer. Verbrechen und Stigma im europäischen-jüdischen Kontext*, edited by Claudia Simone Dorchain and Tommaso Speccher, 19–41. Würzburg: Königshausen and Neumann, 2014.
Lapidot, Elad. "People of Knowers: On Heideggerian and Jewish Political Epistemologies." In *Heidegger and Jewish Thought: Difficult Others*, edited by Elad Lapidot and Micha Brumlik, 269–289. London: Rowman and Littlefield, 2018.
Lapidot, Elad, and Micha Brumlik, eds. *Heidegger and Jewish Thought: Difficult Others*. London: Rowman and Littlefield, 2018.
Latour, Bruno. "The Netz-Works of Greek Deductions." *Social Studies of Science* 38, no. 3 (June 2008): 441–459.
Lee, David C. J. *Ernest Renan: In the Shadow of Faith*. London: Gerald Duckworth and Co., 1996.
Lefort, Claude. "Hannah Arendt—Anti-Semitism in the Nazi System." Translated by Anne O'Byrne. In *Hannah Arendt: Critical Assessments of Leading Political Philosophers*, Vol. I, *Arendt and Political Events*, edited by Garrath Williams, 174–194. New York: Routledge, 2006.
Leopold, David. "The Hegelian Antisemitism of Bruno Bauer." *History of European Ideas* 25 (1999): 179–206.
Lessing, Theodor. *Der jüdische Selbsthaß*. Berlin: Zionistischer Bücherbund, 1930; Nachdruck. Munich: Matthes and Seitz, 2004.

Levinas, Emmanuel. *Être juif: Suivi d'une lettre à Blanchot.* Edited by D. Cohen-Levinas. Paris: Rivages, 2015.

Levinas, Emmanuel. *Les imprévus de l'histoire.* N.p.: Fata Morgana: 1994.

Levinas, Emmanuel. *Totalité et Infini: Essai sur l'extériorité.* Paris: Kluwer Academic, 1991 [1961]. Translated by Alphonso Lingis as *Totality and Infinity: An Essay on Exteriority.* The Hague: Martinus Nijhoff, 1979.

Lévy, Benny. *La Cérémonie de la naissance.* Paris: Verdier, 2005.

Lewis, Bernard. *Semites and Anti-Semites: An Inquiry into Conflict and Prejudice.* New York: W.W. Norton and Company, 1986.

Liedman, Sven-Eric. *A World to Win: The Life and Works of Karl Marx.* Translated by Jeffrey N. Skinner. London: Verso, 2018.

Lyotard, Jean-François. *Heidegger et 'les juifs.'* Paris: Galilée, 1988. Translated by Andreas Michel and Mark Roberts as *Heidegger and "the jews."* Minneapolis: University of Minnesota Press, 1990.

Mack, Michael. *German Idealism and the Jew: The Inner Anti-Semitism of Philosophy and German Jewish Responses.* Chicago: Chicago University Press, 2003.

Mack, Michael. "The Holocaust and Hannah Arendt's Philosophical Critique of Philosophy: 'Eichmann in Jerusalem.'" *New German Critique* 106 (2009): 35–60.

Malpas, Jeff. "On the Philosophical Reading of Heidegger: Situating the *Black Notebooks.*" In *Reading Heidegger's Black Notebooks 1931–1941*, edited by Ingo Farin and Jeff Malpas, 3–22. Cambridge, MA: MIT Press, 2016.

Marafioti, Rosa Maria. "Heideggers vielsagendes ‚Schweigen.'" In *Heidegger und der Anti-Semitismus. Positionen im Widerstreit*, edited by Walter Homolka and Arnulf Heidegger, 277–288. Freiburg: Herder, 2016.

Marr, Wilhelm. *Der Sieg des Judentums über das Germanentum. Vom nicht konfessionellen Standpunkt aus betrachtet.* Bern: Rudolph Costenoble, 1879.

Marr, Wilhelm. *Der Judenspiegel.* Hamburg, 1862.

Marsden, Victor E., trans. *The Protocols of the Meetings of the Learned Elders of Zion.* N.p., 1934.

Marty, Éric. "Alain Badiou: l'avenir d'une négation.» *Les temps modernes* 635/636 (novembre-décembre 2005/janvier 2006): 22–58.

Marty, Éric. *Une querelle avec Alain Badiou, philosophe.* Paris: Gallimard, 2007. Translated by Alan Astro as *Radical French Thought and the Return of the "Jewish Question."* Bloomington: Indiana University Press, 2015.

Marty, Éric. "Réponse à Alain Badiou et Cécile Winter.» *Les temps moderns* 637/638/639, no. 3 (2006): 753–768.

Marty, Éric, and Yves Charles Zarka. "Les manipulations du nom de Juif.» *Cités* 31 (2007): 151–170.

Marx, Karl. "Zur Judenfrage." In Karl Marx and Friedrich Engels, *Werke*, Band I, 347–377. Berlin: Dietz Verlag, 1981; originally published in "Deutsch-Französische Jahrbücher," Paris, 1844.

Marx, Karl. "Zur Kritik der Hegelschen Rechtsphilosophie. Einleitung." In Karl Marx and Friedrich Engels. *Werke*, Band I, 378–391. Berlin: Dietz Verlag, 1981.
Marx, Karl, and Friedrich Engels. "Manifest der Kommunistischen Partei." In Karl Marx and Friedrich Engels, *Werke*, Band IV, 459–493. Berlin: Dietz Verlag, 1977.
Marx, Karl, and Friedrich Engels. "Die deutsche Ideologie. Kritik der neuesten deutschen Philosophie in ihren Repräsentanten Feuerbach, B. Bauer und Stirner, und des deutschen Sozialismus in seinen verschiedenen Propheten." In Karl Marx and Friedrich Engels, *Werke*, Band III, 9–533. Berlin: Dietz Verlag, 1961.
Masuzawa, Tomoko. *The Invention of World Religions, Or, How European Universalism Was Preserved in the Language of Pluralism*. Chicago: University of Chicago Press, 2005.
McLellan, David. *Marx before Marxism*. London: Macmillan, 1970.
Mikkelsen, Jon. "Introduction." In *Kant and the Concept of Race: Late Eighteenth-Century Writings*, edited by Jon Mikkelsen. Albany: State University of New York Press, 2013.
Milner, Jean-Claude. "Le juif de négation.» *Les temps modernes* 635/636 (novembre-décembre 2005/janvier 2006): 12–22.
Milner, Jean-Claude. *Le Juif de savoir*. Paris: Grasset, 2007.
Moggach, Douglas. *The Philosophy and Politics of Bruno Bauer*. Cambridge: Cambridge University Press, 2003.
Mollier, Jean-Yves. *Michel et Calmann Lévy, ou la naissance de l'édition moderne 1836–1891*. Paris: Calmann-Lévy, 1984.
Morris-Reich, Amos. "Argumentative Patterns and Epistemic Considerations: Responses to Anti-Semitism in the Conceptual History of Social Science." *Jewish Quarterly Review* 100, no. 3 (2010): 454–482.
Mosse, George L. *The Crisis of German Ideology: Intellectual Origins of the Third Reich*. New York: Grosset and Dunlap, 1964.
Nancy, Jean-Luc. *Banalité de Heidegger*. Paris: Galilée, 2015. Translated by Jeff Fort as *The Banality of Heidegger*. New York: Fordham University Press, 2017.
Nancy, Jean-Luc. *La communauté désoeuvrée*. Paris: Christian Bourgois Editeur, 1986, 1990. Translated by Peter Connor, Lisa Garbus, Michael Holland, and Simona Sawhney as *The Inoperative Community*. Minneapolis: University of Minnesota Press, 1991.
Nancy, Jean-Luc. *Exclu le juif en nous*. Paris: Galilée, 2018.
Neumann, Franz. *Behemoth. The Structure and Practice of National Socialism 1933–1944*. Chicago: Ivan R. Dee, 2009 [1942].
Nietzsche, Friedrich. *Jenseits von Gut und Böse. Zur Genealogie der Moral*. Kritische Studienausgabe (KSA), Bd. 5, edited by Giorgio Colli und Mazzino Montinari. Munich: de Gruyter, 1993.
Nipperdy, Thomas, and Reinhard Rürup. "Anti-Semitismus." In *Geschichtliche Grundbegriffe. Historisches Lexikon zur politisch-sozialen Sprache in Deutschland*,

edited by Otto Brunner, Werner Conze, Reinhart Koselleck, Bd. 1, 129–153. Stuttgart: Klett Verlag, 1972.

Nirenberg, David. *Anti-Judaism: The Western Tradition*. New York: W. W. Norton, 2013.

Olender, Maurice. *Les langues du Paradis*. Paris: Editions du Seuil, 1989. Translated by Arthur Goldhammer as *The Languages of Paradise: Race, Religion, and Philology in the Nineteenth Century*. Cambridge, MA: Harvard University Press, 1992.

Ophir, Adi, and Ishay Rosen-Zvi. *Goy: Israel's Multiple Others and the Birth of the Gentile*. Oxford: Oxford University Press, 2018.

Peled, Yoav. "From Theology to Sociology: Bruno Bauer and Karl Marx on the Question of Jewish Emancipation." *History of Political Thought* 13 (1992): 463–485.

Phelps, Hollis. *Alain Badiou. Between Theology and Anti-Theology*. Durham: Acumen, 2013.

Poliakov, Léon. *Histoire de l'antisémitisme, tome I: Du Christ aux Juifs de Cour*. Paris: Calmann-Lévy, 1955.

Poliakov, Léon. *Histoire de l'antisémitisme, tome II: De Mahomet aux Marranes*. Paris: Calmann-Lévy, 1961.

Poliakov, Léon. *Histoire de l'antisémitisme, tome III: De Voltaire à Wagner*. Paris: Calmann-Lévy, 1968.

Poliakov, Léon. *Histoire de l'antisémitisme, tome IV: L'Europe suicidaire (1870–1933)*. Paris: Calmann-Lévy, 1977.

Priest, Robert D. "Ernest Renan's Race Problem." *Historical Journal* 58 (2015): 309–330.

Priest, Robert D. *The Gospel according to Renan: Reading, Writing and Religion in Nineteenth-Century France*. Oxford: Oxford University Press, 2015.

Rabinbach, Anson. "Eichmann in New York: The New York Intellectuals and the Hannah Arendt Controversy." *October* 108 (2004): 97–111.

Rabinbach, Anson. "Why Were the Jews Sacrificed? The Place of Anti-Semitism in Dialectic of Enlightenment." *New German Critique* 81 (2000): 49–64.

Ray, Larry. "Marx and the Radical Critique of Difference." *Engage* 3 (2006). https://engageonline.wordpress.com/2015/11/04/marx-and-the-radical-critique-of-difference-larry-ray-engage-journal-issue-3-september-2006/.

Raz-Krakotzkin, Amnon. "Jewish Peoplehood, 'Jewish Politics' and Political Responsibility: Arendt on Zionism and Partitions." *College Literature* 38, no. 1 (2011): 57–74.

Renan, Ernest. *L'Avenir der la science, pensées de 1848*. Paris: Calmann Lévy, 1890.

Renan, Ernest. *Histoire générale et système comparé des langues sémitiques*. Paris: Michel Lévy Frères, 1855.

Renan, Ernest. *Nouvelles considérations sur le caractère général des peuples sémitiques, et en particulier sur leur tendance du monothéisme*. Paris: Michel Lévy Frères, 1859.

Renan, Ernest. *Qu'est-ce qu'une nation? Conférence faite en Sorbonne, Le 11 Mars 1882*. Paris: Calmann-Lévy, 1882.

Rensmann, Lars. *The Politics of Unreason: The Frankfurt School and the Origins of Modern Antisemitism*. Albany: State University of New York Press, 2017.

Rensmann, Lars, and Samir Gandesha, eds. *Arendt and Adorno: Political and Philosophical Investigations*. Stanford, CA: Stanford University Press, 2012.
Ring, Jennifer. *The Political Consequences of Thinking Gender and Judaism in the Work of Hannah Arendt*. Albany: State University of New York Press, 1998.
Rohkrämer, Thomas. "Heidegger and National Socialism: Great Hopes, Despair, and Resilience." In *Reading Heidegger's Black Notebooks 1931–1941*, edited by Ingo Farin and Jeff Malpas, 239–252. Cambridge, MA: MIT Press, 2016.
Rohling, August. *Der Talmudjude*. Münster: Adolph Russells Verlag, 1871.
Rose, Paul Lawrence. *German Question/Jewish Question. Revolutionary Antisemitism in Germany from Kant to Wagner*. Princeton, NJ: Princeton University Press, 1990.
Rose, Paul Lawrence. "Renan versus Gobineau: Semitism and Antisemitism, Ancient Races and Modern Liberal Nations." *History of European Ideas* 39, no. 4 (2013): 528–540.
Rose, Paul Lawrence. *Wagner: Race and Revolution*. New Haven, CT: Yale University Press, 1992.
Rosen, Zvi. *Bruno Bauer and Karl Marx. The Influence of Bruno Bauer on Marx's Thought*. Den Haag: Martinus Nijhoff, 1977.
Rosenberg, Alfred. *Der Mythos des 20. Jahrhunderts*. Munich: Hohenreichen-Verlag, 1934.
Rotenstreich, Nathan. "For and against Emancipation. The Bruno Bauer Controversy." *Leo Baeck Institute Year Book* 4 (1959): 3–36.
Runes, Dagobert D. "Introduction." In Karl Marx. *A World without Jews*, edited and translated by Dagobert D. Runes. New York: Philosophical Library, 1959.
Said, Edward. *Orientalism*. London: Penguin Books, 2003 [1978].
Samuels, Maurice. *The Right to Difference. French Universalism and the Jews*. Chicago: University of Chicago Press, 2016.
Sartre, Jean-Paul. *Critique de la raison dialectique*, Tome I. Paris: Gallimard, 1960.
Sartre, Jean-Paul. *L'être et le néant*. Paris: Gallimard, 1943. Translated by Hazel E. Barnes as *Being and Nothingness*. New York: Washington Square, 1992.
Sartre, Jean-Paul. *Réflexions sur la question juive*. Paris: Gallimard, 1954; Paris: Paul Morihien, 1946. Translated to English by George Becker as *Anti-Semite and Jew*. New York: Schocken Books, 1976 [1948].
Sartre, Jean-Paul, and Benny Lévy. *L'Espoir maintenant. Les entretiens de 1980*. Paris: Verdier, 1991. Translated by Adrian Van den Hoven as *Hope Now: The 1980 Interviews*. Chicago: University of Chicago Press, 1996.
Schleiermacher, Friedrich. "Über die verschiedenen Methoden des Übersetzens." In *Das Problem des Übersetzens*, edited by Hans Joachim Störig, 38–70. Darmstadt: Wissenschaftliche Buchgesellschaft, 1963.
Schlözer, A. L. "Von den Chaldäern." *Repertorium für biblische und morgenländische Litteratur* 8 (1781): 113–176.
Schmitz, Hermann. "Heidegger und der Nationalsozialismus." In *Heidegger und der Anti-Semitismus. Positionen im Widerstreit*, edited by Walter Homolka and Arnulf Heidegger, 326–341. Freiburg: Herder, 2016.

Schulze Wessel, Julia. *Ideologie der Sachlichkeit. Hannah Arendts Politische Theorie des Antisemitismus*. Frankfurt am Main: Suhrkamp, 2006.

Schulze Wessel, Julia, and Lars Rensmann. "The Paralysis of Judgment: Arendt and Adorno on Antisemitism and the Modern Condition." In *Arendt and Adorno: Political and Philosophical Investigations*, edited by Lars Rensmann and Samir Gandesha, 197–225. Stanford, CA: Stanford University Press, 2012.

Segré, Ivan. «Controverse Sur La Question De L'universel (Alain Badiou et Benny Lévy).» *Lignes* 30 (2009): 169–200.

Segré, Ivan. *Les pingouins de l'universel: antijudaïsme, antisémitisme, antisionisme*. Paris: Lignes, 2017.

Segré, Ivan. *Qu'appelle-t-on penser Auschwitz?* Paris: Lignes, 2009.

Segré, Ivan. *La Réaction Philosémite, ou La Trahison des Clercs*. Paris: Lignes, 2009. Translated by David Fernbach as "The Philosemitic Reaction." In Alain Badiou, Eric Hazan, and Ivan Segré, *Reflections on anti-Semitism*. London: Verso, 2013.

Sfez, Gérald. "L'antijudaïsme d'Alain Badiou. Le nom de vérité.» In *Le genre humain: L'antijudaïsme à l'épreuve de la philosophie et de la théologie*, edited by Danielle Cohen-Levinas and Antoine Guggenheim, 463–478. Paris: Seuil, 2016.

Shomali, Alireza. *Politics and the Criteria of Truth*. London: Palgrave Macmillan, 2010.

Silverman, Max. "Re-Figuring 'the Jew' in France." In *Modernity, Culture, and 'the Jew,'* edited by Bryan Cheyette and Laura Marcus, 197–207. Stanford, CA: Stanford University Press, 1998.

Söllner, Alfons. "Hannah Arendt's *The Origins of Totalitarianism* in Its Original Context." In *Hannah Arendt: Critical Assessments of Leading Political Philosophers*, Vol. I, *Arendt and Political Events*, edited by Garrath Williams, 265–285. New York: Routledge, 2006.

Sperber, Jonathan. *Karl Marx: A Nineteenth-Century Life*. New York: Liveright Publishing Corp., 2013.

Staudenmaier, Peter. "Hannah AredNt's Analysis of Antisemitism in *The Origins of Totalitarianism*: A Critical Appraisal." *Patterns of Prejudice* 46, no. 2 (2012): 154–179.

Steinschneider, Moritz. *Hebräische Bibliographie. Blätter für neuere und ältere Literatur des Judenthums* 3, no. 13 (January-February 1860).

Steinthal, H. "Zur Characteristik der semit. Völker." *Zeitschrift für Völkerpsychologie*, edited by M. Lazarus and H. Steinthal, Bd. I. Heft 4, 328–345. Berlin: Ferd. Dümmler's Verlagsbuchhandlung, 1860.

Sternhell, Zeev. *Les anti-Lumières. Du XVIII siècle à la guerre froide*. Paris: Fayard, 2006. Translated by David Maisel as *The Anti-Enlightenment Tradition*. New Haven, CT: Yale University Press, 2009.

Stoetzler, Marcel, ed. *Antisemitism and the Constitution of Sociology*. Lincoln: University of Nebraska Press, 2014.

Strong, Tracy. "On Relevant Events, Then and Now." In *Reading Heidegger's Black Notebooks 1931–1941*, edited by Ingo Farin and Jeff Malpas, 223–238. Cambridge, MA: MIT Press, 2016.

Thomä, Dieter. "Wie antisemitisch ist Heidegger? Über die Schwarzen Hefte und die gegenwärtige Lage der Heidegger-Kritik." In *Martin Heideggers "Schwarze Hefte." Eine philosophische-politische Debatte*, edited by Marion Heinz and Sidonie Kellerer, 211–233. Berlin: Suhrkamp, 2016.

Thomson, Iain. "Technology, Ontotheology." In *Heidegger on Technology*, edited by Aaron James Wendland et al., 174–193. New York: Taylor and Francis, 2018.

Toury, Jacob. "'The Jewish Question': A Semantic Approach." *Leo Baeck Institute Year Book* 11 (1966): 85–106.

Trawny, Peter. *Heidegger und der Mythos der jüdischen Weltverschwörung*. Frankfurt am Main: Vittorio Klostermann, 2014.

Trawny, Peter, and Andrew J. Mitchell, eds. *Heidegger, die Juden, noch einmal*. Frankfurt am Main: Vittorio Klostermann, 2015.

Treitschke, Heinrich von. "Unsere Ansichten." *Preußische Jahrbücher* 44 (1879): 559–576.

Treß, Werner, ed. *Verbrannte Bücher 1933. Mit Feuer gegen die Freiheit des Geistes. Eine Anthologie*. Bonn: Bundeszentrale für politische Bildung, 2009.

Treß, Werner. *Wider den undeutschen Geist. Bücherverbrennung 1933*. Berlin: Parthas, 2003.

Tsao, Roy. "The Three Phases of Arendt's Theory of Totalitarianism." In *Hannah Arendt: Critical Assessments of Leading Political Philosophers*, Vol. I, *Arendt and Political Events*, edited by Garrath Williams, 195–223. New York: Routledge, 2006.

Vallega-Neu, Daniela. "The Black Notebooks and Heidegger's Writing on the Event (1936–1942)." In *Reading Heidegger's Black Notebooks 1931–1941*, edited by Ingo Farin and Jeff Malpas, 127–144. Cambridge, MA: MIT Press, 2016.

Vašek, Thomas. "Schluss mit Heidegger?" In *Heidegger und der Anti-Semitismus. Positionen im Widerstreit*, edited by Walter Homolka and Arnulf Heidegger, 392–404. Freiburg: Herder, 2016.

Vial, Theodore. *Modern Religion, Modern Race*. Oxford: Oxford University Press, 2016.

Vietta, Silvio. "Heideggers seinesgeschichtliche Kovergenztheorie." In *Heidegger und der Anti-Semitismus. Positionen im Widerstreit*, edited by Walter Homolka and Arnulf Heidegger, 405–427. Freiburg: Herder, 2016.

Voegelin, Eric. "Concluding Remark." *Review of Politics* 15, no. 1 (1953): 84–85.

Voegelin, Eric. "The Origins of Totalitarianism." *Review of Politics* 15, no. 1 (1953): 68–76.

Volkov, Shulamit. *German, Jews, and Antisemites: Trials in Emancipation*. Cambridge: Cambridge University Press, 2006.

Wagner, Richard. *Das Judentum in der Musik*. Leipzig: Weber, 1869 [1850].

Wallace, Max. *The American Axis: Henry Ford, Charles Lindbergh, and the Rise of the Third Reich*. New York: St. Martin's/Griffin, 2003.

Wimpfheimer, Barry. *The Talmud: A Biography*. Princeton, NJ: Princeton University Press, 2018.

Wistrich, Robert S. *A Lethal Obsession: Anti-Semitism from Antiquity to the Global Jihad*. New York: Random House, 2010.

Wistrich, Robert S. "Radical Antisemitism in France and Germany (1840–1880)." *Modern Judaism* 15 (1995): 109–135.

Woeste, Victoria Saker. *Henry Ford's War on Jews and the Legal Battle against Hate Speech*. Stanford, CA: Stanford University Press, 2012.

Wolfson, Elliot. *Alef, Mem, Tau: Kabbalistic Musings on Time, Truth, and Death*. Berkeley: University of California Press, 2006.

Wolfson, Elliot. *The Duplicity of Philosophy's Shadow: Heidegger, Nazism, and the Jewish Other*. New York: Columbia University Press, 2018.

Wolfson, Elliot. *Giving beyond the Gift: Apophasis and Overcoming Theomania*. New York: Fordham University Press, 2014.

Wolfson, Elliot. *Heidegger and Kabbalah: Hidden Gnosis and the Path of Poiēsis*. Bloomington: Indiana University Press, 2019.

Wolfson, Elliot. *Language, Eros, and Being: Kabbalistic Hermeneutics and the Poetic Imagination*. New York: Fordham University Press, 2005.

Wolin, Richard. "Vernunftkritik nach den Schwarzen Heften." In *Martin Heideggers "Schwarze Hefte." Eine philosophische-politische Debatte*, edited by Marion Heinz and Sidonie Kellerer, 397–415. Berlin: Suhrkamp, 2016.

Yakira, Elhanan. "Hannah Arendt, the Holocaust, and Zionism: A Story of Failure." *Israel Studies* 11, no. 3 (2006): 31–61.

Yerushalmi, Yosef Hayim. "L'antisémitisme racial est-il apparu au XXe siècle? De la limpieza de sangre espagnol au nazisme: continuités et ruptures.» Translated by Jacqueline Carnaud. *Esprit* 190, no. 3/4 (1993): 5–35.

Zarader, Marlène. *La Dette impensée. Heidegger et l'héritage hébraïque*. Paris: Seuil, 1990. Translated by Bettina Bergo as *The Unthought Debt: Heidegger and the Hebraic Heritage*. Stanford, CA: Stanford University Press, 2006.

Zelinsky, H. *Richard Wagner—Ein deutsches Thema. Eine Dokumentation der Wirkungsgeschichte Richard Wagners 1876–1976*. Vienna/Berlin: Medusa, 1983.

Zertal, Idith. "A State of Trial: Hannah Arendt vs. the State of Israel." *Social Research* 74, no. 4 (2007): 1127–1158.

Zimmermann, Moshe. *Wilhelm Marr, the Patriarch of anti-Semitism*. New York: Oxford University Press, 1986.

Index

Adorno, Theodor, 6–7, 20, 53–72, 74–75, 83, 88, 90, 95–96, 101, 109, 121, 147, 150, 154, 156, 186, 262
Aloni, Udi, 137, 139
Angelus Silesius, 176
Anidjar, Gil, 5, 7, 10, 12–15, 17, 271
Anti-Christ, 28
Anti-Judaism (also anti-Jewish), 8–10, 15–16, 18, 30, 66, 152, 155, 188, 236, 239–250; Christian, 259; religious, 260; theological, 259
Anti-Semite and Jew, see Reflections on the Jewish Question
Antisemitismusforschung, 7
Arendt, Hannah, 4, 6–7, 16, 20, 49, 66, 76, 85–122, 129, 148, 150–151, 153–155, 162, 171, 186–187, 193, 227
Aristotle (also Aristotelian), 53, 204
Aryan, 75, 131–132, 191, 206–207, 217–218, 261, 279
Assimilation, 21–22, 113, 118, 221, 224–225, 238, 248, 256, 261–262, 265, 271, 283, 285
Auerbach, Erich, 302
Augustine, 176
Auschwitz, 4, 15–16, 53, 56, 58, 90, 173, 186, 281, 283, 285, 300
The Authoritarian Personality, 63

Babylon (also Babylonian), 116, 209, 287
Badiou, Alain, 15, 20, 76, 85, 120–148, 153, 160, 180, 234
Balibar, Etienne, 146
The Banality of Evil, 87, 90, 119, 150
Baron, Saul, 105
Baudelaire, Charles, 277
Bauer, Bruno, 22, 194, 225–252, 256, 258–259, 269, 271, 275
BDS Movement, 2
Bein, Alex, 187, 190, 194, 257, 281
Being and Nothingness, 74
Being, the question of, 160–161
Benhabib, Seyla, 109–110
Benjamin, Walter, 167, 300
Bernstein, Richard, 86, 110
Bible, 208, 213, 288, 299, 302; Christian, 297; Hebrew, Jewish, 220, 286, 288, 290, 293, 296–297
Black Notebooks, 11, 25–26, 29–30, 33, 39, 42, 46, 49, 51, 58, 168, 288–289, 296
Black Skin, White Masks, 78
Blanchot, Maurice, 166, 180–181, 301
Bloom, Harold, 302
Boers, 116–117
Bowie, Andrew, 40, 43
Boyarin, Daniel, 36–37, 139–143, 146, 159–160, 178–182, 303

Boyarin, Jonathan, 36–37, 179–182, 197, 222
Buber, Martin, 48, 104, 167

Canovan, Margaret, 88, 91, 117
Capitalism, 62
Caputo, John, 49, 289–290, 292, 299
Catholicism, Roman, 13
Chamberlain, Houston Stewart, 264
Chosenness, 48, 52, 76, 105, 118–119, 220, 280
Chosen people, 50, 76, 117, 233, 269, 280
Christ, 133, 141–142, 144; belonging to, 200; birth of, 158; death of, 296; resurrection of, 143, 146
Christianity (also Christian, Christic), 11, 13, 20–21, 28, 30–31, 39, 47, 63, 66, 69, 82, 92, 95, 115, 142, 158–161, 215–216, 218, 221, 231, 234–237, 239, 241, 247, 257; being, 239; birth of, 159; canon, 169; claim to exclusive possession of truth, 119; content of Paul's Gospel, 133; doctrine of the common origin of men, 117; early, 132; Europe, 262; event, 133–134, 158, 162, 169, 206, 215; foundational text, 132; Jew-hatred, 166; Judeo- (also Jewish-), 100, 117, 288, 290–303; modern, 225; nation, 216; non-, 138, 140; perspective, 169; political theology, 213; principle, 152, 235, 259; project, 211; protestant, 235; religion, 234; self, 159–160; spirit, 219, 261; subject, 133, 136; supersession, 160; theology, 140, 245, 258; tradition, 180; universalism, 180; universality, 133; West, 161, 165
Christianism, 158, 174
Christology, 141, 144
Class, 72–73, 81; struggle, 106
Cohen, Hermann, 48, 167
Cold War, 89, 122
Colonialism, 15
Communism (also communist), 81, 93, 106, 136, 251–253; The Manifesto, 243, 251–253

Conspiracy, 44, 101, 104, 269–274

Daniel, Jean, 77
Dastur, Françoise, 49, 289–290
David, Alain, 1, 2
Deleuze, Gilles, 167
Derrida, Jacques, 164, 167, 172, 204, 302
The Dialectics of Enlightenment, 20, 53, 55–69, 88, 95, 164
Diaspora, 36, 87, 159, 171, 175, 177, 179–182
Di Cesare, Donatella, 26, 37–38, 41, 173–175
Dis-figuration (also disfiguration, disfigured), 10, 17–18, 21–22, 177–178, 300–301
Dolgopolski, Sergey, 182, 287, 303
Dreyfus, affair, 73, 191
Drumond, Edouard, 257, 265
Dühring, Eugen, 264

Eichhorn, 210
Eichmann, Adolf, 87, 120, 150–151, 268; trial, 119
Eisenmenger, Johann Andreas, 274
Elbogen, Ismar, 190, 195
Elements of Anti-Semitism, 55–57, 63–64
Emancipation, 21, 113, 221, 224, 228–229, 231–241, 246, 251, 256, 261, 269, 276, 282
Engels, Friedrich, 60–61
Enlightenment, 54–62, 68, 95, 127, 154, 187, 192, 228, 232–235, 262; the Concept of, 68; progress of, 277
Epistemology, political (see political epistemology)
Erasmus, 286
Eschatology (also eschatological), 56, 59, 80, 82, 133, 186, 199, 228, 232, 246
Exile, 116, 182

Fagenblat, Michael, 302
Fanon, Frantz, 78
Farias, Victor, 288
Farin, Ingo, 42

Fascism, 63, 93, 163
Faye, Emmanuel, 32, 41, 87
Feuerbach, Ludwig, 245
Final Solution, 22, 114, 281–283
Ford, Henry, 273
Foucault, Michel, 167
Fourier, Charles, 251
The Frankfurt School, 68
Freud, Sigmund, 48, 65, 84, 136, 302
Friedländer, Saul, 281
Fritsch, Theodor, 188, 194, 260

Gabriel, Markus, 40
Geschichtliche Grundbegriffe, 188–191, 195
Gobineau, Arthur de, 200–201
Grondin, Jean, 32
Grousillier, Hector de, 259

Hammerschlag, Sarah, 36–37, 70, 74, 80, 134, 141–142, 177–179
Handelman, Sarah, 302
Harries, Karsten, 29
Hazan, Eric, 121–124, 126
Hegel, Georg Wilhelm Friedrich, 18, 28, 56–57, 69, 73, 83, 91, 156, 162, 212–213, 240, 244–245, 251
Hegelianism (also Hegelian), 27, 56, 68, 80, 90, 164, 172, 229, 234; dialectics, 236, 242; Geist, 242; Young, 230
Heidegger, Martin (also Heideggerian), 11–12, 16, 18–19, 21–22, 25–54, 57–59, 65, 72, 75–76, 87–88, 150–151, 156–158, 160, 162, 164, 167–168, 172–173, 175, 225, 287–303; anti-Semitism, 167, 183, 287; Being and Time, 227–229; debate, 25–54, 101, 149–154, 167, 227, 259, 287–290; on Hölderlin, 290–299; and language, 204; and National-Socialism, 287–288, 290, 296; post-, 165; question of being, 227–228; text, 168–169; work, 176
Heinz, Marion, 32, 43
Hermeneutics (also hermeneutic, hermeneutical), 9, 18–19, 29–30, 32, 46, 85–86; biblical, 208; deconstructive, 116; philological, 208; of "with-against", 142
Herzl, Theodor, 48, 104
Hess, Moses, 245
Himmler, Heinrich, 117
Historiography (also historiographical), 98, 105–108, 113, 145; Christian, 220; Jewish (see Jewish); modern, 200; Semitic, 213; Western, 159; Zionist, 116, 123
Hitler, Adolf, 22, 194, 255, 258, 261, 263, 265, 267–268, 276–282, 286
Hochberg, Gil, 14–15, 17
Hölderlin, Friedrich, 176, 290–302
Holocaust, 87, 281, 283, 288
Homeric, 302
Hope Now, 82
Horkheimer, Max, 20, 53–72, 74–75, 83, 88, 90, 95–96, 101, 109, 121, 147, 150, 156, 186, 262
Hosea, 50
The Human Condition, 92, 94
Husserl, Edmund, 5, 8–9, 27, 37–38, 164, 225

Ideology, 60–61, 95, 105–106, 109, 151
Idolatry, 68, 246
Imperialism, 96, 99, 106, 111, 113, 116–118; British, 104
Indo-European, 206–207, 217–218
Islam (also Muslim), 14–17, 69, 215–216, 220–221
Israel, 50, 73; State of, 2, 123–126, 128, 137–138

Jacob, François, 77
Jaspers, Karl, 151
Jesus, 140–141
Jew, anti-anti-Semitic, 149
Jewish, 168, 177–180, 288; agent, 276; alterity, 167, 169, 172–173; being, 126, 145, 147, 149, 162, 171–172, 174–175, 178, 180–182, 194, 230, 236–238, 244–245, 248, 255, 259, 261–262;

Jewish (cont'd)
body, 222; community, 133, 135; conspiracy, 272–275; consciousness, 149; discourse, 135; dispersion, 114; event, 170; episteme, 115, 127, 132, 147–148, 152, 162, 165–166, 171, 174–175, 177; existence, 181; figure, 299; God, 168; history, 105, 138–139; historiography, 103–105, 112, 114, 119, 138; intellectual tradition, 127, 132, 138–139, 179; justice, 169; knowledge, 132, 148, 165, 287; limitation, 247; nationalist, 104; otherness, 175; particularism, 132, 180, 250; particularity, 133, 136; people, 97, 115–116, 118, 126, 128, 132, 136, 152, 160, 220, 233–235, 246, 248; political epistemology (see Political Epistemology); politics, 274; polity, 272; principle, 119, 166, 172; project, 180; Question, 11, 22, 46, 59, 70, 75, 80, 86, 124, 126, 134, 174, 188, 223–256, 258, 268, 281–285; race, 238, 263, 272, 281; reality, 177; religion (see Religion); site, 135; Self-Hate, 169–170; specificity, 170; state, 128, 137, 268, 272–276; study, 145–146; textual tradition, 302; theology, 134, 243; thought, 18, 22, 126, 139–140, 167, 285–287; tradition, 138–139, 176;
Jewishness, 18, 20, 37, 68, 72, 74, 76, 85, 103, 118, 122, 124, 126, 147–148, 182, 271, 274; carnal, 139; epistemic, 174; performance of, 149
The Jewish Question (Bauer), 225–243
Judaism, 14, 27, 115, 118, 126, 132, 136, 159, 166, 174, 178, 181–183, 215–216, 220–222, 231–237, 244–245, 257, 261; biblical, 296; as a political project, 124; rabbinic, 144, 159, 177, 233; spirit of, 259; world, 28, 31
Judaken, Jonathan, 11–12, 58–59, 70, 80

Kabbalah, 289
Kant, Immanuel, (also Kantian), 8, 62, 202, 275

Katz, Jacob, 115, 187, 192, 194, 224, 239, 245, 257–258, 260, 264–265, 272, 276, 281
Klemperer, Victor, 282

Lacan, Jacques, 167, 302
Lacoue-Labarthe, Philippe, 16, 154, 178, 181, 297–303
Lanzmann, Claude, 77, 82, 125
Latour, Bruno, 3
Lazarus, Moritz, 195
Lefort, Claude, 113–114
Lessing, Theodor, 169
Levinas, Emmanuel, 77, 79, 83, 134, 144, 167, 173–175, 178, 288
Lévy, Benny, 82–83, 142, 147
Liberalism, 64
The Life of the Mind, 109–110
Literature, 13
Luther, Martin (also Lutheran), 169, 263
Lyotard, Jean-François, 35–38, 167, 173, 180

Messianic, 50
Machination, 27–29
Mack, Michael, 95, 108, 110
Malpas, Jeff, 31
Marafioti, Rosa Maria, 30, 41
Marr, Wilhelm, 22, 189–190, 194, 225, 248, 255–257, 259, 261, 265, 268, 276
Marty, Éric, 125, 137
Marx, Karl, 22, 28, 46, 60–61, 136–137, 139, 164, 194, 218, 226–227, 230–232, 239–256, 258–261, 263, 268–269, 278
Marxism (also Marxist), 72–73, 81, 83–84, 91, 277; science, 242; theory, 242
Mein Kampf, 258, 278–280, 286
Mendelssohn, 237
Messianism (also Messianic), 50, 82, 118, 133, 151, 299
Metaphysics (also metaphysical), 11, 27–28, 31, 37–38, 40–41, 58, 82, 154, 157–158, 173; of being, 172; metaphysical anti-Semitism, 37–38; Western tradition of, 290
Midrash, 289, 302

Milner, Jean-Claude, 125–126, 154
Mimesis, 65
Minima Moralia, 56
Misrahi, Robert, 77
Monotheism, 196, 205, 211–222, 233, 245, 292
Morin, Edgar, 77
Muhammad, 216
Myth (also Mythology), 59–61, 67–69, 95, 101, 104–105, 109, 112, 116, 118, 143, 152, 154, 158, 164, 177–178, 298–299; Jewish, 299; Jewish rejection of, 166, 180, 301; of the nation-state, 175; Nazi, see National-Socialism; of autochthony, 181; Western, 300

Nancy, Jean-Luc, 21, 36, 149–182, 187, 203, 218, 298, 303
Nation, 21, 73, 79, 116, 118, 198, 203, 218, 224; imagined, 240; modern, 279; principle of, 238; -state, see State
Nationalism (also nationalist), 99, 118
Nationality, 118–119
National-Socialism (also Nazism, Nazi), 5, 16, 29, 32, 50, 57, 63, 72, 75, 90–93, 96, 104, 112, 117–118–120, 128, 131–132, 135, 155, 174, 255, 260, 278, 290, 298–299; anti-Jewish politics, 223, 238, 282, 288; bible of, 286; crimes, 151; language, 188; myth, 163, 298; Propaganda Ministry, 188; semantics, 286
Neo-Kantian, 27
New Testament, 169
Nietzsche (also Nietzschean), 65, 164, 250, 277, 290
Nihilism (also nihilist), 107
Nirenberg, David, 66, 155
Nuremberg Laws, 188

Odysseus, 68
Old Testament, 49, 116, 159, 169, 289, 291, 299, 301, 303
Olender, Maurice, 191, 206, 208, 215
On the Jewish Question, 46, 226–227, 239–255, 259

Ontology (also ontological), 48, 74; difference, 161
Orientalism, 14, 196
Ottoman, Imperial Caliphate, 216
The Origins of Totalitarianism, 6, 20, 88–120, 151
Owen, Robert, 251

Palestine, 221
Paranoia (also paranoid), 62, 68–69, 71, 112, 149, 155, 173
Paul, Saint, 20, 132, 135–143, 145–146, 160, 180, 197–198; gospel, 133
Paulinian, 36; discourse, 206; event, 134, 142, 146, 198; logic, 231; Platonic, 141; tradition, 169; universalism, 141–142
Phenomenology (also phenomenological), 18–19, 27, 59; of Spirit, 56
Philippson, Ludwig, 191, 225
Philology, 21
Philosemitism (also philosemitic), 5, 15, 17
Plato (also Platonic, Platonism), 92, 100–102, 104–105, 139–143, 145, 298–299
Poliakov, Léon, 154, 187, 189
Political epistemology, 2–14, 18–19, 21–22, 26, 39, 44, 52, 55, 88, 93, 95, 106, 113, 181, 260; alternative, 176; anti-Semitic, 262; anti-anti-Semitic, 186; contemporary, 163; Jewish, 175, 179, 182, 194, 237; Marxist, 252–253; modern, 194, 198, 224, 239, 242, 252, 282; negative, 151, 154, 157, 182, 185, 219, 251; non-Jewish, 182; positive, 140, 145, 154, 157, 178, 253, 281; rabbinic, 182; racist, 262; tradition, 221
Political, civilization, 212; contemporary, 130; critical, 130; Jewish political epistemology, 115, 117–118, 250; philosophy (also philosopher), 4–5, 19, 88; theology, 3; thought, 4, 88
Politics, epistemo- (or epistemo-political), 2, 3, 47–48, 51, 57, 59, 61, 66, 69–73, 78–83, 85, 87, 95; Communist, 253; Jewish, 124; Nazi, 129

Positivism, 62–64, 67, 95, 109
Postcolonial, sophist, 141; thought, 78
Prinz, Joachim, 48
Protestantism, 235
The Protocols of the Elders of Zion, 44, 49, 99, 101, 104, 151, 272–275
Psychoanalysis, 48

Rabbinic, political epistemology, see political epistemology; hermeneutics, 302; literature, 287, 302; tradition, 180–181
Race (also racial), 13, 21–22, 27–28, 31, 34, 40, 50, 65, 72–74, 79, 115–116, 151, 191, 229–230, 233, 238, 247, 260–262, 267, 271, 278–279, 285; Aryan, 279–280; category, 118; discourse, 212; epistemology, 212, 215; Indo-European, 211; of Israel, 280–281; logic, 200, 276, 279; murder, 285; Muslim, 215; negative of spirit, 198; origins of, 208; perversion, 119; politics, 269, 279; principle, 279; science, 196–222, 265, 279; Semitic, 211–215, 261; spirit, 202–222, 264, 267; spiritual 217–218; state, 269–275, 283; theory, 117, 208, 278–279
Racism (also racist), 14, 34, 50, 104, 106, 138, 196, 198, 200; politics, 267, 278
Rathenau, Walther, 49
Réflexions sur la question juive (also Reflections on the Jewish Question), 20, 53, 62–84, 88, 121
Reformation, 13
Religion, 13, 22, 69, 119, 132–133, 214, 230–232, 240, 247; critique of, 240; Indo-European, 211, 217; Jewish, 68–69, 73, 118, 127, 246, 259; Semitic, 210–222; question of, 231–232
Renan, Ernst, 21–22, 119, 190–191, 193, 195–222, 224, 227–230, 233–234, 236, 238–241, 245–247, 256, 260–262, 264–267, 269, 278–279
Rensmann, Lars, 6–8, 96
Revolution, 82

Ricoeur, Paul, 290
Robespierre, 229
Rohrkrämer, Thomas, 40
Rosenberg, Alfred, 265
Rosenzweig, Franz, 49, 167

Said, Edward, 14, 198, 207
Saint Paul: The Foundation of Universalism, 132–136
Saint-Simon, Henry de, 251
Sartre, Jean-Paul, 11, 20, 48, 53, 62, 70–84, 88, 96, 104, 121–122, 129, 147, 167, 174
Shoah, 89, 138, 281
Science, Studies, 3
Schleiermacher, Friedrich, 266
Schmitt, Carl, 4
Scholem, Gershom, 120, 302
Schulze Wessel, Julia, 6–8, 96–97
Secularism, 13
Secularization, 118, 236, 296
Segré, Ivan, 5, 15–16, 139–140, 142–147
Seinsgeschichte, 30, 41–42, 50, 152
Semitism, Semites, 6–10, 13–18, 21–22, 188, 191, 194–202, 234, 246, 259, 262, 279; language, 206–211, 214; religion, 211–222; spirit, 215, 262, 275
Septuagint, 168
Shema Yisrael, 169
Socrates, 4
Spinoza, 136–137, 139
Spirit, 21, 27–28
Stalinism, 91, 96
State, 22, 93, 297; modern, 229, 236–238, 241, 293; nation-, 92–94, 113, 125–126, 224–225, 235, 238–239, 241, 261, 274; Prussian, 241; question of the, 239; secular, 237
Steinthal, Heymann, 195–196, 211
Steinschneider, Moritz, 190, 195–196, 209, 211

Taine, 119
Talmud (also Talmudic), 18, 247, 268–269, 274–275, 285–288, 297, 301, 303;

330 Index

literature, 290; thinker, 139; tradition, 138–140, 144–145
Tanach, 50
Technology, 16, 30
Les Temps Modernes, 125
Third Reich, 50, 280
Thomä, Dieter, 32
Torah, 140, 178
Totalitarianism, 88, 91–97, 103, 105–111, 122–123, 130, 162; modern, 163, 186
Tower of Babel, 209–210
Trawny, Peter, 11, 25–26, 33–34, 37, 39–42, 44, 48–50, 152
Trenitsch, Arthur, 169
Trotsky, 136

Use of the Word 'Jew', 125

Vallega-Neu, Daniela, 31–32, 42
Veil, Simone, 77
Voegelin, Eric, 106–108, 110–111
Voltaire, 119
Von Hermann, Friedrich Wilhelm, 30, 41
Von Treitschke, Heinrich, 194, 264

Wagner, Richard, 194, 257, 265–266
Weininger, Otto, 169
Wiesel, Elie, 283
Wissenschaft des Judentums, 196
Wissenschaft der Logik, 57
Wittgenstein, Ludwig, 164
Wolfson, Elliot, 1, 26, 29, 182, 302–303
Wolin, Richard, 29
World War II, 4–5, 19, 53, 55, 57, 89, 123, 213, 288; post, 52, 63, 69, 86, 88, 123, 154, 177, 185, 187, 283
The Wretched of the Earth, 78

Xenophobia, 99

Yerushalmi, Yosef Hayim, 270

Zarader, Marlène, 288–290, 294, 302
Zarka, Yves Charles, 125
Zeus, 302
Zimmermann, Moshe, 259
Zionism (also Zionist), 14, 79, 87, 104, 120, 123, 181, 268; anti-, 2, 15; discourse, 274; First Congress, 274; pro-, 2; World Organization, 49